CONTENTS

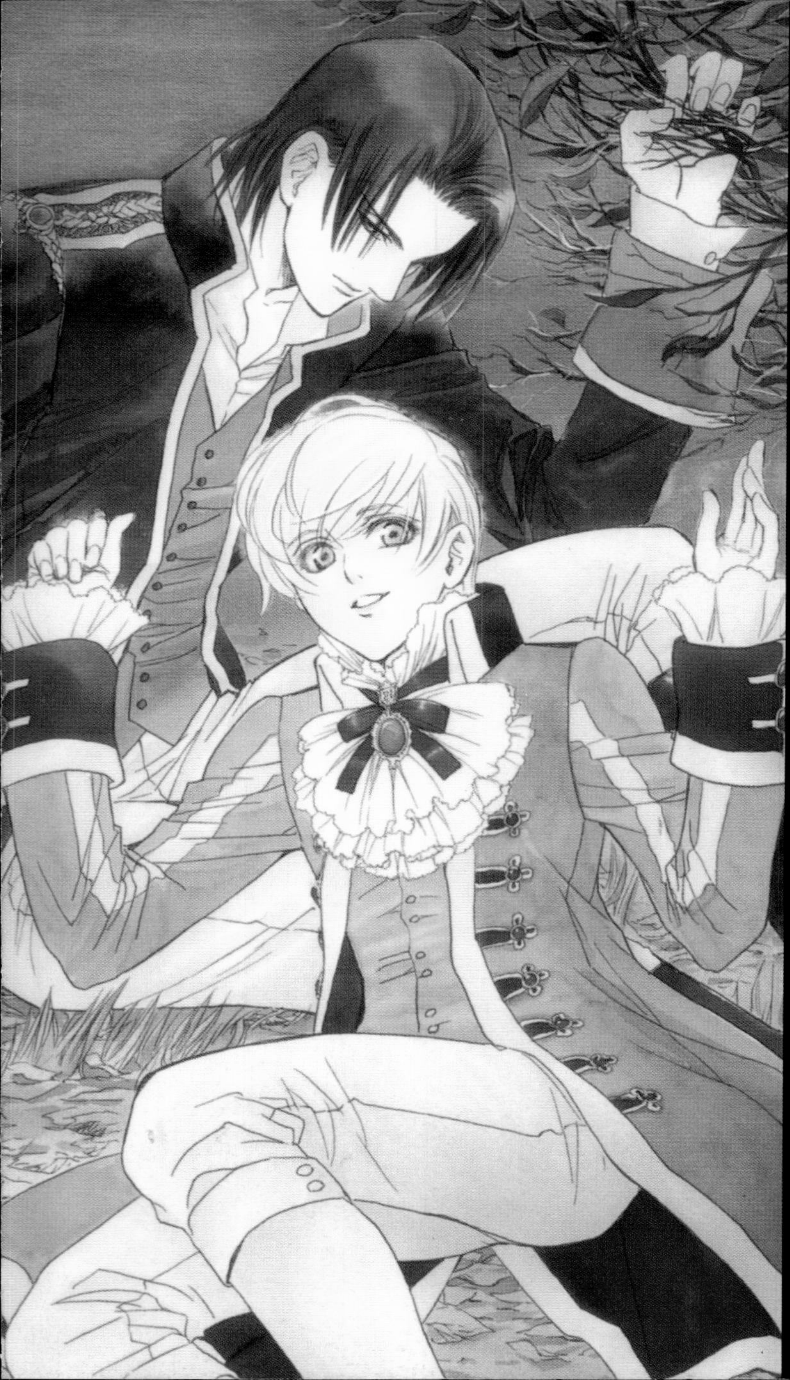

Our story thus far…

Welcome to the peaceful kingdom of Aran, where kings and queens reign with a gentle hand, assassins prowl the woodland, and knights battle for the honor of their lord.

Prince Christian and his loyal Black Knight Zeke play out their romance amidst the political unrest of the land. Just as the Kingdom of Aran was finally won over by Chris' lord father, the neighboring Dundalk Empire threatens to end any chance of peaceful unification of the land. Now that diplomatic relations have been cut off completely, a new face appears at the King's door — Prince James, alleged second prince of the Dundalk Empire!

His plan? To enter Dundalk's court with Prince Christian in tow as a hostage. But there are forces greater than they imagined who will do anything to stop them…

Prince Christian Wilson Jeremy:
As third son of the king of Aran, Chris is far behind in line to the crown, and so has lived his entire life relaxing in the life of luxury. Although the physical training at the knighthood academy did little for him, it was there that he met his knight and lover, Zeke. He now strives to prove his reliability in the kingdom.

Zeke O'Brien:
A master of the sword and newest holder of the title of "Black Knight." When not dueling with swords, Zeke actually has a gentle demeanor, and would do anything for master and lover Chris.

King Aran:
Chris' loving father and king of Aran. He strives to maintain peace throughout his kingdom while keeping a jovial outlook on life. His past was one filled with betrayal, suffering, but also an undying love.

Master Brigadoon Rossetti:
The happy-go-lucky merchant who has made the Kingdom of Aran his current residence. His plans are still somewhat mysterious.

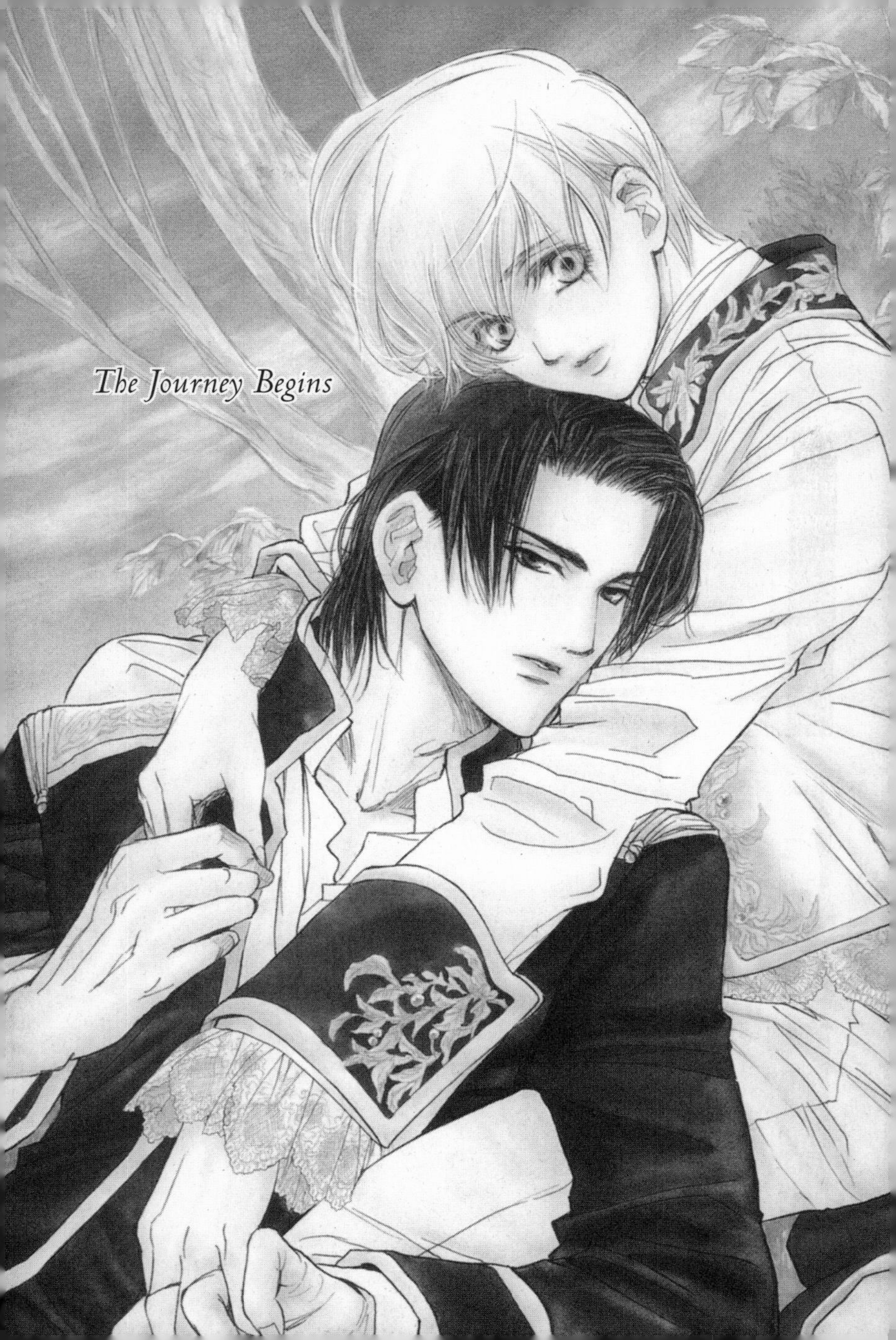
The Journey Begins

THE BLACK KNIGHT

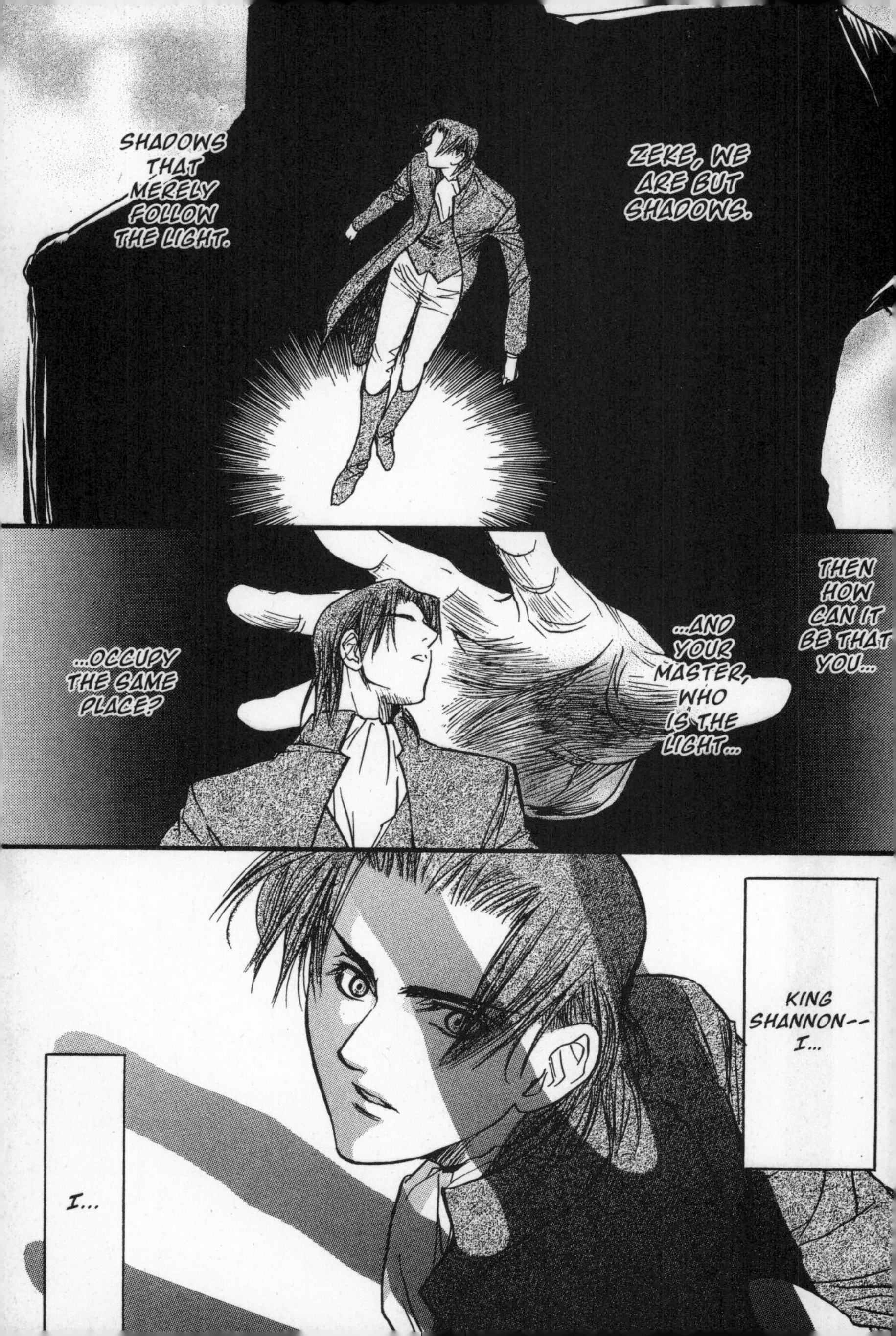
ZEKE, WE ARE BUT SHADOWS.
SHADOWS THAT MERELY FOLLOW THE LIGHT.
THEN HOW CAN IT BE THAT YOU...
...AND YOUR MASTER, WHO IS THE LIGHT...
...OCCUPY THE SAME PLACE?
KING SHANNON-- I...
I...

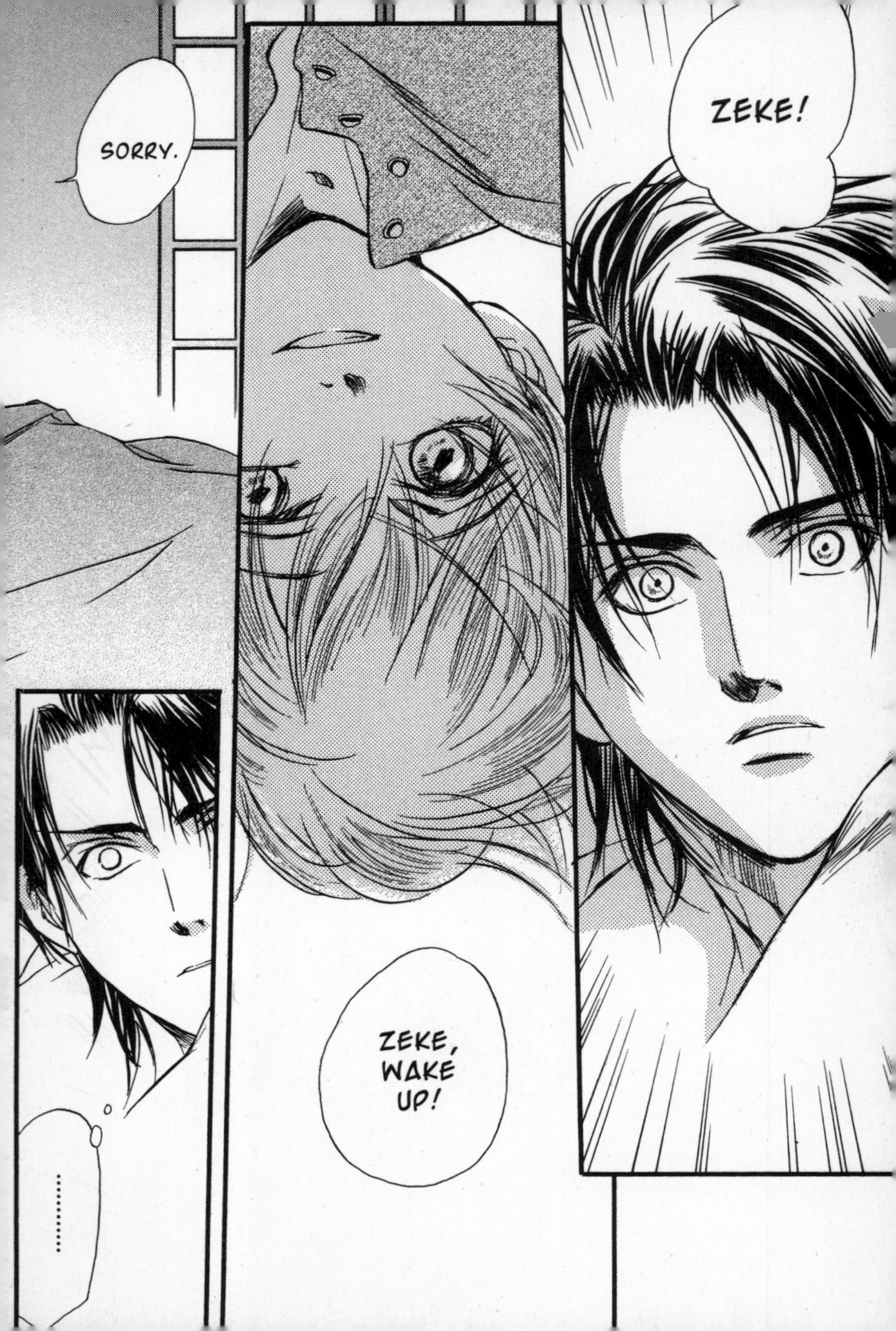
ZEKE!
ZEKE, WAKE UP!
SORRY.
....

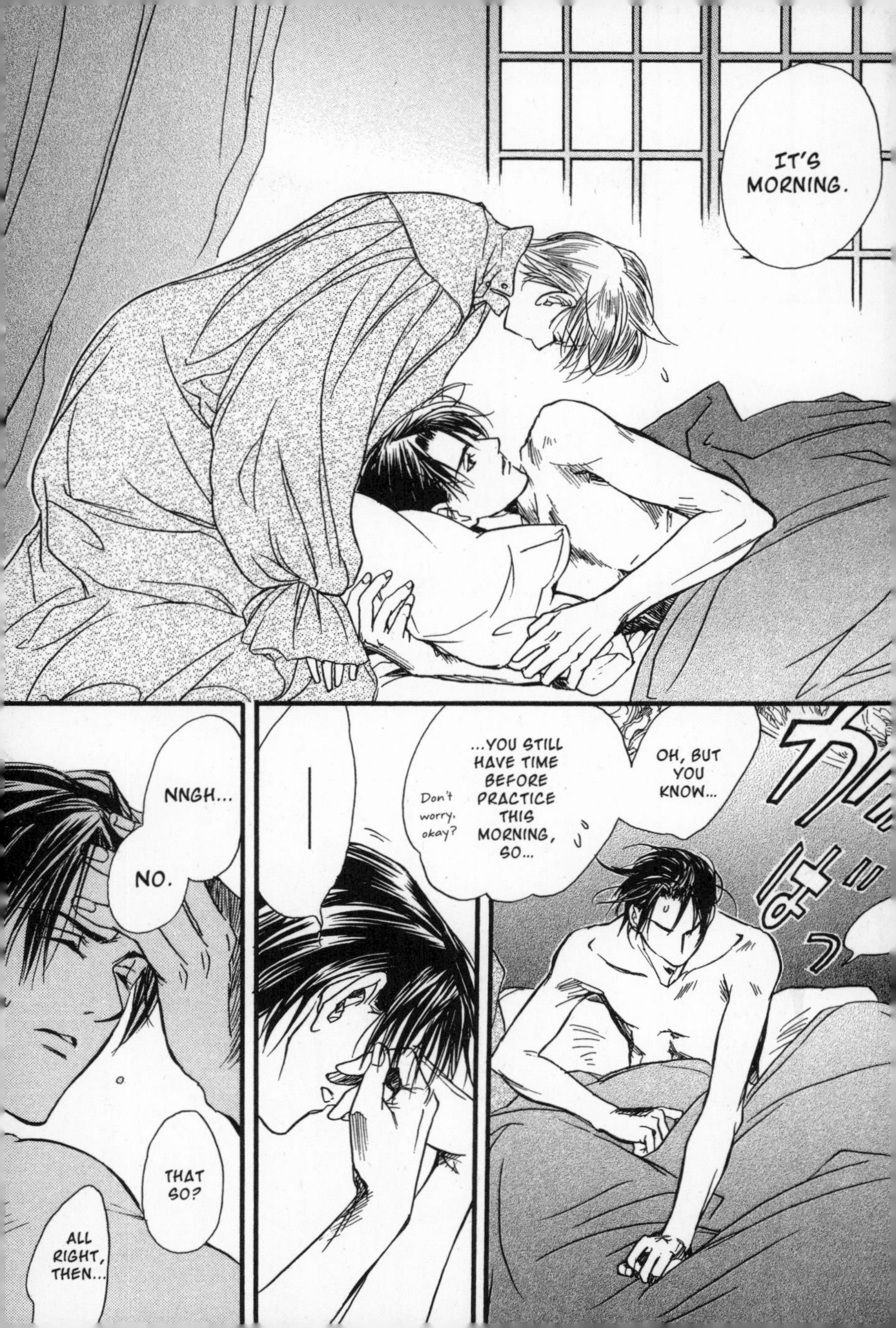
IT'S MORNING.
OH, BUT YOU KNOW...
...YOU STILL HAVE TIME BEFORE PRACTICE THIS MORNING, SO...
Don't worry, okay?
NNGH...
NO.
THAT SO?
ALL RIGHT, THEN...

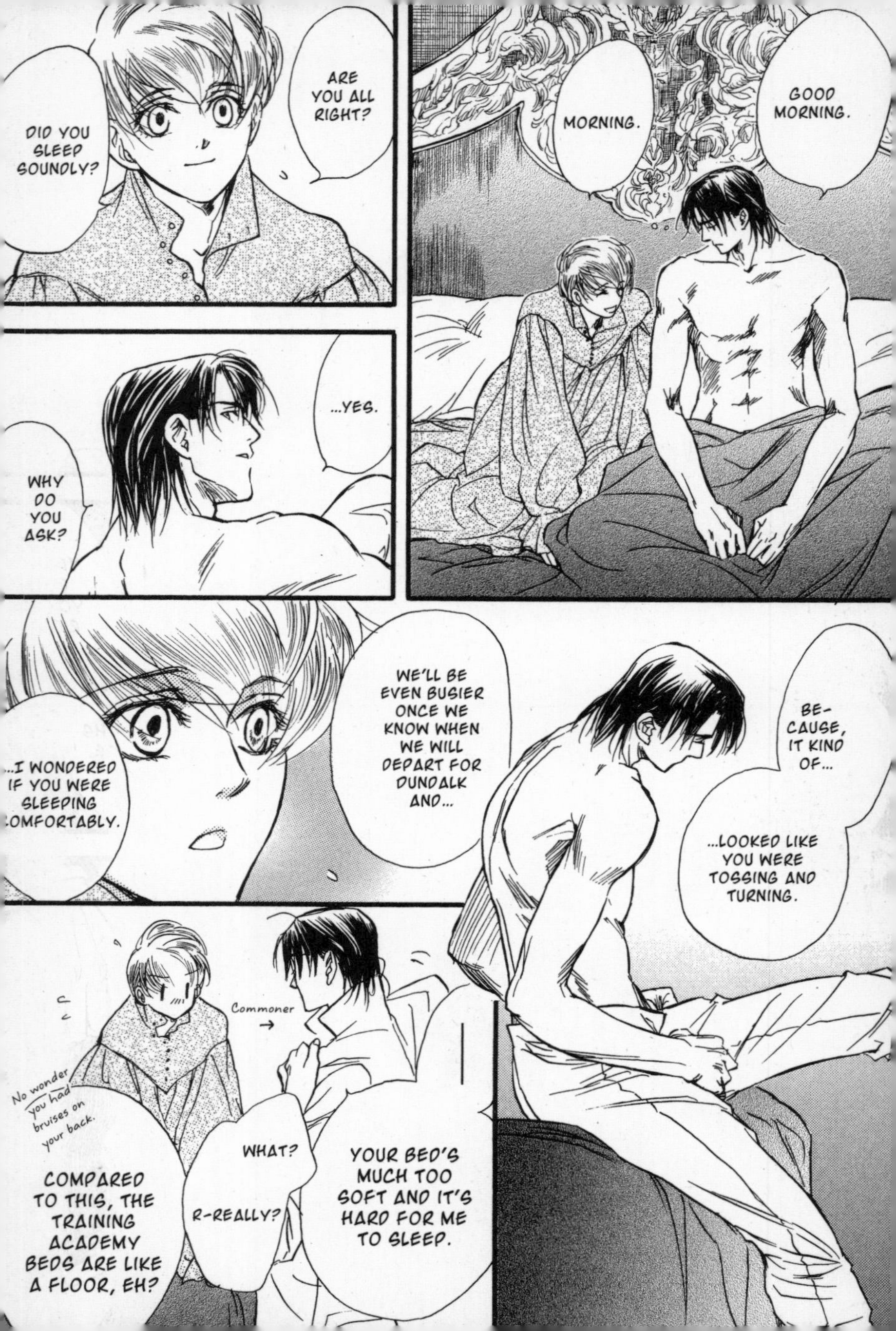
GOOD MORNING.
MORNING.
ARE YOU ALL RIGHT?
DID YOU SLEEP SOUNDLY?
...YES.
WHY DO YOU ASK?
BE-CAUSE, IT KIND OF...
...LOOKED LIKE YOU WERE TOSSING AND TURNING.
WE'LL BE EVEN BUSIER ONCE WE KNOW WHEN WE WILL DEPART FOR DUNDALK AND...
...I WONDERED IF YOU WERE SLEEPING COMFORTABLY.
YOUR BED'S MUCH TOO SOFT AND IT'S HARD FOR ME TO SLEEP.
WHAT?
Commoner →
R-REALLY?
No wonder you had bruises on your back.
COMPARED TO THIS, THE TRAINING ACADEMY BEDS ARE LIKE A FLOOR, EH?

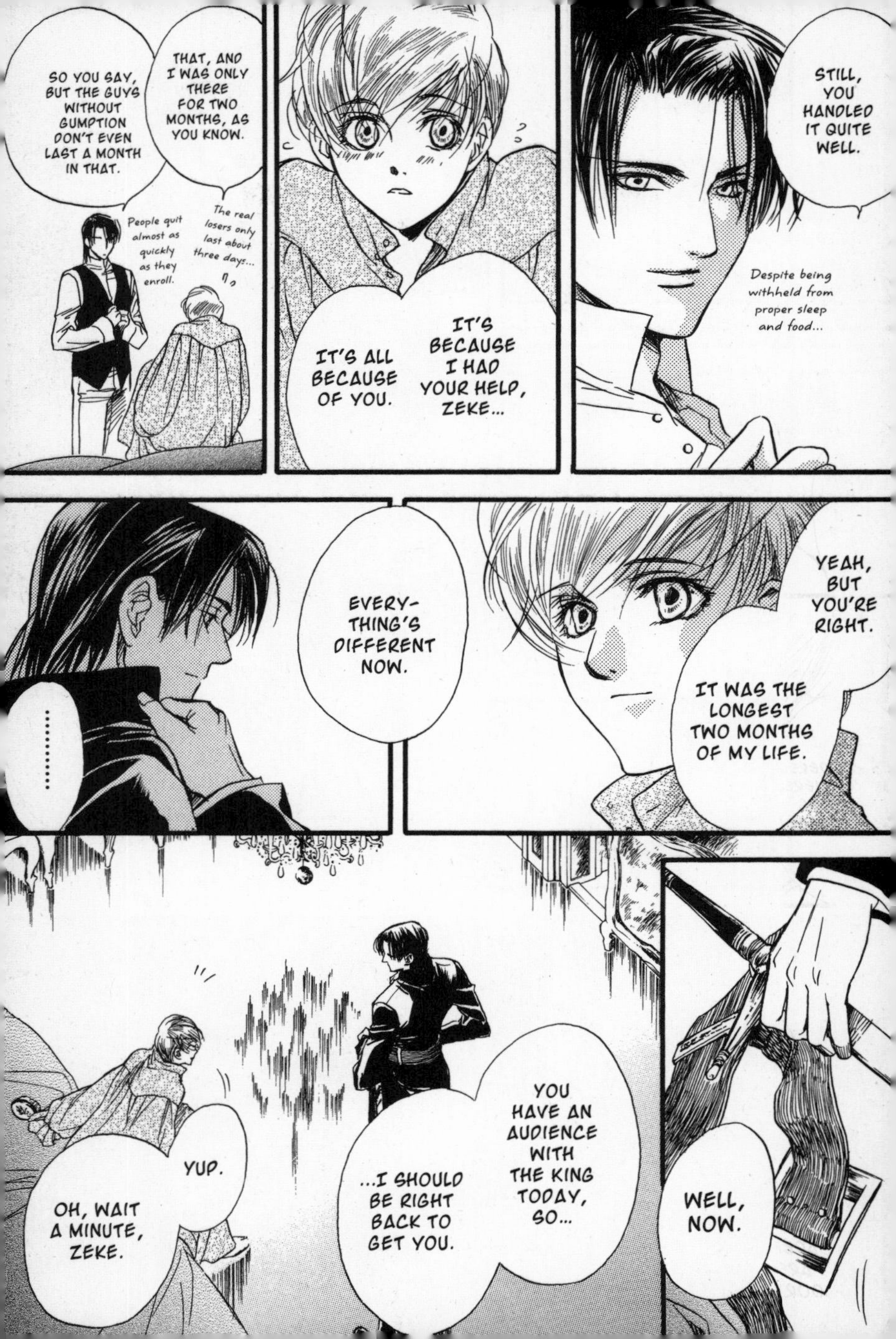
STILL, YOU HANDLED IT QUITE WELL.
Despite being withheld from proper sleep and food...
IT'S BECAUSE I HAD YOUR HELP, ZEKE...
IT'S ALL BECAUSE OF YOU.
THAT, AND I WAS ONLY THERE FOR TWO MONTHS, AS YOU KNOW.
SO YOU SAY, BUT THE GUYS WITHOUT GUMPTION DON'T EVEN LAST A MONTH IN THAT.
The real losers only last about three days...
People quit almost as quickly as they enroll.
YEAH, BUT YOU'RE RIGHT.
IT WAS THE LONGEST TWO MONTHS OF MY LIFE.
EVERY-THING'S DIFFERENT NOW.
......
WELL, NOW.
YOU HAVE AN AUDIENCE WITH THE KING TODAY, SO...
...I SHOULD BE RIGHT BACK TO GET YOU.
YUP.
OH, WAIT A MINUTE, ZEKE.

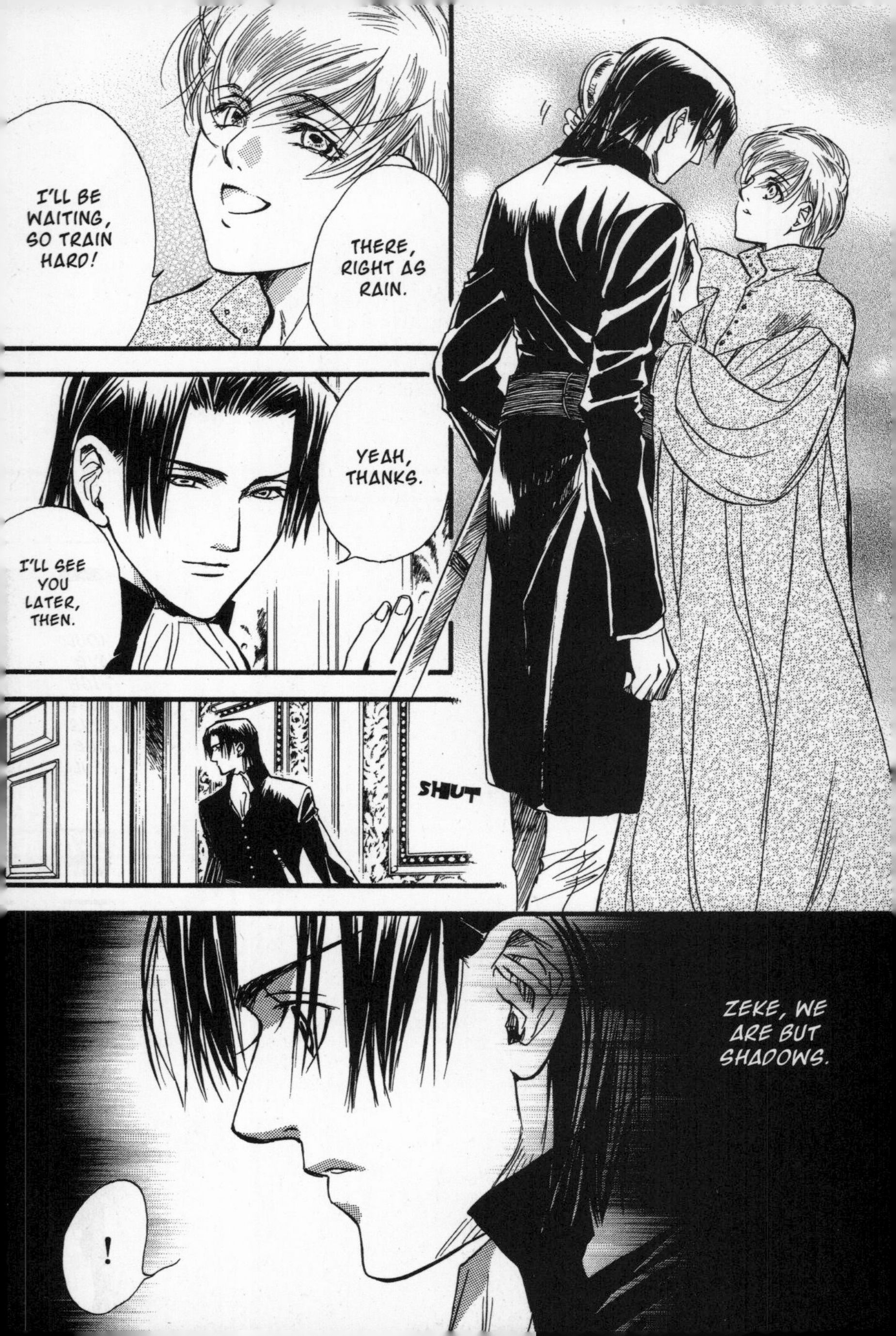
THERE, RIGHT AS RAIN.
I'LL BE WAITING, SO TRAIN HARD!
YEAH, THANKS.
I'LL SEE YOU LATER, THEN.
SHUT
ZEKE, WE ARE BUT SHADOWS.
!

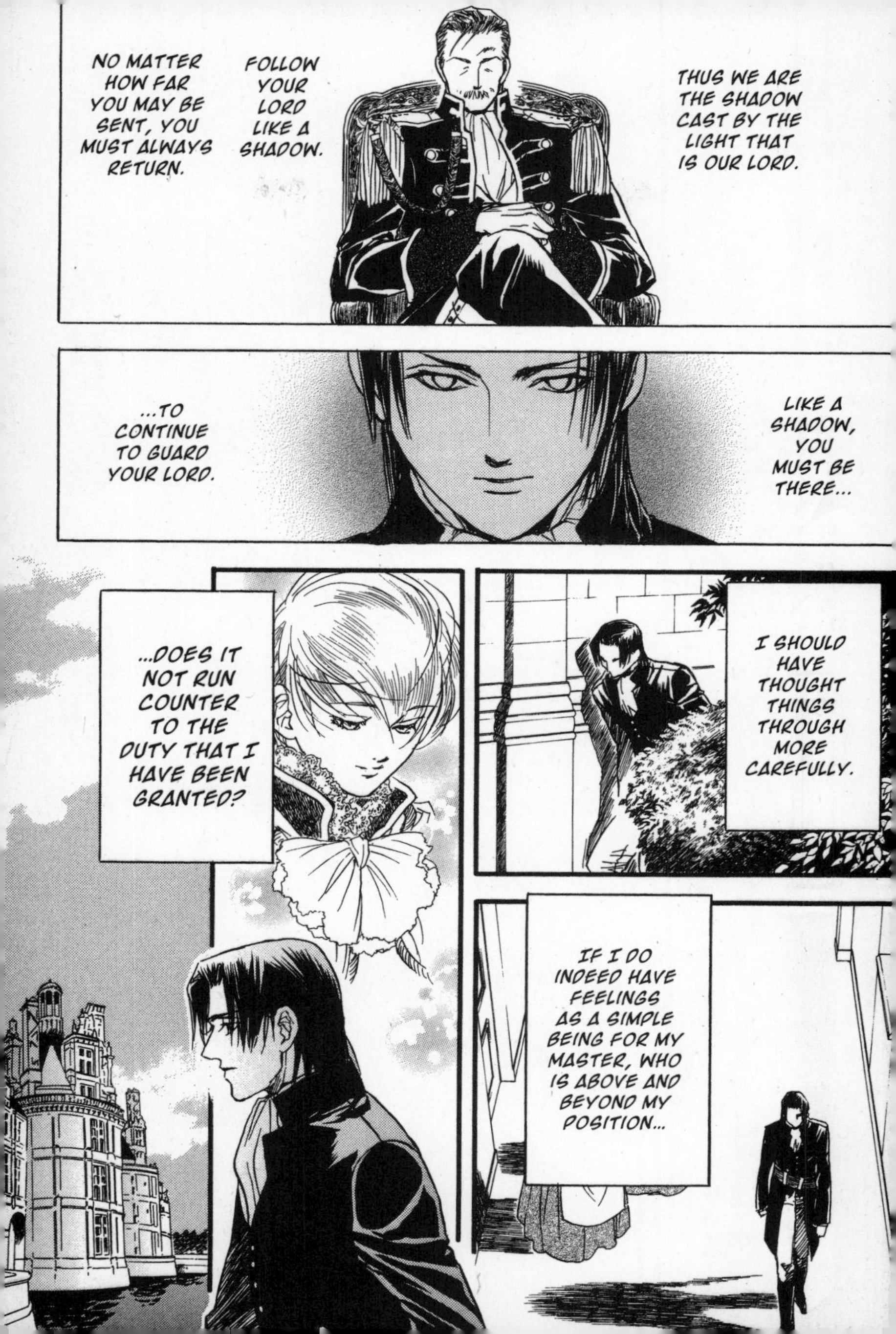
THUS WE ARE THE SHADOW CAST BY THE LIGHT THAT IS OUR LORD.
FOLLOW YOUR LORD LIKE A SHADOW.
NO MATTER HOW FAR YOU MAY BE SENT, YOU MUST ALWAYS RETURN.
LIKE A SHADOW, YOU MUST BE THERE...
...TO CONTINUE TO GUARD YOUR LORD.
I SHOULD HAVE THOUGHT THINGS THROUGH MORE CAREFULLY.
IF I DO INDEED HAVE FEELINGS AS A SIMPLE BEING FOR MY MASTER, WHO IS ABOVE AND BEYOND MY POSITION...
...DOES IT NOT RUN COUNTER TO THE DUTY THAT I HAVE BEEN GRANTED?

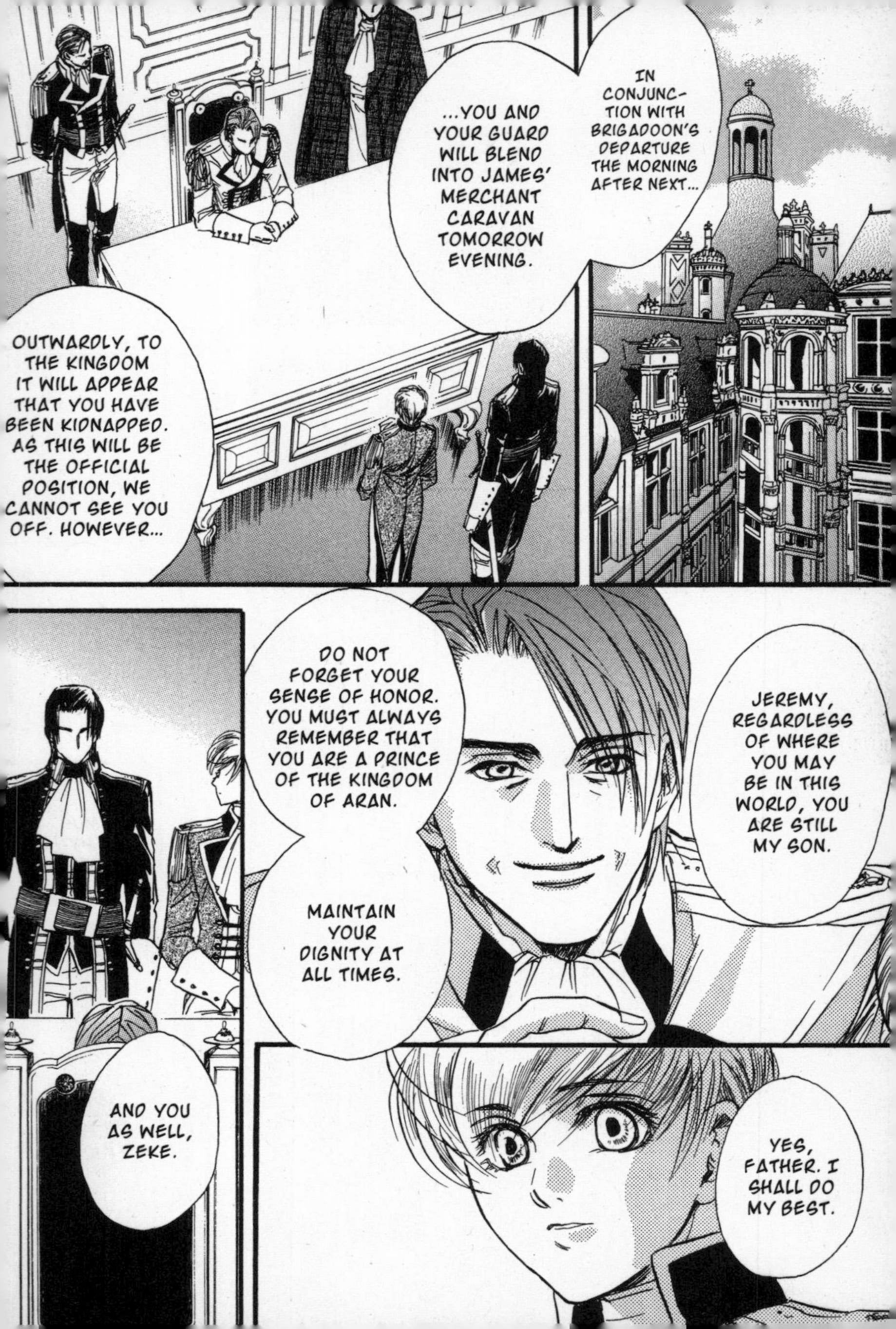
IN CONJUNCTION WITH BRIGADOON'S DEPARTURE THE MORNING AFTER NEXT...
...YOU AND YOUR GUARD WILL BLEND INTO JAMES' MERCHANT CARAVAN TOMORROW EVENING.
OUTWARDLY, TO THE KINGDOM IT WILL APPEAR THAT YOU HAVE BEEN KIDNAPPED. AS THIS WILL BE THE OFFICIAL POSITION, WE CANNOT SEE YOU OFF. HOWEVER...
JEREMY, REGARDLESS OF WHERE YOU MAY BE IN THIS WORLD, YOU ARE STILL MY SON.
DO NOT FORGET YOUR SENSE OF HONOR. YOU MUST ALWAYS REMEMBER THAT YOU ARE A PRINCE OF THE KINGDOM OF ARAN.
MAINTAIN YOUR DIGNITY AT ALL TIMES.
YES, FATHER. I SHALL DO MY BEST.
AND YOU AS WELL, ZEKE.

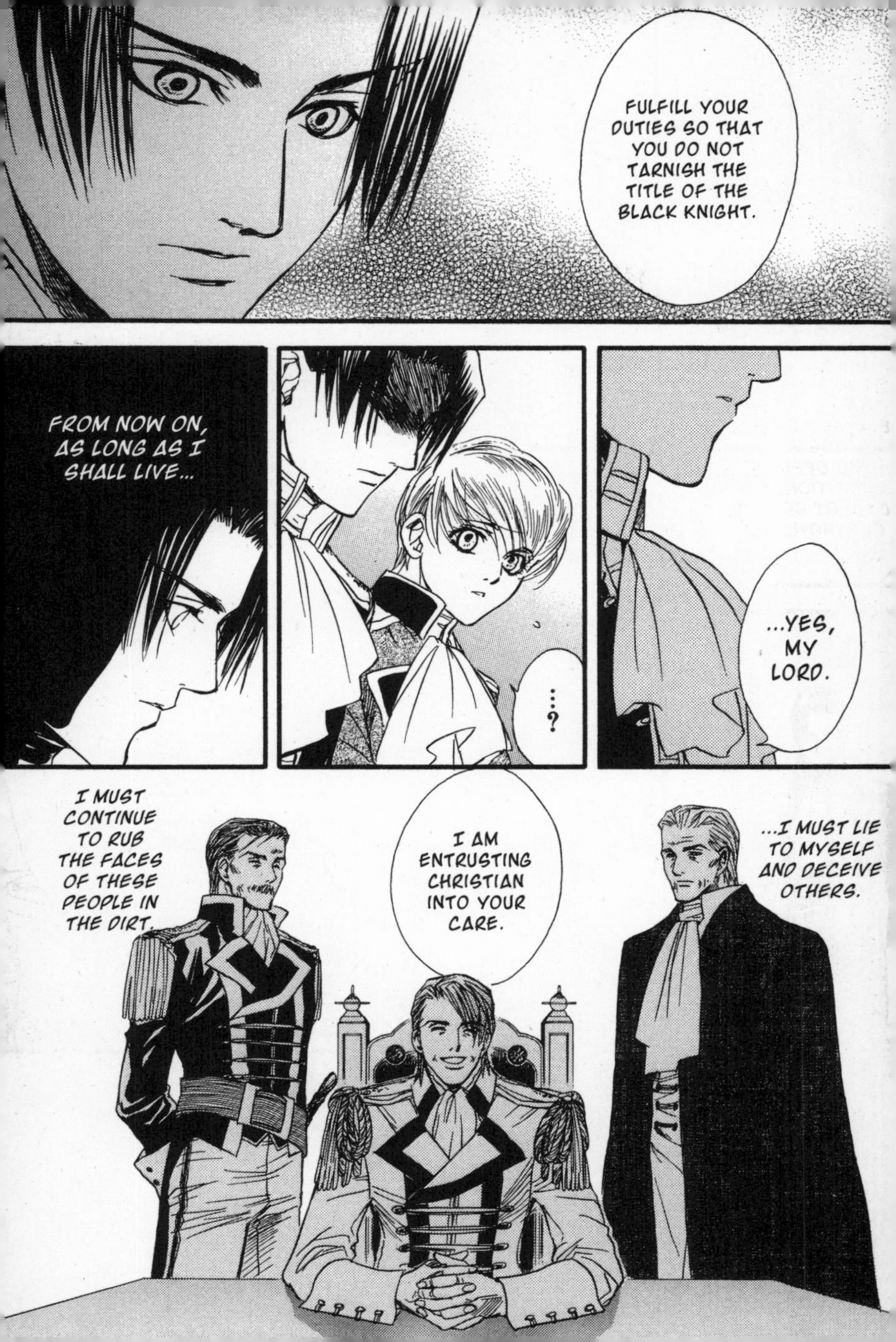
FULFILL YOUR DUTIES SO THAT YOU DO NOT TARNISH THE TITLE OF THE BLACK KNIGHT.
...YES, MY LORD.
...?
FROM NOW ON, AS LONG AS I SHALL LIVE...
...I MUST LIE TO MYSELF AND DECEIVE OTHERS.
I AM ENTRUSTING CHRISTIAN INTO YOUR CARE.
I MUST CONTINUE TO RUB THE FACES OF THESE PEOPLE IN THE DIRT.

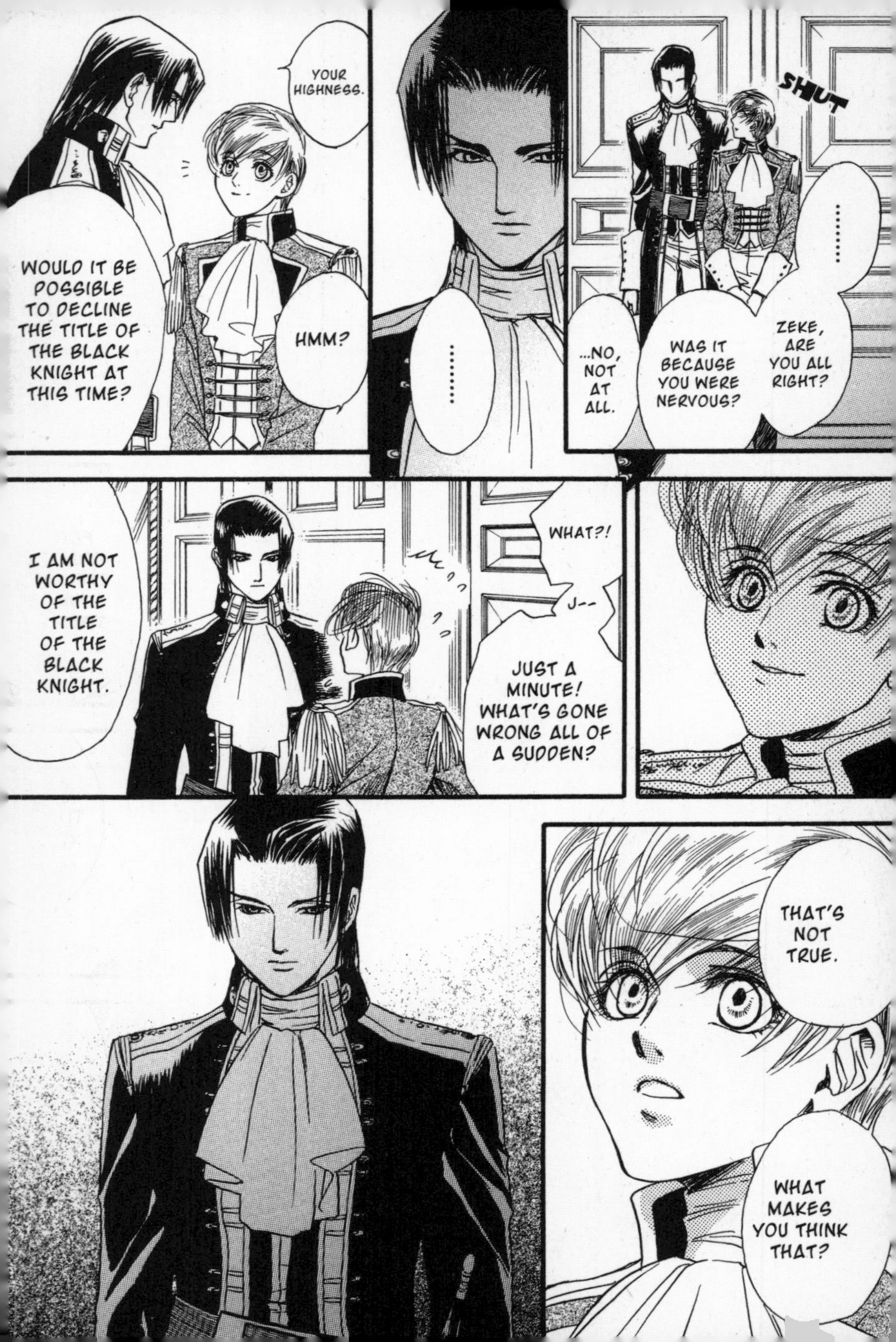
SHUT
......
ZEKE, ARE YOU ALL RIGHT?
WAS IT BECAUSE YOU WERE NERVOUS?
...NO, NOT AT ALL.
....
YOUR HIGHNESS.
HMM?
WOULD IT BE POSSIBLE TO DECLINE THE TITLE OF THE BLACK KNIGHT AT THIS TIME?
I AM NOT WORTHY OF THE TITLE OF THE BLACK KNIGHT.
WHAT?!
J--
JUST A MINUTE! WHAT'S GONE WRONG ALL OF A SUDDEN?
THAT'S NOT TRUE.
WHAT MAKES YOU THINK THAT?

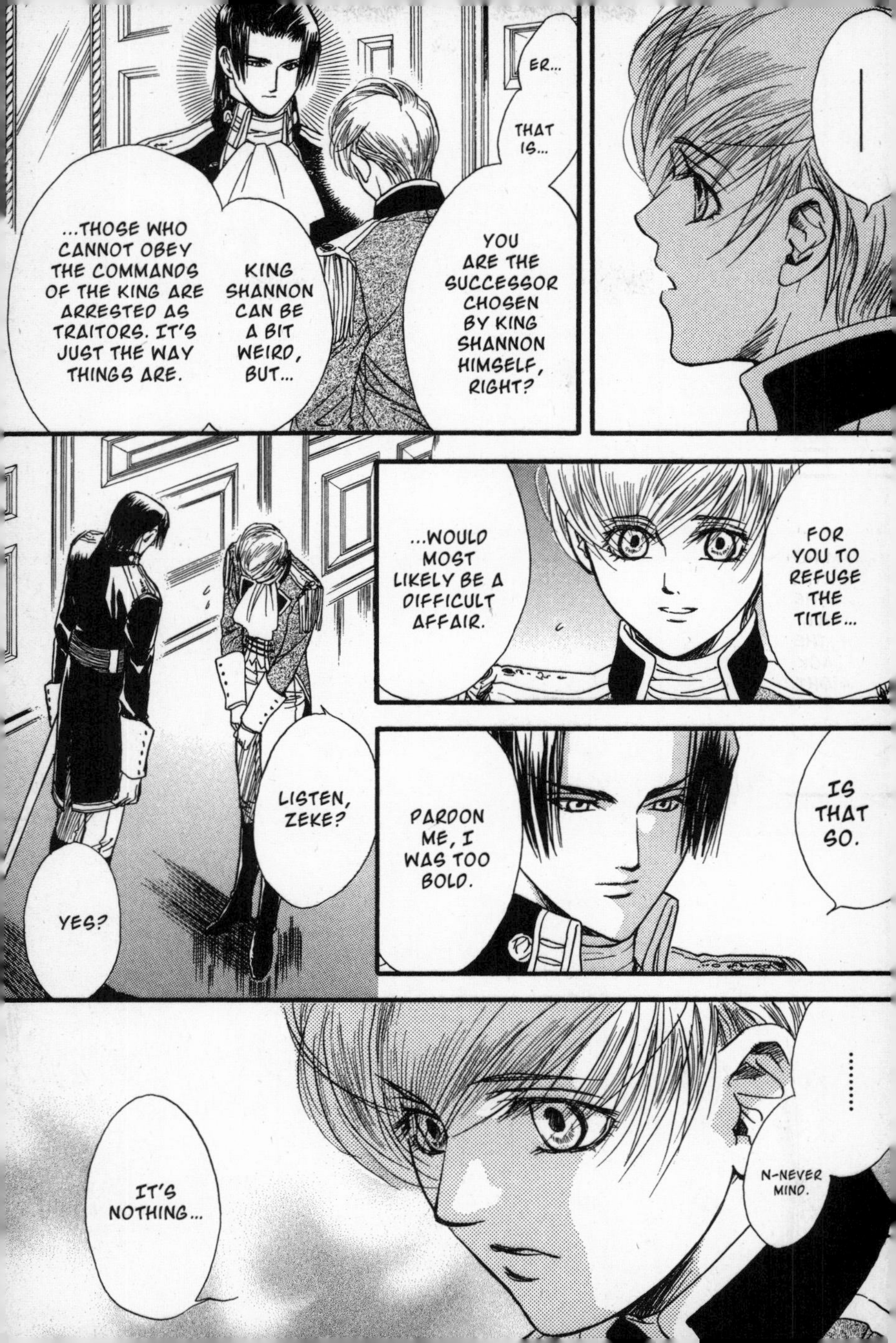
ER...
THAT IS...
YOU ARE THE SUCCESSOR CHOSEN BY KING SHANNON HIMSELF, RIGHT?
KING SHANNON CAN BE A BIT WEIRD, BUT...
...THOSE WHO CANNOT OBEY THE COMMANDS OF THE KING ARE ARRESTED AS TRAITORS. IT'S JUST THE WAY THINGS ARE.
FOR YOU TO REFUSE THE TITLE...
...WOULD MOST LIKELY BE A DIFFICULT AFFAIR.
IS THAT SO.
PARDON ME, I WAS TOO BOLD.
LISTEN, ZEKE?
YES?
....
N-NEVER MIND.
IT'S NOTHING...

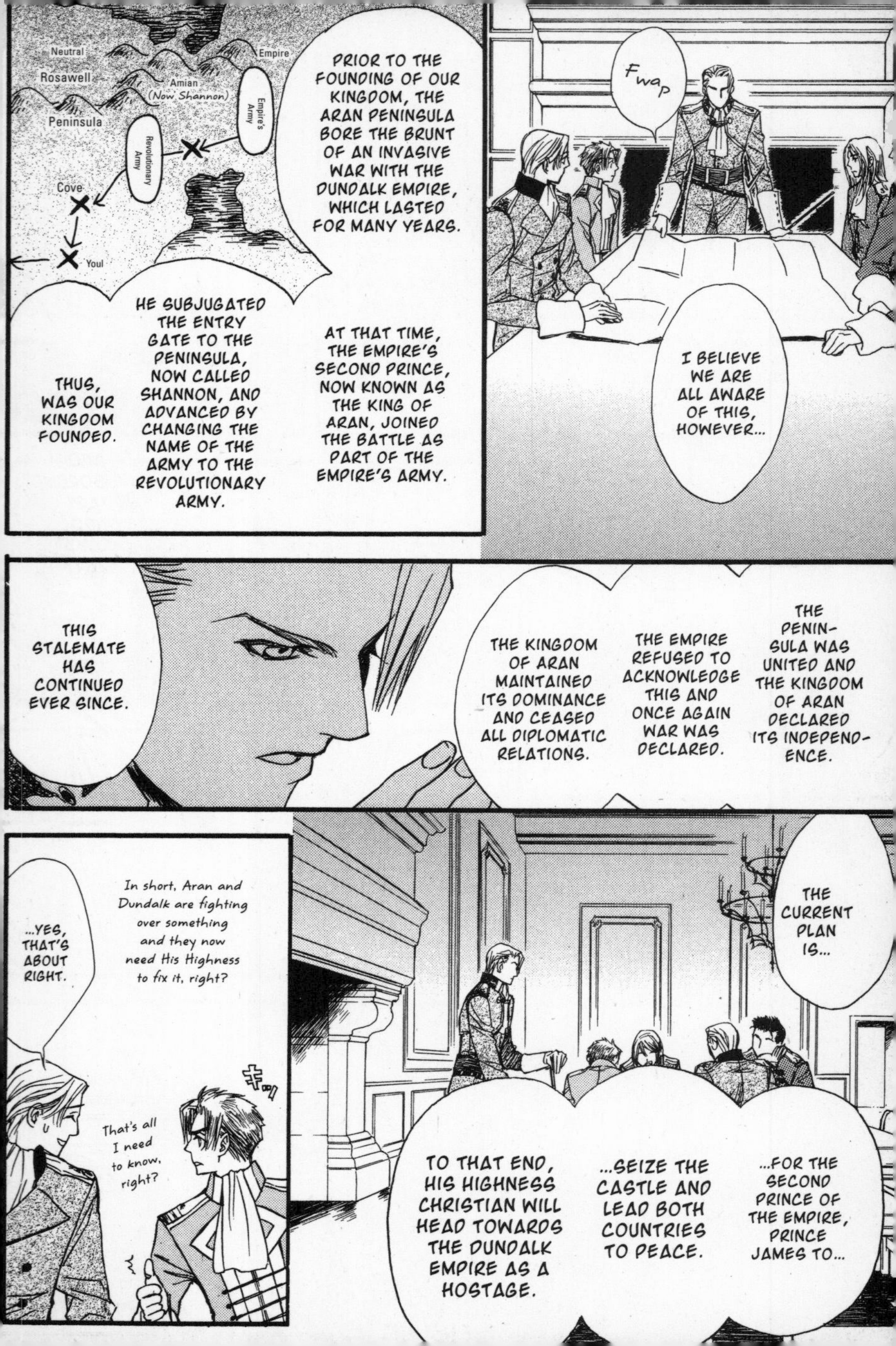
Fwap
I BELIEVE WE ARE ALL AWARE OF THIS, HOWEVER...
Neutral
Empire
Rosawell
Amian (Now Shannon)
Peninsula
Empire's Army
Revolutionary Army
Cove
Youl
PRIOR TO THE FOUNDING OF OUR KINGDOM, THE ARAN PENINSULA BORE THE BRUNT OF AN INVASIVE WAR WITH THE DUNDALK EMPIRE, WHICH LASTED FOR MANY YEARS.
AT THAT TIME, THE EMPIRE'S SECOND PRINCE, NOW KNOWN AS THE KING OF ARAN, JOINED THE BATTLE AS PART OF THE EMPIRE'S ARMY.
HE SUBJUGATED THE ENTRY GATE TO THE PENINSULA, NOW CALLED SHANNON, AND ADVANCED BY CHANGING THE NAME OF THE ARMY TO THE REVOLUTIONARY ARMY.
THUS, WAS OUR KINGDOM FOUNDED.
THE PENIN-SULA WAS UNITED AND THE KINGDOM OF ARAN DECLARED ITS INDEPENDENCE.
THE EMPIRE REFUSED TO ACKNOWLEDGE THIS AND ONCE AGAIN WAR WAS DECLARED.
THE KINGDOM OF ARAN MAINTAINED ITS DOMINANCE AND CEASED ALL DIPLOMATIC RELATIONS.
THIS STALEMATE HAS CONTINUED EVER SINCE.
THE CURRENT PLAN IS...
...FOR THE SECOND PRINCE OF THE EMPIRE, PRINCE JAMES TO...
...SEIZE THE CASTLE AND LEAD BOTH COUNTRIES TO PEACE.
TO THAT END, HIS HIGHNESS CHRISTIAN WILL HEAD TOWARDS THE DUNDALK EMPIRE AS A HOSTAGE.
In short, Aran and Dundalk are fighting over something and they now need His Highness to fix it, right?
...YES, THAT'S ABOUT RIGHT.
That's all I need to know, right?

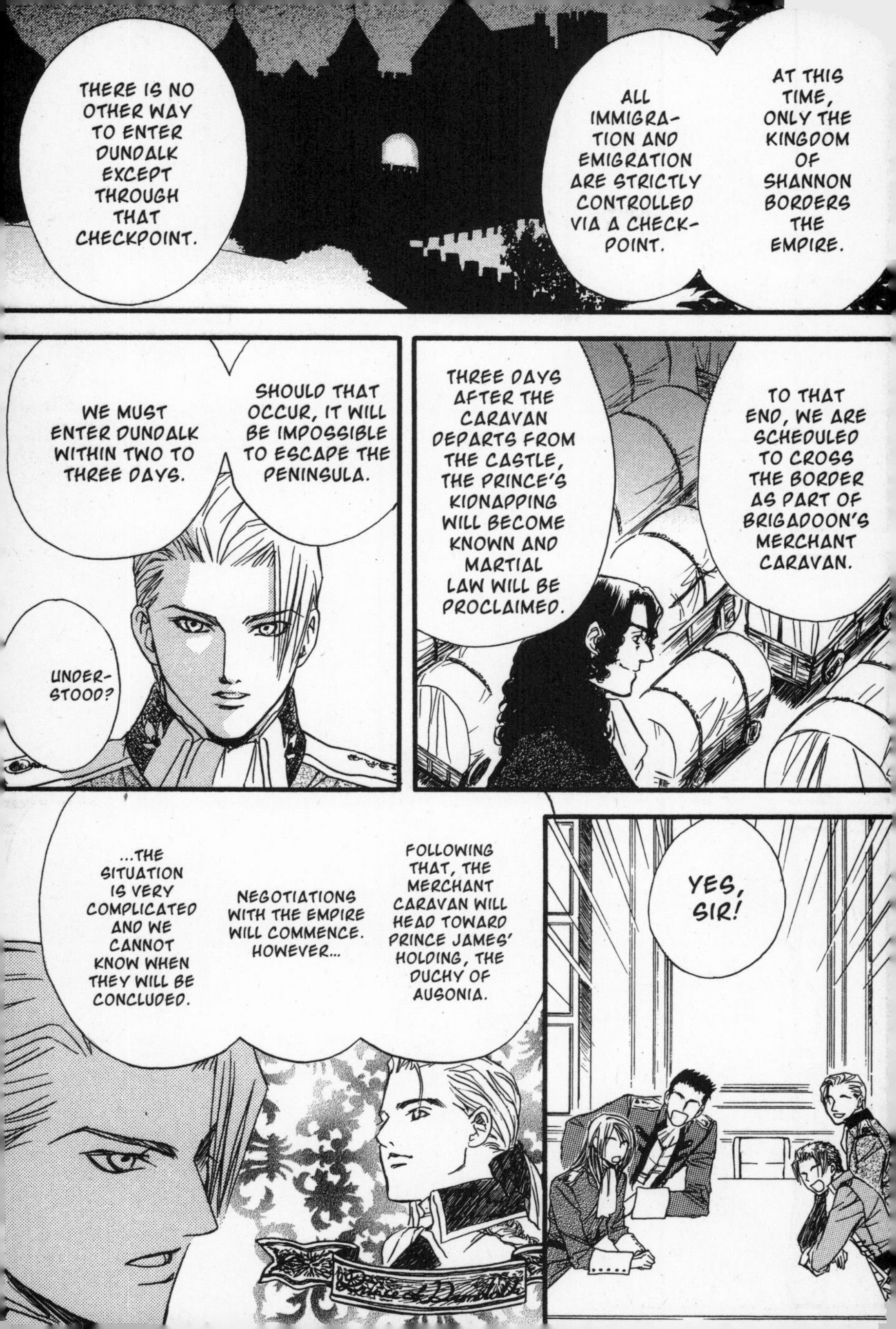
AT THIS TIME, ONLY THE KINGDOM OF SHANNON BORDERS THE EMPIRE.
ALL IMMIGRATION AND EMIGRATION ARE STRICTLY CONTROLLED VIA A CHECKPOINT.
THERE IS NO OTHER WAY TO ENTER DUNDALK EXCEPT THROUGH THAT CHECKPOINT.
TO THAT END, WE ARE SCHEDULED TO CROSS THE BORDER AS PART OF BRIGADOON'S MERCHANT CARAVAN.
THREE DAYS AFTER THE CARAVAN DEPARTS FROM THE CASTLE, THE PRINCE'S KIDNAPPING WILL BECOME KNOWN AND MARTIAL LAW WILL BE PROCLAIMED.
SHOULD THAT OCCUR, IT WILL BE IMPOSSIBLE TO ESCAPE THE PENINSULA.
WE MUST ENTER DUNDALK WITHIN TWO TO THREE DAYS.
UNDERSTOOD?
YES, SIR!
FOLLOWING THAT, THE MERCHANT CARAVAN WILL HEAD TOWARD PRINCE JAMES' HOLDING, THE DUCHY OF AUSONIA.
NEGOTIATIONS WITH THE EMPIRE WILL COMMENCE. HOWEVER...
...THE SITUATION IS VERY COMPLICATED AND WE CANNOT KNOW WHEN THEY WILL BE CONCLUDED.

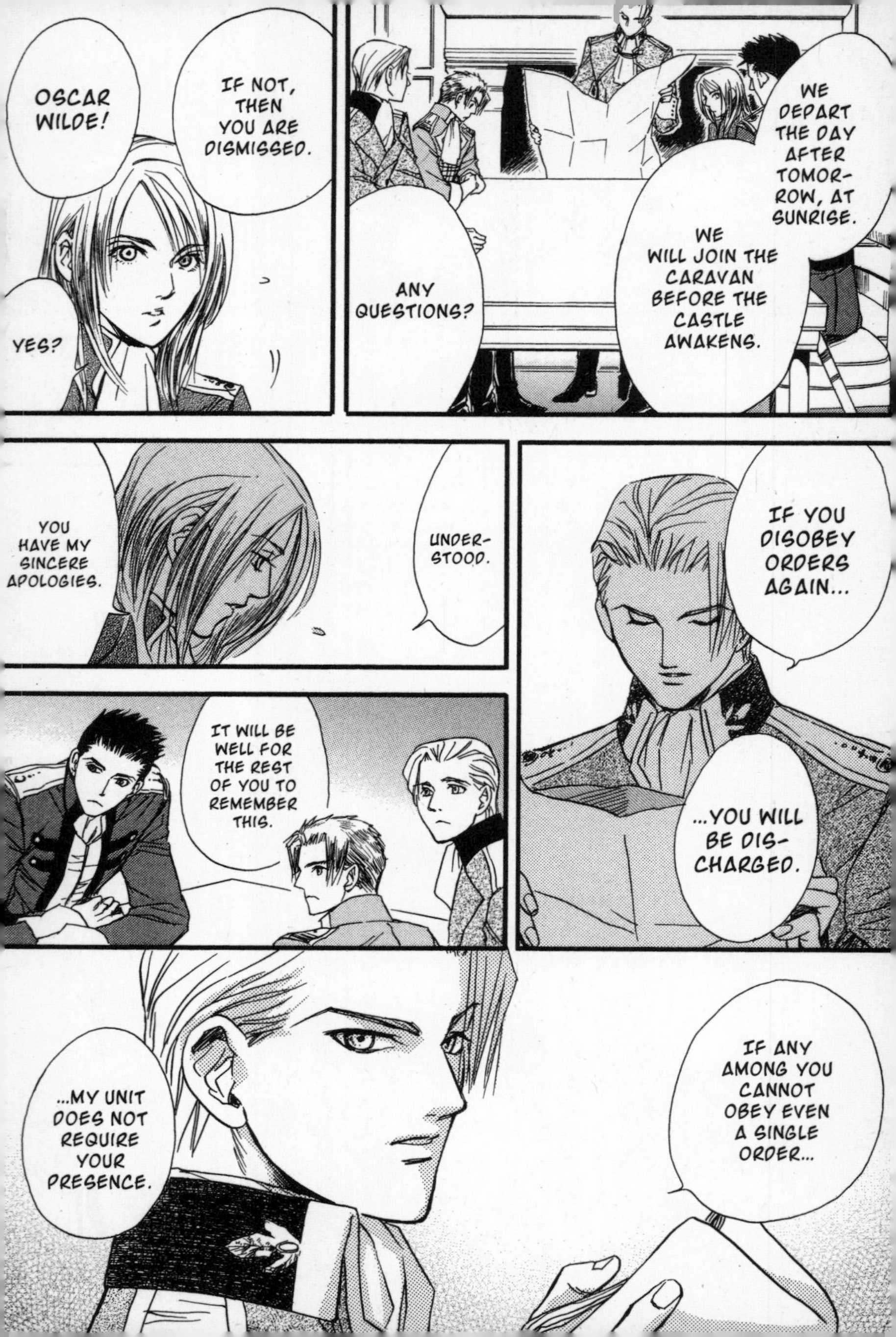
WE DEPART THE DAY AFTER TOMOR-ROW, AT SUNRISE.
WE WILL JOIN THE CARAVAN BEFORE THE CASTLE AWAKENS.
ANY QUESTIONS?
IF NOT, THEN YOU ARE DISMISSED.
OSCAR WILDE!
YES?
IF YOU DISOBEY ORDERS AGAIN...
...YOU WILL BE DIS-CHARGED.
UNDER-STOOD.
YOU HAVE MY SINCERE APOLOGIES.
IT WILL BE WELL FOR THE REST OF YOU TO REMEMBER THIS.
IF ANY AMONG YOU CANNOT OBEY EVEN A SINGLE ORDER...
...MY UNIT DOES NOT REQUIRE YOUR PRESENCE.

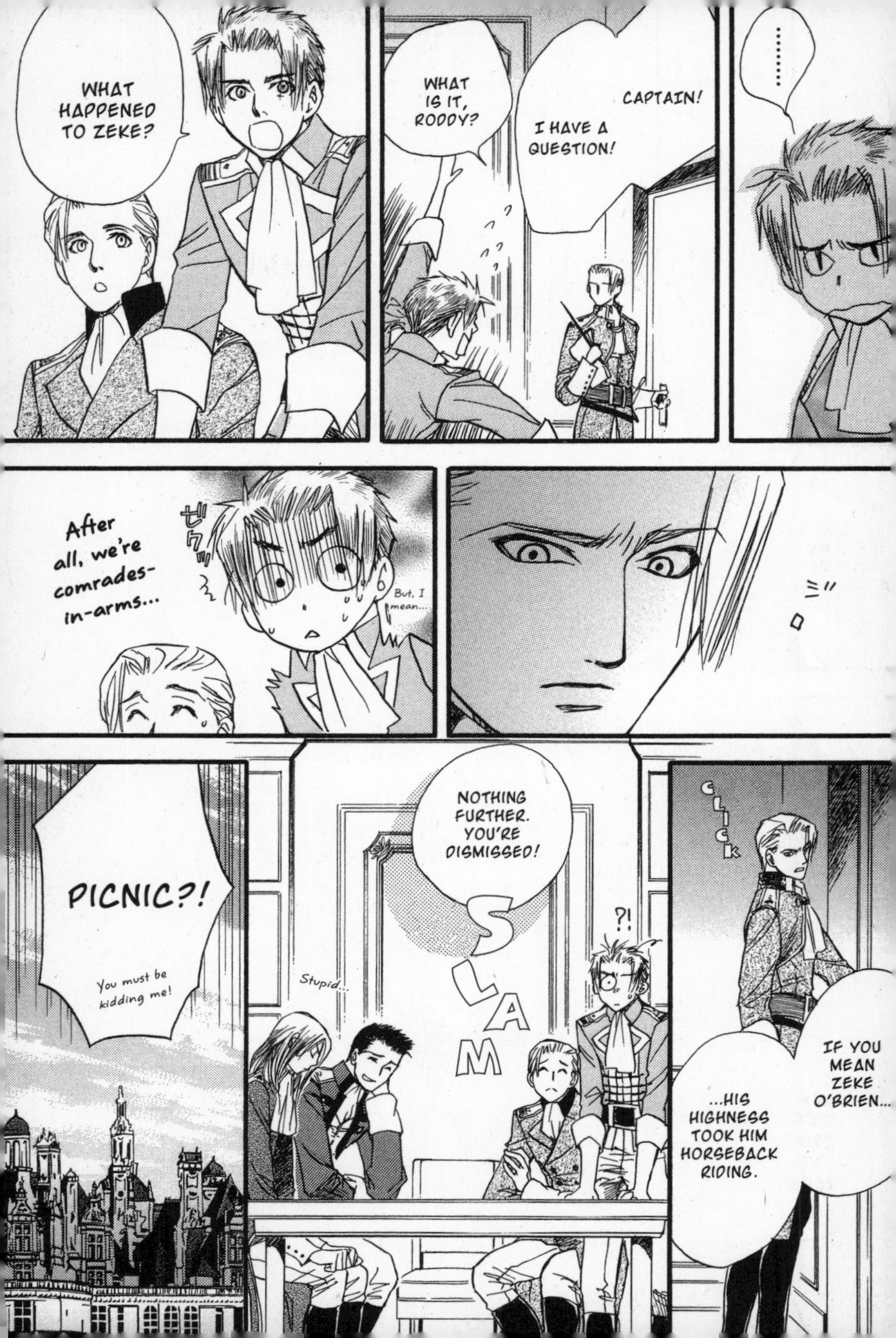
......
CAPTAIN!
I HAVE A QUESTION!
WHAT IS IT, RODDY?
WHAT HAPPENED TO ZEKE?
ジ
ロ
But, I mean...
After all, we're comrades-in-arms...
CLICK
IF YOU MEAN ZEKE O'BRIEN...
...HIS HIGHNESS TOOK HIM HORSEBACK RIDING.
NOTHING FURTHER. YOU'RE DISMISSED!
?!
SLAM
Stupid...
PICNIC?!
You must be kidding me!

THE
BLACK
KNIGHT

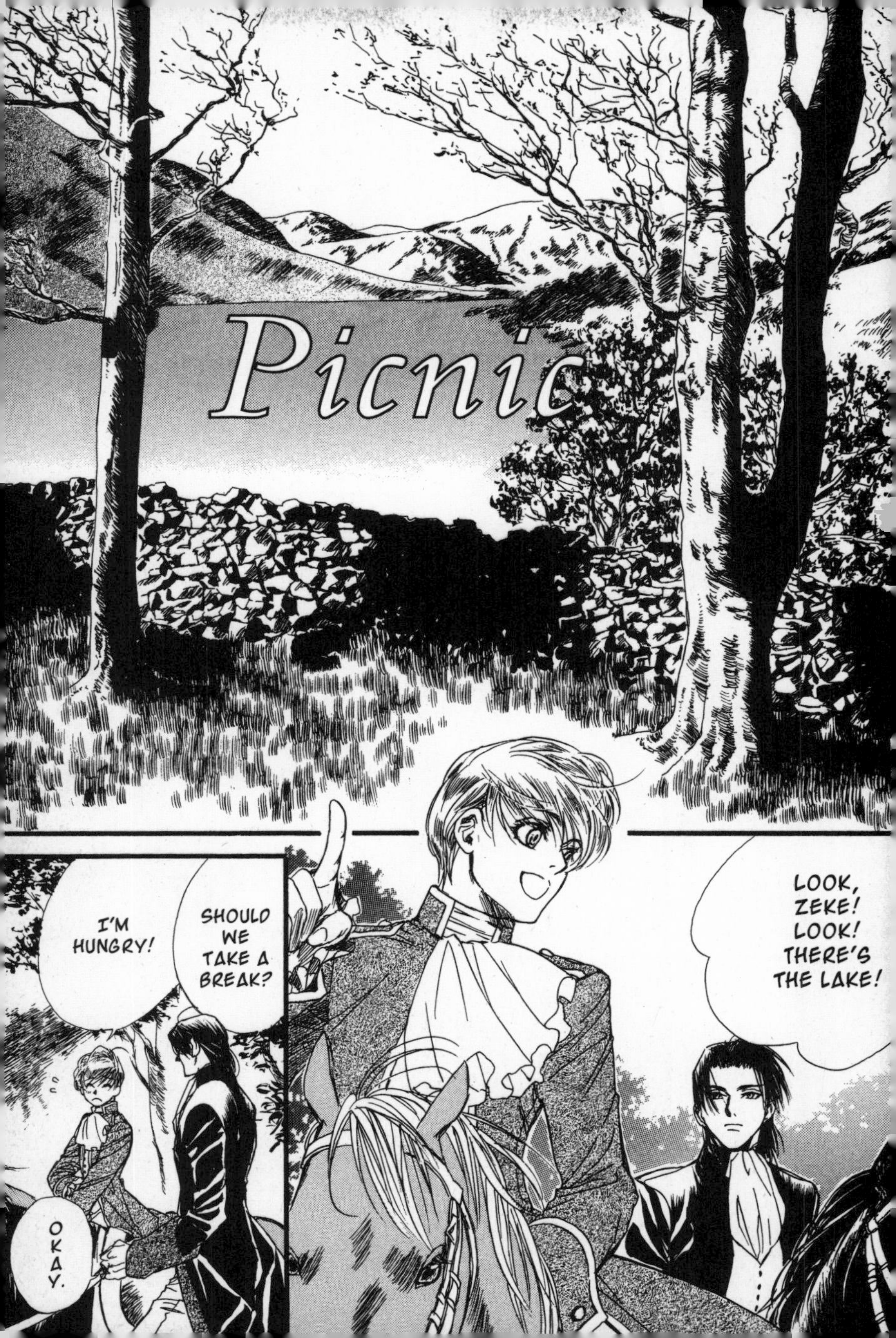
Picnic
LOOK, ZEKE! LOOK! THERE'S THE LAKE!
SHOULD WE TAKE A BREAK?
I'M HUNGRY!
OKAY.

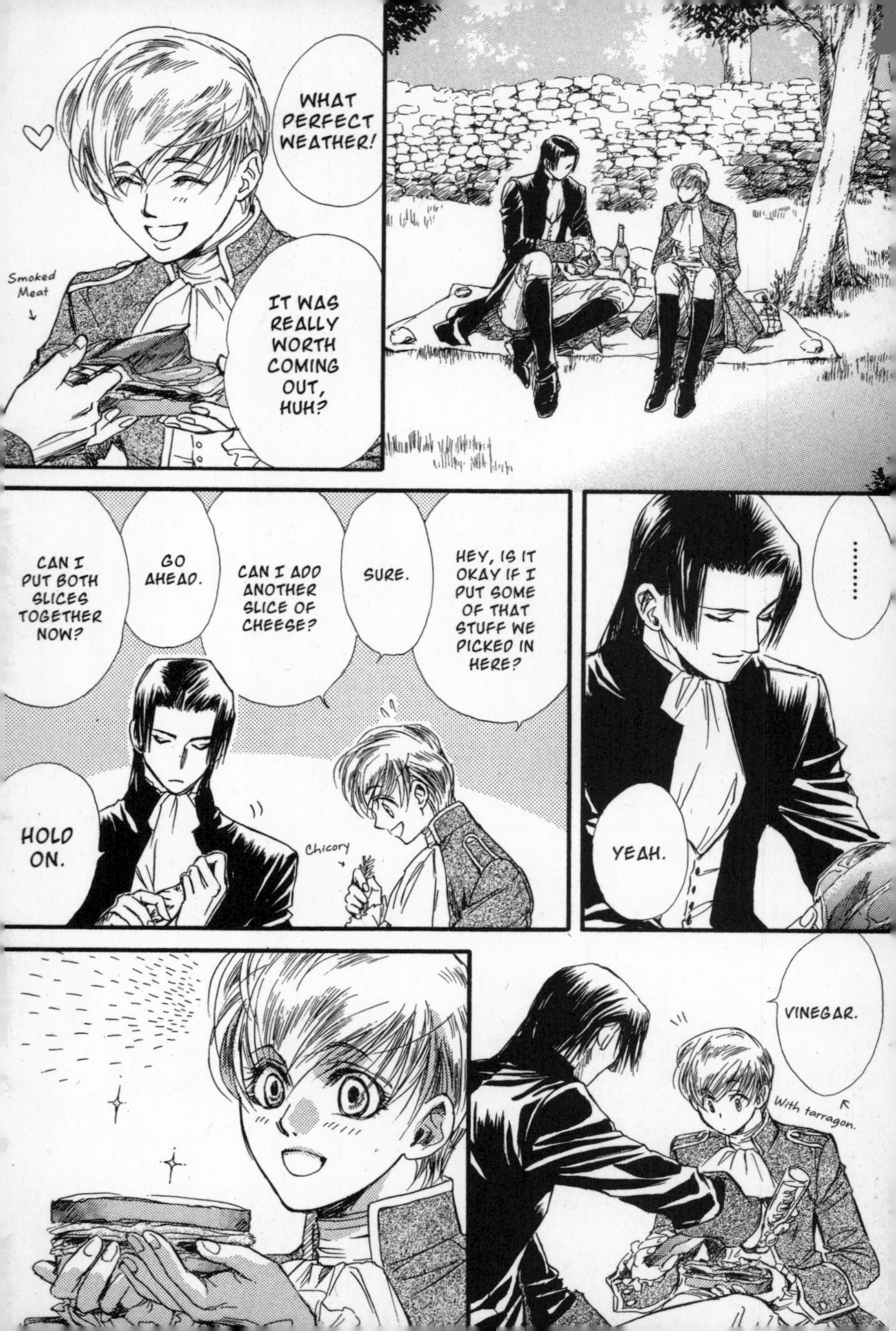
WHAT PERFECT WEATHER!
IT WAS REALLY WORTH COMING OUT, HUH?
Smoked Meat
......
YEAH.
HEY, IS IT OKAY IF I PUT SOME OF THAT STUFF WE PICKED IN HERE?
SURE.
CAN I ADD ANOTHER SLICE OF CHEESE?
GO AHEAD.
CAN I PUT BOTH SLICES TOGETHER NOW?
Chicory
HOLD ON.
VINEGAR.
With tarragon.

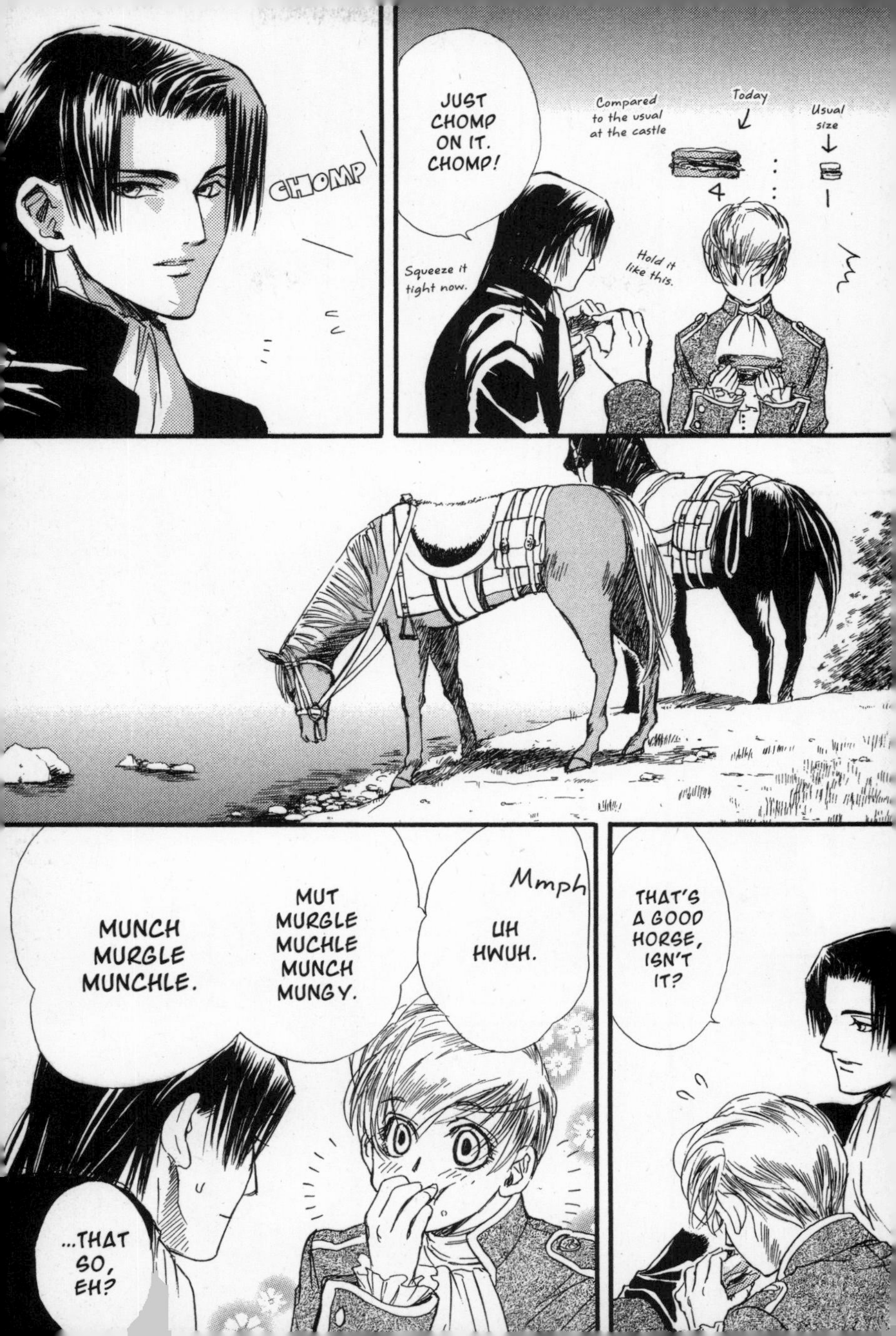
Usual size
Today
Compared to the usual at the castle
4
1
Hold it like this.
JUST CHOMP ON IT. CHOMP!
Squeeze it tight now.
CHOMP
THAT'S A GOOD HORSE, ISN'T IT?
Mmph
UH HWUH.
MUT MURGLE MUCHLE MUNCH MUNGY.
MUNCH MURGLE MUNCHLE.
...THAT SO, EH?

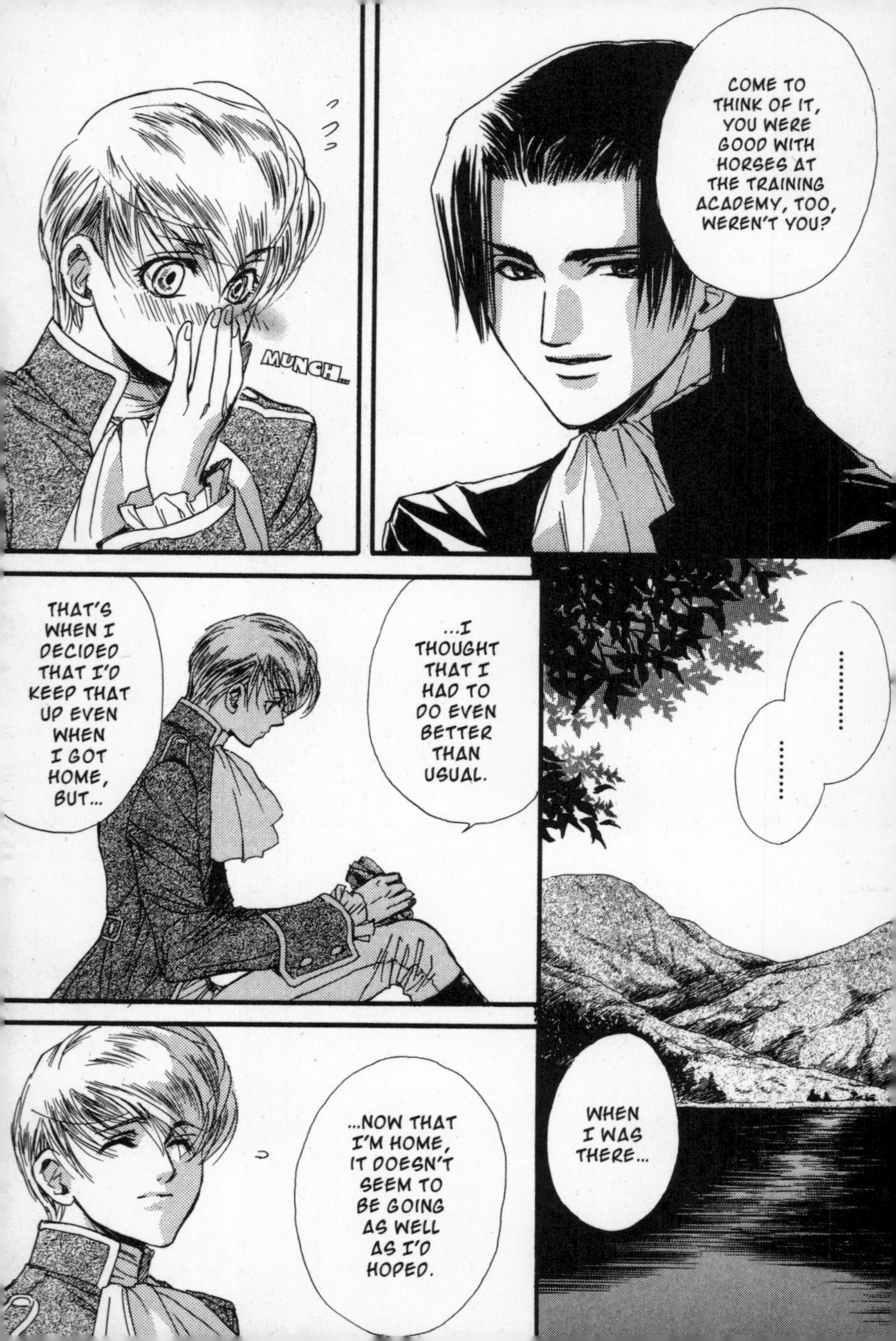
COME TO THINK OF IT, YOU WERE GOOD WITH HORSES AT THE TRAINING ACADEMY, TOO, WEREN'T YOU?
MUNCH...
......
......
WHEN I WAS THERE...
...I THOUGHT THAT I HAD TO DO EVEN BETTER THAN USUAL.
THAT'S WHEN I DECIDED THAT I'D KEEP THAT UP EVEN WHEN I GOT HOME, BUT...
...NOW THAT I'M HOME, IT DOESN'T SEEM TO BE GOING AS WELL AS I'D HOPED.

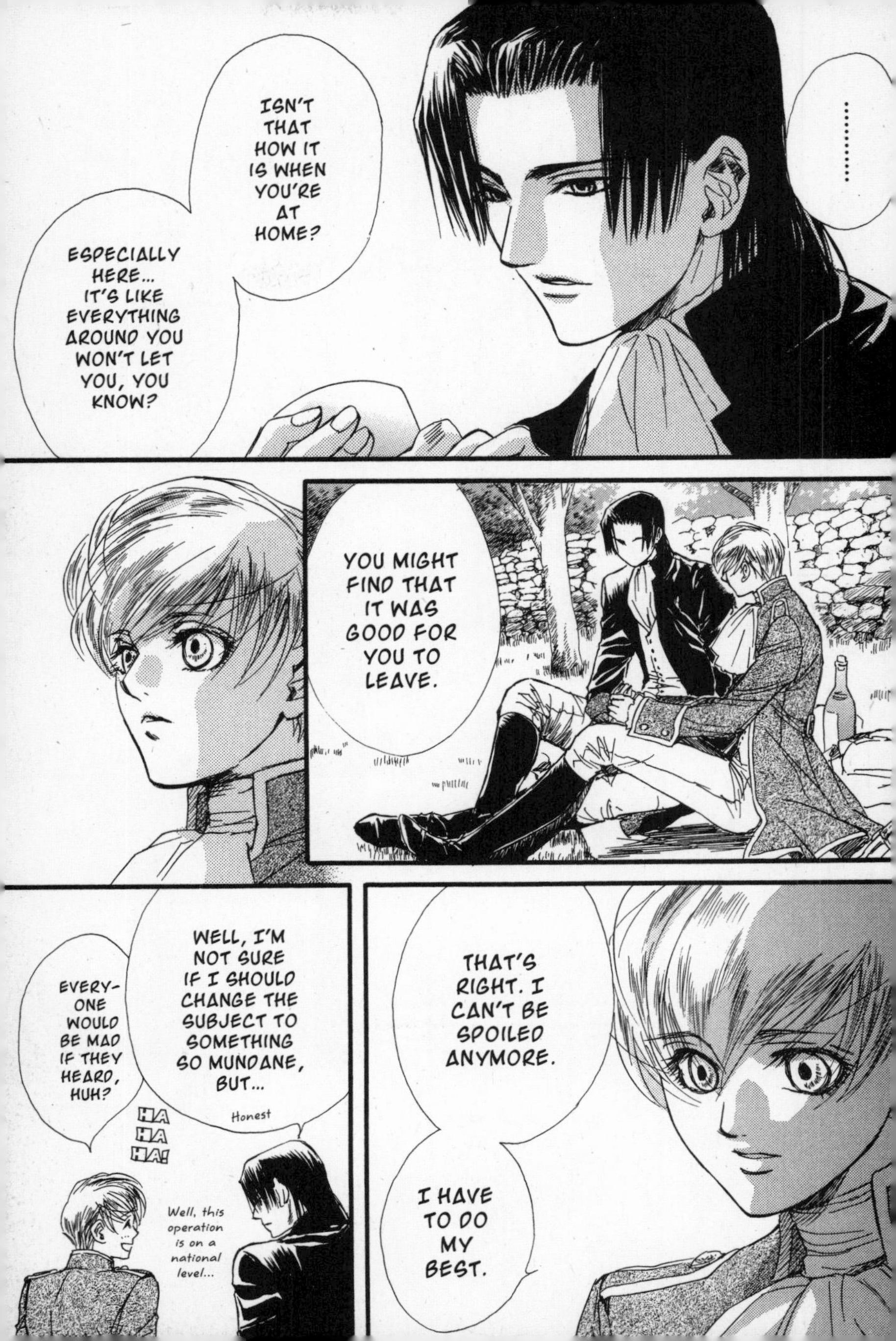
……
ISN'T THAT HOW IT IS WHEN YOU'RE AT HOME?
ESPECIALLY HERE... IT'S LIKE EVERYTHING AROUND YOU WON'T LET YOU, YOU KNOW?
YOU MIGHT FIND THAT IT WAS GOOD FOR YOU TO LEAVE.
THAT'S RIGHT. I CAN'T BE SPOILED ANYMORE.
I HAVE TO DO MY BEST.
WELL, I'M NOT SURE IF I SHOULD CHANGE THE SUBJECT TO SOMETHING SO MUNDANE, BUT...
Honest
EVERY-ONE WOULD BE MAD IF THEY HEARD, HUH?
HA HA HA!
Well, this operation is on a national level...

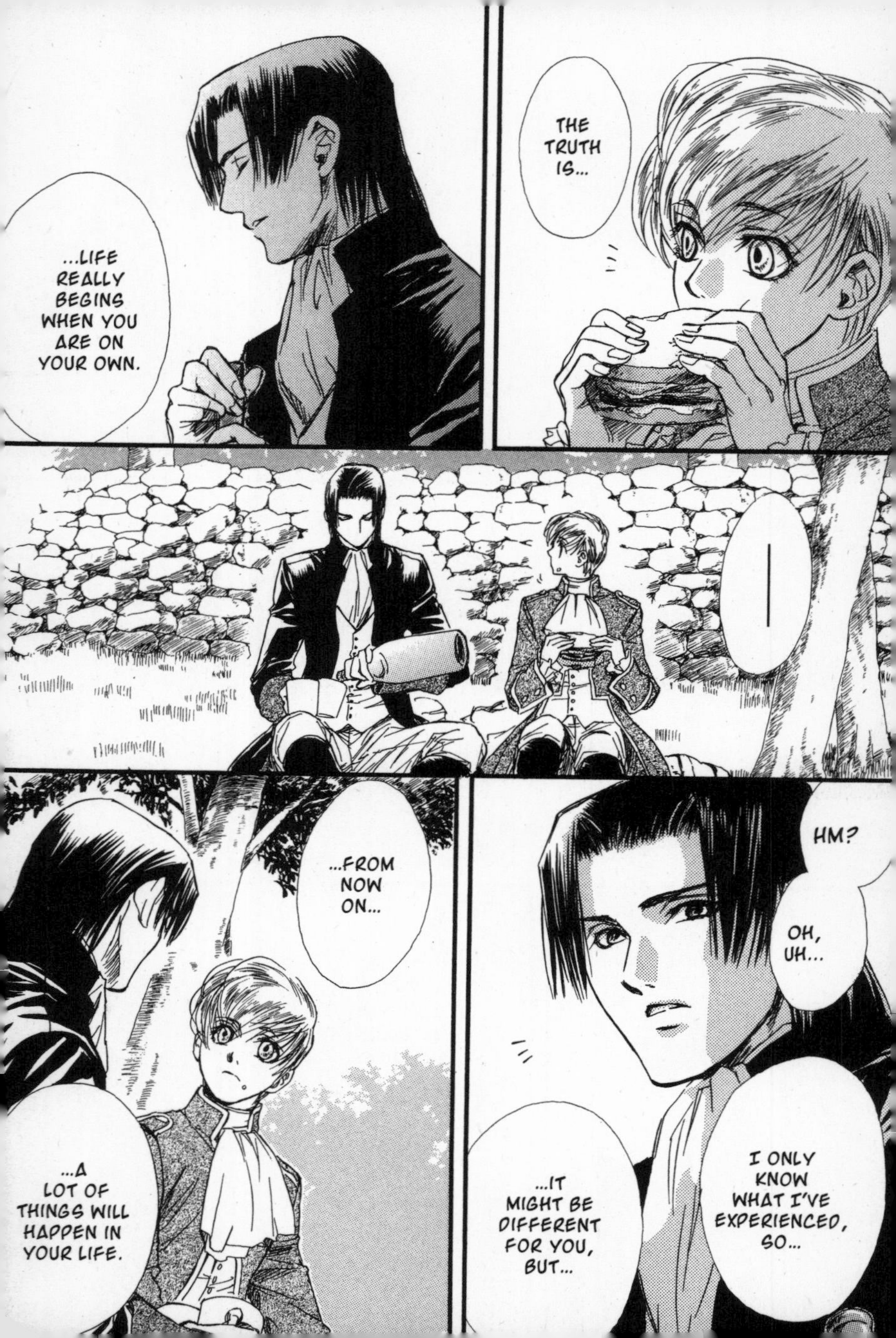
THE TRUTH IS...
...LIFE REALLY BEGINS WHEN YOU ARE ON YOUR OWN.
HM?
OH, UH...
I ONLY KNOW WHAT I'VE EXPERIENCED, SO...
...IT MIGHT BE DIFFERENT FOR YOU, BUT...
...FROM NOW ON...
...A LOT OF THINGS WILL HAPPEN IN YOUR LIFE.

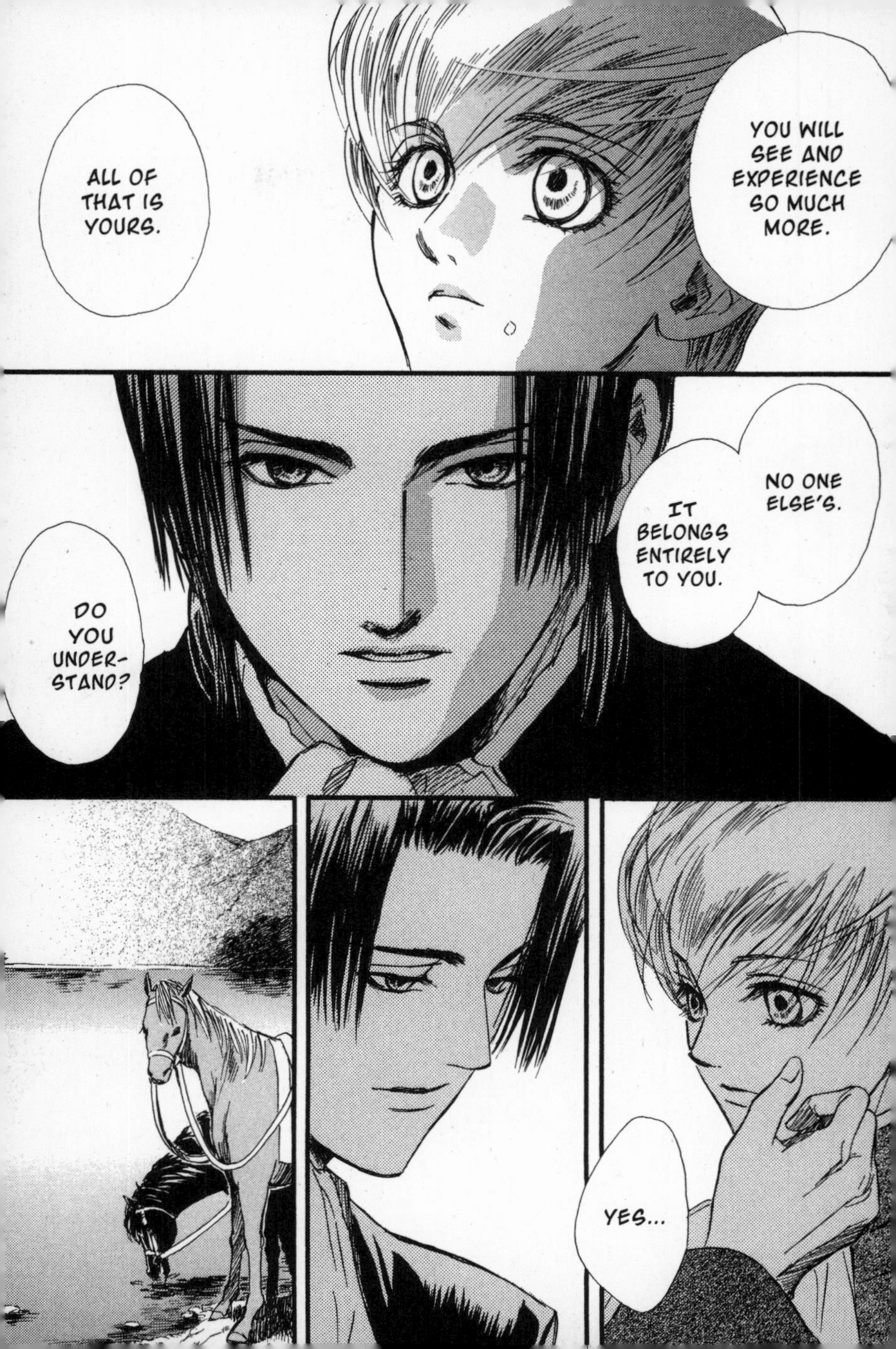
YOU WILL SEE AND EXPERIENCE SO MUCH MORE.
ALL OF THAT IS YOURS.
NO ONE ELSE'S.
IT BELONGS ENTIRELY TO YOU.
DO YOU UNDER-STAND?
YES...

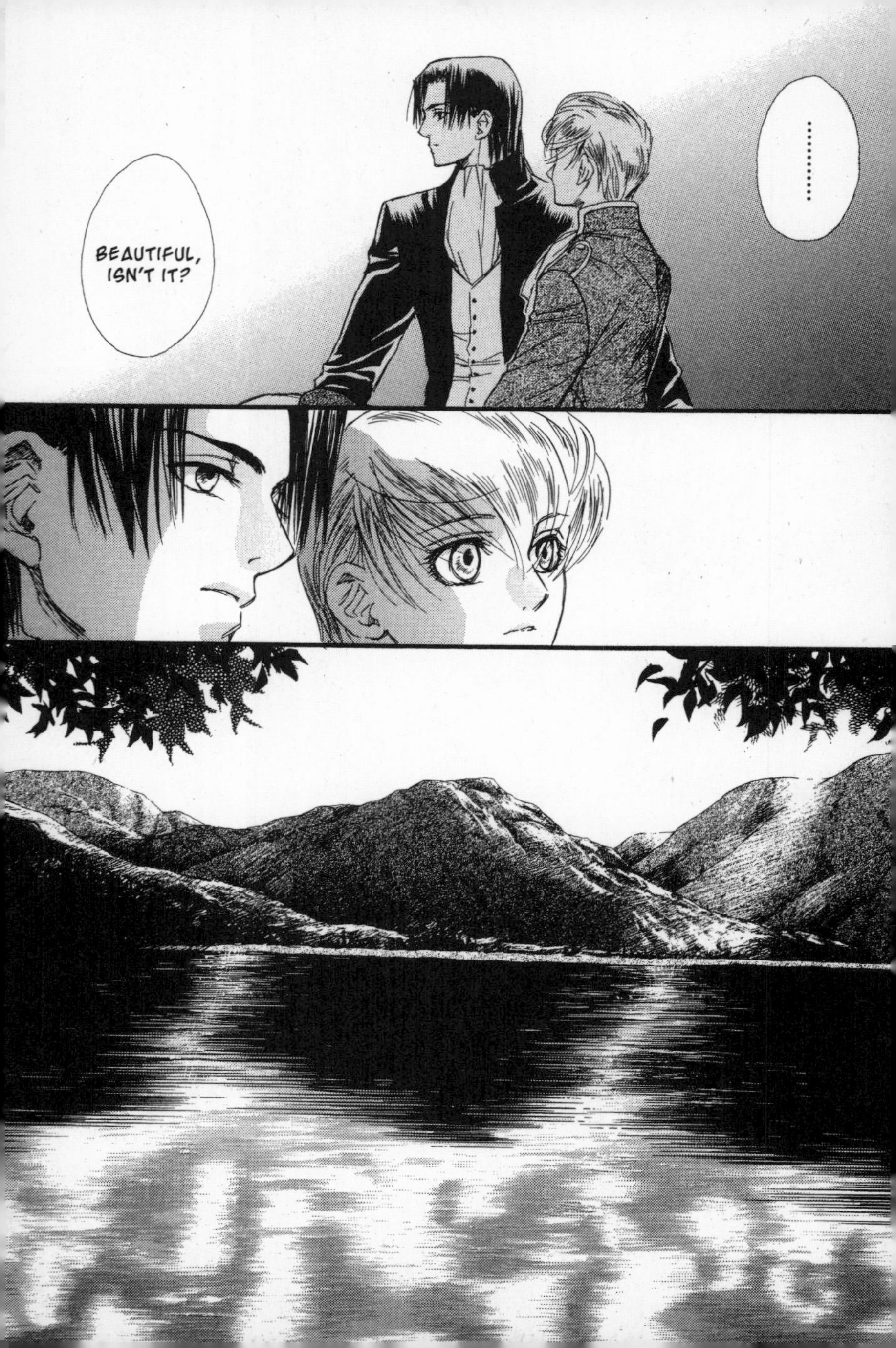
……
BEAUTIFUL, ISN'T IT?

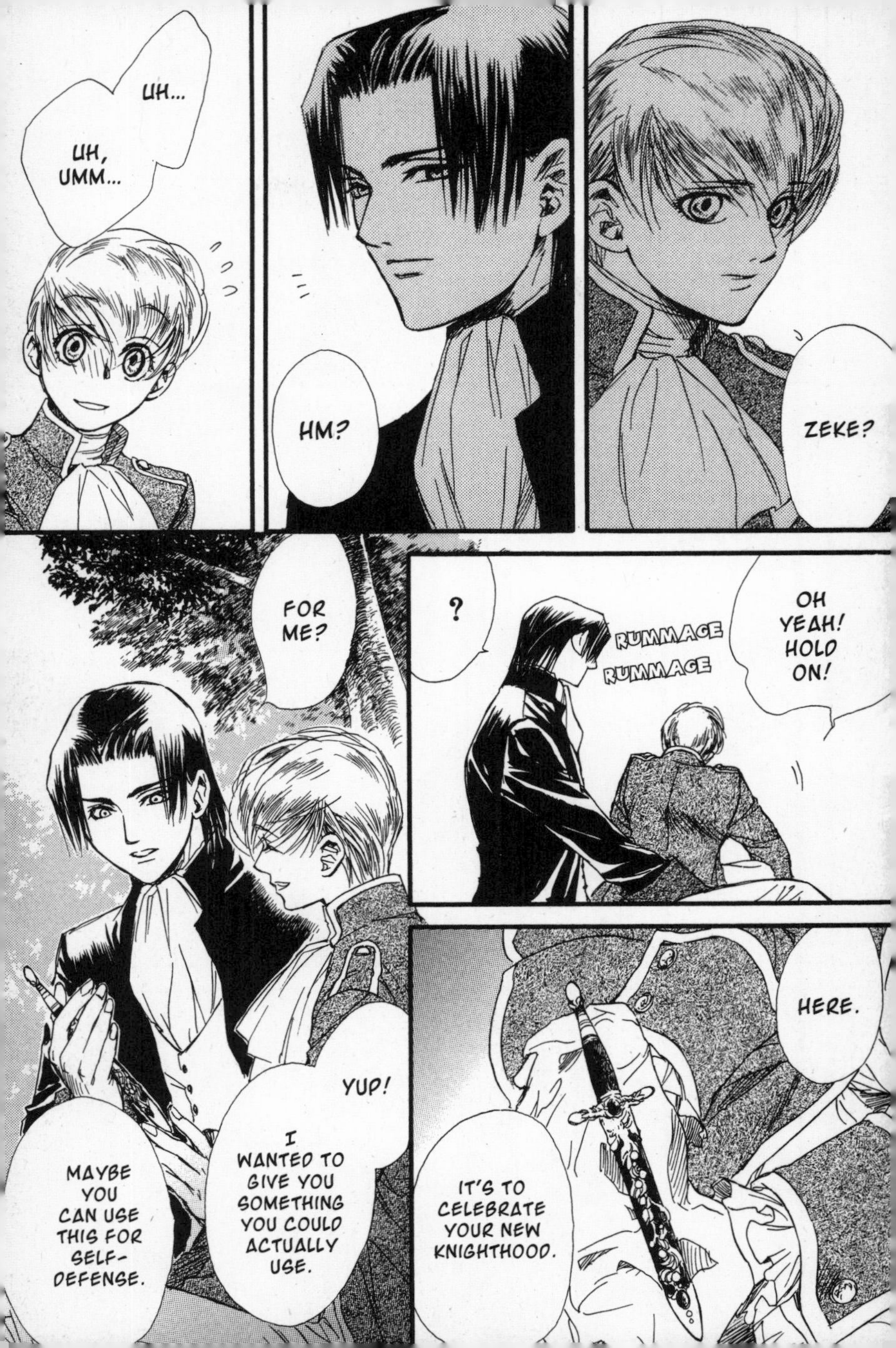
ZEKE?
HM?
UH...
UH, UMM...
OH YEAH! HOLD ON!
RUMMAGE
RUMMAGE
?
HERE.
IT'S TO CELEBRATE YOUR NEW KNIGHTHOOD.
FOR ME?
YUP!
I WANTED TO GIVE YOU SOMETHING YOU COULD ACTUALLY USE.
MAYBE YOU CAN USE THIS FOR SELF-DEFENSE.

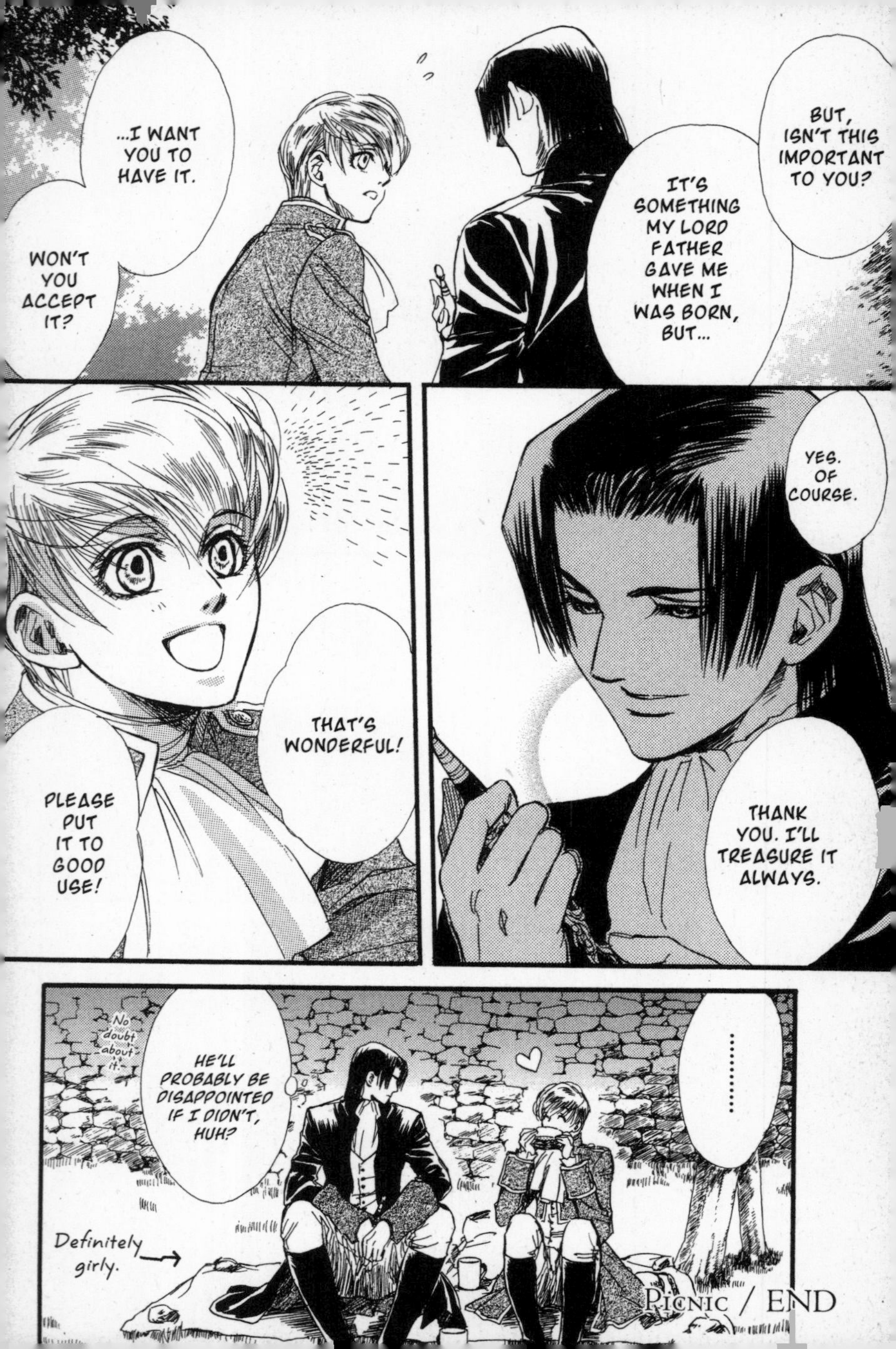

BUT, ISN'T THIS IMPORTANT TO YOU?
IT'S SOMETHING MY LORD FATHER GAVE ME WHEN I WAS BORN, BUT...
...I WANT YOU TO HAVE IT.
WON'T YOU ACCEPT IT?
YES. OF COURSE.
THANK YOU. I'LL TREASURE IT ALWAYS.
THAT'S WONDERFUL!
PLEASE PUT IT TO GOOD USE!
....
HE'LL PROBABLY BE DISAPPOINTED IF I DIDN'T, HUH?
No doubt about it.
Definitely girly.
PICNIC / END

THE
BLACK
KNIGHT

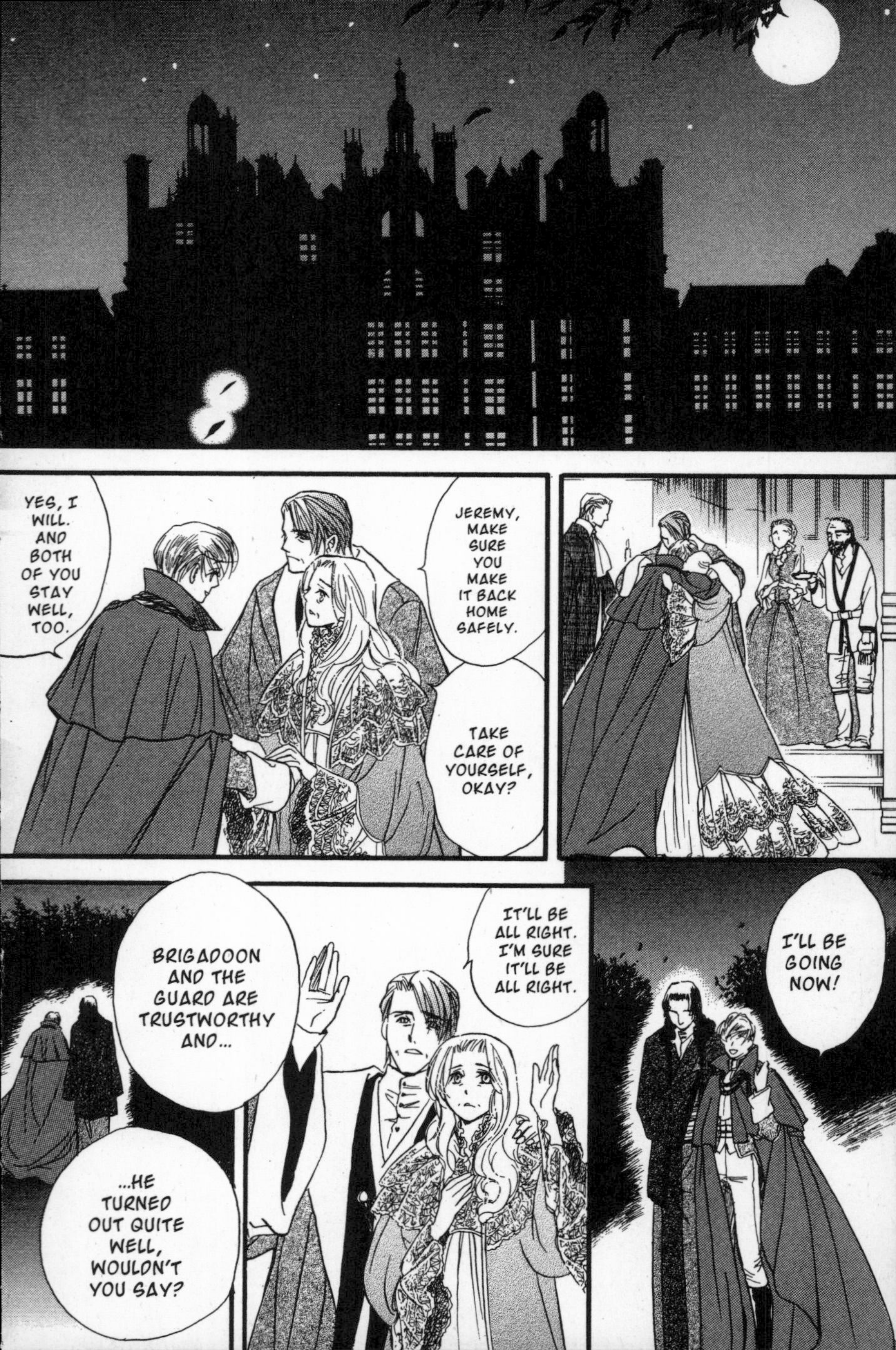
JEREMY, MAKE SURE YOU MAKE IT BACK HOME SAFELY.
TAKE CARE OF YOURSELF, OKAY?
YES, I WILL. AND BOTH OF YOU STAY WELL, TOO.
I'LL BE GOING NOW!
IT'LL BE ALL RIGHT. I'M SURE IT'LL BE ALL RIGHT.
BRIGADOON AND THE GUARD ARE TRUSTWORTHY AND...
...HE TURNED OUT QUITE WELL, WOULDN'T YOU SAY?

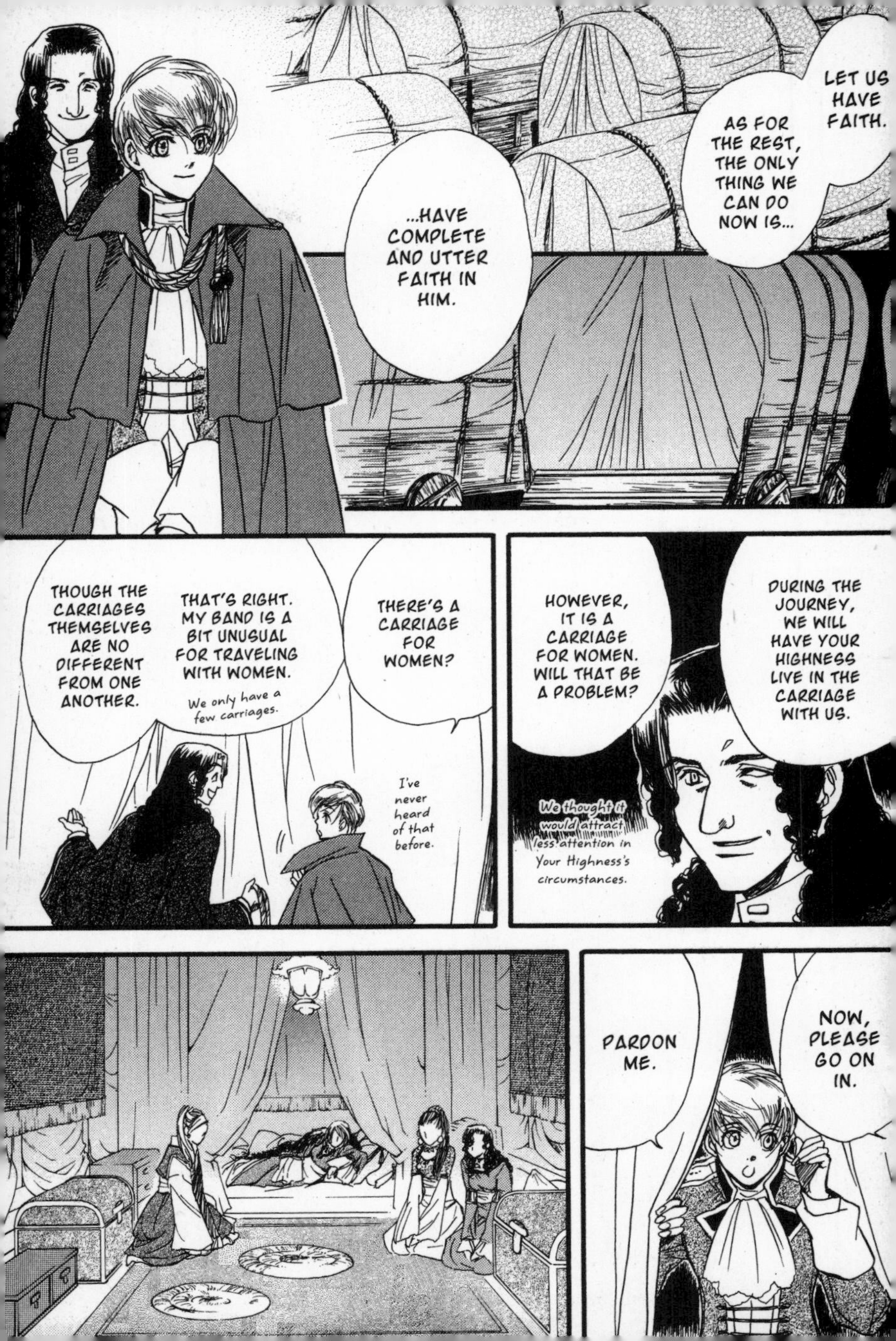
LET US HAVE FAITH.
AS FOR THE REST, THE ONLY THING WE CAN DO NOW IS...
...HAVE COMPLETE AND UTTER FAITH IN HIM.
DURING THE JOURNEY, WE WILL HAVE YOUR HIGHNESS LIVE IN THE CARRIAGE WITH US.
HOWEVER, IT IS A CARRIAGE FOR WOMEN. WILL THAT BE A PROBLEM?
We thought it would attract less attention in Your Highness's circumstances.
THERE'S A CARRIAGE FOR WOMEN?
I've never heard of that before.
THAT'S RIGHT. MY BAND IS A BIT UNUSUAL FOR TRAVELING WITH WOMEN.
We only have a few carriages.
THOUGH THE CARRIAGES THEMSELVES ARE NO DIFFERENT FROM ONE ANOTHER.
NOW, PLEASE GO ON IN.
PARDON ME.

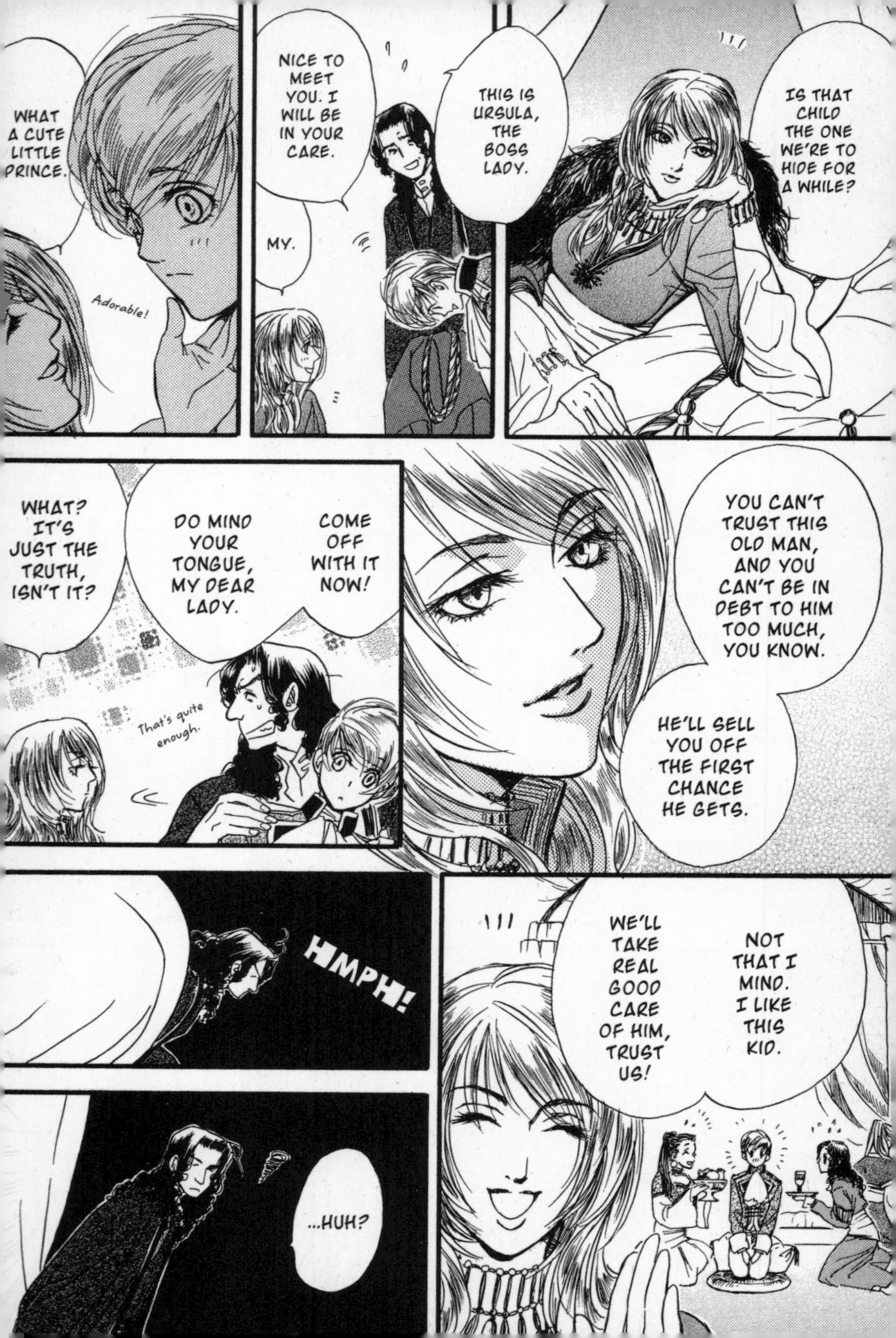
IS THAT CHILD THE ONE WE'RE TO HIDE FOR A WHILE?
THIS IS URSULA, THE BOSS LADY.
NICE TO MEET YOU. I WILL BE IN YOUR CARE.
MY.
WHAT A CUTE LITTLE PRINCE.
Adorable!
YOU CAN'T TRUST THIS OLD MAN, AND YOU CAN'T BE IN DEBT TO HIM TOO MUCH, YOU KNOW.
HE'LL SELL YOU OFF THE FIRST CHANCE HE GETS.
COME OFF WITH IT NOW!
DO MIND YOUR TONGUE, MY DEAR LADY.
WHAT? IT'S JUST THE TRUTH, ISN'T IT?
That's quite enough.
NOT THAT I MIND. I LIKE THIS KID.
WE'LL TAKE REAL GOOD CARE OF HIM, TRUST US!
HMPH!
...HUH?

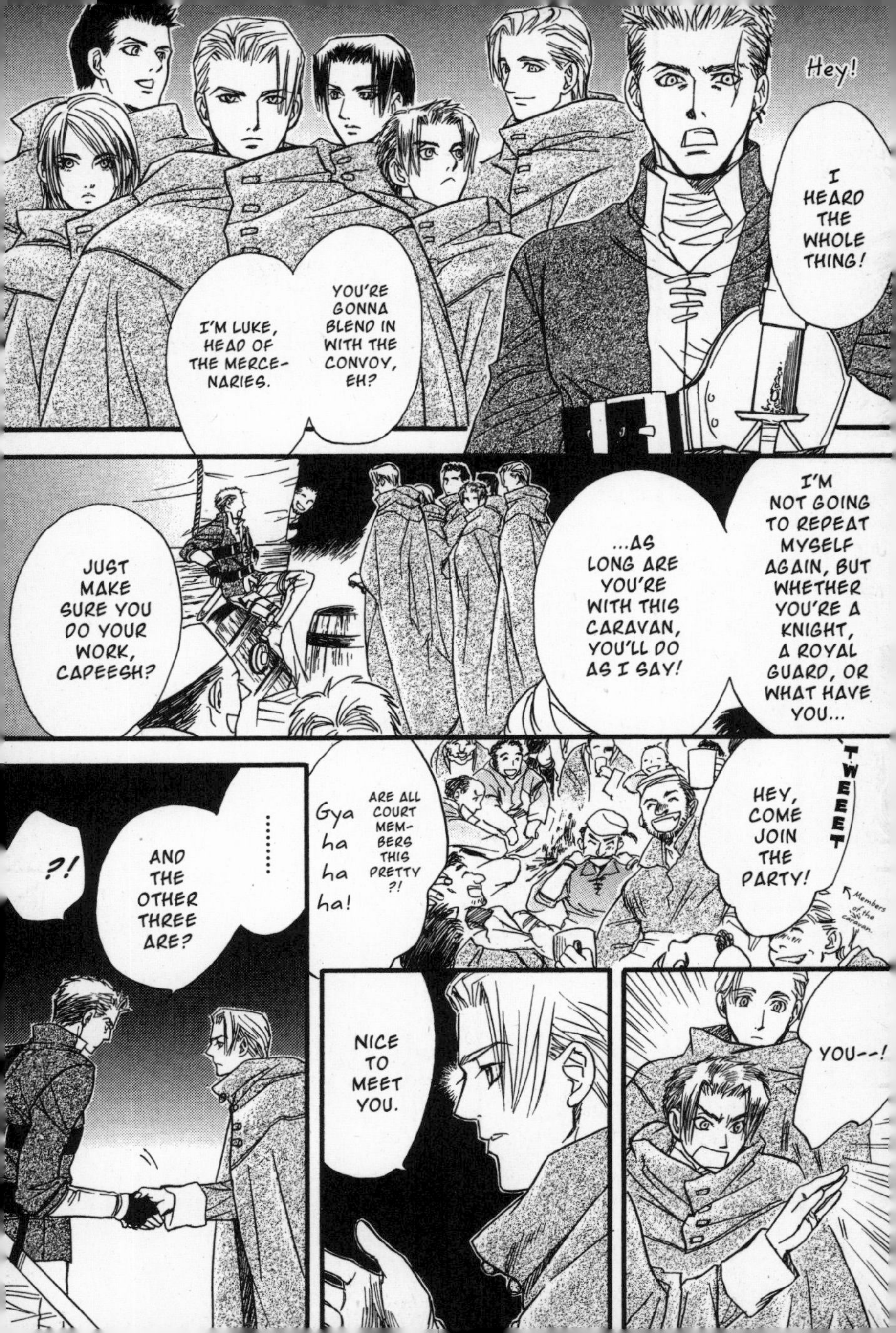
Hey!
I HEARD THE WHOLE THING!
YOU'RE GONNA BLEND IN WITH THE CONVOY, EH?
I'M LUKE, HEAD OF THE MERCE-NARIES.
I'M NOT GOING TO REPEAT MYSELF AGAIN, BUT WHETHER YOU'RE A KNIGHT, A ROYAL GUARD, OR WHAT HAVE YOU...
...AS LONG ARE YOU'RE WITH THIS CARAVAN, YOU'LL DO AS I SAY!
JUST MAKE SURE YOU DO YOUR WORK, CAPEESH?
TWEEET
HEY, COME JOIN THE PARTY!
Members of the caravan.
ARE ALL COURT MEM-BERS THIS PRETTY ?!
Gya ha ha ha!
YOU--!
NICE TO MEET YOU.
......
AND THE OTHER THREE ARE?
?!

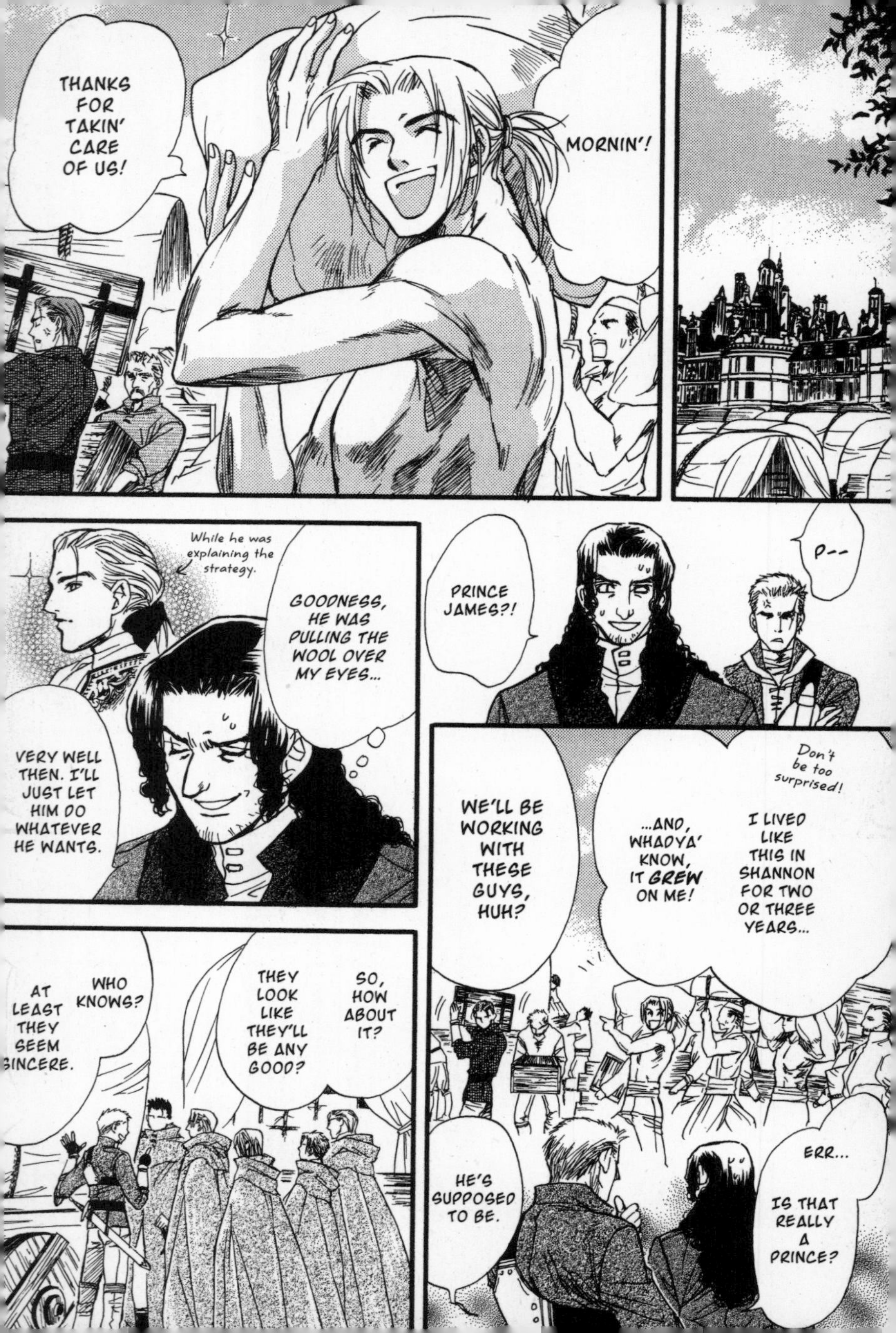
MORNIN'!
THANKS FOR TAKIN' CARE OF US!
P--
PRINCE JAMES?!
GOODNESS, HE WAS PULLING THE WOOL OVER MY EYES...
While he was explaining the strategy.
VERY WELL THEN. I'LL JUST LET HIM DO WHATEVER HE WANTS.
Don't be too surprised!
I LIVED LIKE THIS IN SHANNON FOR TWO OR THREE YEARS...
...AND, WHADYA' KNOW, IT GREW ON ME!
WE'LL BE WORKING WITH THESE GUYS, HUH?
ERR... IS THAT REALLY A PRINCE?
HE'S SUPPOSED TO BE.
SO, HOW ABOUT IT?
THEY LOOK LIKE THEY'LL BE ANY GOOD?
WHO KNOWS?
AT LEAST THEY SEEM SINCERE.

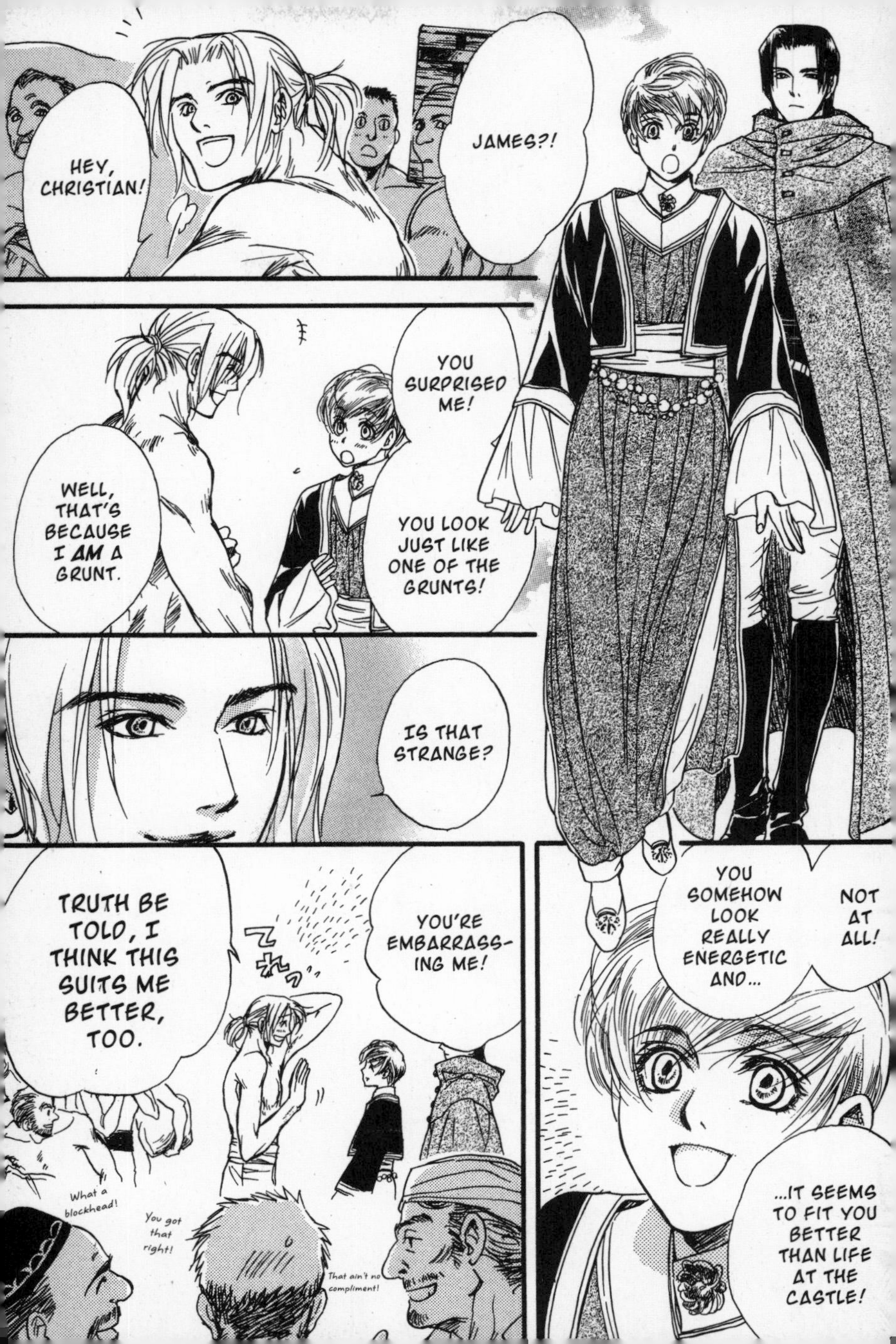
JAMES?!
HEY, CHRISTIAN!
YOU SURPRISED ME!
YOU LOOK JUST LIKE ONE OF THE GRUNTS!
WELL, THAT'S BECAUSE I *AM* A GRUNT.
IS THAT STRANGE?
NOT AT ALL!
YOU SOMEHOW LOOK REALLY ENERGETIC AND...
...IT SEEMS TO FIT YOU BETTER THAN LIFE AT THE CASTLE!
YOU'RE EMBARRASSING ME!
TRUTH BE TOLD, I THINK THIS SUITS ME BETTER, TOO.
What a blockhead!
You got that right!
That ain't no compliment!

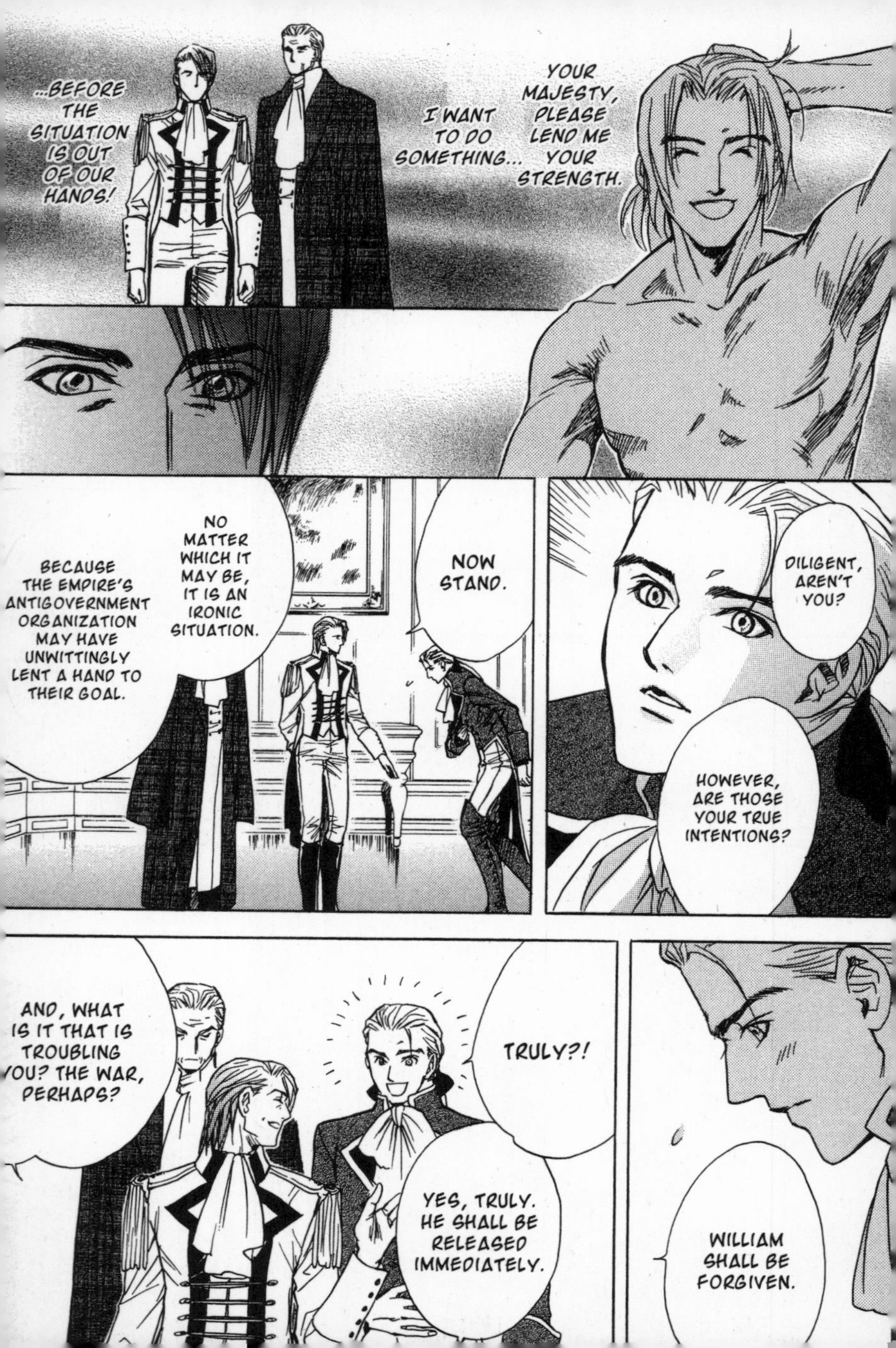
YOUR MAJESTY, PLEASE LEND ME YOUR STRENGTH.
I WANT TO DO SOMETHING...
...BEFORE THE SITUATION IS OUT OF OUR HANDS!
DILIGENT, AREN'T YOU?
HOWEVER, ARE THOSE YOUR TRUE INTENTIONS?
NOW STAND.
NO MATTER WHICH IT MAY BE, IT IS AN IRONIC SITUATION.
BECAUSE THE EMPIRE'S ANTIGOVERNMENT ORGANIZATION MAY HAVE UNWITTINGLY LENT A HAND TO THEIR GOAL.
WILLIAM SHALL BE FORGIVEN.
TRULY?!
YES, TRULY. HE SHALL BE RELEASED IMMEDIATELY.
AND, WHAT IS IT THAT IS TROUBLING YOU? THE WAR, PERHAPS?

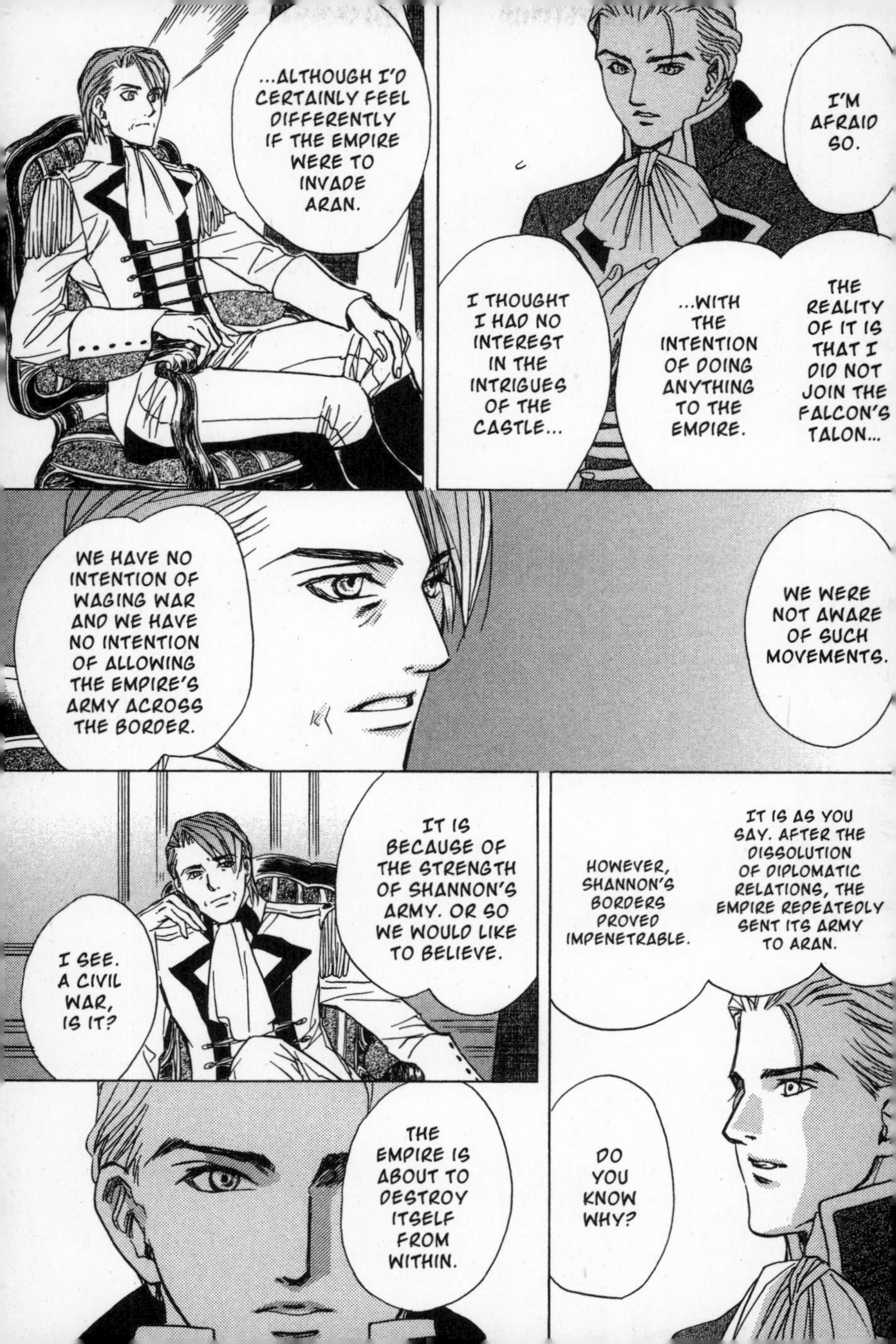
I'M AFRAID SO.
THE REALITY OF IT IS THAT I DID NOT JOIN THE FALCON'S TALON...
...WITH THE INTENTION OF DOING ANYTHING TO THE EMPIRE.
I THOUGHT I HAD NO INTEREST IN THE INTRIGUES OF THE CASTLE...
...ALTHOUGH I'D CERTAINLY FEEL DIFFERENTLY IF THE EMPIRE WERE TO INVADE ARAN.
WE WERE NOT AWARE OF SUCH MOVEMENTS.
WE HAVE NO INTENTION OF WAGING WAR AND WE HAVE NO INTENTION OF ALLOWING THE EMPIRE'S ARMY ACROSS THE BORDER.
IT IS AS YOU SAY. AFTER THE DISSOLUTION OF DIPLOMATIC RELATIONS, THE EMPIRE REPEATEDLY SENT ITS ARMY TO ARAN.
HOWEVER, SHANNON'S BORDERS PROVED IMPENETRABLE.
DO YOU KNOW WHY?
IT IS BECAUSE OF THE STRENGTH OF SHANNON'S ARMY. OR SO WE WOULD LIKE TO BELIEVE.
I SEE. A CIVIL WAR, IS IT?
THE EMPIRE IS ABOUT TO DESTROY ITSELF FROM WITHIN.

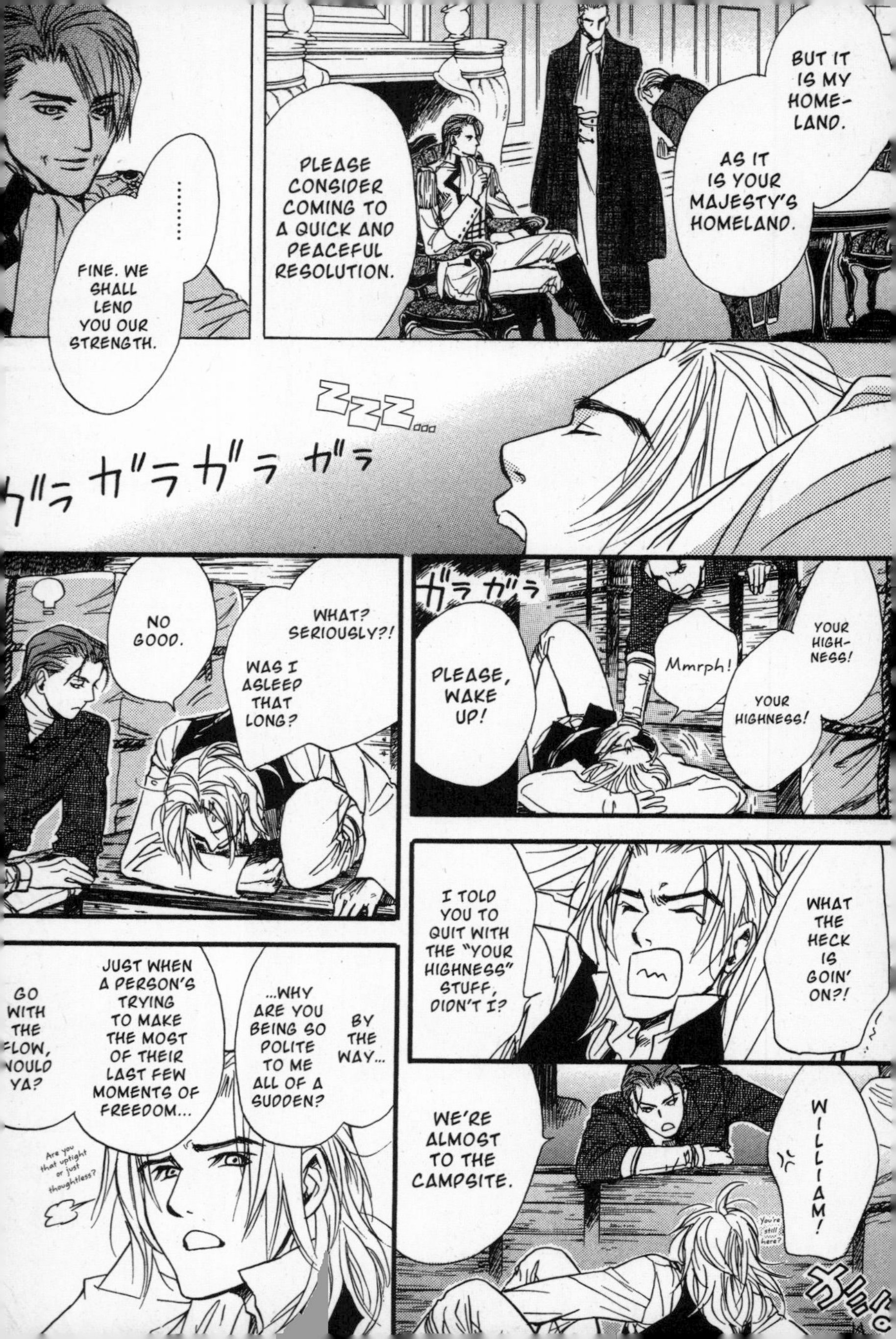
BUT IT IS MY HOME-LAND.
AS IT IS YOUR MAJESTY'S HOMELAND.
PLEASE CONSIDER COMING TO A QUICK AND PEACEFUL RESOLUTION.
......
FINE. WE SHALL LEND YOU OUR STRENGTH.
ZZZ...
ガラ ガラガラ ガラ
ガラガラ
YOUR HIGH-NESS!
YOUR HIGHNESS!
Mmrph!
PLEASE, WAKE UP!
WHAT? SERIOUSLY?!
WAS I ASLEEP THAT LONG?
NO GOOD.
WHAT THE HECK IS GOIN' ON?!
I TOLD YOU TO QUIT WITH THE "YOUR HIGHNESS" STUFF, DIDN'T I?
WILLIAM!
You're still here?
WE'RE ALMOST TO THE CAMPSITE.
BY THE WAY...
...WHY ARE YOU BEING SO POLITE TO ME ALL OF A SUDDEN?
JUST WHEN A PERSON'S TRYING TO MAKE THE MOST OF THEIR LAST FEW MOMENTS OF FREEDOM...
GO WITH THE FLOW, WOULD YA?
Are you that uptight or just thoughtless?

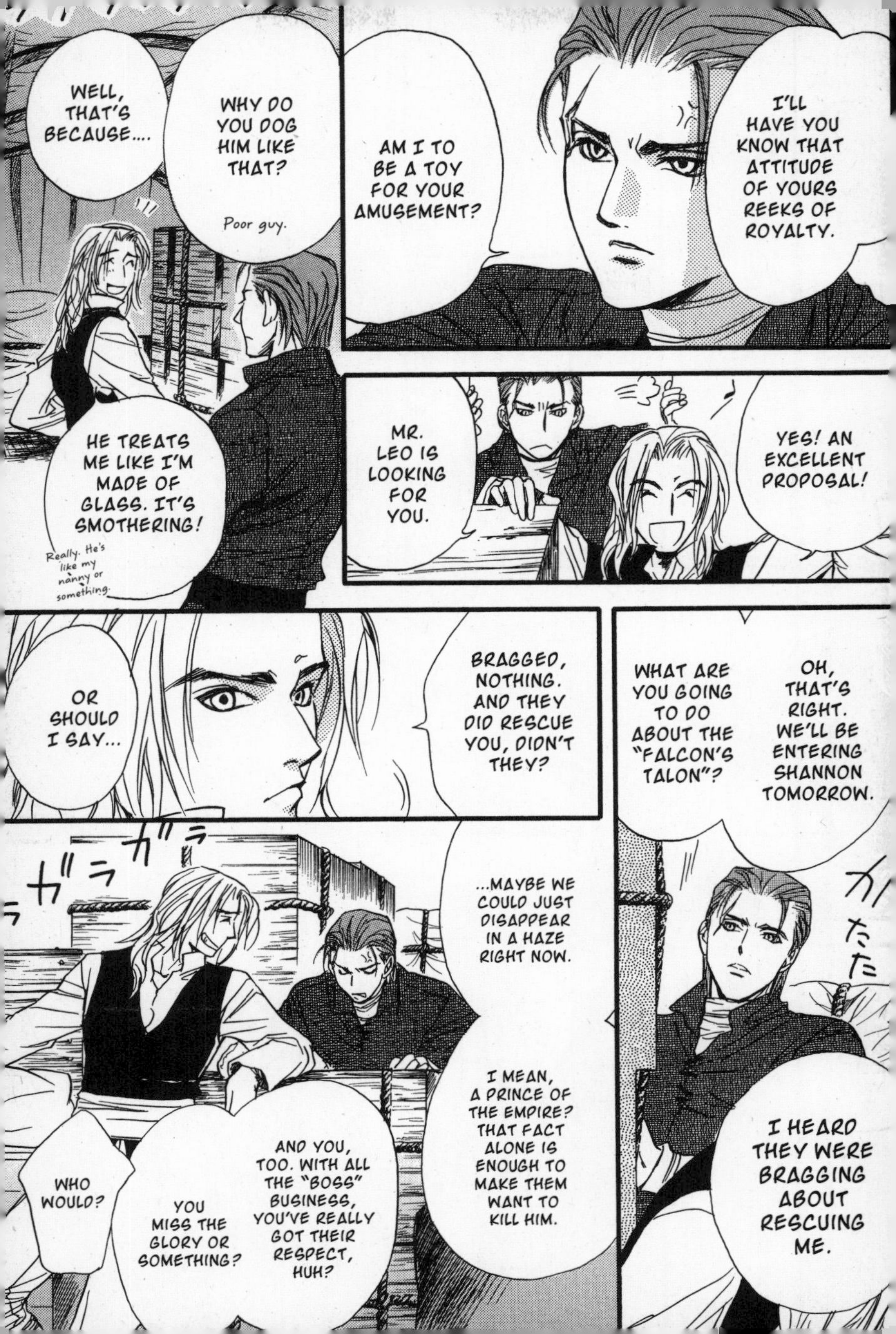
I'LL HAVE YOU KNOW THAT ATTITUDE OF YOURS REEKS OF ROYALTY.
AM I TO BE A TOY FOR YOUR AMUSEMENT?
YES! AN EXCELLENT PROPOSAL!
MR. LEO IS LOOKING FOR YOU.
WHY DO YOU DOG HIM LIKE THAT?
Poor guy.
WELL, THAT'S BECAUSE....
HE TREATS ME LIKE I'M MADE OF GLASS. IT'S SMOTHERING!
Really. He's like my nanny or something.
OH, THAT'S RIGHT. WE'LL BE ENTERING SHANNON TOMORROW.
WHAT ARE YOU GOING TO DO ABOUT THE "FALCON'S TALON"?
カたた
I HEARD THEY WERE BRAGGING ABOUT RESCUING ME.
BRAGGED, NOTHING. AND THEY DID RESCUE YOU, DIDN'T THEY?
OR SHOULD I SAY...
ガラ
ガラ
...MAYBE WE COULD JUST DISAPPEAR IN A HAZE RIGHT NOW.
I MEAN, A PRINCE OF THE EMPIRE? THAT FACT ALONE IS ENOUGH TO MAKE THEM WANT TO KILL HIM.
AND YOU, TOO. WITH ALL THE "BOSS" BUSINESS, YOU'VE REALLY GOT THEIR RESPECT, HUH?
YOU MISS THE GLORY OR SOMETHING?
WHO WOULD?

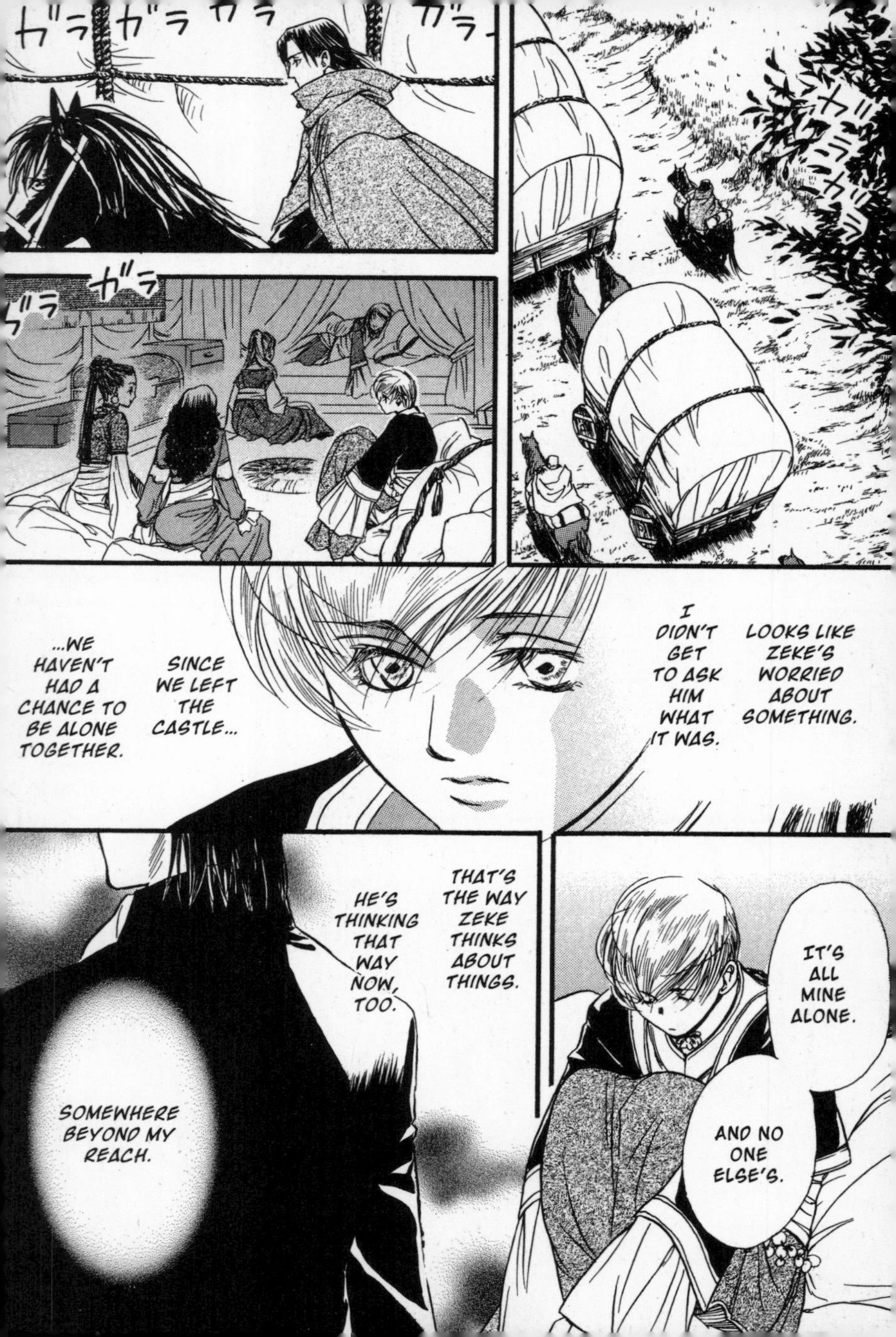
ガラガラガラ
ガラガラガラ
ガラ
ガラ
ガラ
LOOKS LIKE ZEKE'S WORRIED ABOUT SOMETHING.
I DIDN'T GET TO ASK HIM WHAT IT WAS.
SINCE WE LEFT THE CASTLE...
...WE HAVEN'T HAD A CHANCE TO BE ALONE TOGETHER.
IT'S ALL MINE ALONE.
AND NO ONE ELSE'S.
THAT'S THE WAY ZEKE THINKS ABOUT THINGS.
HE'S THINKING THAT WAY NOW, TOO.
SOMEWHERE BEYOND MY REACH.

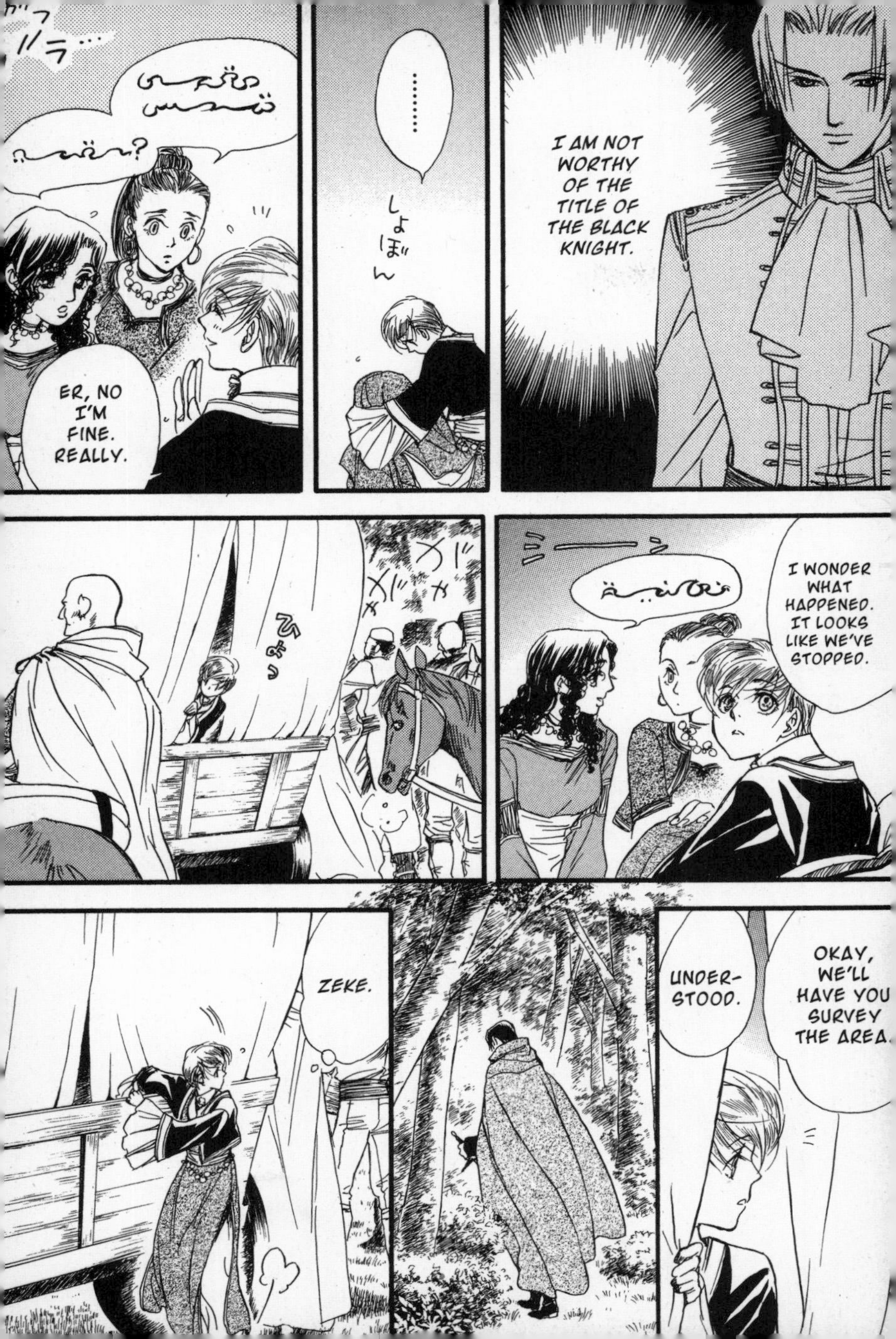

I AM NOT WORTHY OF THE TITLE OF THE BLACK KNIGHT.
……
しょぼん
ER, NO I'M FINE. REALLY.
シーン
I WONDER WHAT HAPPENED. IT LOOKS LIKE WE'VE STOPPED.
ひょっ
OKAY, WE'LL HAVE YOU SURVEY THE AREA.
UNDER-STOOD.
ZEKE.

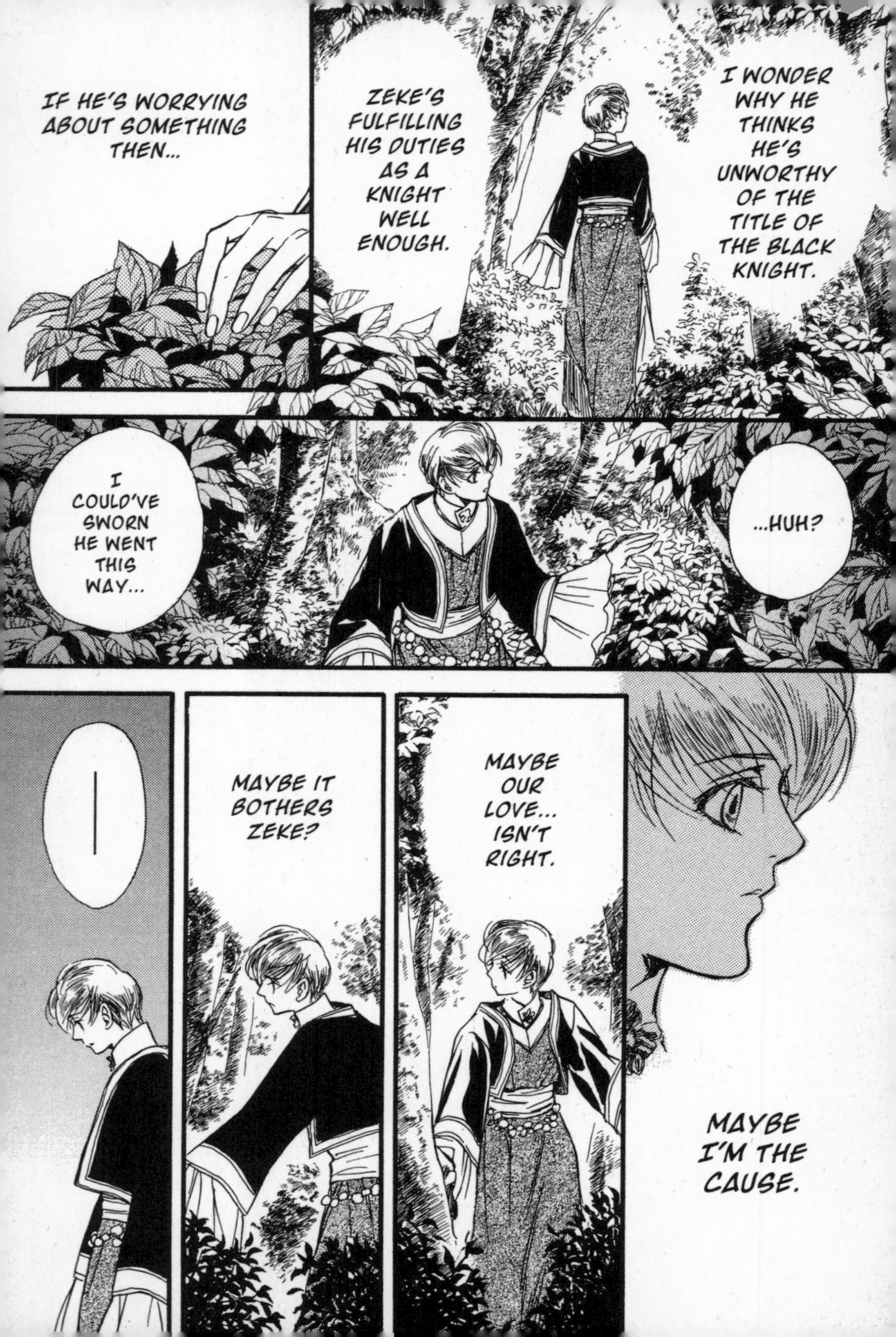
I WONDER WHY HE THINKS HE'S UNWORTHY OF THE TITLE OF THE BLACK KNIGHT.
ZEKE'S FULFILLING HIS DUTIES AS A KNIGHT WELL ENOUGH.
IF HE'S WORRYING ABOUT SOMETHING THEN...
...HUH?
I COULD'VE SWORN HE WENT THIS WAY...
MAYBE I'M THE CAUSE.
MAYBE OUR LOVE... ISN'T RIGHT.
MAYBE IT BOTHERS ZEKE?
—

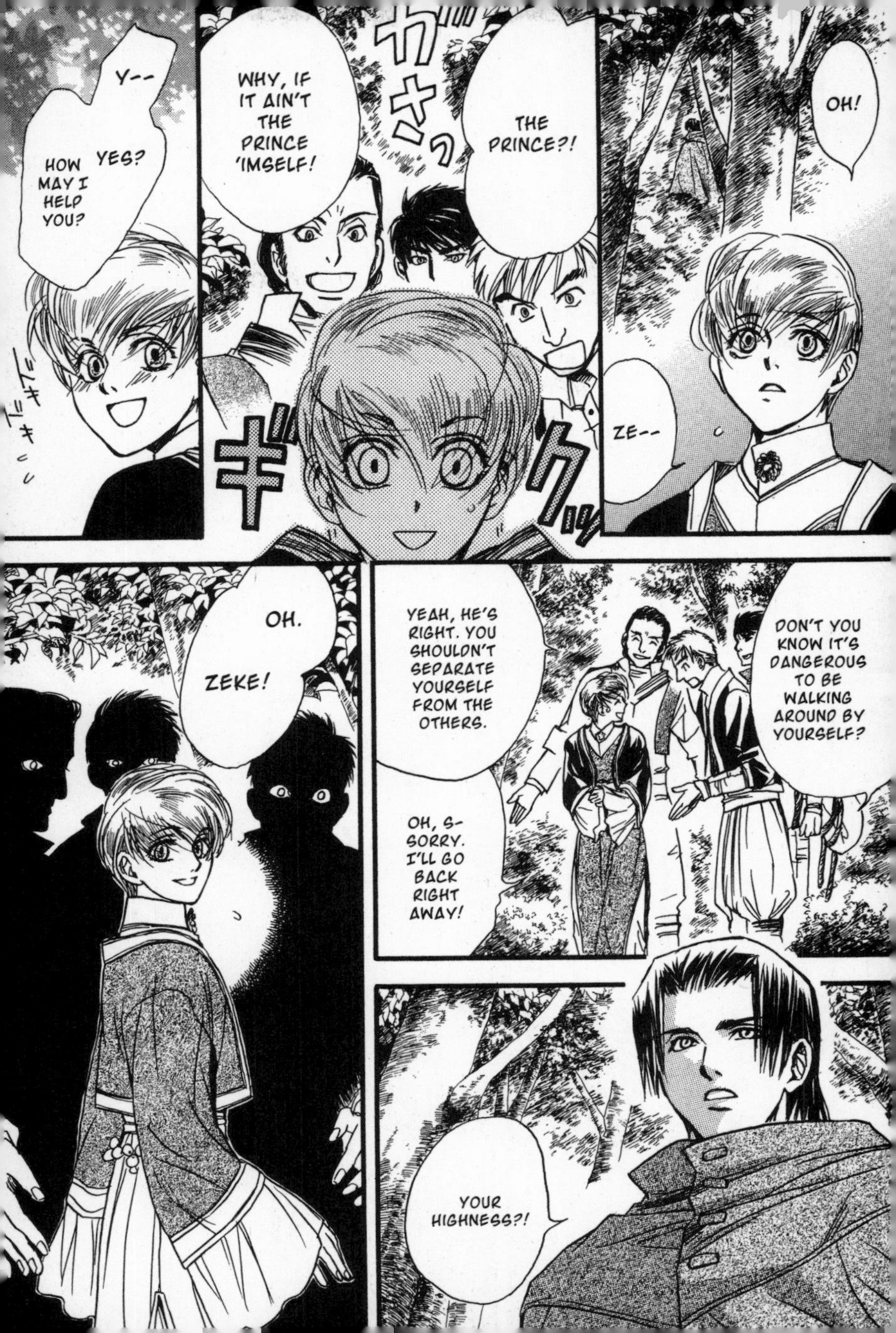
OH!
ZE--
THE PRINCE?!
WHY, IF IT AIN'T THE PRINCE 'IMSELF!
わさっ
ギクッ
Y--
YES? HOW MAY I HELP YOU?
DON'T YOU KNOW IT'S DANGEROUS TO BE WALKING AROUND BY YOURSELF?
YEAH, HE'S RIGHT. YOU SHOULDN'T SEPARATE YOURSELF FROM THE OTHERS.
OH, S-SORRY. I'LL GO BACK RIGHT AWAY!
YOUR HIGHNESS?!
OH.
ZEKE!

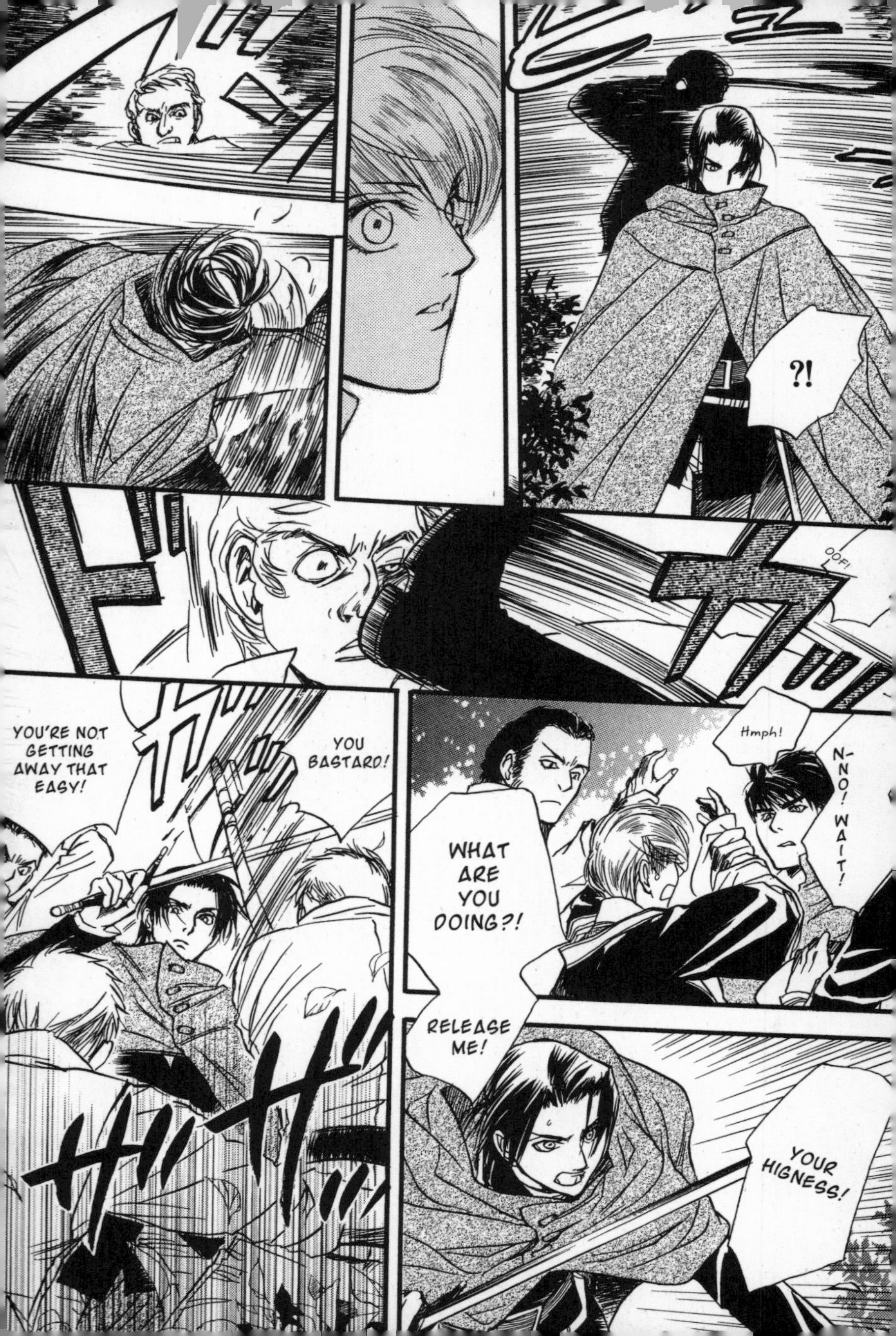
?!
OOF!
Hmph!
N-NO! WAIT!
WHAT ARE YOU DOING?!
YOUR HIGNESS!
RELEASE ME!
YOU BASTARD!
YOU'RE NOT GETTING AWAY THAT EASY!

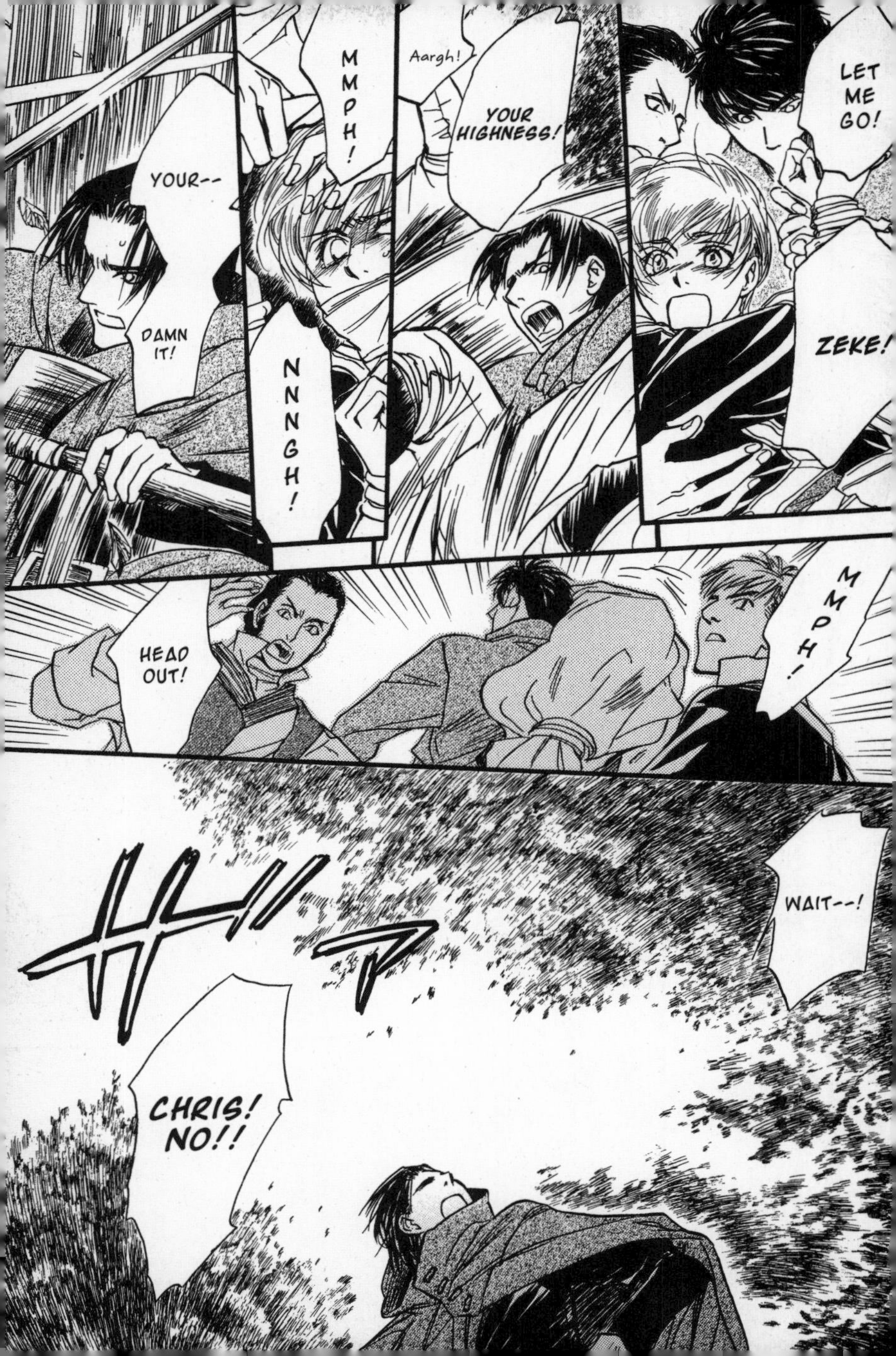
LET ME GO!
ZEKE!
YOUR HIGHNESS!
Aargh!
MMPH!
NNNGH!
YOUR--
DAMN IT!
MMPH!
HEAD OUT!
WAIT--!
CHRIS! NO!!

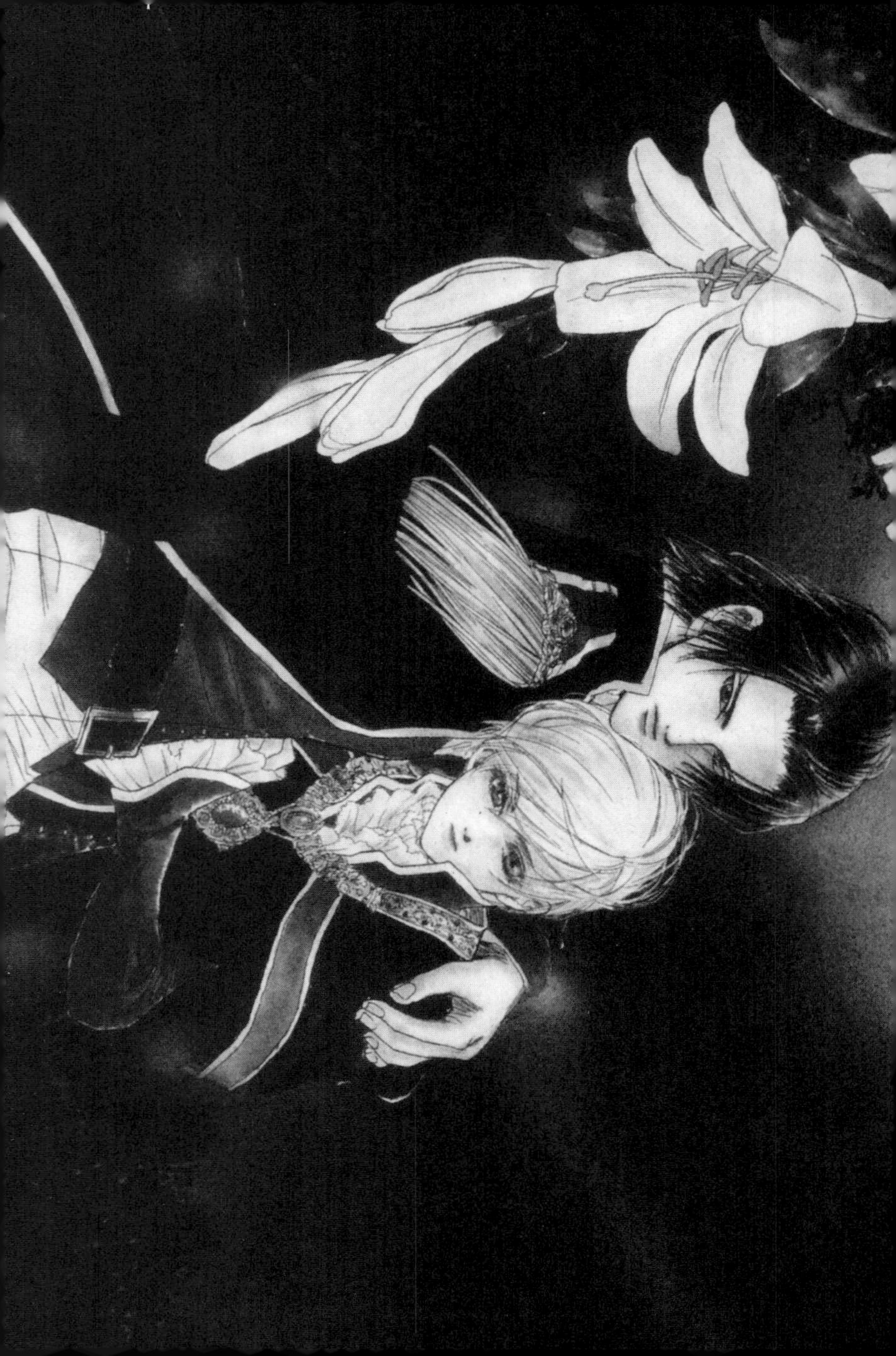

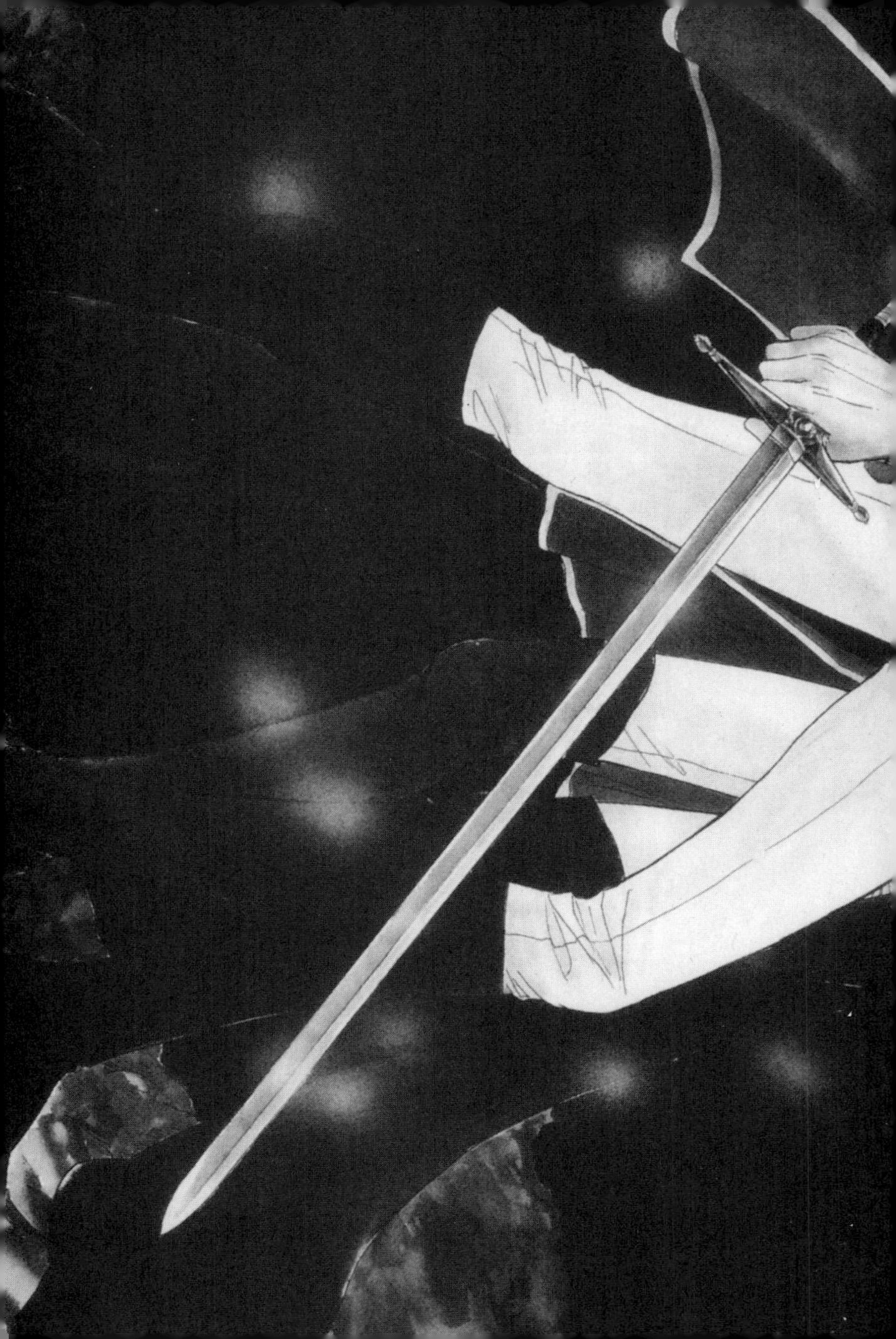

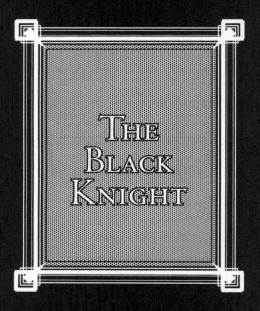

THE
BLACK
KNIGHT

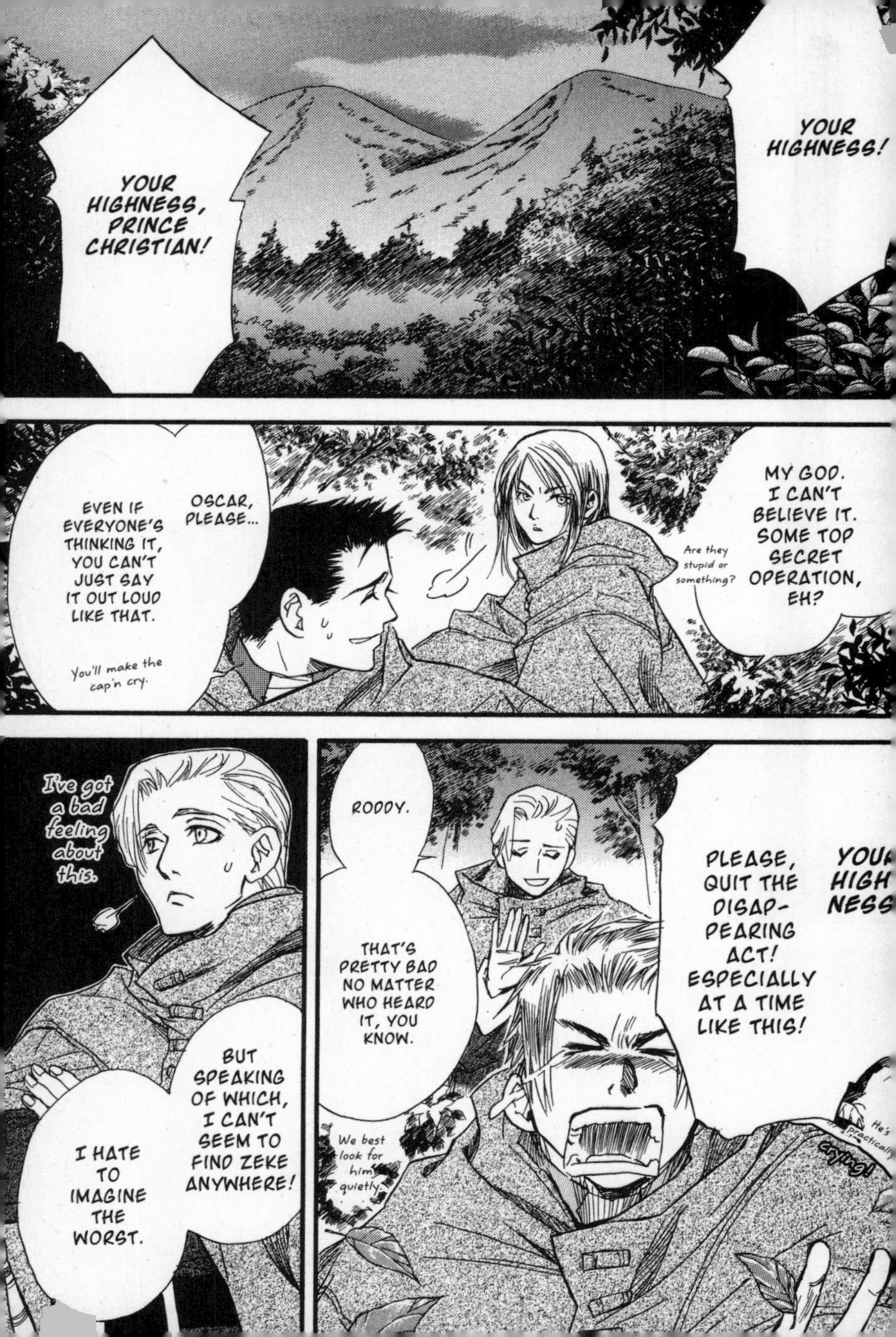
YOUR HIGHNESS!
YOUR HIGHNESS, PRINCE CHRISTIAN!
MY GOD. I CAN'T BELIEVE IT. SOME TOP SECRET OPERATION, EH?
Are they stupid or something?
OSCAR, PLEASE...
EVEN IF EVERYONE'S THINKING IT, YOU CAN'T JUST SAY IT OUT LOUD LIKE THAT.
You'll make the cap'n cry.
PLEASE, QUIT THE DISAP-PEARING ACT! ESPECIALLY AT A TIME LIKE THIS!
He's practically crying!
RODDY.
THAT'S PRETTY BAD NO MATTER WHO HEARD IT, YOU KNOW.
We best look for him quietly.
I've got a bad feeling about this.
BUT SPEAKING OF WHICH, I CAN'T SEEM TO FIND ZEKE ANYWHERE!
I HATE TO IMAGINE THE WORST.

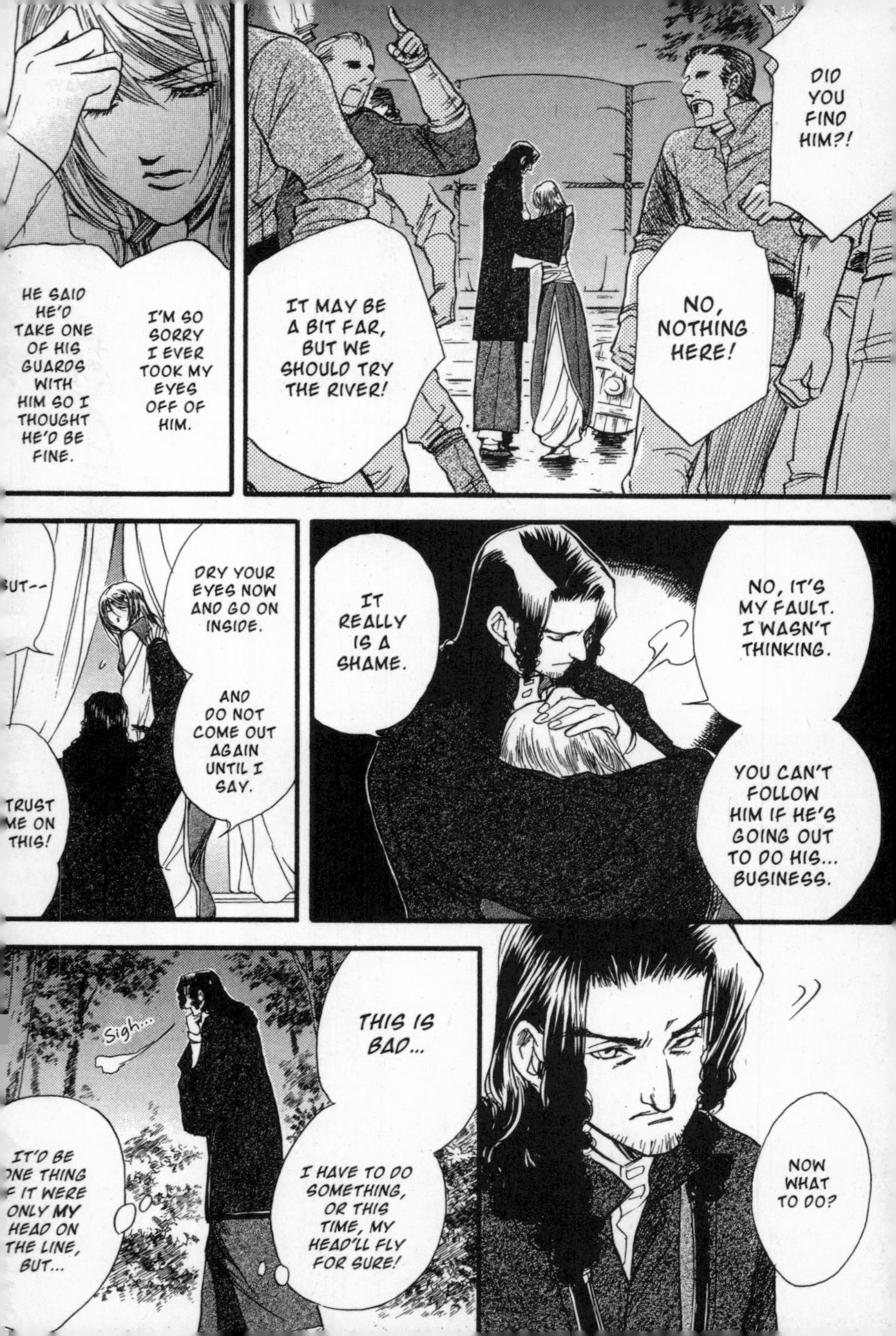
DID YOU FIND HIM?!
NO, NOTHING HERE!
IT MAY BE A BIT FAR, BUT WE SHOULD TRY THE RIVER!
I'M SO SORRY I EVER TOOK MY EYES OFF OF HIM.
HE SAID HE'D TAKE ONE OF HIS GUARDS WITH HIM SO I THOUGHT HE'D BE FINE.
NO, IT'S MY FAULT. I WASN'T THINKING.
IT REALLY IS A SHAME.
YOU CAN'T FOLLOW HIM IF HE'S GOING OUT TO DO HIS... BUSINESS.
DRY YOUR EYES NOW AND GO ON INSIDE.
UT--
AND DO NOT COME OUT AGAIN UNTIL I SAY.
TRUST ME ON THIS!
NOW WHAT TO DO?
THIS IS BAD...
Sigh...
I HAVE TO DO SOMETHING, OR THIS TIME, MY HEAD'LL FLY FOR SURE!
IT'D BE ONE THING IF IT WERE ONLY MY HEAD ON THE LINE, BUT...

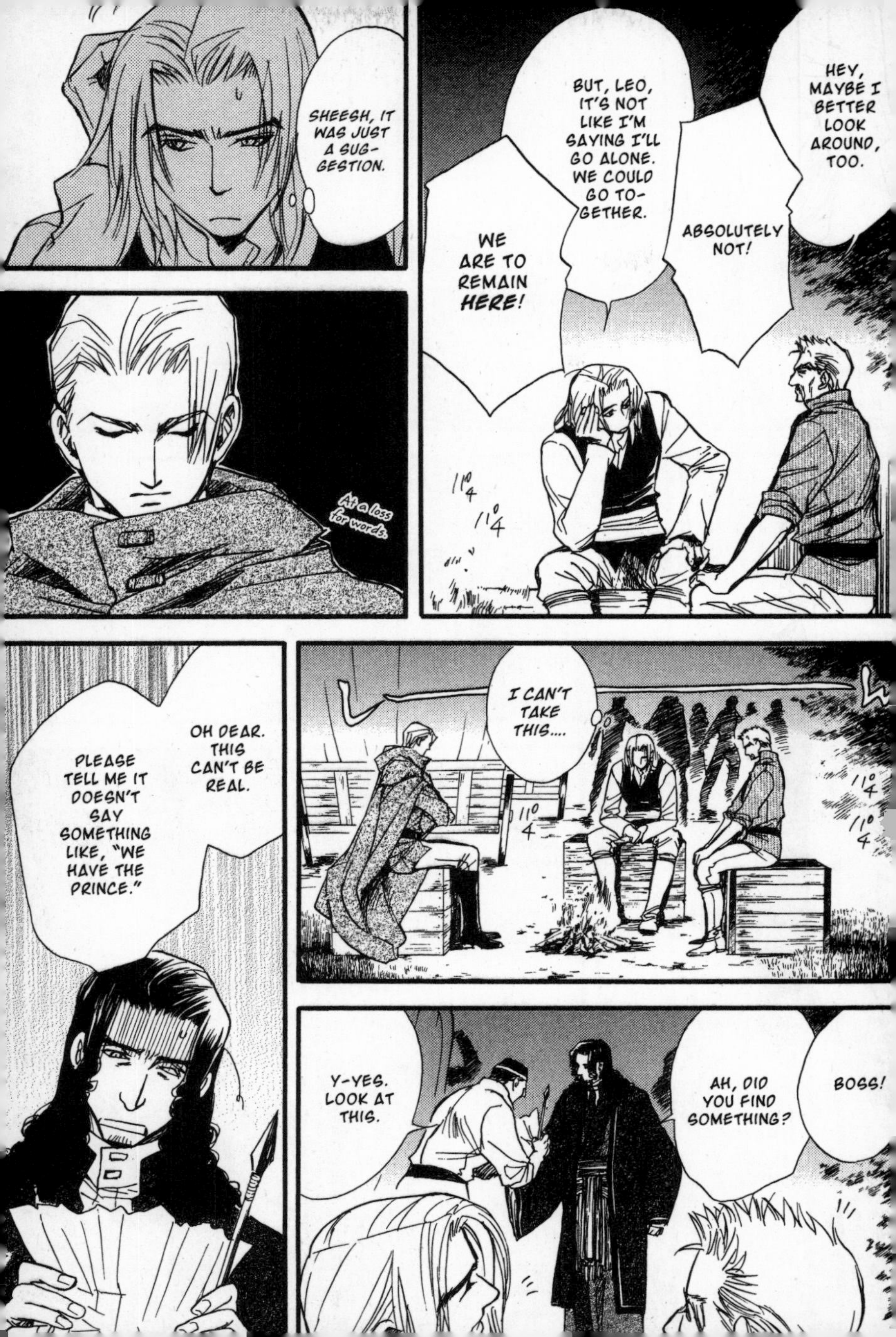
HEY, MAYBE I BETTER LOOK AROUND, TOO.
ABSOLUTELY NOT!
BUT, LEO, IT'S NOT LIKE I'M SAYING I'LL GO ALONE. WE COULD GO TO-GETHER.
WE ARE TO REMAIN HERE!
SHEESH, IT WAS JUST A SUG-GESTION.
At a loss for words.
I CAN'T TAKE THIS....
BOSS!
AH, DID YOU FIND SOMETHING?
Y-YES. LOOK AT THIS.
OH DEAR. THIS CAN'T BE REAL.
PLEASE TELL ME IT DOESN'T SAY SOMETHING LIKE, "WE HAVE THE PRINCE."

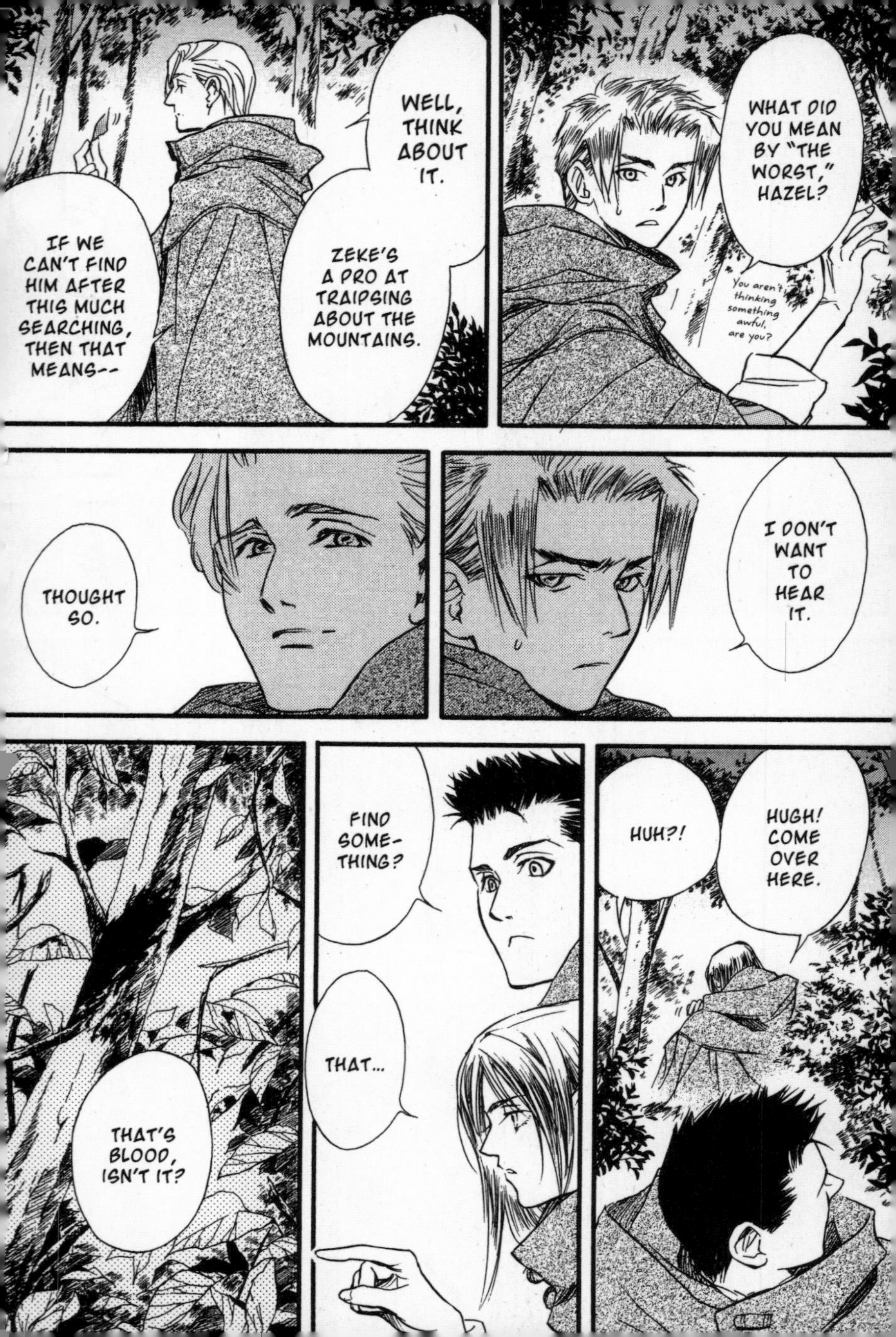
WHAT DID YOU MEAN BY "THE WORST," HAZEL?
You aren't thinking something awful, are you?
WELL, THINK ABOUT IT.
ZEKE'S A PRO AT TRAIPSING ABOUT THE MOUNTAINS.
IF WE CAN'T FIND HIM AFTER THIS MUCH SEARCHING, THEN THAT MEANS--
I DON'T WANT TO HEAR IT.
THOUGHT SO.
HUGH! COME OVER HERE.
HUH?!
FIND SOME-THING?
THAT...
THAT'S BLOOD, ISN'T IT?

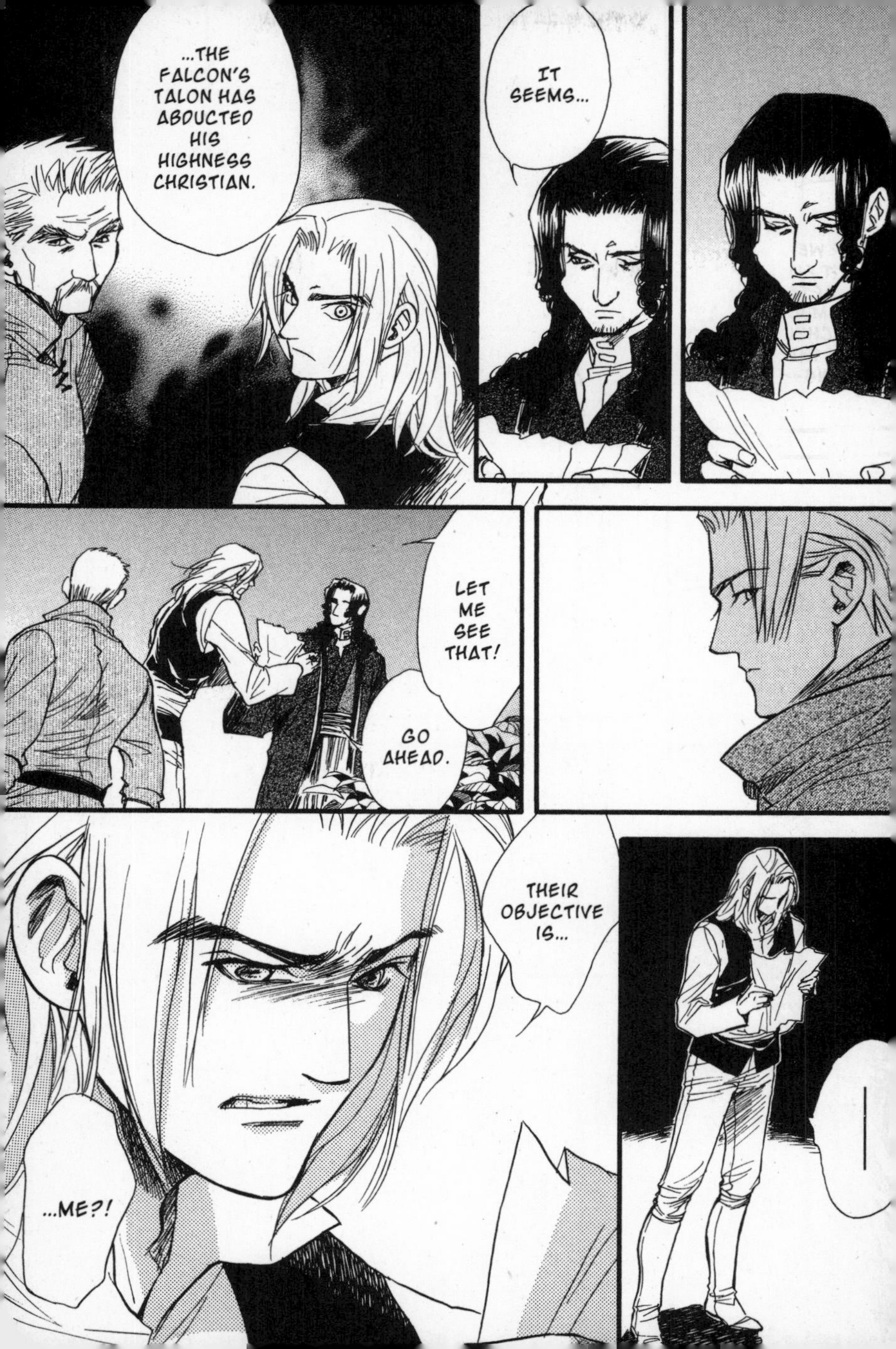
IT SEEMS...
...THE FALCON'S TALON HAS ABDUCTED HIS HIGHNESS CHRISTIAN.
LET ME SEE THAT!
GO AHEAD.
THEIR OBJECTIVE IS...
...ME?!

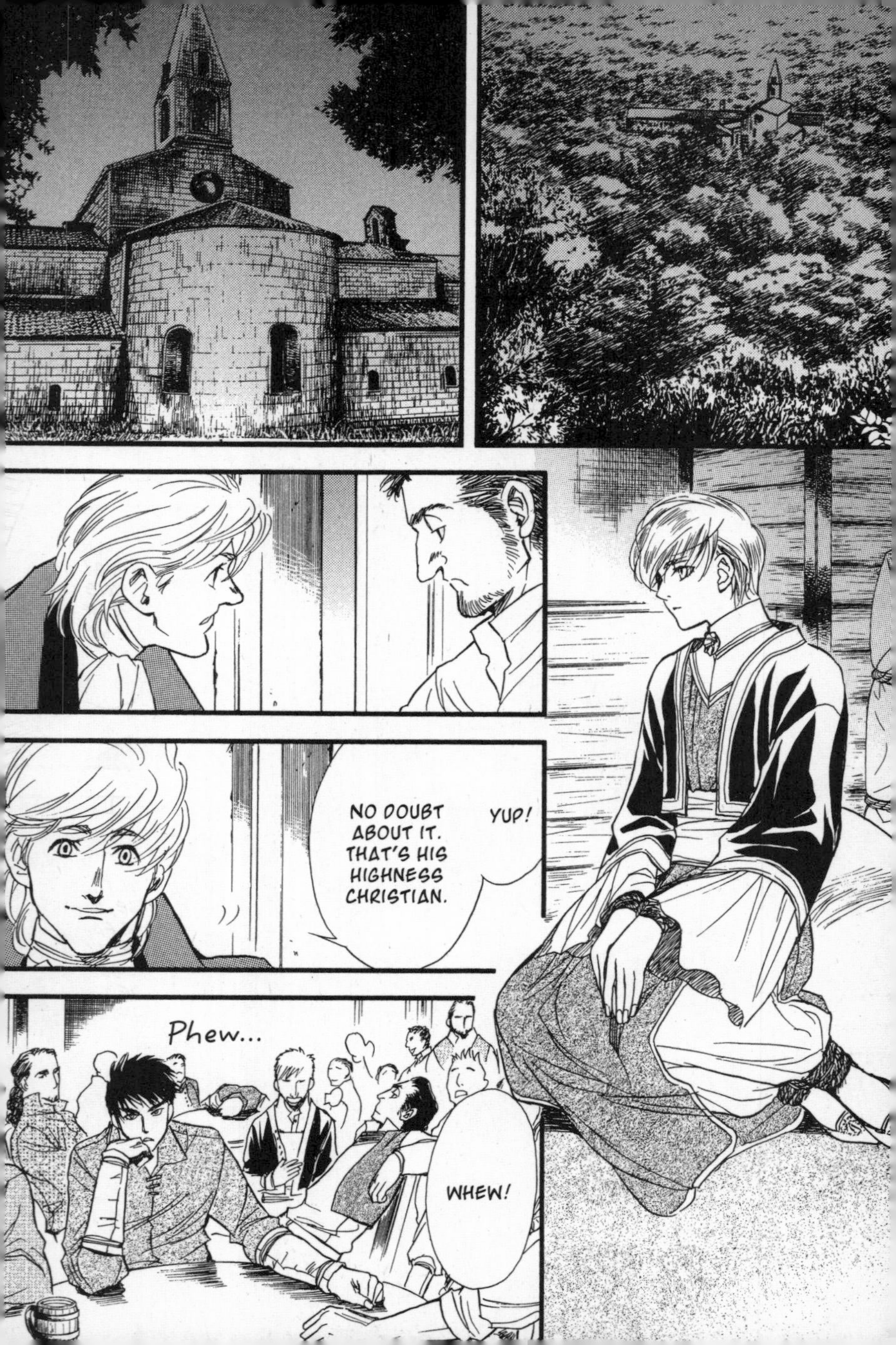
NO DOUBT ABOUT IT. THAT'S HIS HIGHNESS CHRISTIAN.
YUP!
Phew...
WHEW!

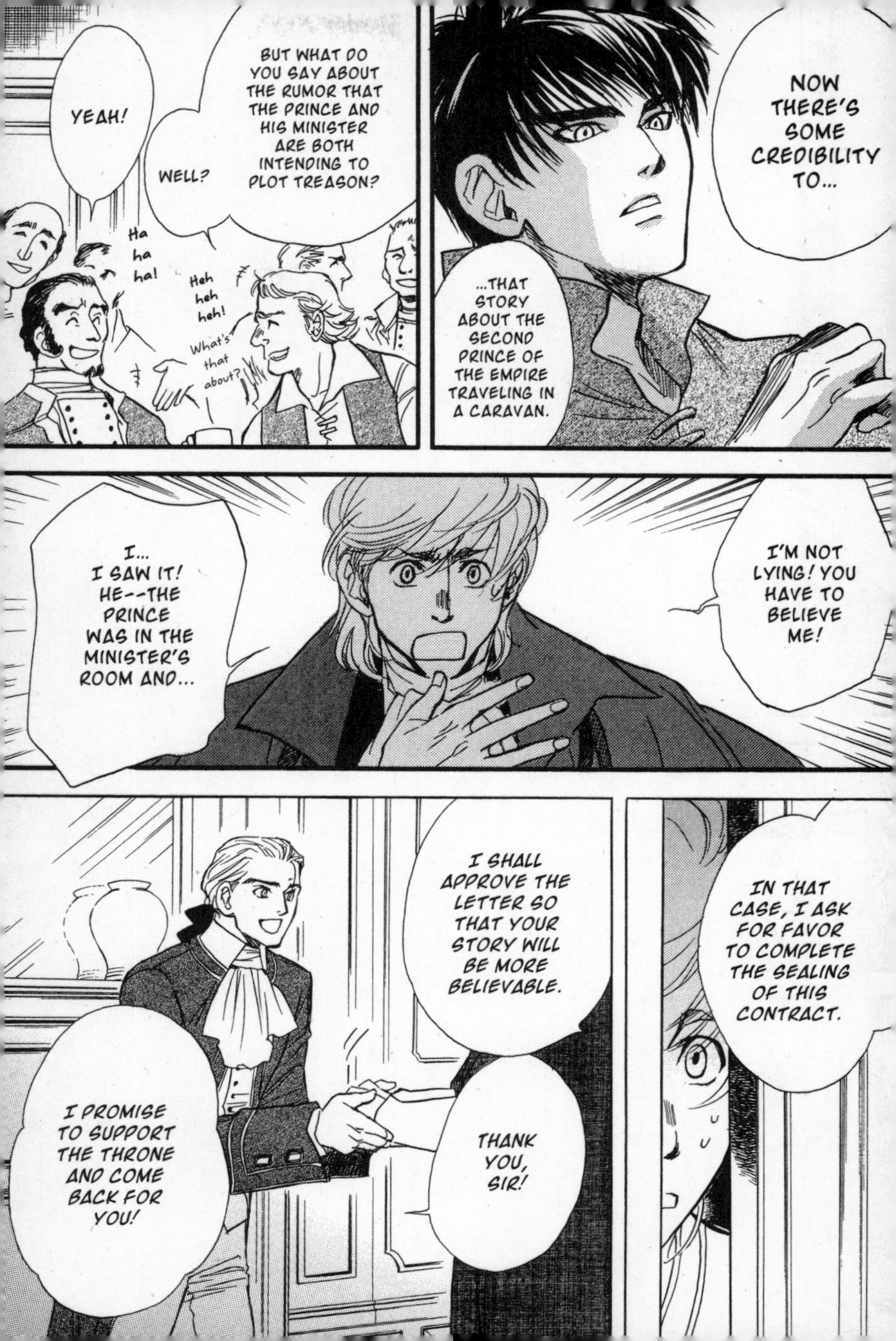
NOW THERE'S SOME CREDIBILITY TO...
...THAT STORY ABOUT THE SECOND PRINCE OF THE EMPIRE TRAVELING IN A CARAVAN.
BUT WHAT DO YOU SAY ABOUT THE RUMOR THAT THE PRINCE AND HIS MINISTER ARE BOTH INTENDING TO PLOT TREASON?
WELL?
YEAH!
Heh heh heh!
Ha ha ha!
What's that about?
I'M NOT LYING! YOU HAVE TO BELIEVE ME!
I... I SAW IT! HE--THE PRINCE WAS IN THE MINISTER'S ROOM AND...
IN THAT CASE, I ASK FOR FAVOR TO COMPLETE THE SEALING OF THIS CONTRACT.
I SHALL APPROVE THE LETTER SO THAT YOUR STORY WILL BE MORE BELIEVABLE.
THANK YOU, SIR!
I PROMISE TO SUPPORT THE THRONE AND COME BACK FOR YOU!

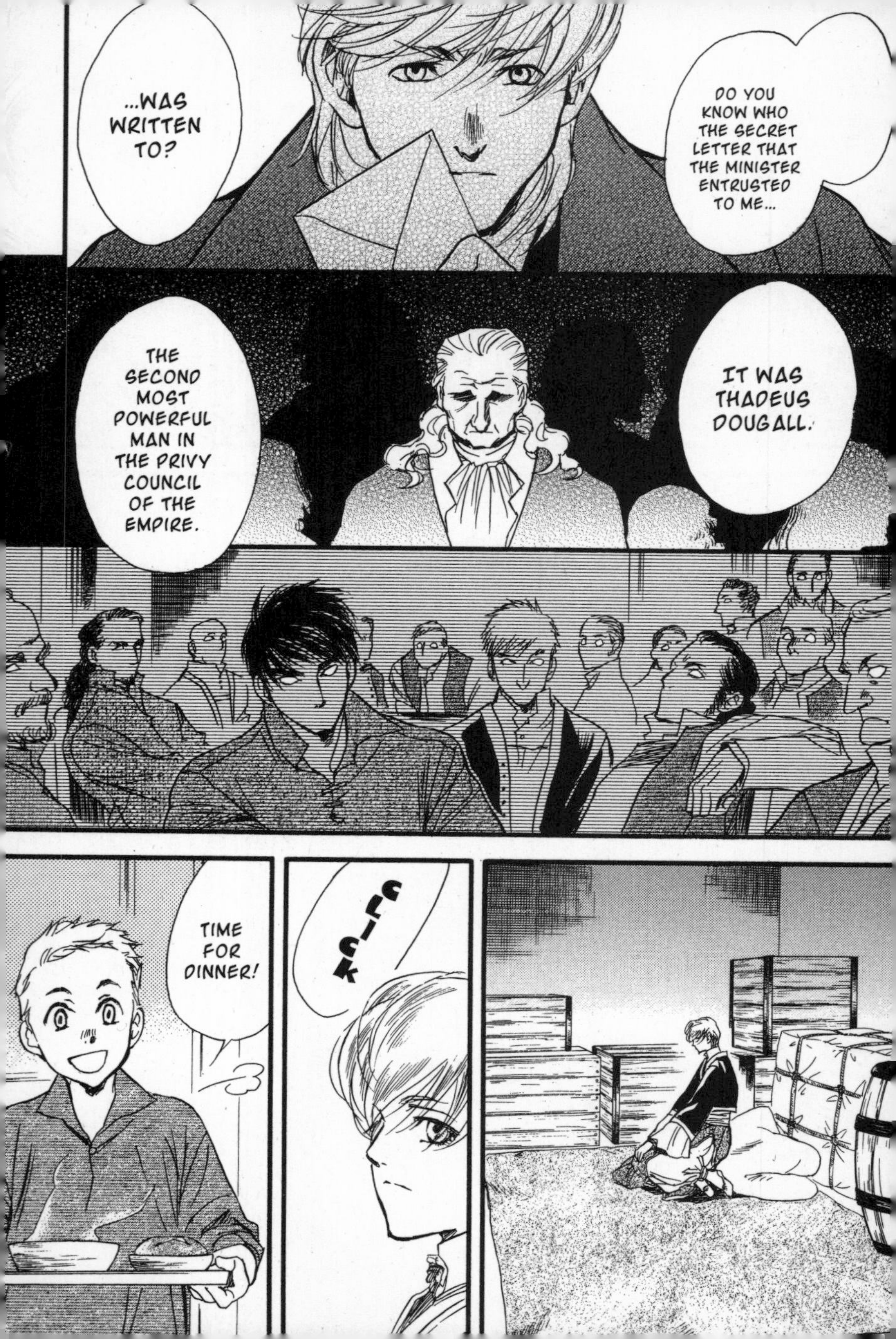
DO YOU KNOW WHO THE SECRET LETTER THAT THE MINISTER ENTRUSTED TO ME...
...WAS WRITTEN TO?
IT WAS THADEUS DOUGALL.
THE SECOND MOST POWERFUL MAN IN THE PRIVY COUNCIL OF THE EMPIRE.
CLICK
TIME FOR DINNER!

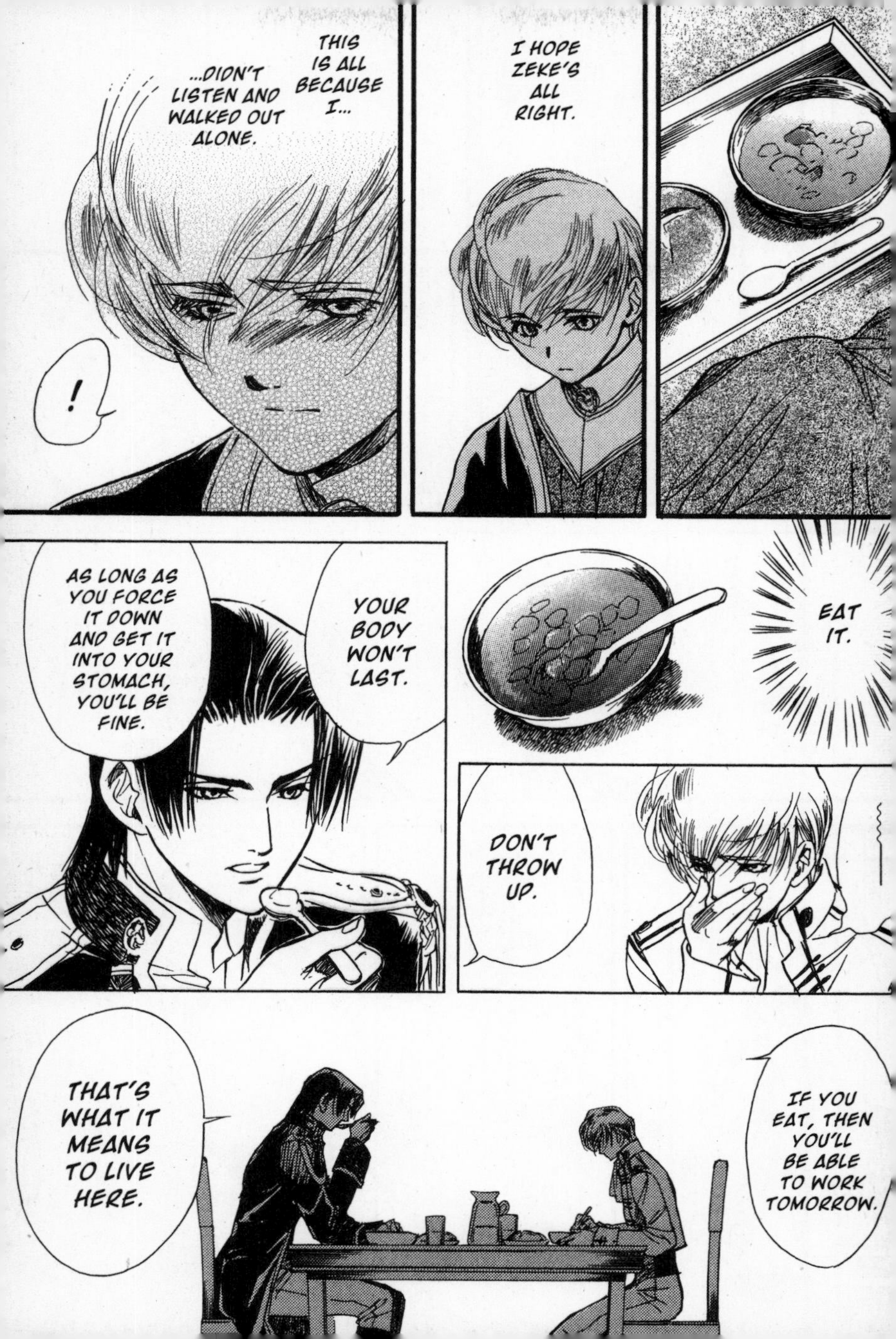
I HOPE ZEKE'S ALL RIGHT.
THIS IS ALL BECAUSE I...
...DIDN'T LISTEN AND WALKED OUT ALONE.
!
EAT IT.
DON'T THROW UP.
YOUR BODY WON'T LAST.
AS LONG AS YOU FORCE IT DOWN AND GET IT INTO YOUR STOMACH, YOU'LL BE FINE.
IF YOU EAT, THEN YOU'LL BE ABLE TO WORK TOMORROW.
THAT'S WHAT IT MEANS TO LIVE HERE.

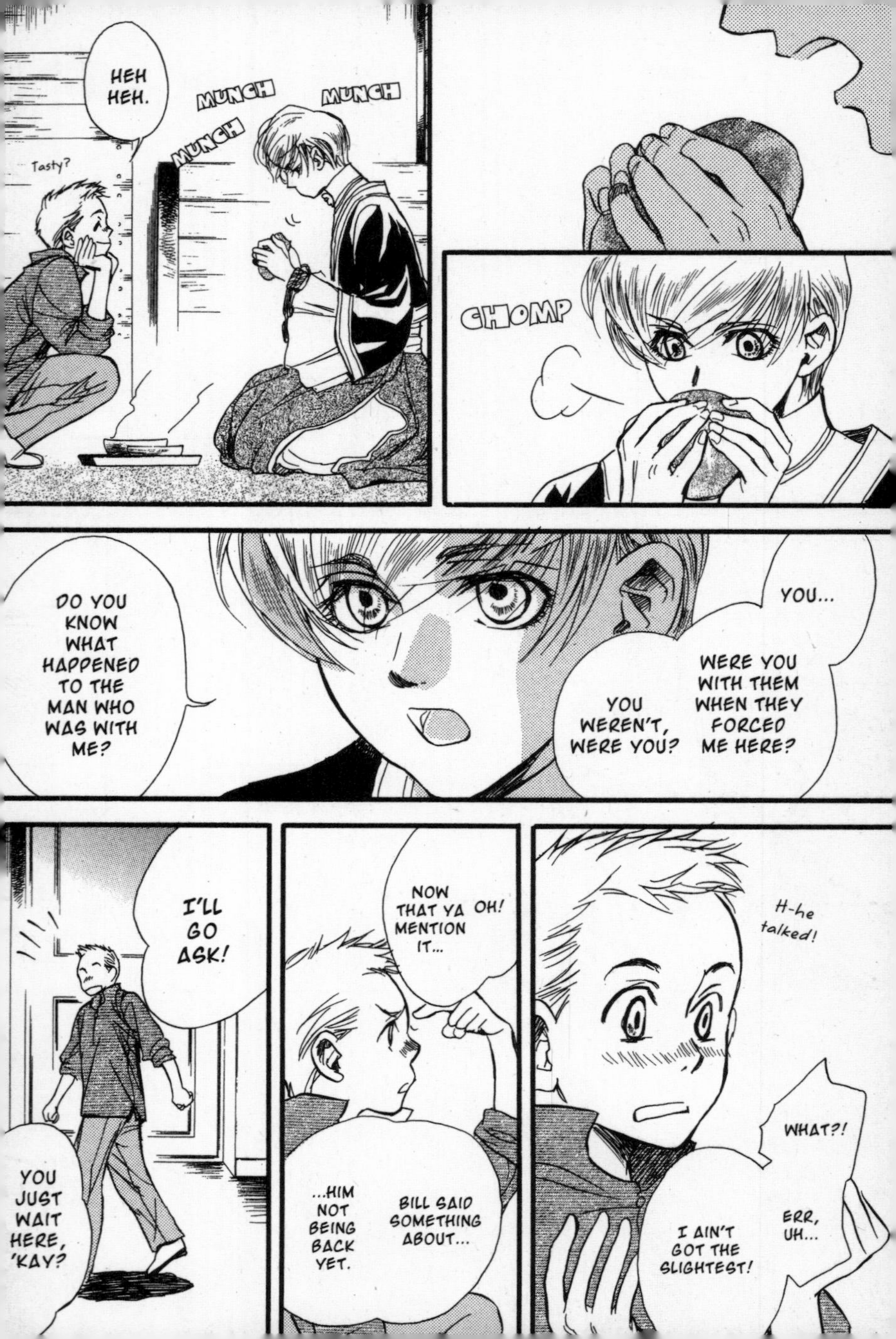
CHOMP
HEH HEH.
MUNCH
MUNCH
MUNCH
Tasty?
YOU...
WERE YOU WITH THEM WHEN THEY FORCED ME HERE?
YOU WEREN'T, WERE YOU?
DO YOU KNOW WHAT HAPPENED TO THE MAN WHO WAS WITH ME?
H-he talked!
WHAT?!
ERR, UH...
I AIN'T GOT THE SLIGHTEST!
OH!
NOW THAT YA MENTION IT...
BILL SAID SOMETHING ABOUT...
...HIM NOT BEING BACK YET.
I'LL GO ASK!
YOU JUST WAIT HERE, 'KAY?

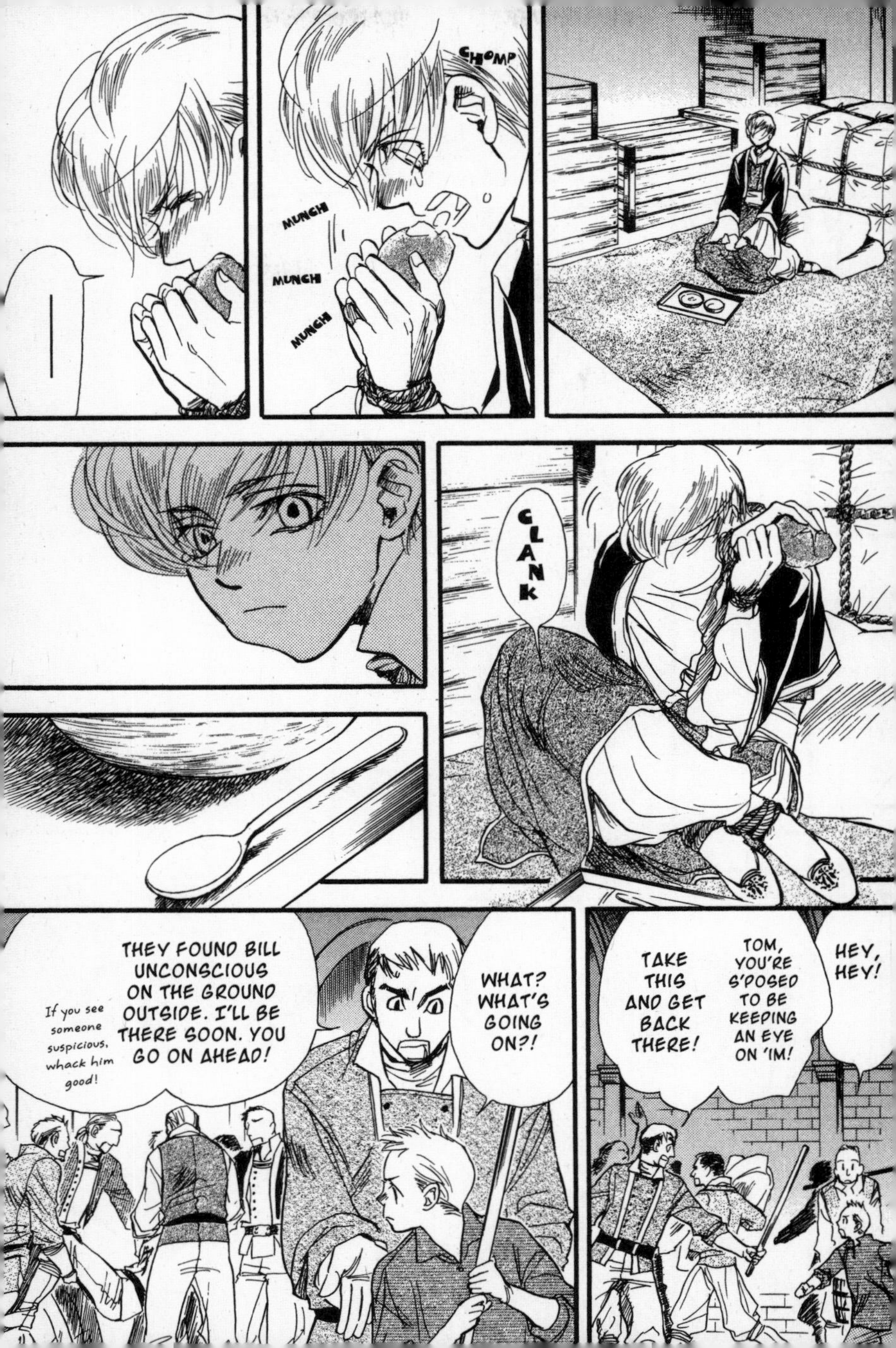
CHOMP
MUNCH
MUNCH
MUNCH
CLANK
HEY, HEY!
TOM, YOU'RE S'POSED TO BE KEEPING AN EYE ON 'IM!
TAKE THIS AND GET BACK THERE!
WHAT? WHAT'S GOING ON?!
THEY FOUND BILL UNCONSCIOUS ON THE GROUND OUTSIDE. I'LL BE THERE SOON. YOU GO ON AHEAD!
If you see someone suspicious, whack him good!

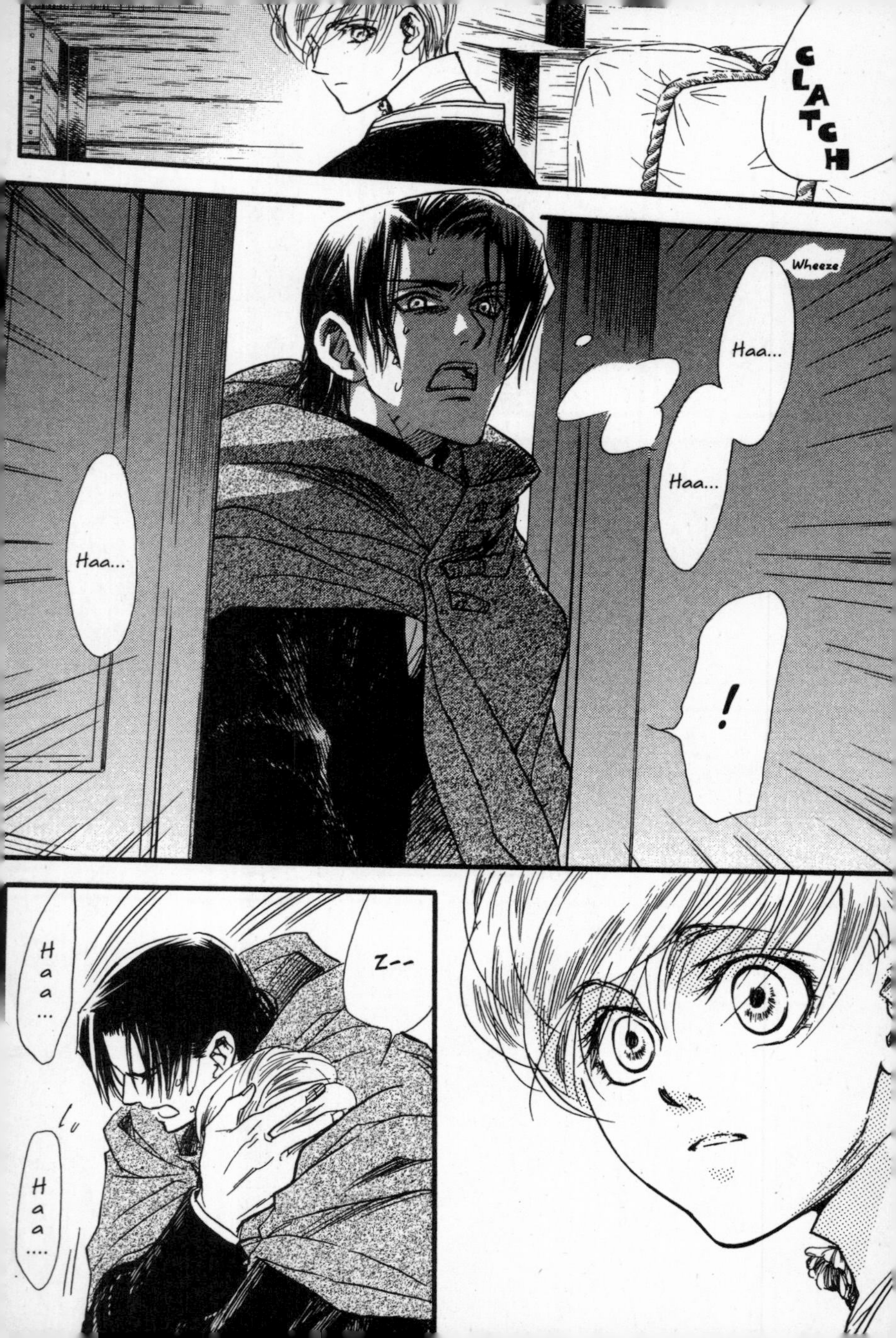
CLATCH
Wheeze
Haa...
Haa...
!
Haa...
Z--
Haa...
Haa....

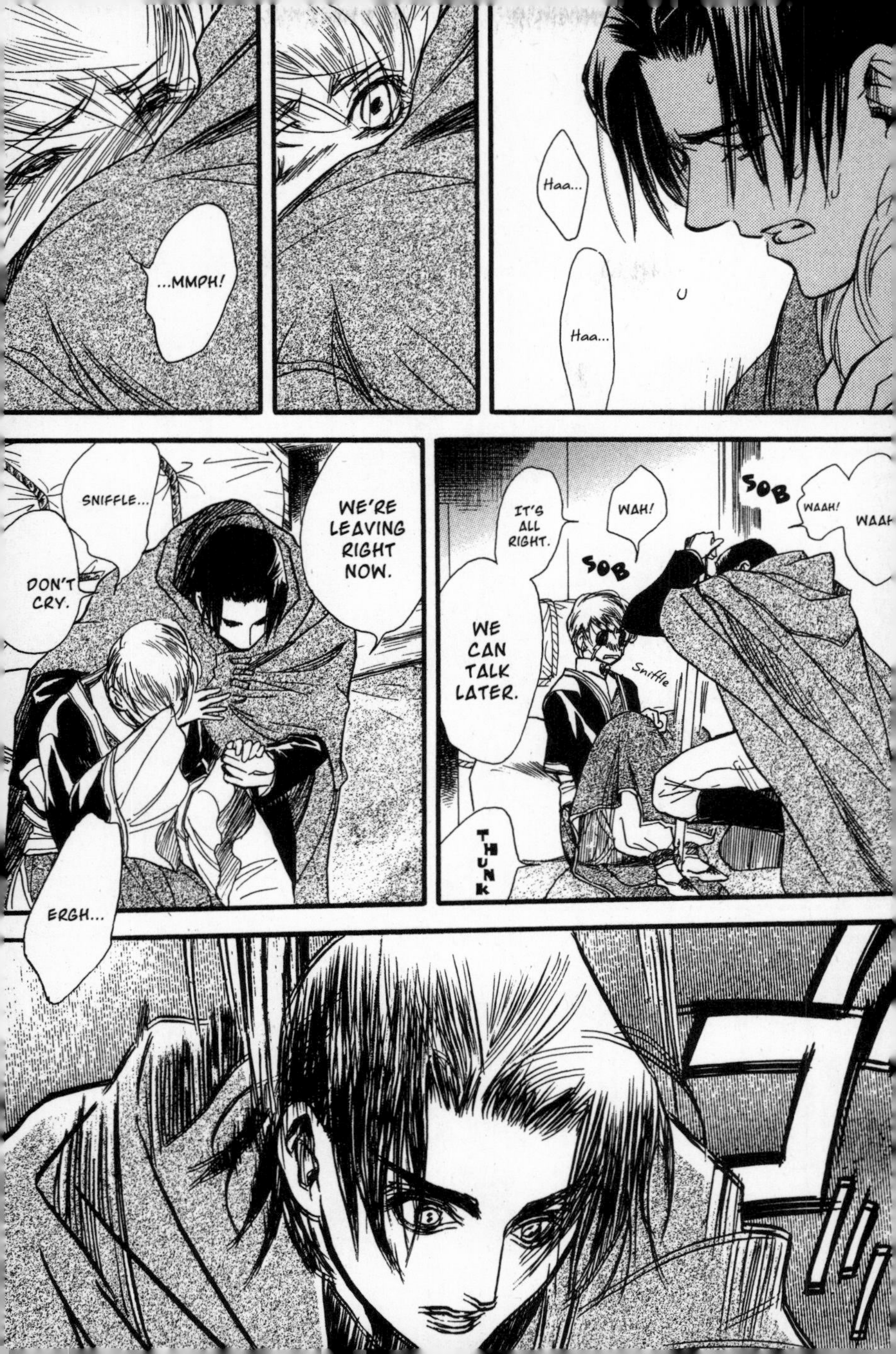
Haa...
Haa...
...MMPH!
WAAH!
WAAH
SOB
WAH!
IT'S ALL RIGHT.
SOB
Sniffle
WE CAN TALK LATER.
THUNK
WE'RE LEAVING RIGHT NOW.
SNIFFLE...
DON'T CRY.
ERGH...

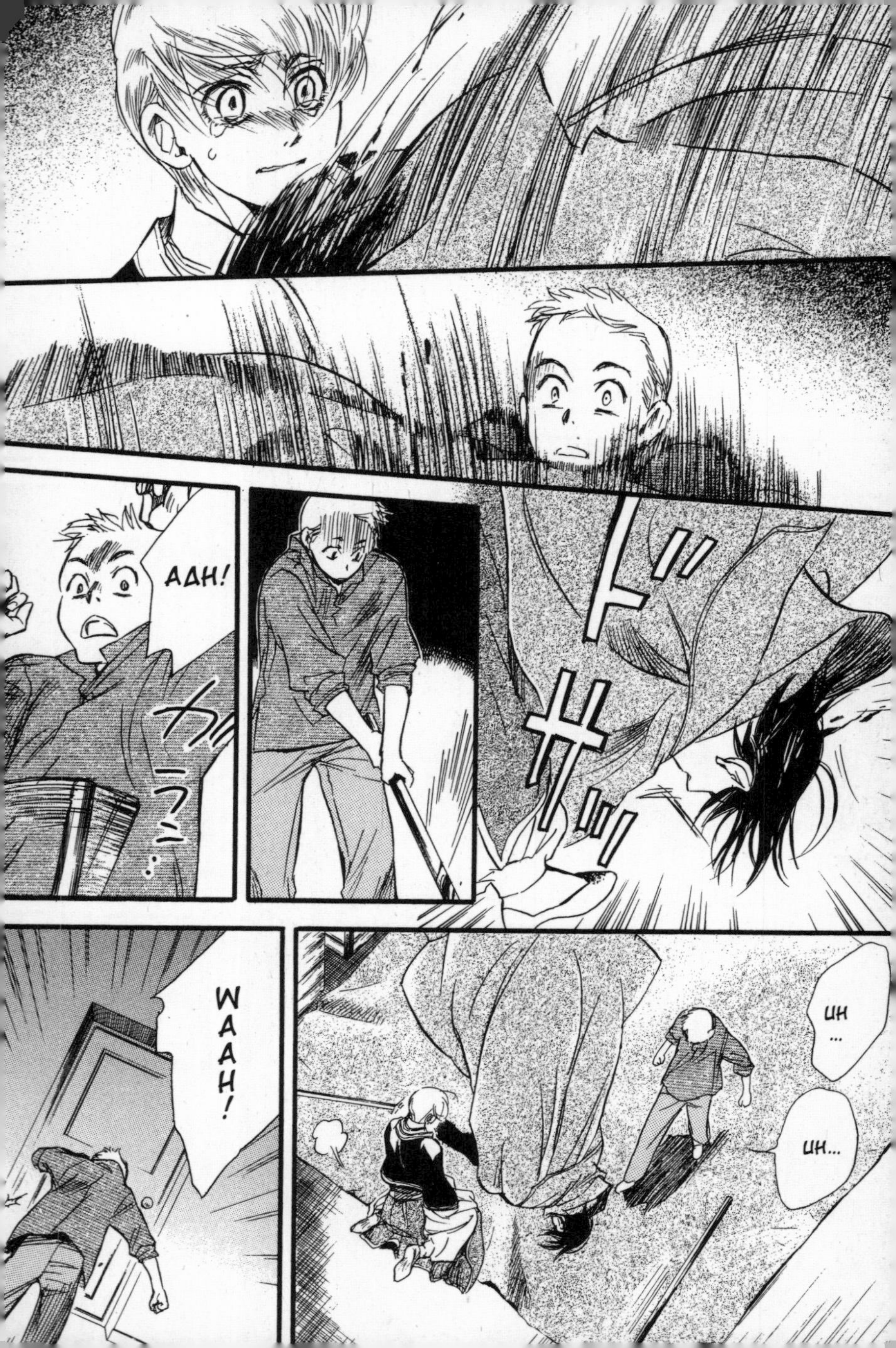
ドサッ
AAH!
ガラン‥
UH ...
UH...
WAAAH!

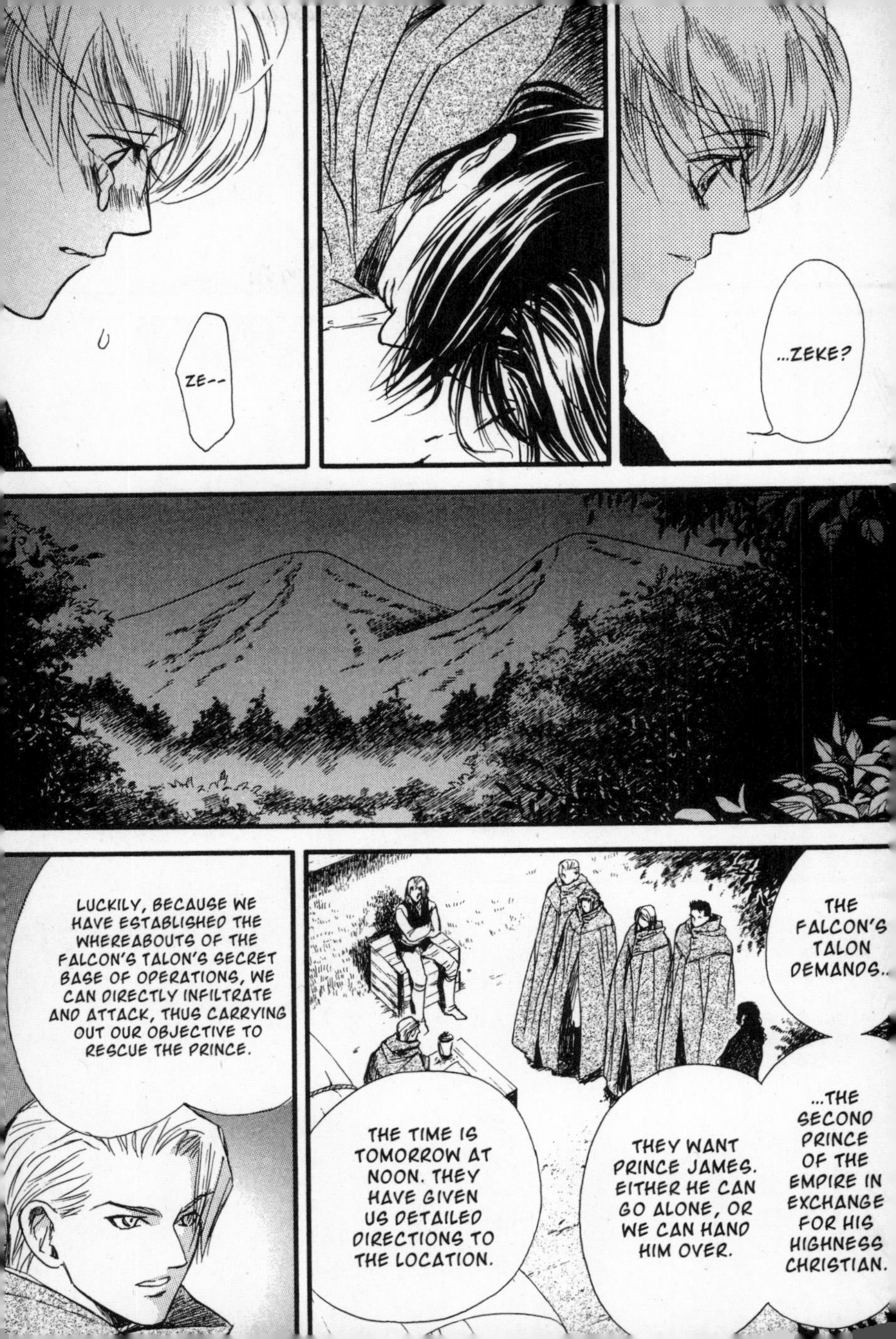
...ZEKE?
ZE--
THE FALCON'S TALON DEMANDS..
...THE SECOND PRINCE OF THE EMPIRE IN EXCHANGE FOR HIS HIGHNESS CHRISTIAN.
THEY WANT PRINCE JAMES. EITHER HE CAN GO ALONE, OR WE CAN HAND HIM OVER.
THE TIME IS TOMORROW AT NOON. THEY HAVE GIVEN US DETAILED DIRECTIONS TO THE LOCATION.
LUCKILY, BECAUSE WE HAVE ESTABLISHED THE WHEREABOUTS OF THE FALCON'S TALON'S SECRET BASE OF OPERATIONS, WE CAN DIRECTLY INFILTRATE AND ATTACK, THUS CARRYING OUT OUR OBJECTIVE TO RESCUE THE PRINCE.

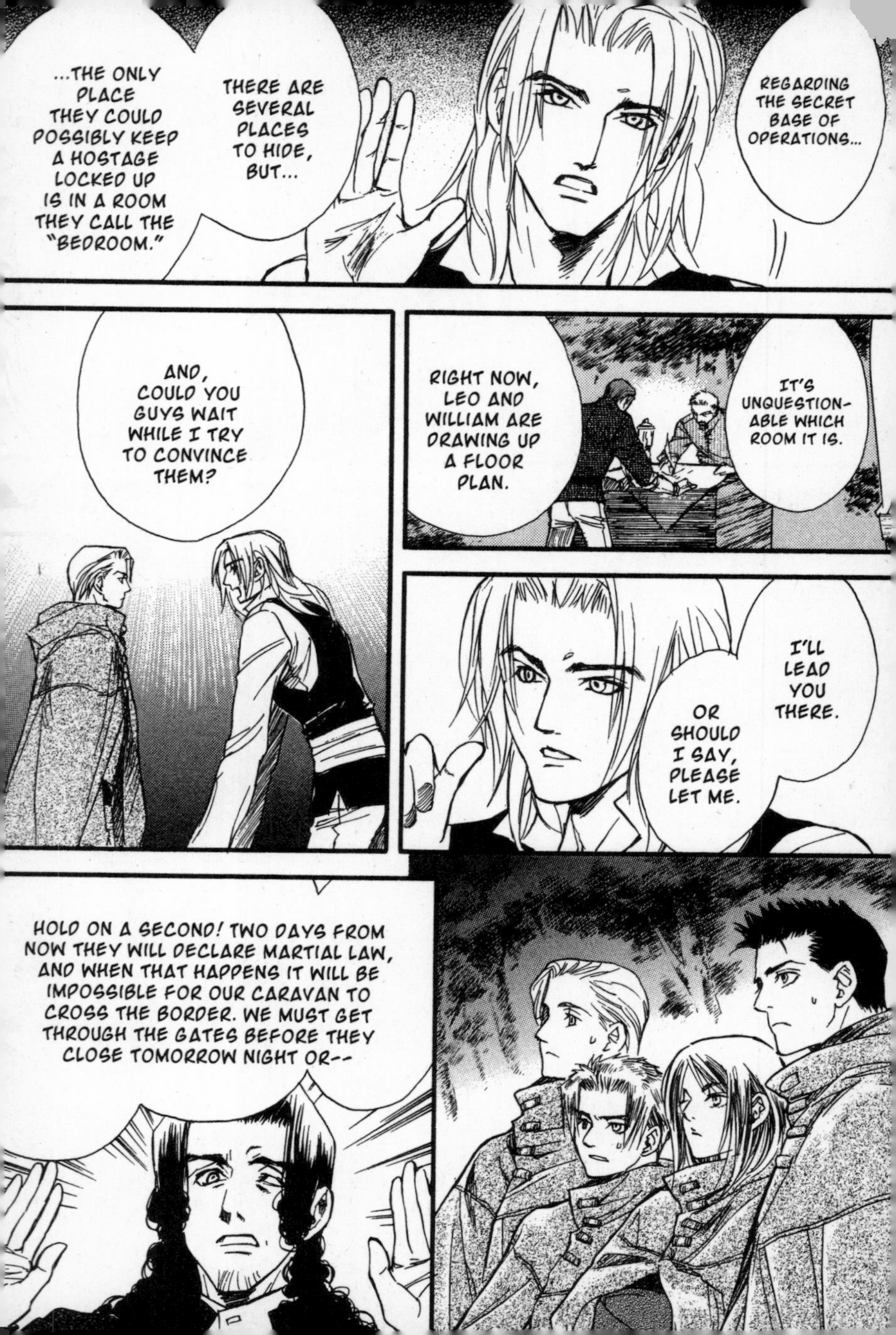
REGARDING THE SECRET BASE OF OPERATIONS...
THERE ARE SEVERAL PLACES TO HIDE, BUT...
...THE ONLY PLACE THEY COULD POSSIBLY KEEP A HOSTAGE LOCKED UP IS IN A ROOM THEY CALL THE "BEDROOM."
IT'S UNQUESTION-ABLE WHICH ROOM IT IS.
RIGHT NOW, LEO AND WILLIAM ARE DRAWING UP A FLOOR PLAN.
I'LL LEAD YOU THERE.
OR SHOULD I SAY, PLEASE LET ME.
AND, COULD YOU GUYS WAIT WHILE I TRY TO CONVINCE THEM?
HOLD ON A SECOND! TWO DAYS FROM NOW THEY WILL DECLARE MARTIAL LAW, AND WHEN THAT HAPPENS IT WILL BE IMPOSSIBLE FOR OUR CARAVAN TO CROSS THE BORDER. WE MUST GET THROUGH THE GATES BEFORE THEY CLOSE TOMORROW NIGHT OR--

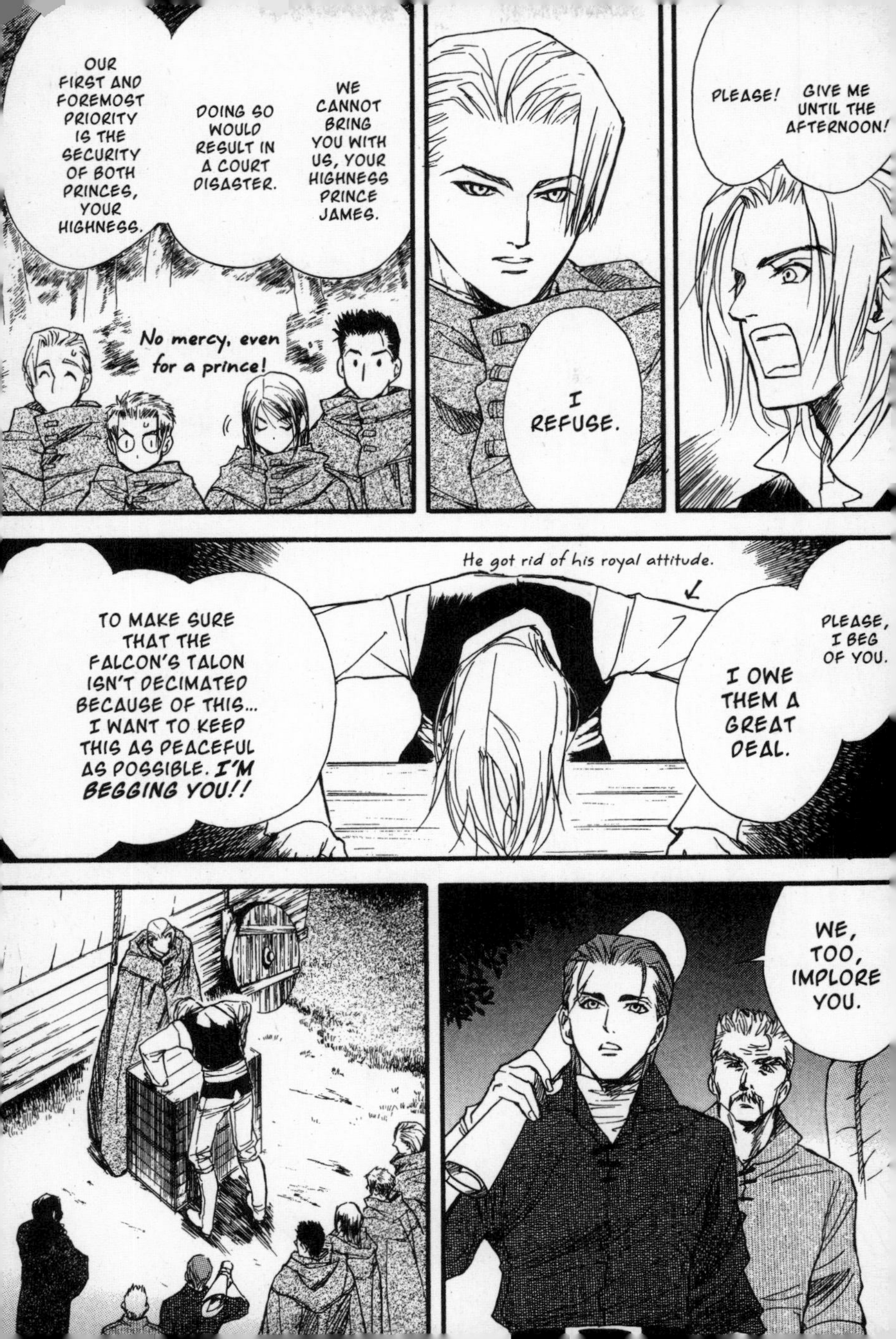
PLEASE! GIVE ME UNTIL THE AFTERNOON!
I REFUSE.
WE CANNOT BRING YOU WITH US, YOUR HIGHNESS PRINCE JAMES.
DOING SO WOULD RESULT IN A COURT DISASTER.
OUR FIRST AND FOREMOST PRIORITY IS THE SECURITY OF BOTH PRINCES, YOUR HIGHNESS.
No mercy, even for a prince!
He got rid of his royal attitude.
PLEASE, I BEG OF YOU.
I OWE THEM A GREAT DEAL.
TO MAKE SURE THAT THE FALCON'S TALON ISN'T DECIMATED BECAUSE OF THIS... I WANT TO KEEP THIS AS PEACEFUL AS POSSIBLE. I'M BEGGING YOU!!
WE, TOO, IMPLORE YOU.

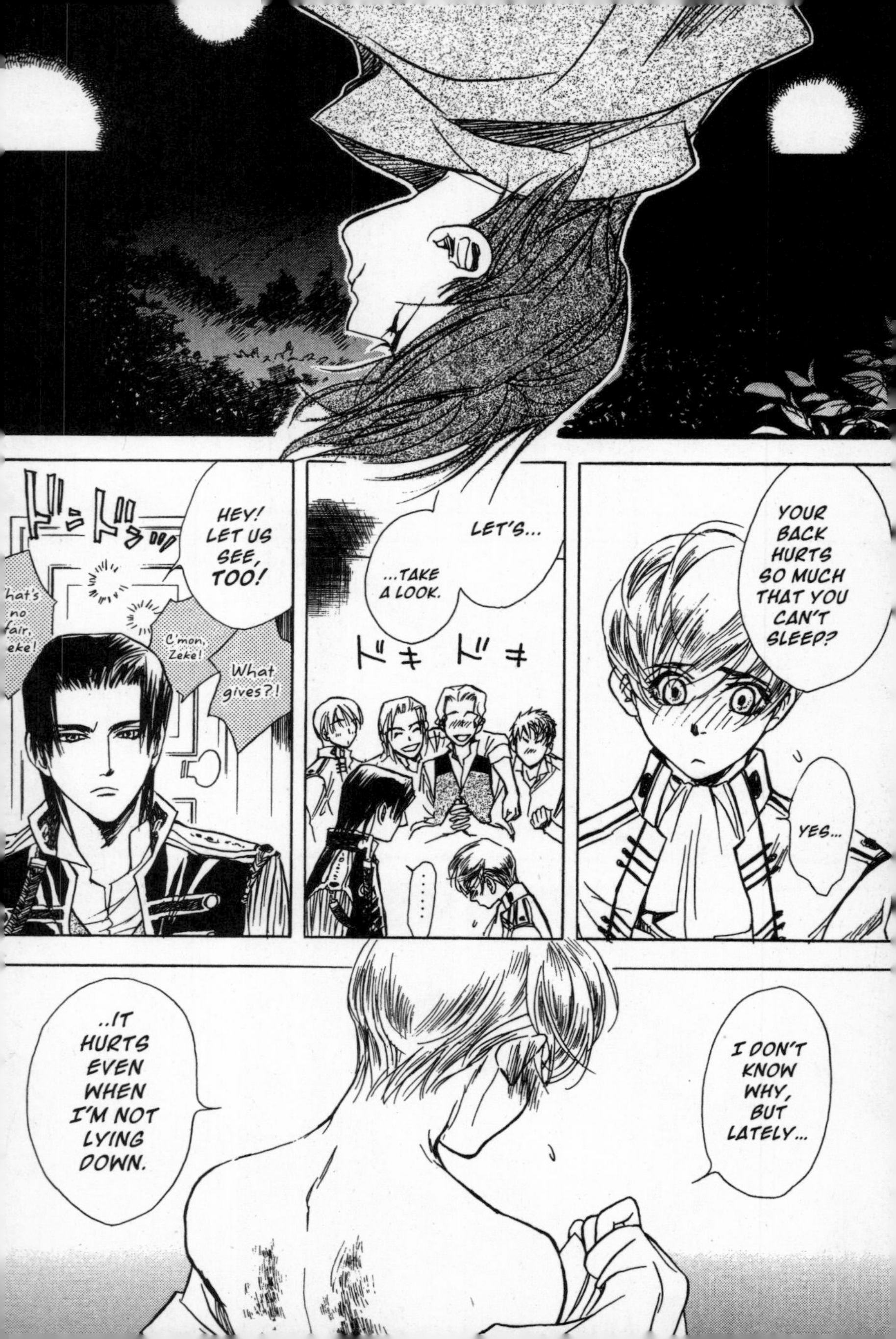
YOUR BACK HURTS SO MUCH THAT YOU CAN'T SLEEP?
YES...
LET'S...
...TAKE A LOOK.
ドキ ドキ
......
HEY! LET US SEE, TOO!
ドッドッ
hat's no fair, eke!
C'mon, Zeke!
What gives?!
I DON'T KNOW WHY, BUT LATELY...
..IT HURTS EVEN WHEN I'M NOT LYING DOWN.

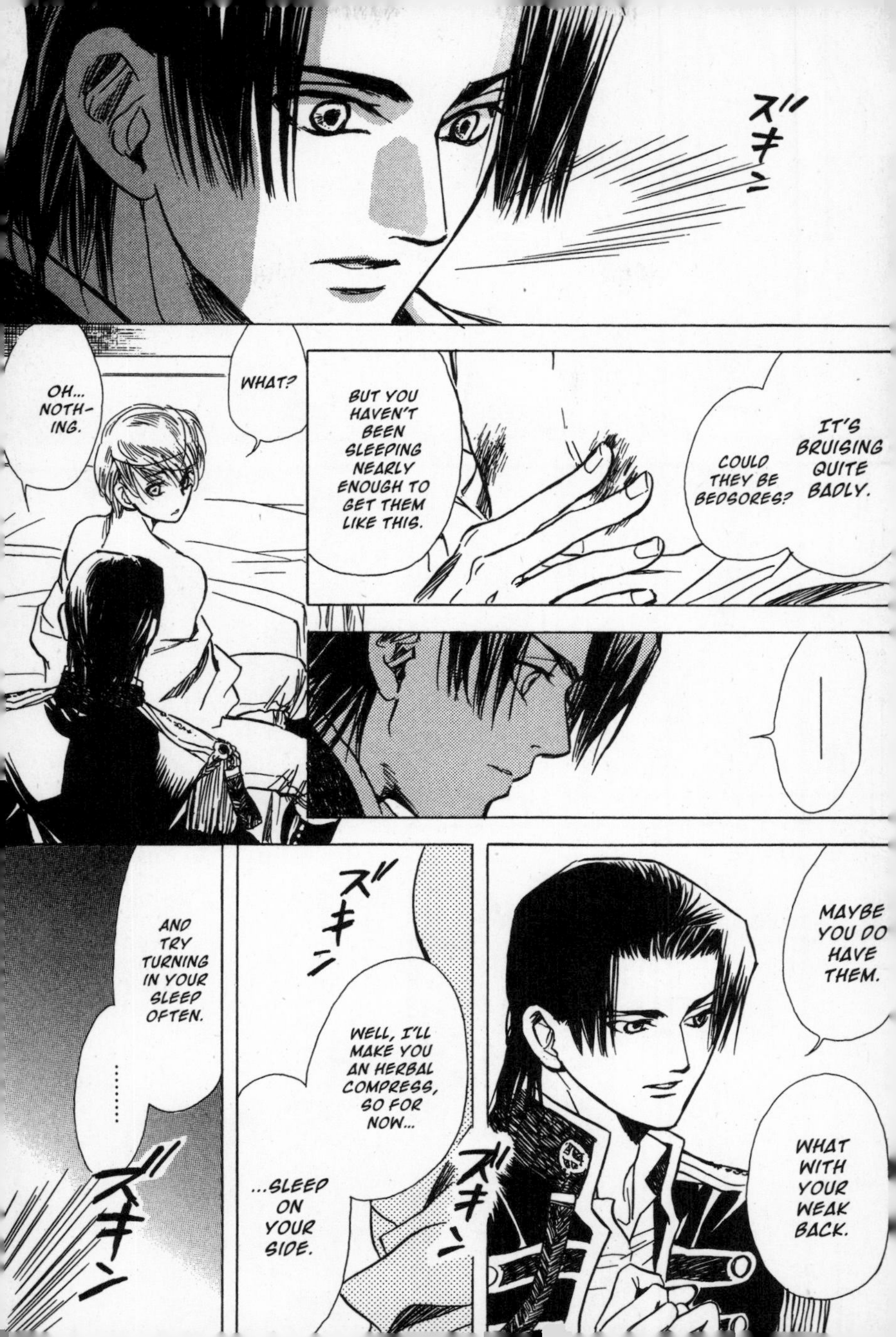
ズキン
IT'S BRUISING QUITE BADLY.
COULD THEY BE BEDSORES?
BUT YOU HAVEN'T BEEN SLEEPING NEARLY ENOUGH TO GET THEM LIKE THIS.
—
WHAT?
OH... NOTHING.
MAYBE YOU DO HAVE THEM.
WHAT WITH YOUR WEAK BACK.
ズキン
ズキン
WELL, I'LL MAKE YOU AN HERBAL COMPRESS, SO FOR NOW...
...SLEEP ON YOUR SIDE.
AND TRY TURNING IN YOUR SLEEP OFTEN.
......
ズキン

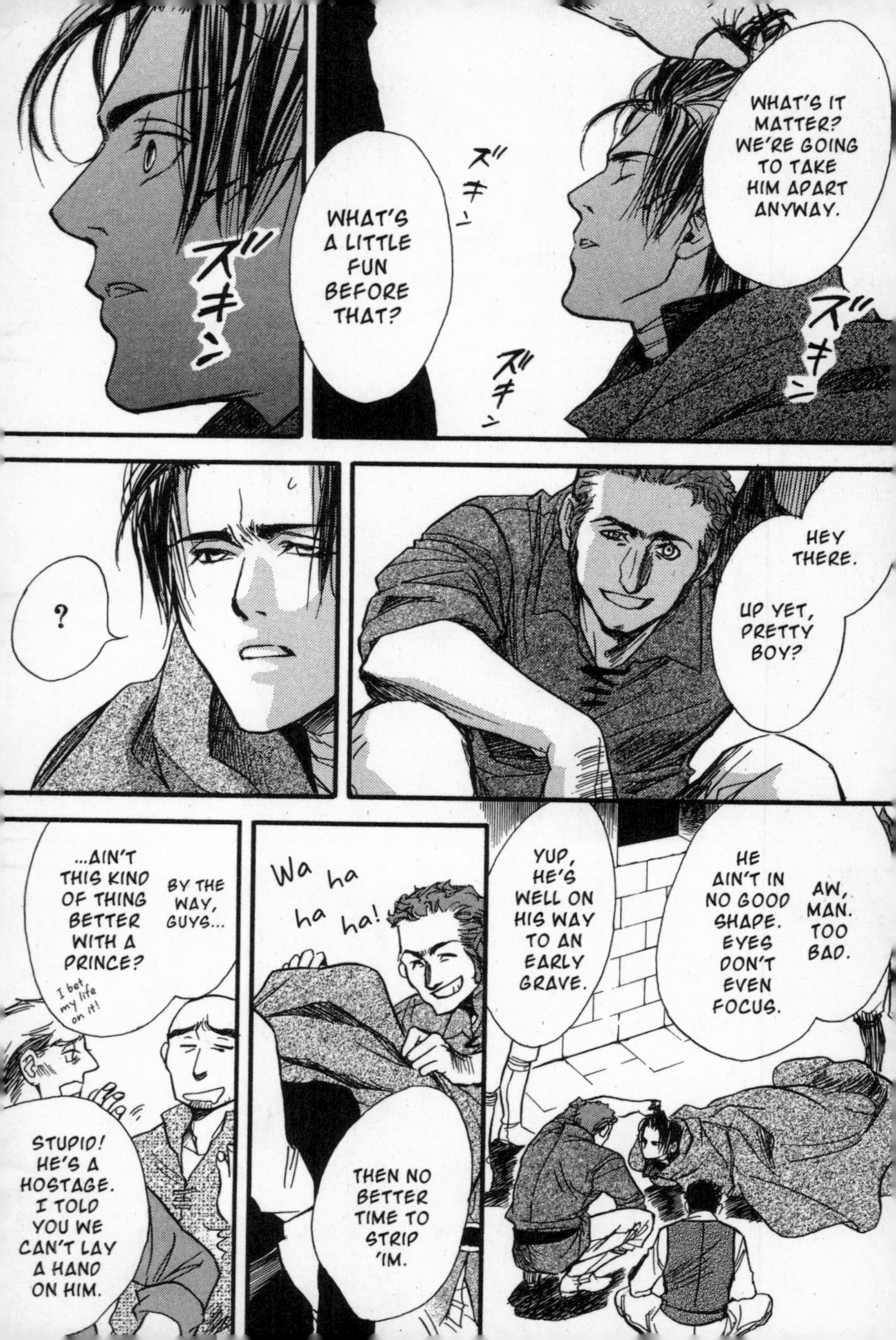
WHAT'S IT MATTER? WE'RE GOING TO TAKE HIM APART ANYWAY.
ズキン
ズキン
ズキン
WHAT'S A LITTLE FUN BEFORE THAT?
ズキン
HEY THERE.
UP YET, PRETTY BOY?
?
AW, MAN. TOO BAD.
HE AIN'T IN NO GOOD SHAPE. EYES DON'T EVEN FOCUS.
YUP, HE'S WELL ON HIS WAY TO AN EARLY GRAVE.
Wa ha ha ha!
THEN NO BETTER TIME TO STRIP 'IM.
BY THE WAY, GUYS...
...AIN'T THIS KIND OF THING BETTER WITH A PRINCE?
I bet my life on it!
STUPID! HE'S A HOSTAGE. I TOLD YOU WE CAN'T LAY A HAND ON HIM.

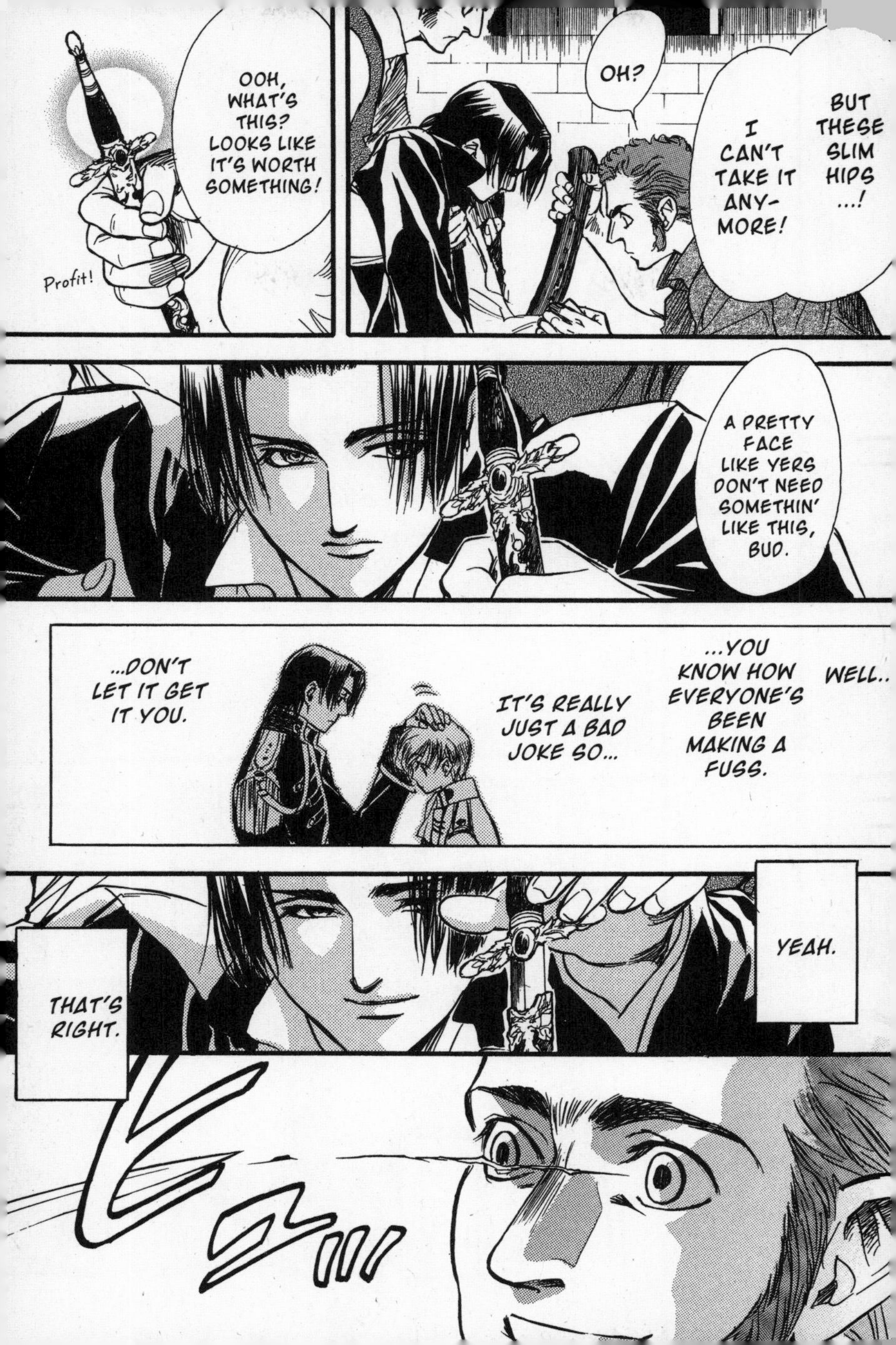
BUT THESE SLIM HIPS ...!
I CAN'T TAKE IT ANY-MORE!
OH?
OOH, WHAT'S THIS? LOOKS LIKE IT'S WORTH SOMETHING!
Profit!
A PRETTY FACE LIKE YERS DON'T NEED SOMETHIN' LIKE THIS, BUD.
WELL..
...YOU KNOW HOW EVERYONE'S BEEN MAKING A FUSS.
IT'S REALLY JUST A BAD JOKE SO...
...DON'T LET IT GET IT YOU.
YEAH.
THAT'S RIGHT.

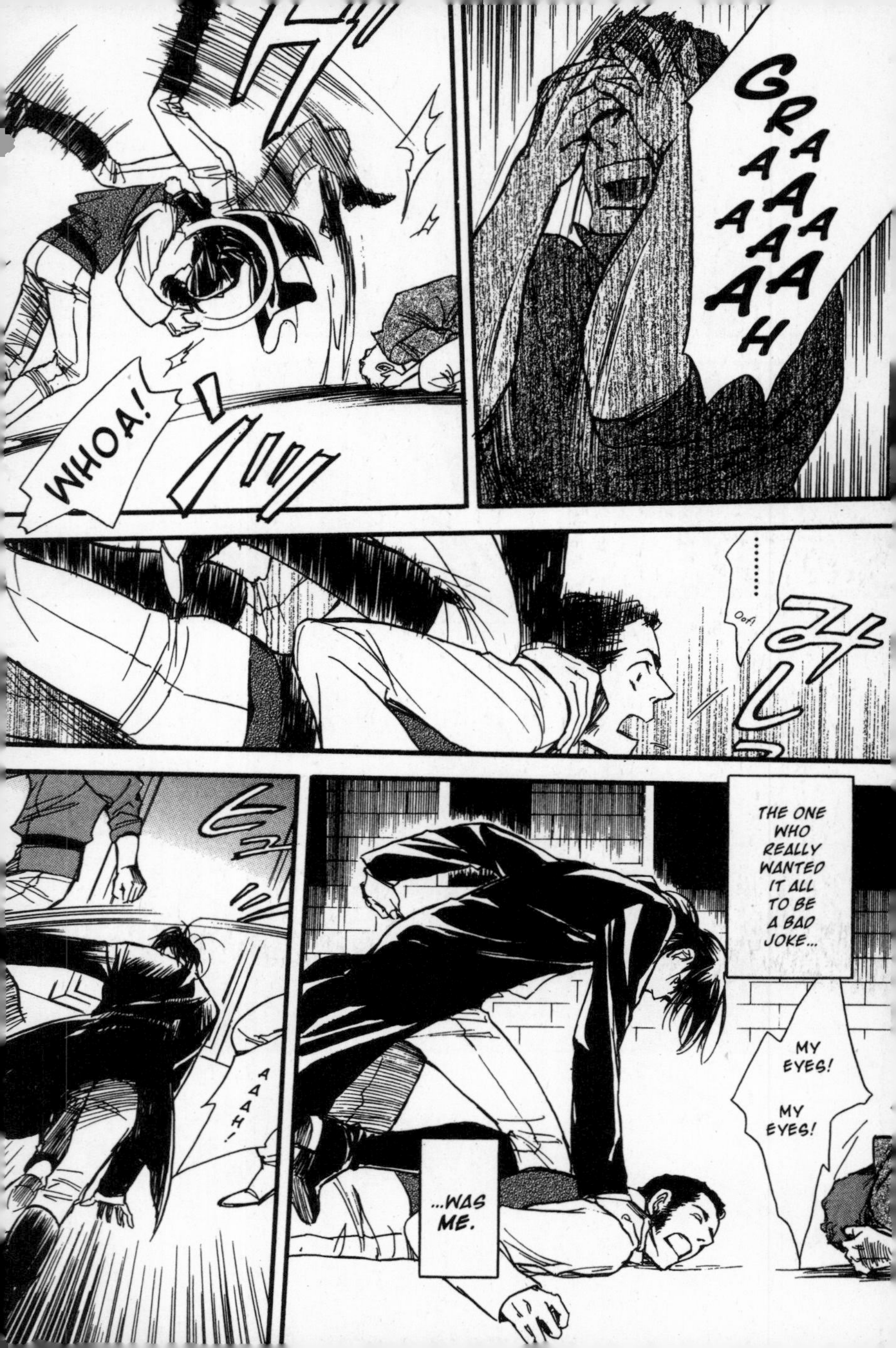
GRAAAAAAAAH
WHOA!
......
Oof!
THE ONE WHO REALLY WANTED IT ALL TO BE A BAD JOKE...
MY EYES!
MY EYES!
...WAS ME.
AAAH!

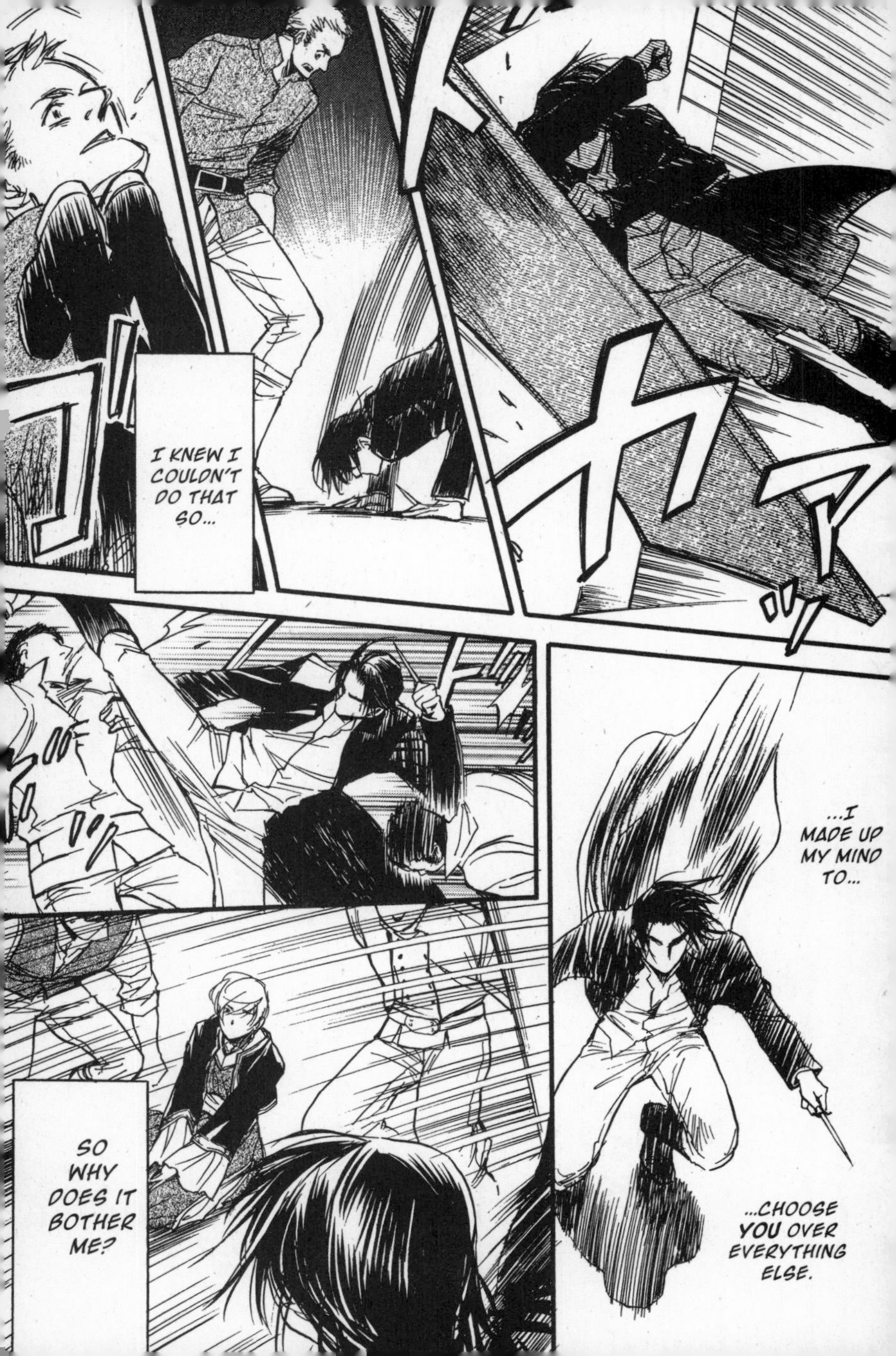
I KNEW I COULDN'T DO THAT SO...
...I MADE UP MY MIND TO...
...CHOOSE YOU OVER EVERYTHING ELSE.
SO WHY DOES IT BOTHER ME?

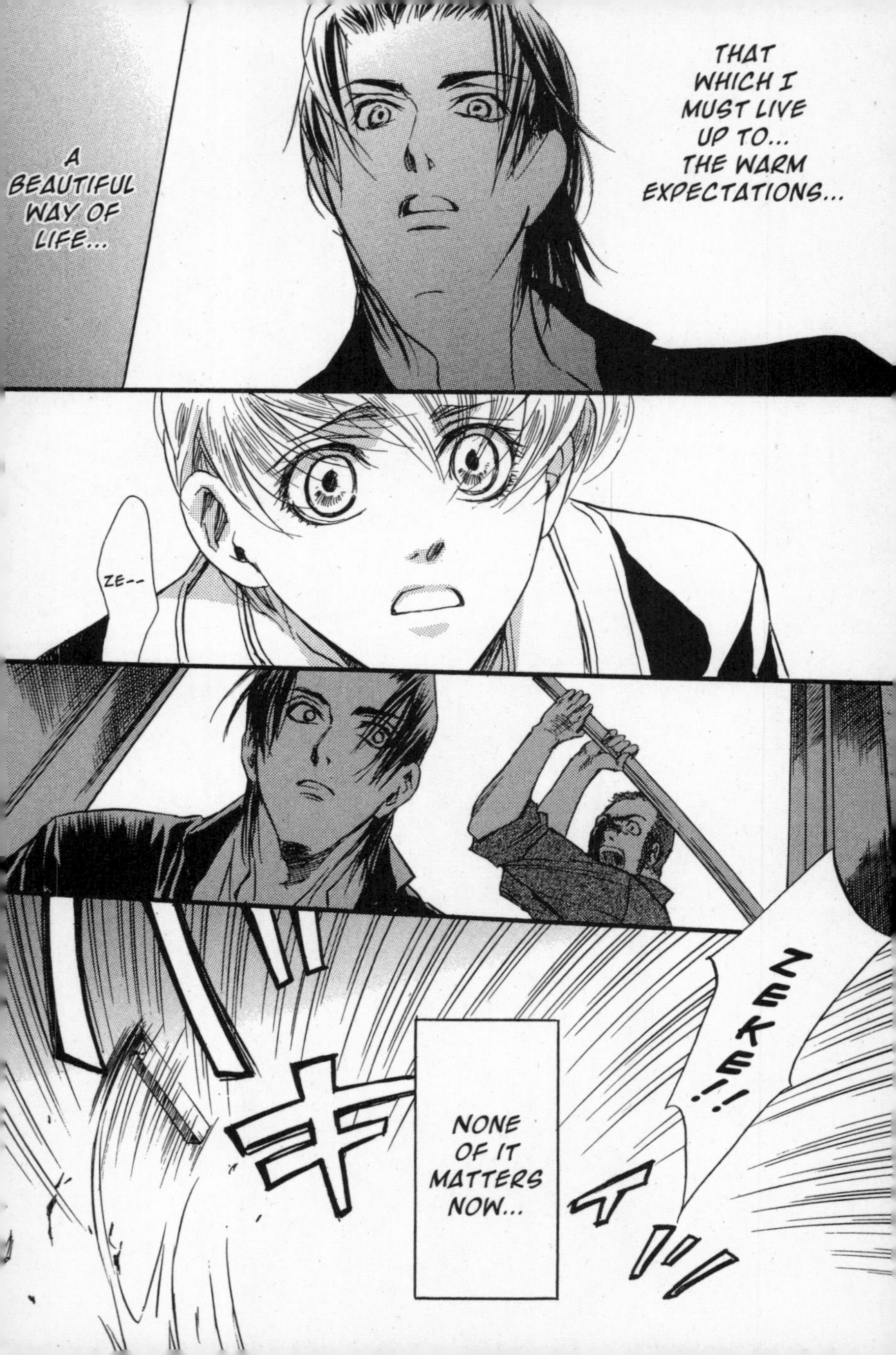
THAT WHICH I MUST LIVE UP TO... THE WARM EXPECTATIONS...
A BEAUTIFUL WAY OF LIFE...
ZE--
ZEKE!!
NONE OF IT MATTERS NOW...
キィ!!

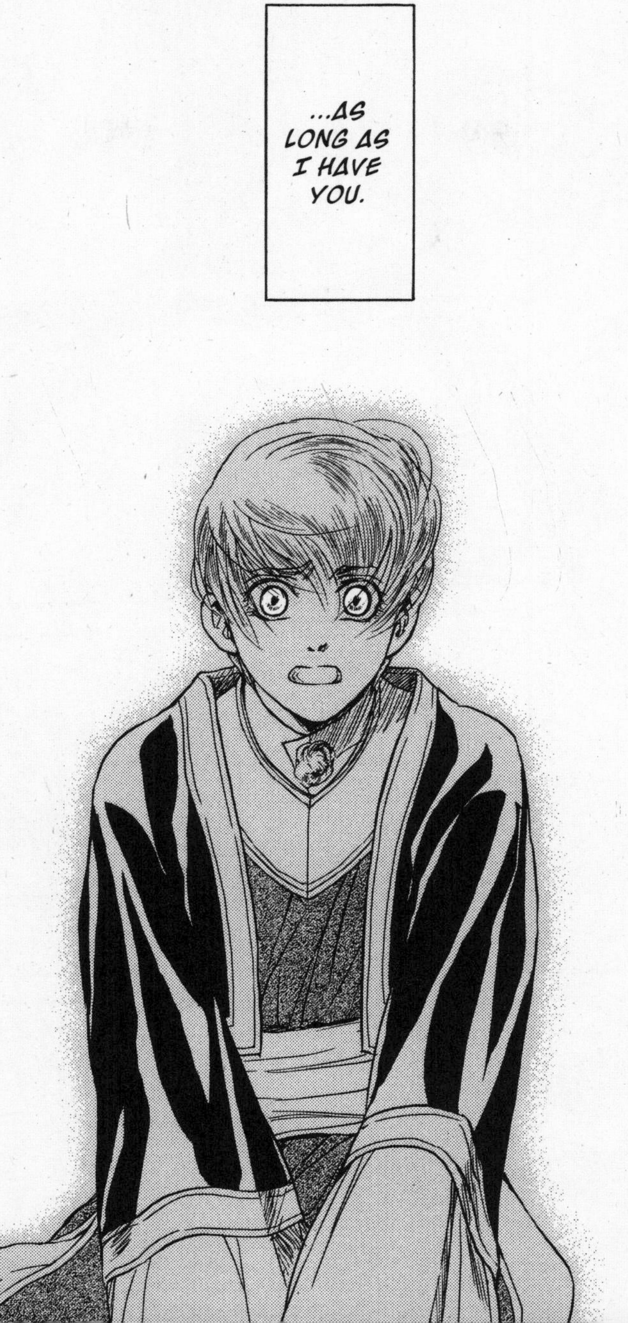
...AS LONG AS I HAVE YOU.

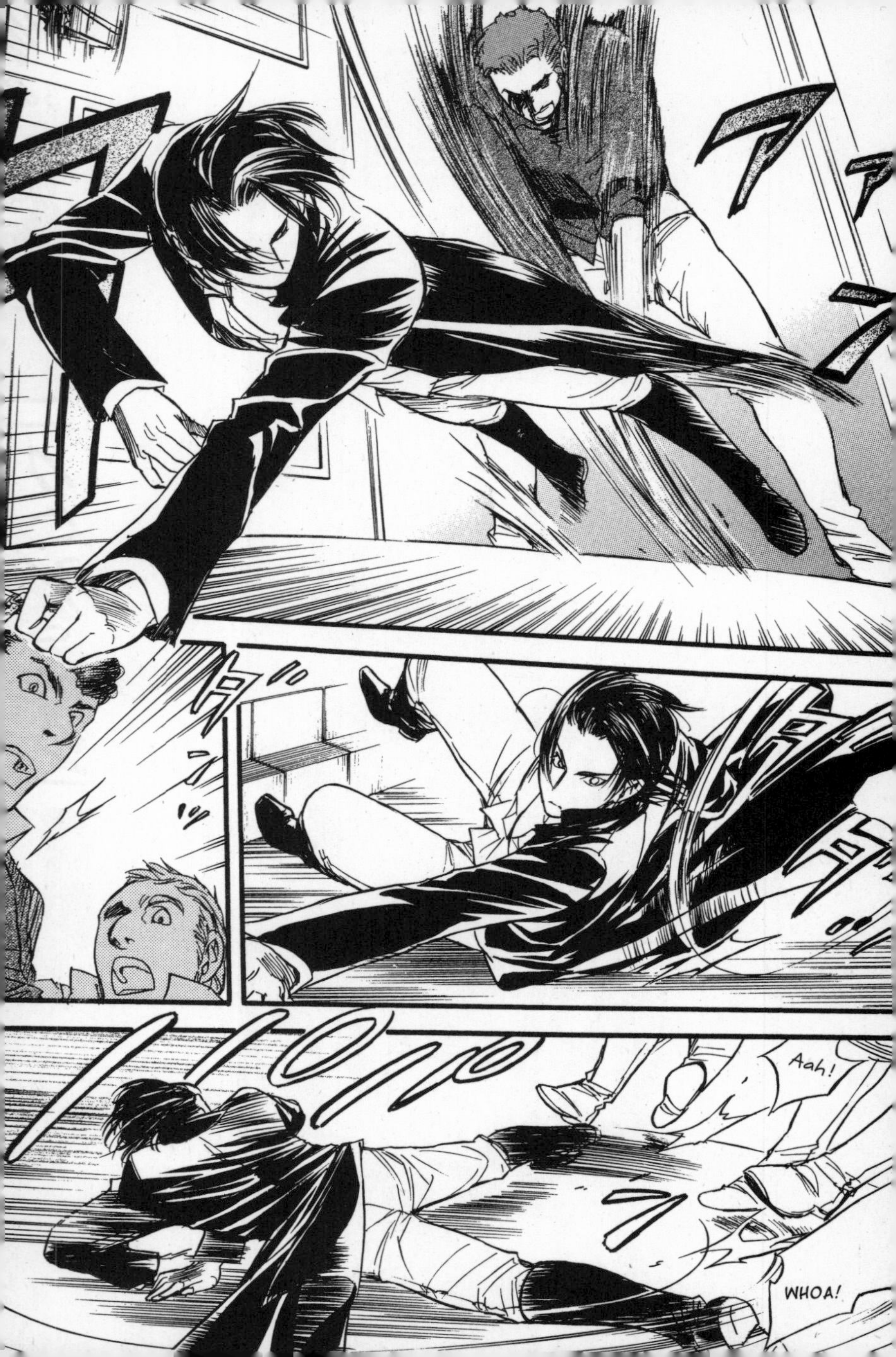
Aah!
WHOA!

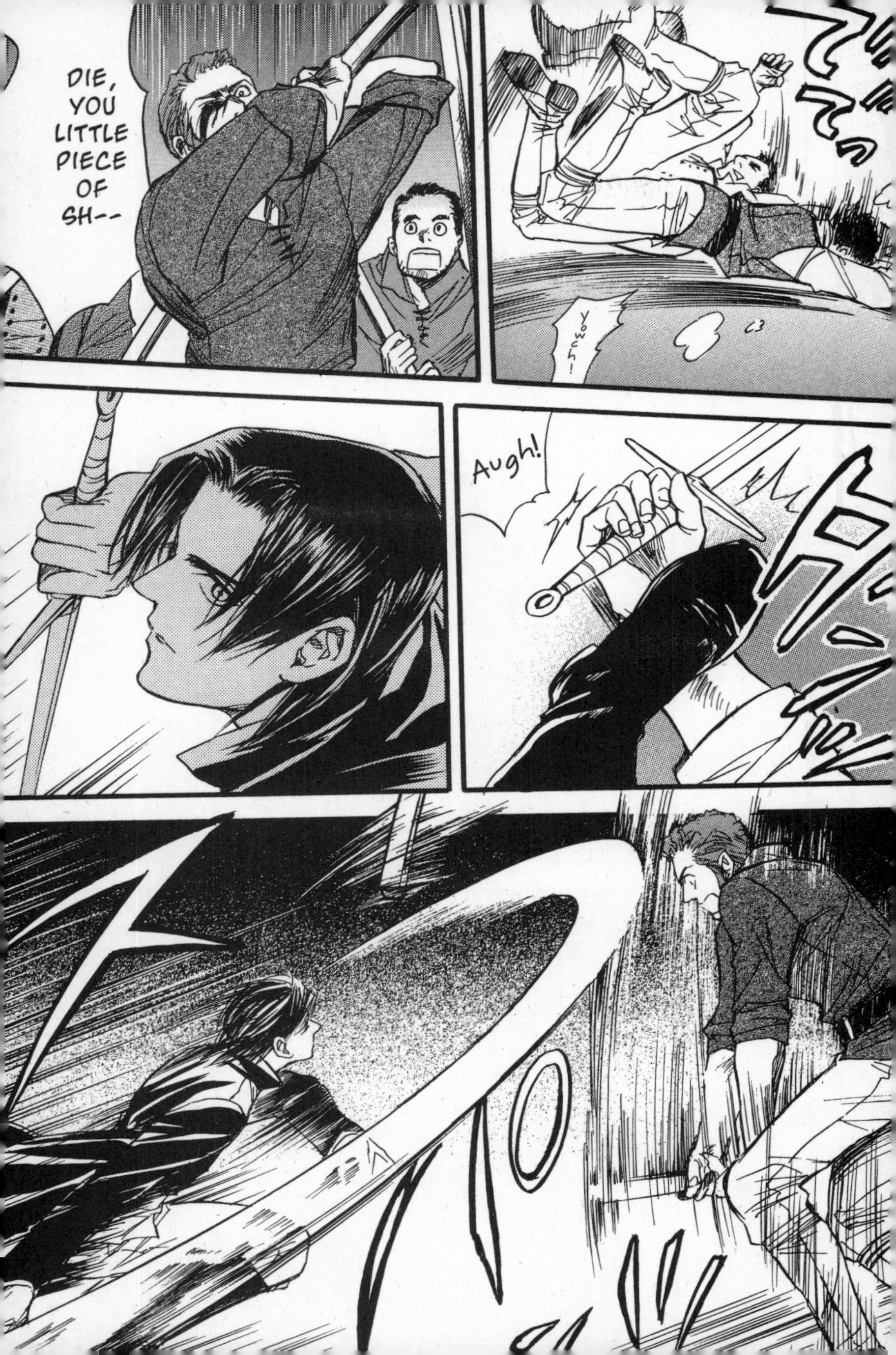
Yowch!
DIE, YOU LITTLE PIECE OF SH--
Augh!

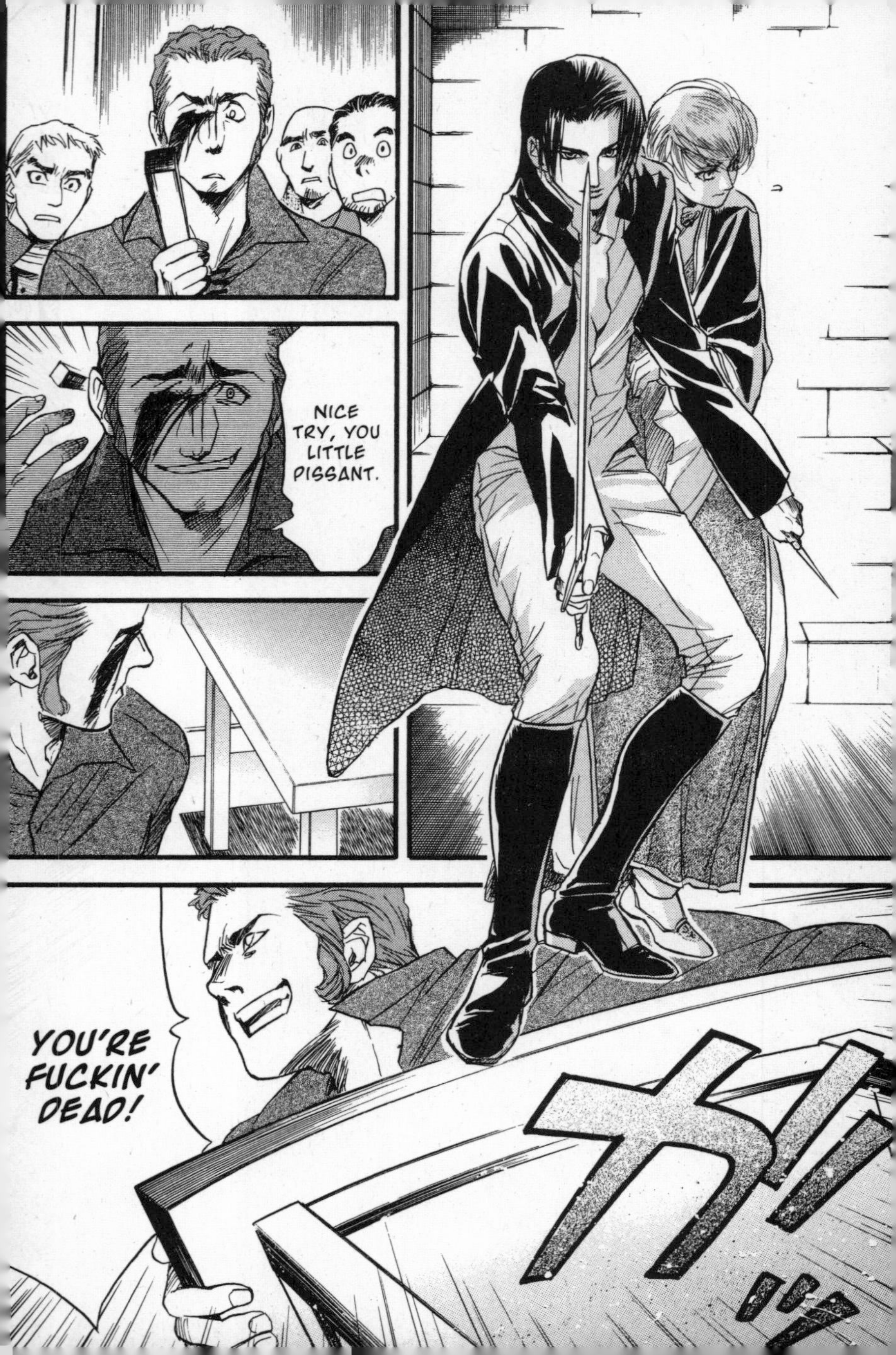
NICE TRY, YOU LITTLE PISSANT.
YOU'RE FUCKIN' DEAD!

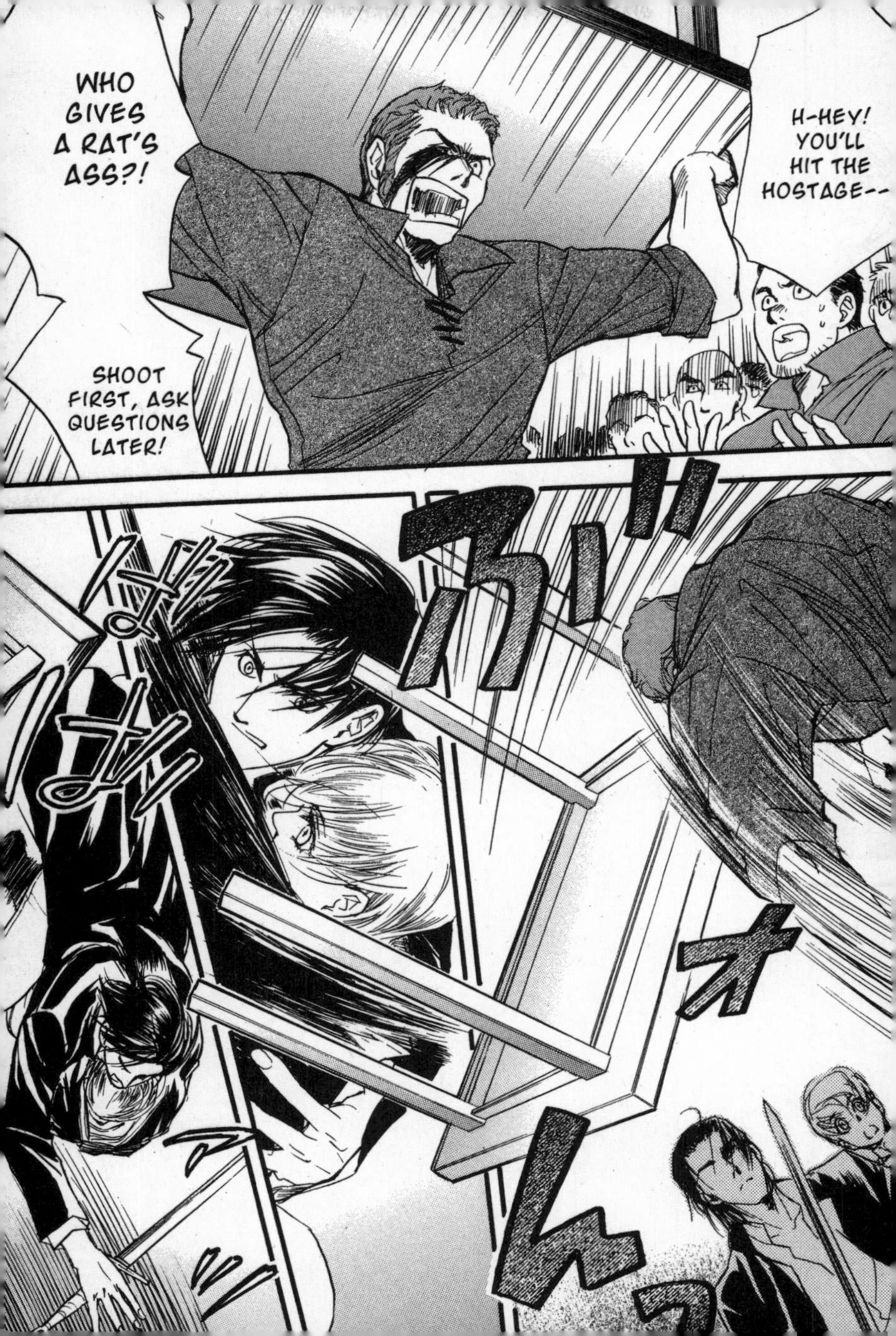

H-HEY! YOU'LL HIT THE HOSTAGE--
WHO GIVES A RAT'S ASS?!
SHOOT FIRST, ASK QUESTIONS LATER!

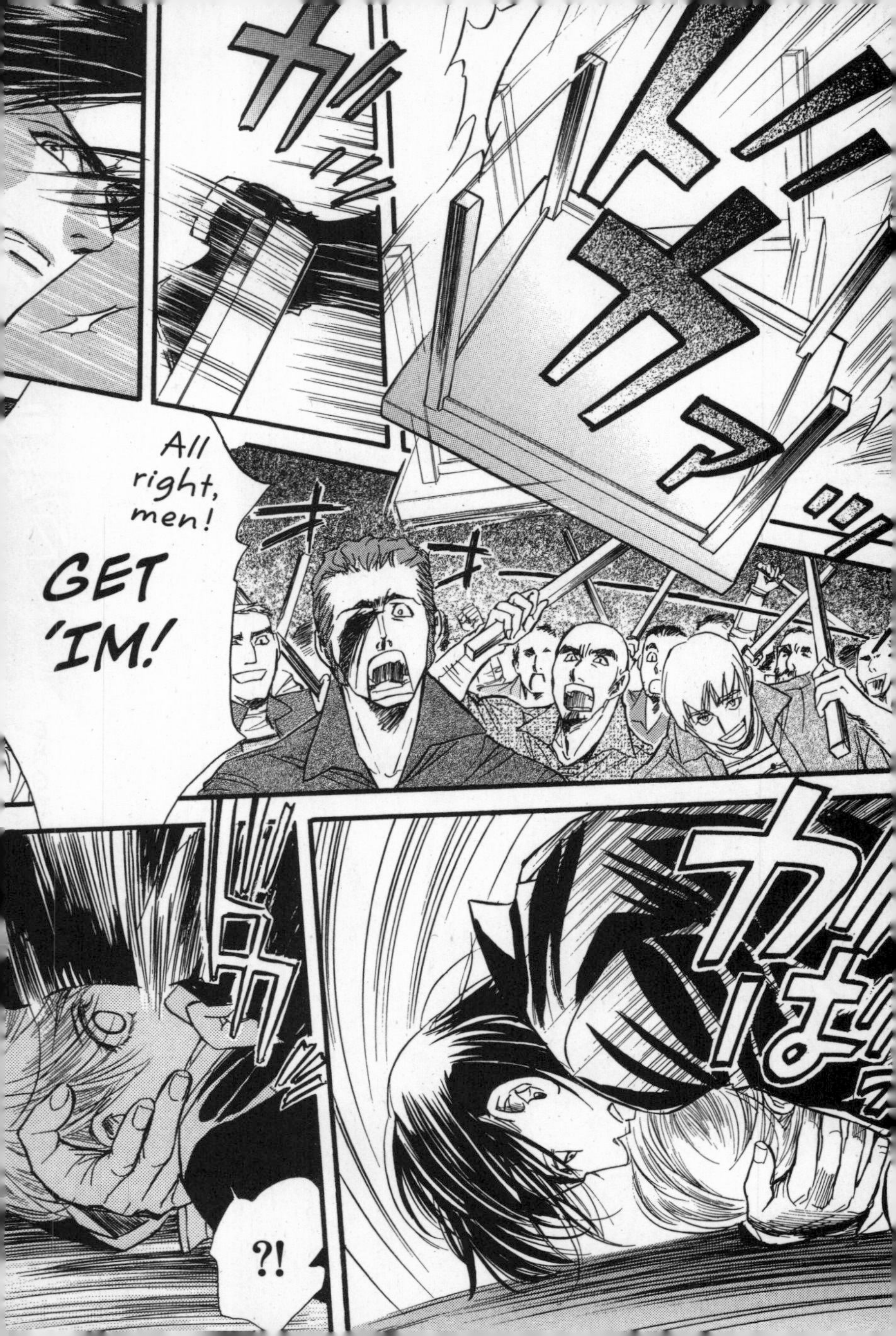
All right, men!
GET 'IM!
?!

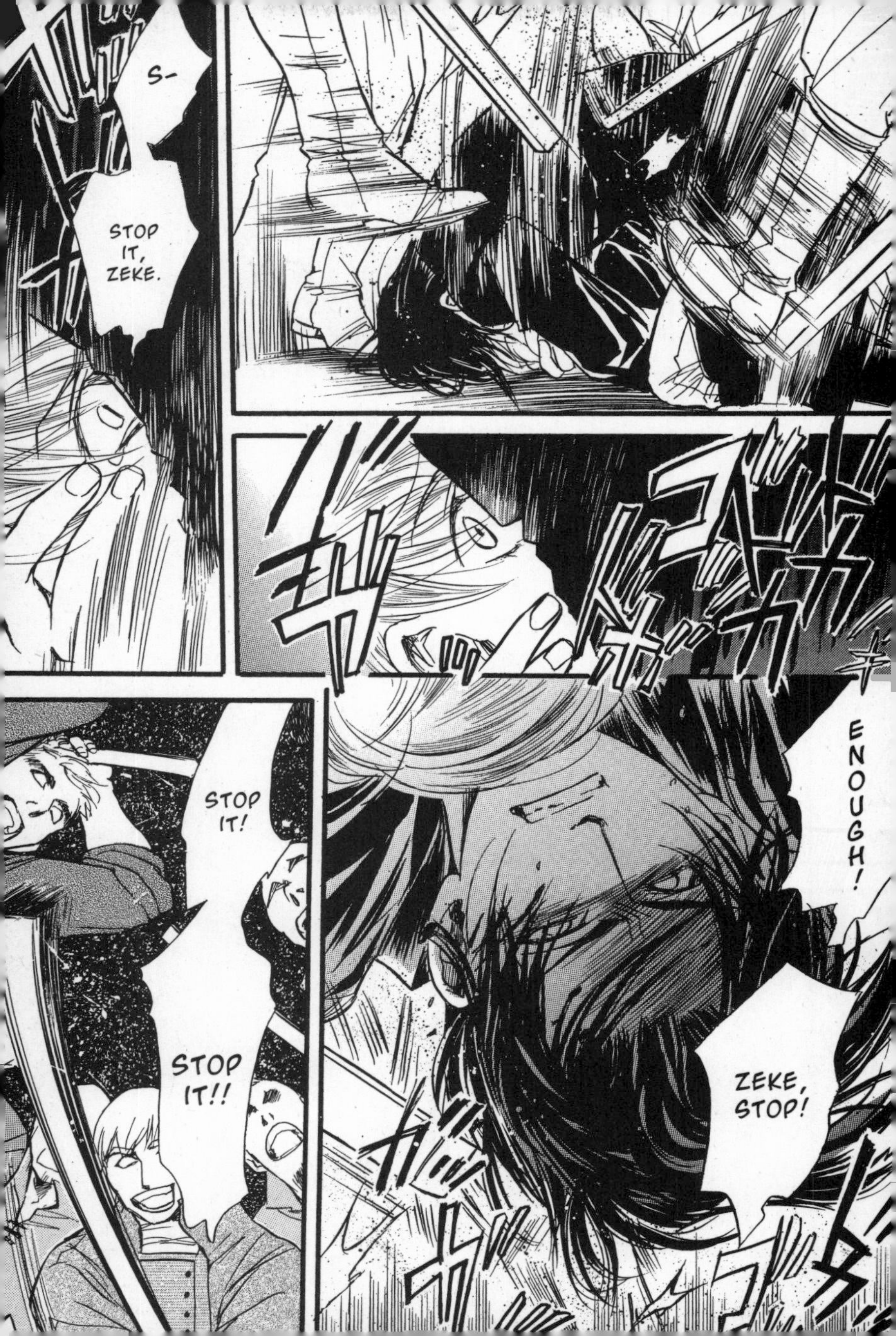
S-
STOP IT, ZEKE.
ENOUGH!
ZEKE, STOP!
STOP IT!
STOP IT!!

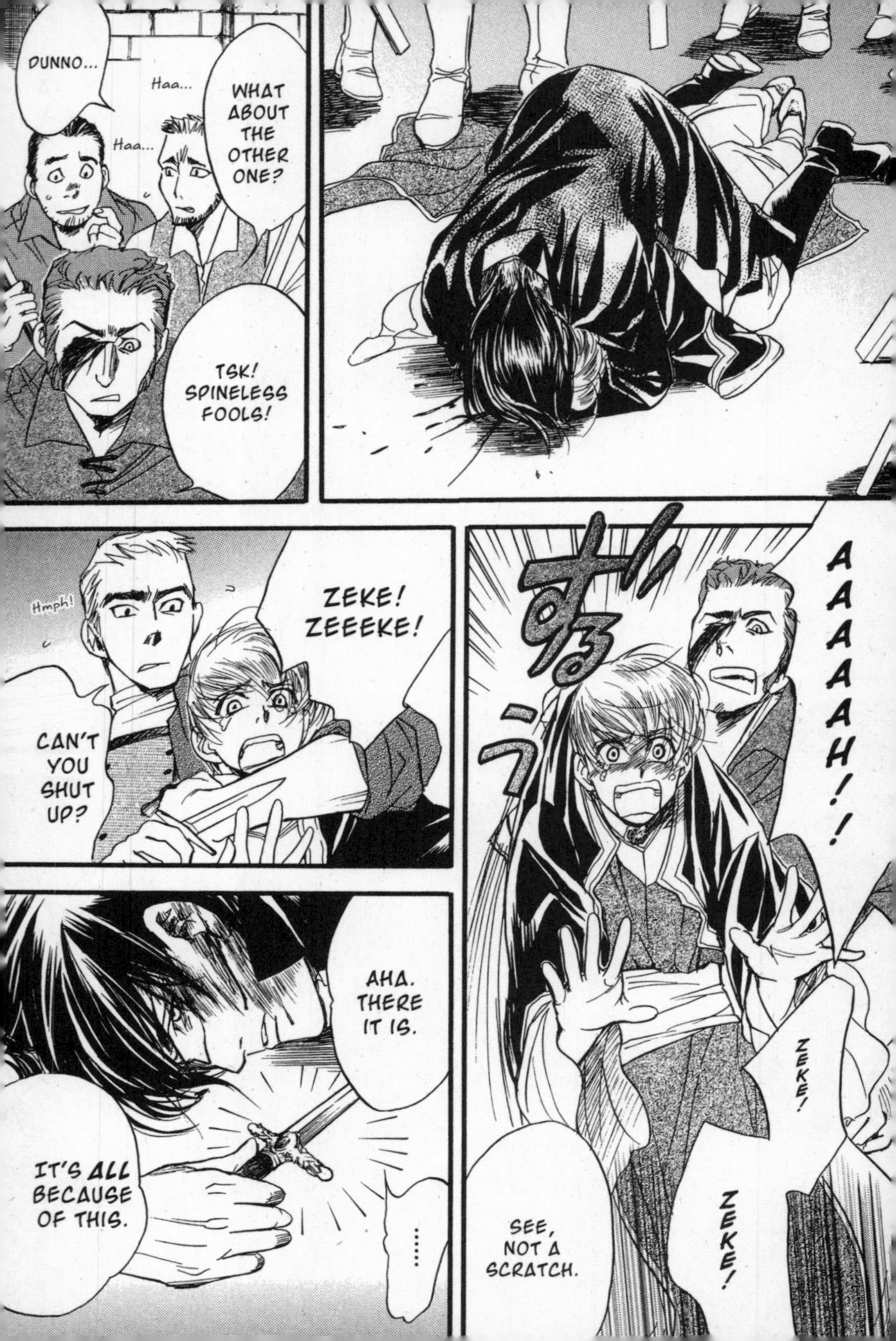
WHAT ABOUT THE OTHER ONE?
Haa...
Haa...
DUNNO...
TSK! SPINELESS FOOLS!
ずるう
AAAAAH!!
ZEKE!
ZEKE!
SEE, NOT A SCRATCH.
ZEKE! ZEEEKE!
Hmph!
CAN'T YOU SHUT UP?
AHA. THERE IT IS.
......
IT'S ALL BECAUSE OF THIS.

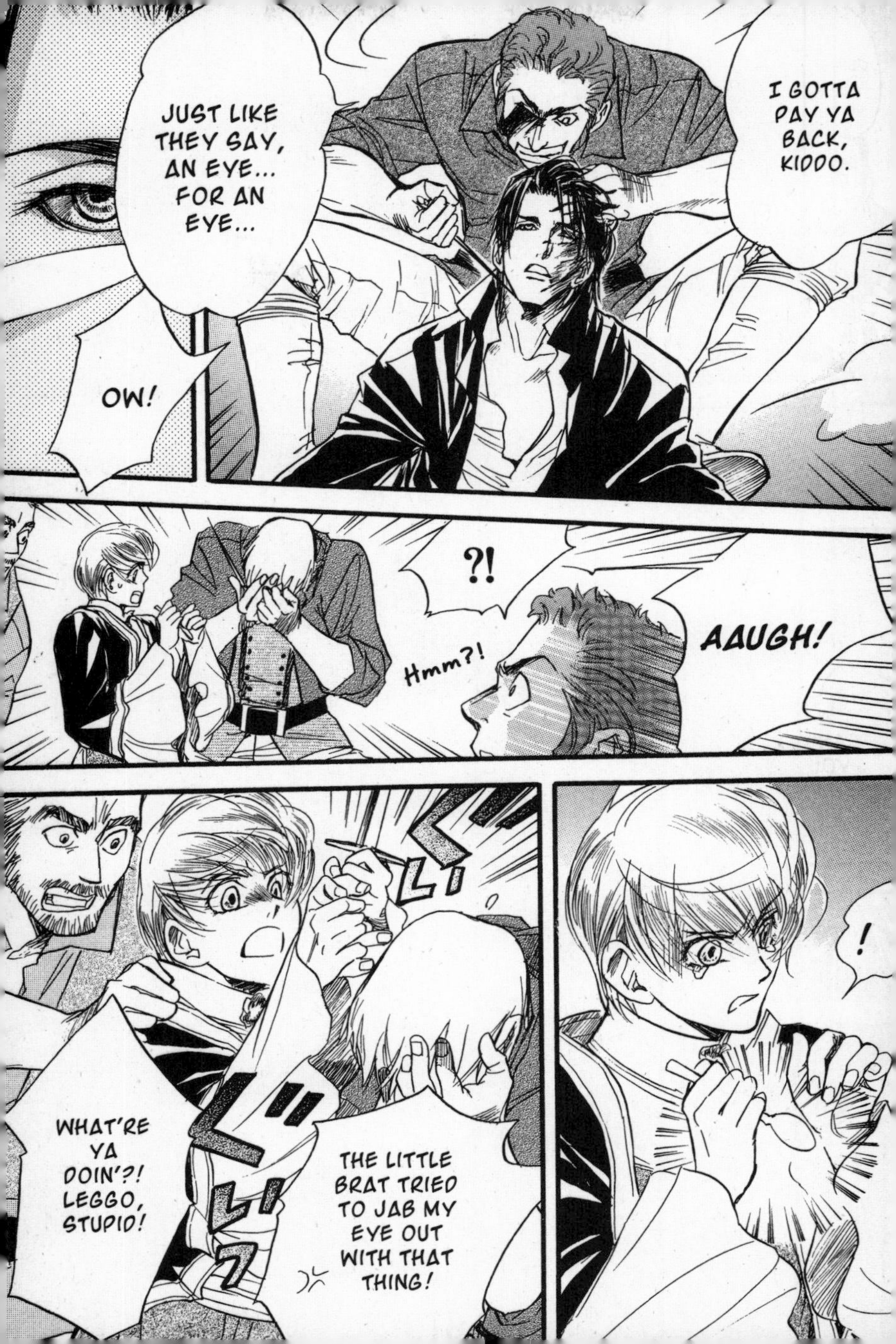
I GOTTA PAY YA BACK, KIDDO.
JUST LIKE THEY SAY, AN EYE... FOR AN EYE...
OW!
AAUGH!
?!
Hmm?!
!
THE LITTLE BRAT TRIED TO JAB MY EYE OUT WITH THAT THING!
WHAT'RE YA DOIN'?! LEGGO, STUPID!

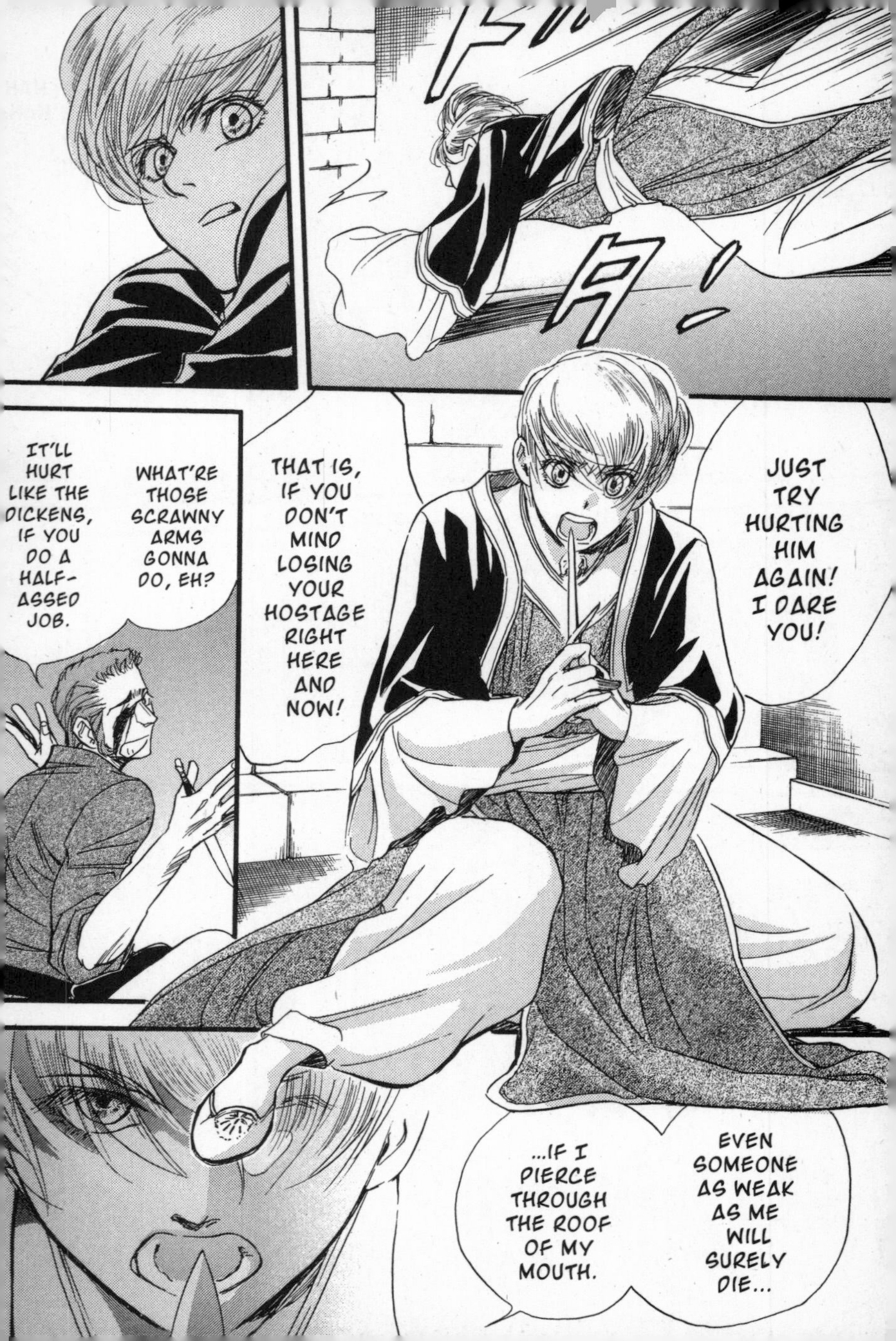
JUST TRY HURTING HIM AGAIN! I DARE YOU!
THAT IS, IF YOU DON'T MIND LOSING YOUR HOSTAGE RIGHT HERE AND NOW!
WHAT'RE THOSE SCRAWNY ARMS GONNA DO, EH?
IT'LL HURT LIKE THE DICKENS, IF YOU DO A HALF-ASSED JOB.
EVEN SOMEONE AS WEAK AS ME WILL SURELY DIE...
...IF I PIERCE THROUGH THE ROOF OF MY MOUTH.

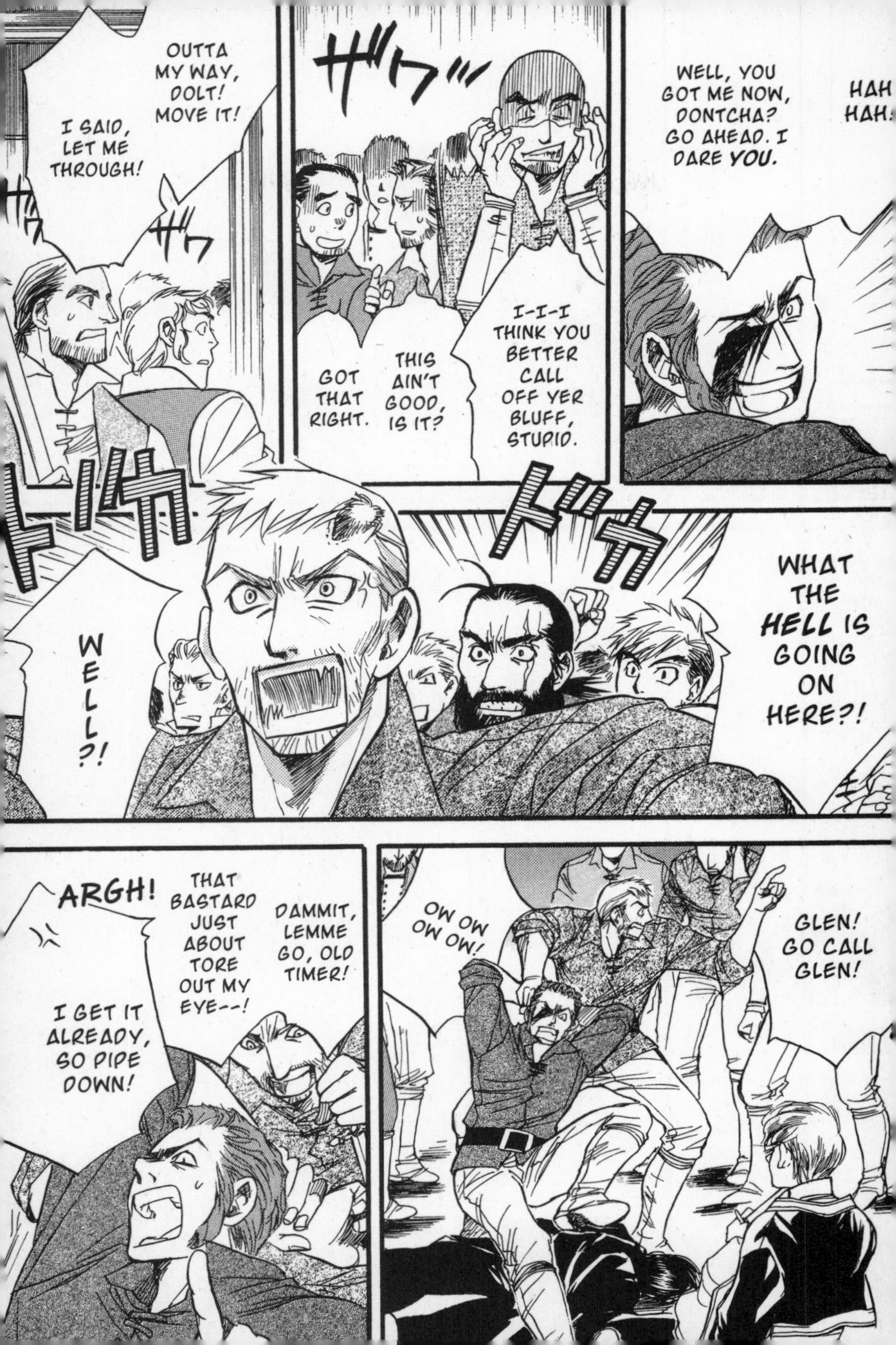
HAH HAH.
WELL, YOU GOT ME NOW, DONTCHA? GO AHEAD. I DARE **YOU**.
I-I-I THINK YOU BETTER CALL OFF YER BLUFF, STUPID.
THIS AIN'T GOOD, IS IT?
GOT THAT RIGHT.
OUTTA MY WAY, DOLT! MOVE IT!
I SAID, LET ME THROUGH!
WHAT THE **HELL** IS GOING ON HERE?!
WELL?!
GLEN! GO CALL GLEN!
OW OW OW OW!
DAMMIT, LEMME GO, OLD TIMER!
THAT BASTARD JUST ABOUT TORE OUT MY EYE--!
ARGH!
I GET IT ALREADY, SO PIPE DOWN!

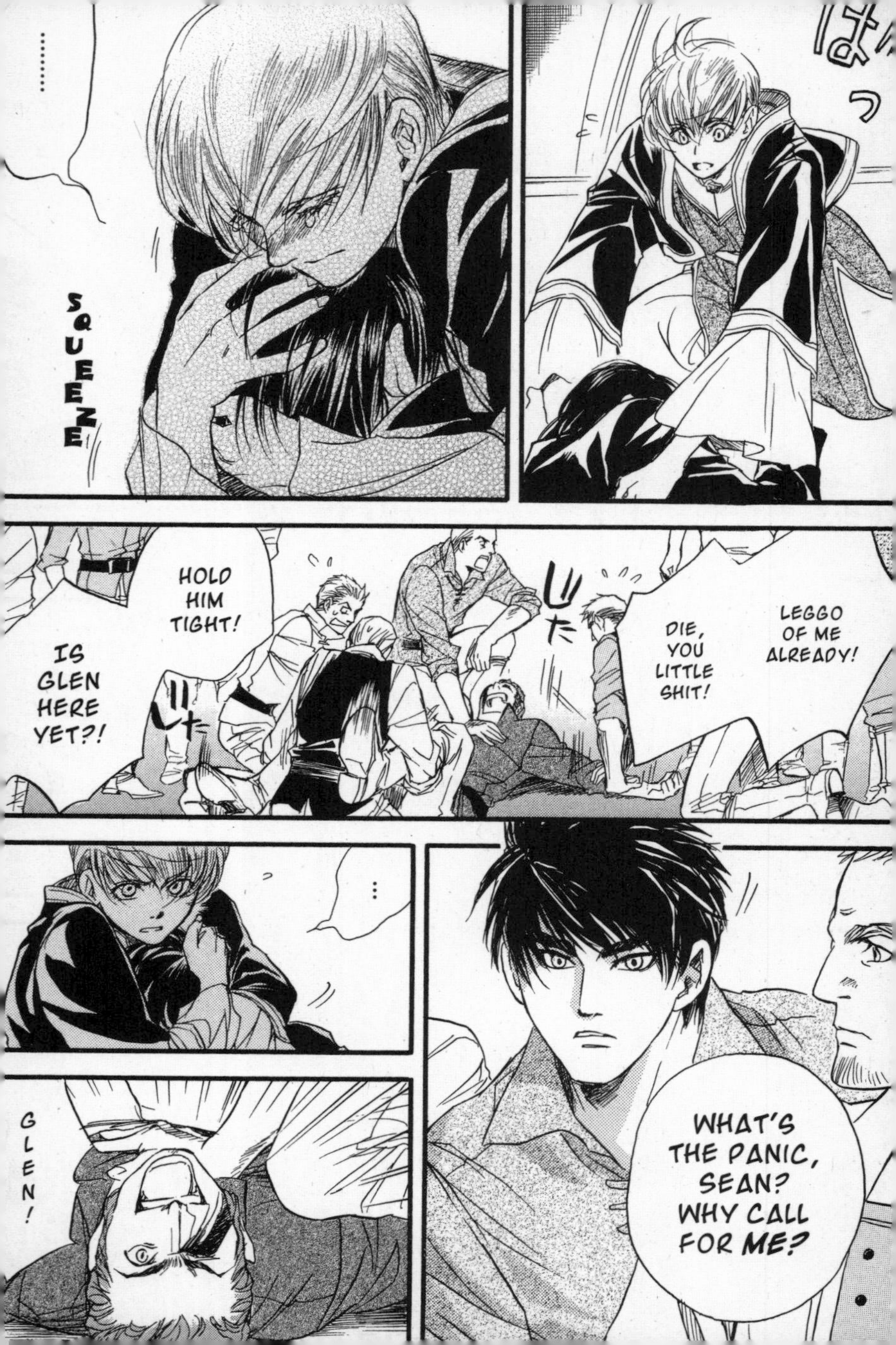
はっ
……
SQUEEZE
LEGGO OF ME ALREADY!
DIE, YOU LITTLE SHIT!
HOLD HIM TIGHT!
IS GLEN HERE YET?!
WHAT'S THE PANIC, SEAN? WHY CALL FOR ME?
…
GLEN!

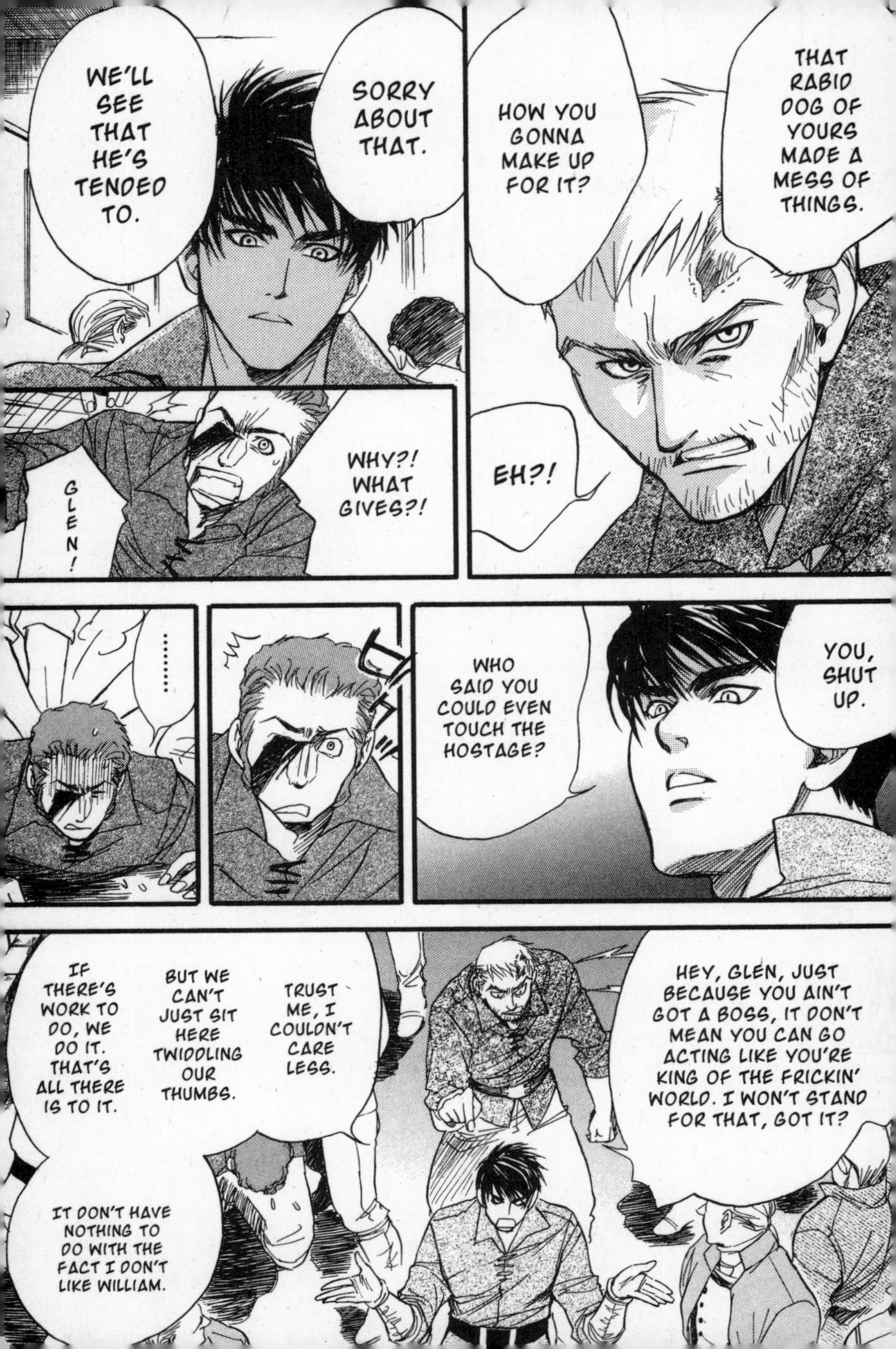

THAT RABID DOG OF YOURS MADE A MESS OF THINGS.
HOW YOU GONNA MAKE UP FOR IT?
EH?!
SORRY ABOUT THAT.
WE'LL SEE THAT HE'S TENDED TO.
WHY?! WHAT GIVES?!
GLEN!
YOU, SHUT UP.
WHO SAID YOU COULD EVEN TOUCH THE HOSTAGE?
......
HEY, GLEN, JUST BECAUSE YOU AIN'T GOT A BOSS, IT DON'T MEAN YOU CAN GO ACTING LIKE YOU'RE KING OF THE FRICKIN' WORLD. I WON'T STAND FOR THAT, GOT IT?
TRUST ME, I COULDN'T CARE LESS.
BUT WE CAN'T JUST SIT HERE TWIDDLING OUR THUMBS.
IF THERE'S WORK TO DO, WE DO IT. THAT'S ALL THERE IS TO IT.
IT DON'T HAVE NOTHING TO DO WITH THE FACT I DON'T LIKE WILLIAM.

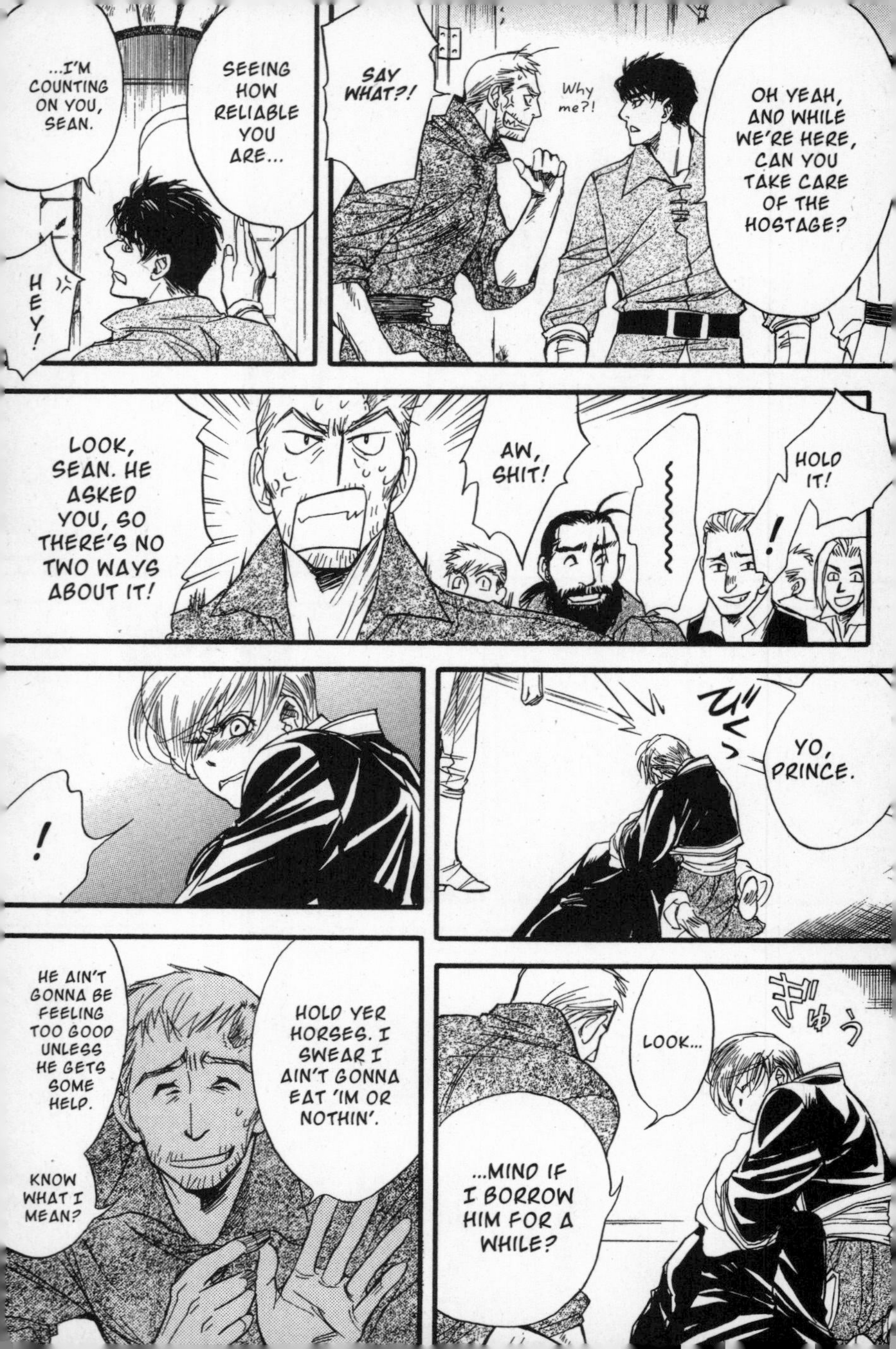
OH YEAH, AND WHILE WE'RE HERE, CAN YOU TAKE CARE OF THE HOSTAGE?
Why me?!
SAY WHAT?!
SEEING HOW RELIABLE YOU ARE...
...I'M COUNTING ON YOU, SEAN.
HEY!
HOLD IT!
!
AW, SHIT!
LOOK, SEAN. HE ASKED YOU, SO THERE'S NO TWO WAYS ABOUT IT!
YO, PRINCE.
びくっ
!
ぎゅう
LOOK...
...MIND IF I BORROW HIM FOR A WHILE?
HOLD YER HORSES. I SWEAR I AIN'T GONNA EAT 'IM OR NOTHIN'.
HE AIN'T GONNA BE FEELING TOO GOOD UNLESS HE GETS SOME HELP.
KNOW WHAT I MEAN?

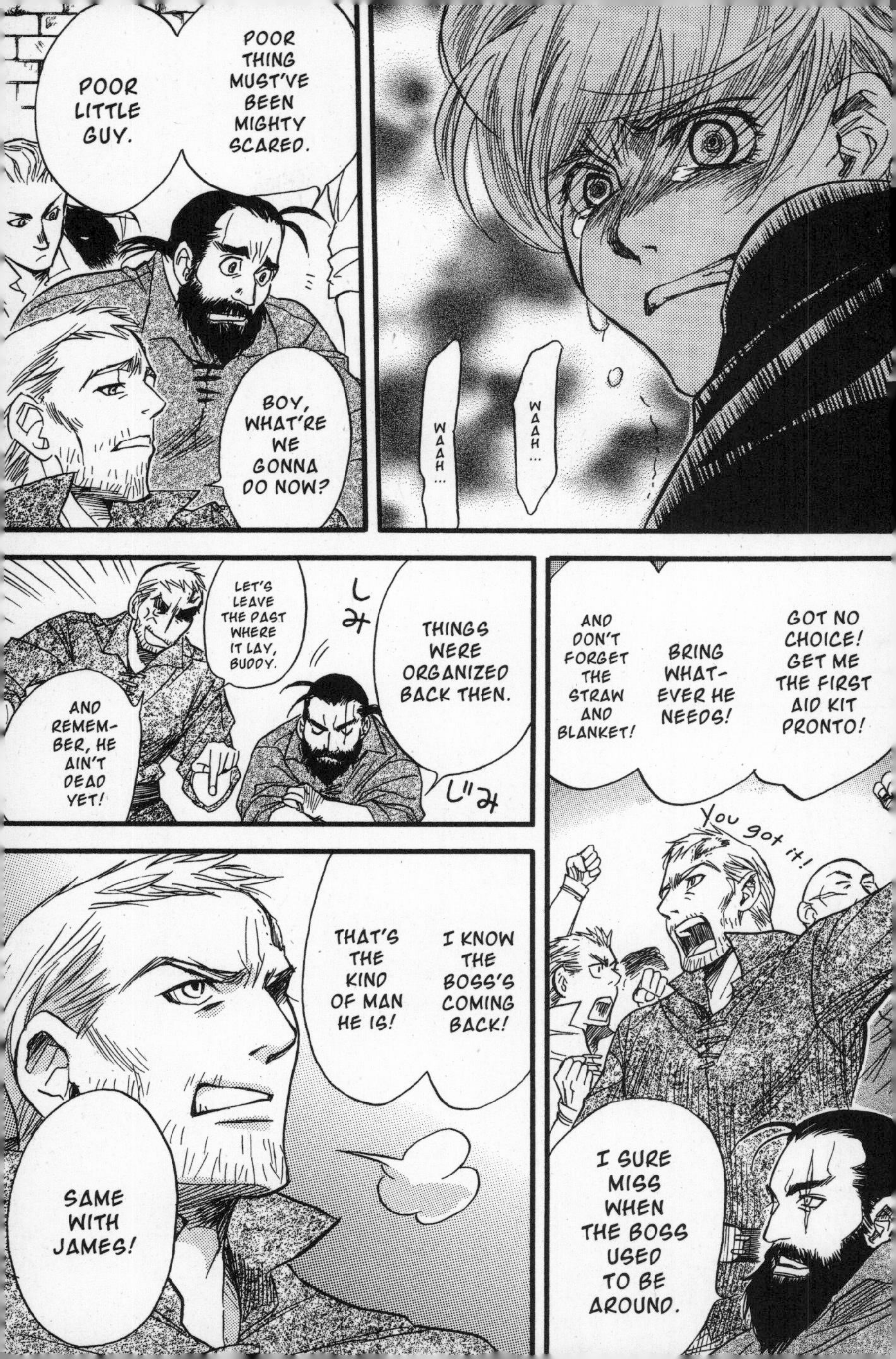
WAAH...
WAAH...
POOR THING MUST'VE BEEN MIGHTY SCARED.
POOR LITTLE GUY.
BOY, WHAT'RE WE GONNA DO NOW?
GOT NO CHOICE! GET ME THE FIRST AID KIT PRONTO!
BRING WHAT-EVER HE NEEDS!
AND DON'T FORGET THE STRAW AND BLANKET!
You got it!
I SURE MISS WHEN THE BOSS USED TO BE AROUND.
THINGS WERE ORGANIZED BACK THEN.
しみ
じみ
LET'S LEAVE THE PAST WHERE IT LAY, BUDDY.
AND REMEM-BER, HE AIN'T DEAD YET!
I KNOW THE BOSS'S COMING BACK!
THAT'S THE KIND OF MAN HE IS!
SAME WITH JAMES!

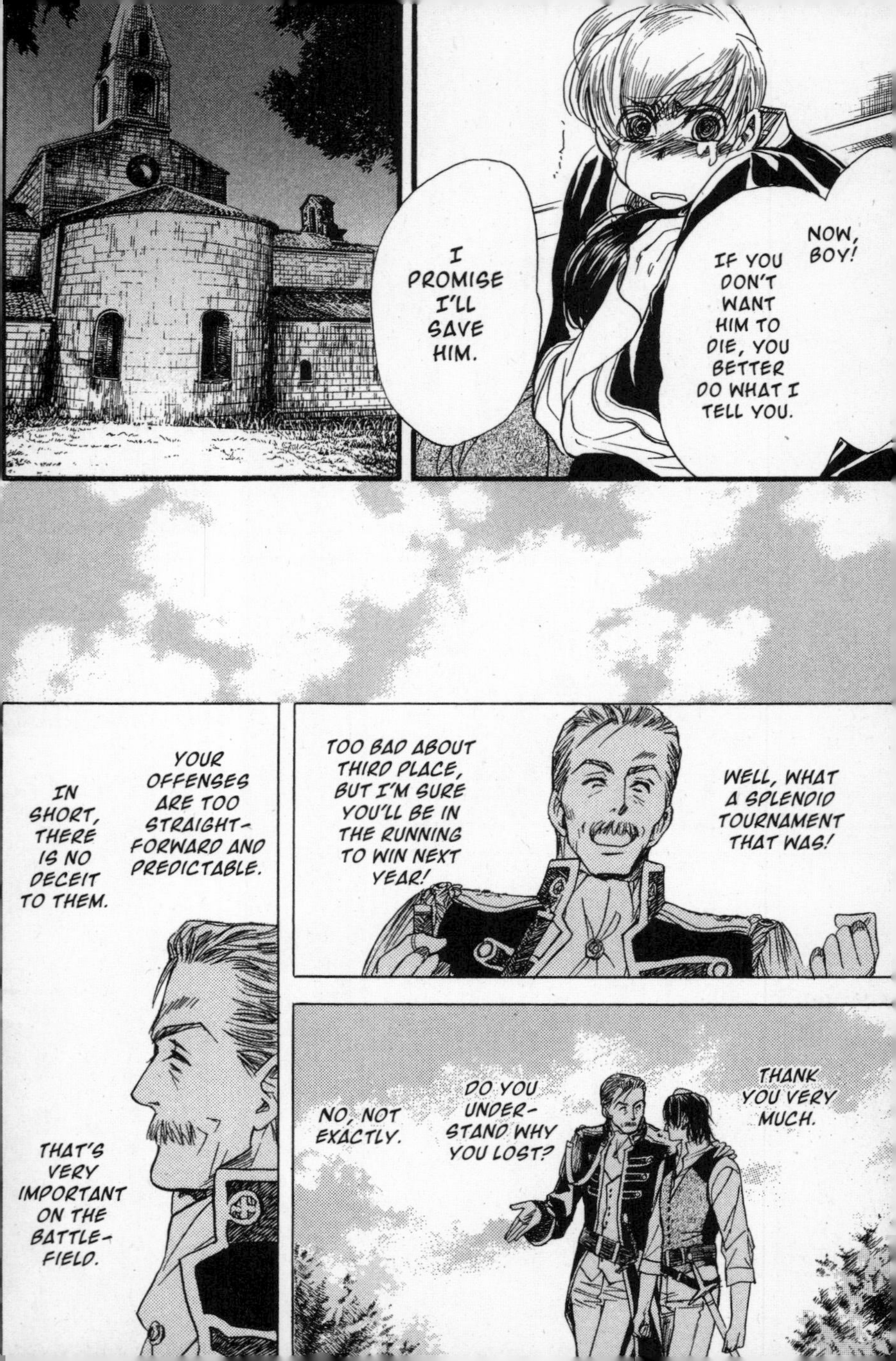
NOW, BOY!
IF YOU DON'T WANT HIM TO DIE, YOU BETTER DO WHAT I TELL YOU.
I PROMISE I'LL SAVE HIM.
WELL, WHAT A SPLENDID TOURNAMENT THAT WAS!
TOO BAD ABOUT THIRD PLACE, BUT I'M SURE YOU'LL BE IN THE RUNNING TO WIN NEXT YEAR!
THANK YOU VERY MUCH.
DO YOU UNDER-STAND WHY YOU LOST?
NO, NOT EXACTLY.
YOUR OFFENSES ARE TOO STRAIGHT-FORWARD AND PREDICTABLE.
IN SHORT, THERE IS NO DECEIT TO THEM.
THAT'S VERY IMPORTANT ON THE BATTLE-FIELD.

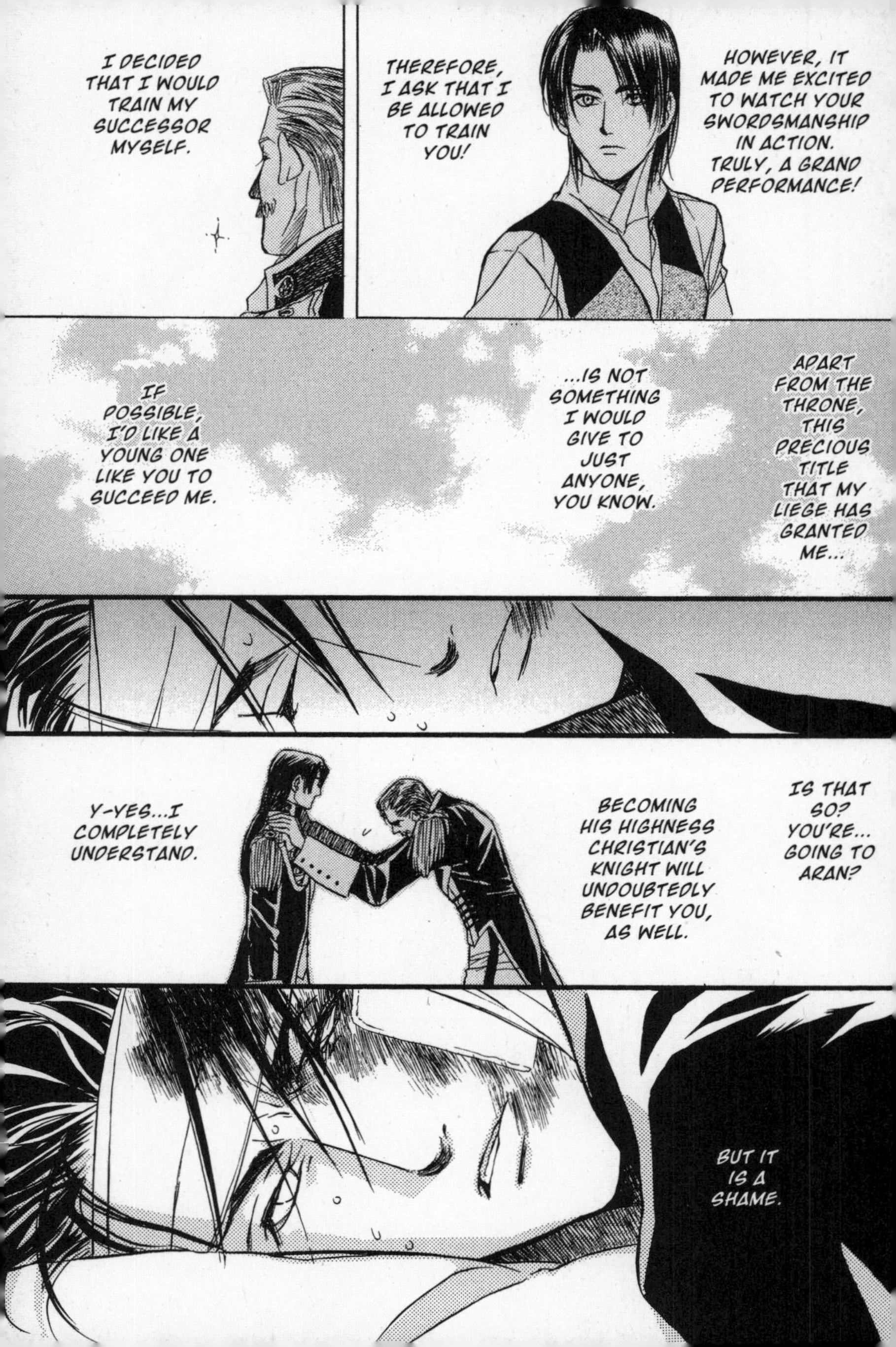
HOWEVER, IT MADE ME EXCITED TO WATCH YOUR SWORDSMANSHIP IN ACTION. TRULY, A GRAND PERFORMANCE!
THEREFORE, I ASK THAT I BE ALLOWED TO TRAIN YOU!
I DECIDED THAT I WOULD TRAIN MY SUCCESSOR MYSELF.
APART FROM THE THRONE, THIS PRECIOUS TITLE THAT MY LIEGE HAS GRANTED ME...
...IS NOT SOMETHING I WOULD GIVE TO JUST ANYONE, YOU KNOW.
IF POSSIBLE, I'D LIKE A YOUNG ONE LIKE YOU TO SUCCEED ME.
IS THAT SO? YOU'RE... GOING TO ARAN?
BECOMING HIS HIGHNESS CHRISTIAN'S KNIGHT WILL UNDOUBTEDLY BENEFIT YOU, AS WELL.
Y-YES...I COMPLETELY UNDERSTAND.
BUT IT IS A SHAME.

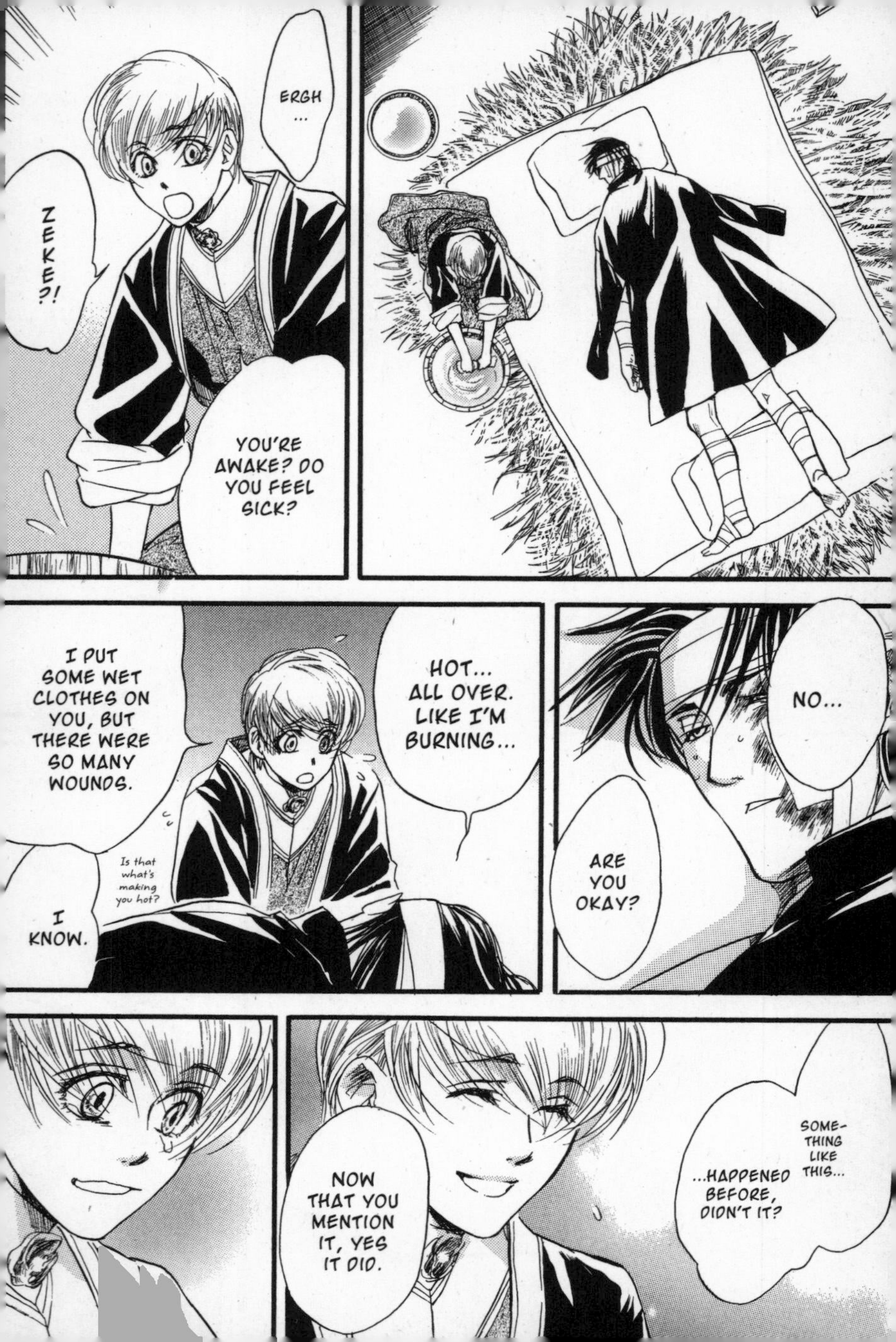
ERGH ...
ZEKE?!
YOU'RE AWAKE? DO YOU FEEL SICK?
NO...
ARE YOU OKAY?
HOT... ALL OVER. LIKE I'M BURNING...
I PUT SOME WET CLOTHES ON YOU, BUT THERE WERE SO MANY WOUNDS.
Is that what's making you hot?
I KNOW.
SOME-THING LIKE THIS...
...HAPPENED BEFORE, DIDN'T IT?
NOW THAT YOU MENTION IT, YES IT DID.

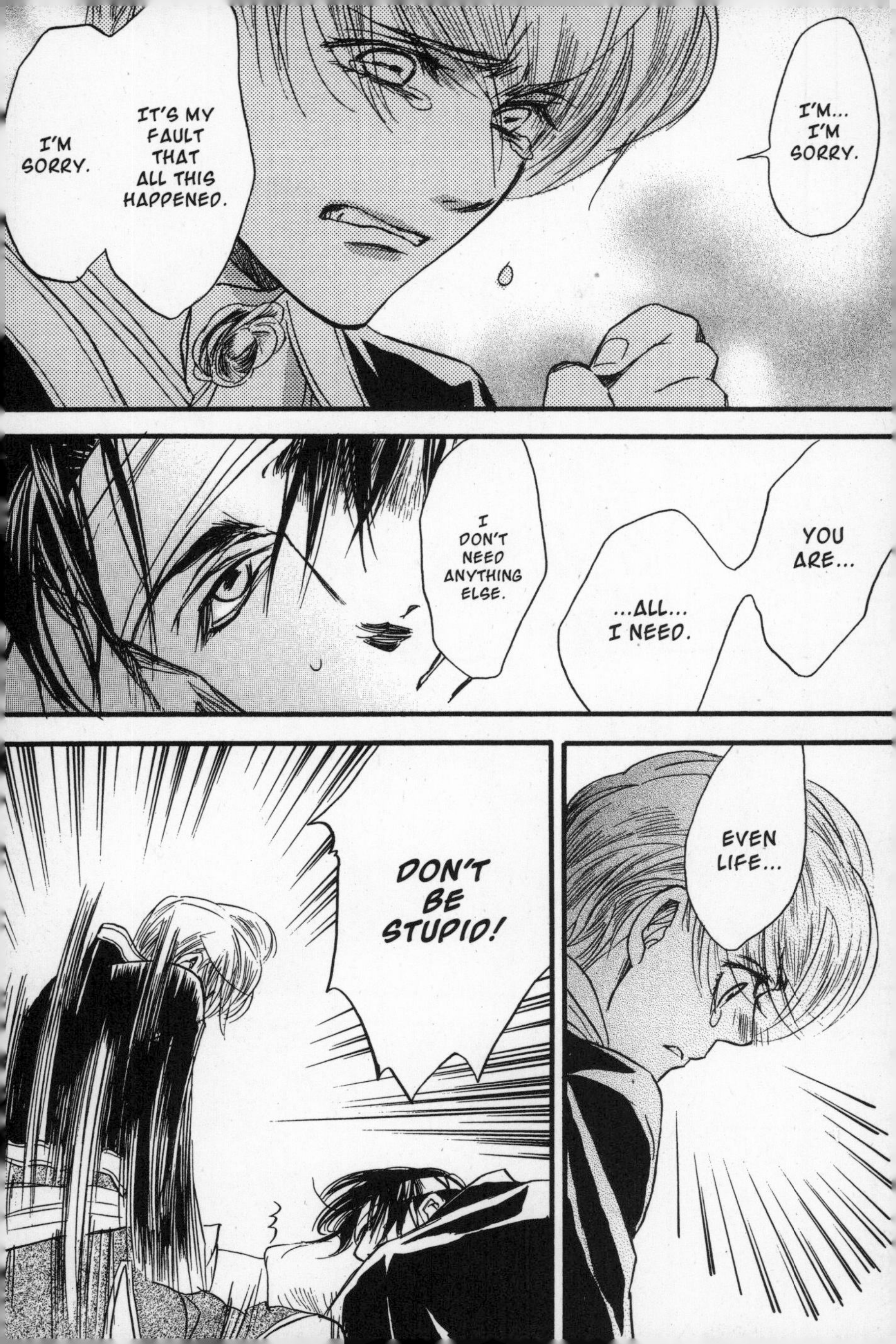
I'M... I'M SORRY.
IT'S MY FAULT THAT ALL THIS HAPPENED.
I'M SORRY.
YOU ARE...
...ALL... I NEED.
I DON'T NEED ANYTHING ELSE.
EVEN LIFE...
DON'T BE STUPID!

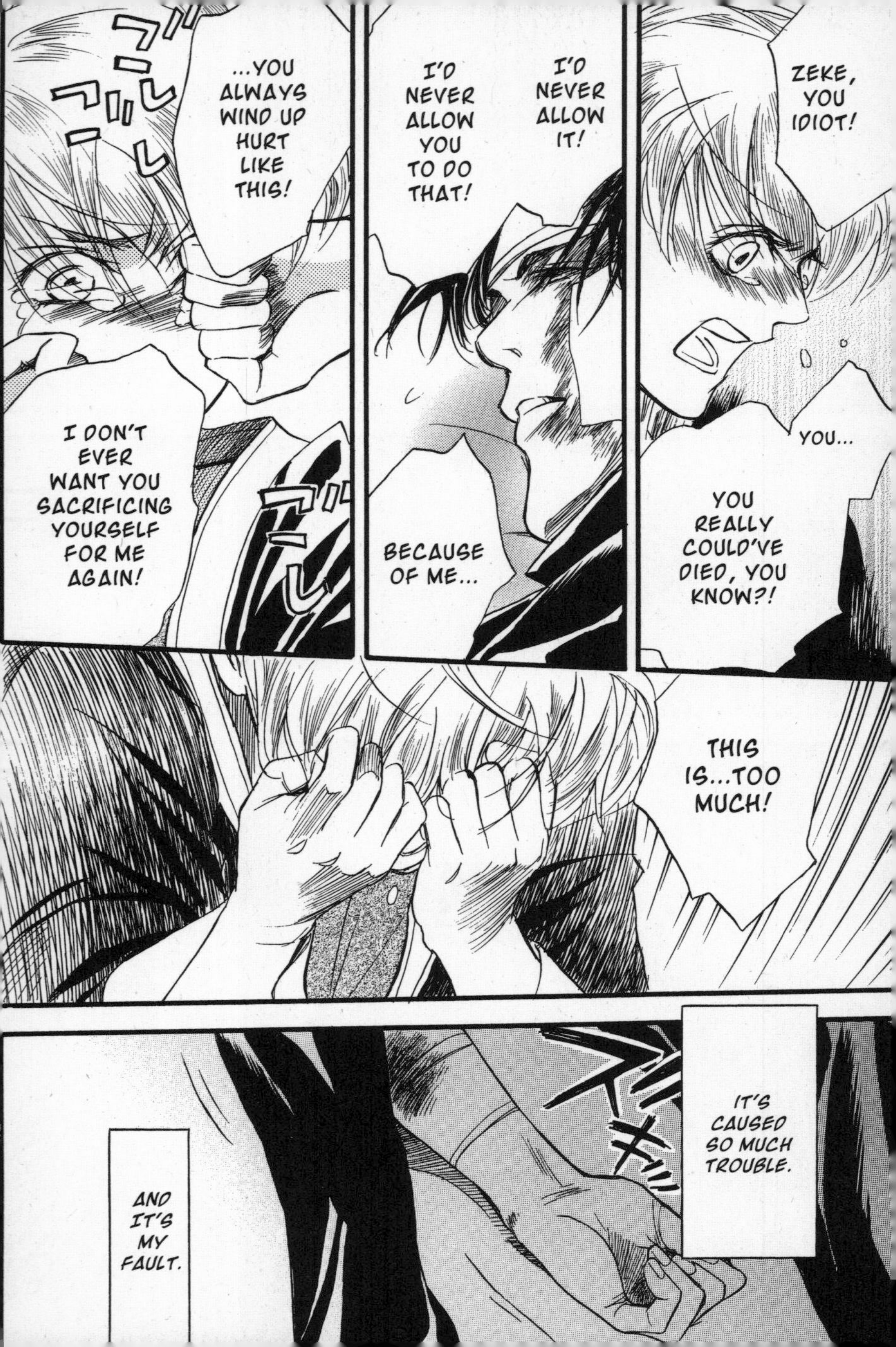
ZEKE, YOU IDIOT!
YOU...
YOU REALLY COULD'VE DIED, YOU KNOW?!
I'D NEVER ALLOW IT!
I'D NEVER ALLOW YOU TO DO THAT!
BECAUSE OF ME...
...YOU ALWAYS WIND UP HURT LIKE THIS!
I DON'T EVER WANT YOU SACRIFICING YOURSELF FOR ME AGAIN!
THIS IS...TOO MUCH!
IT'S CAUSED SO MUCH TROUBLE.
AND IT'S MY FAULT.

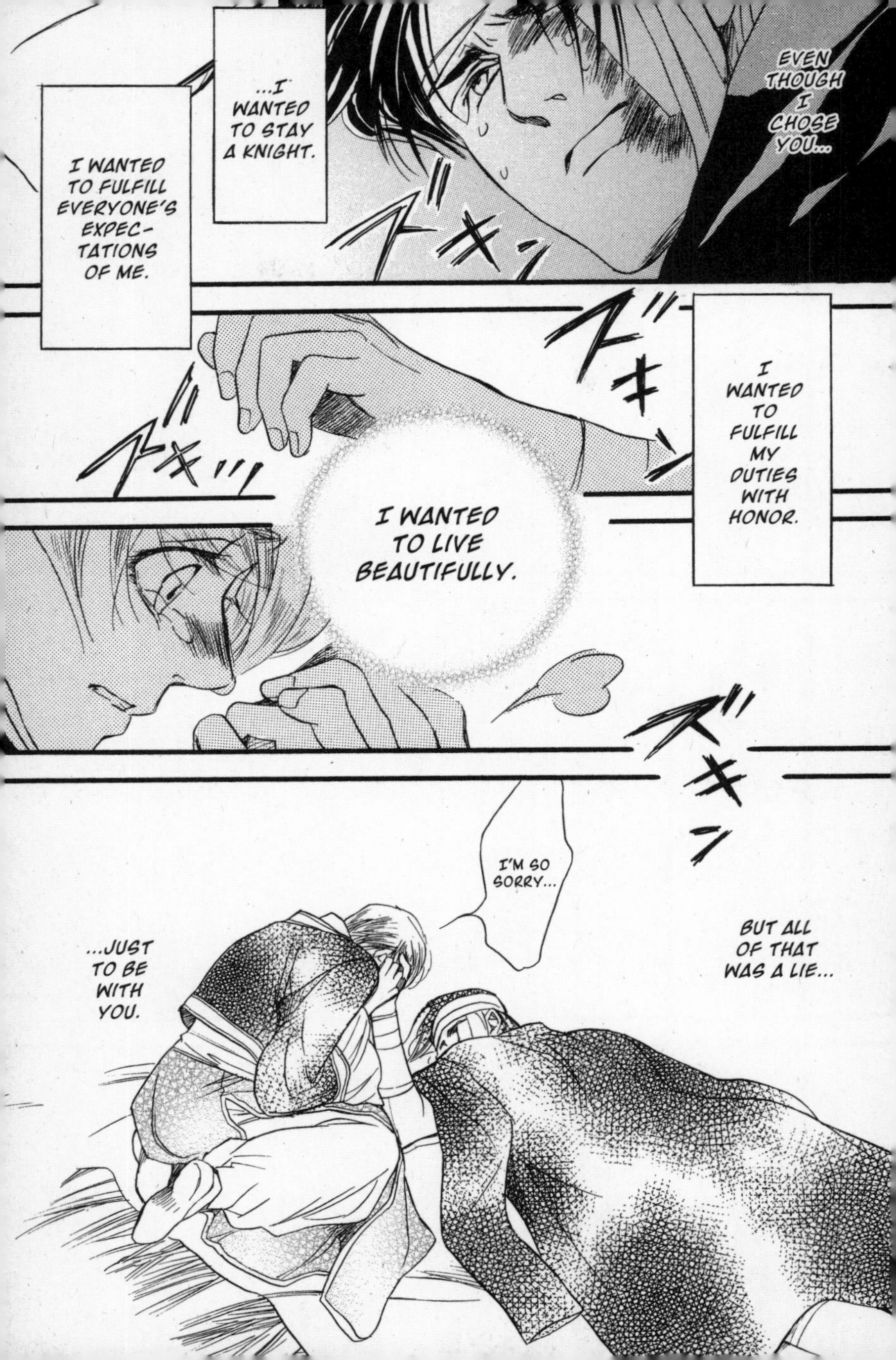
EVEN THOUGH I CHOSE YOU...
...I WANTED TO STAY A KNIGHT.
I WANTED TO FULFILL EVERYONE'S EXPECTATIONS OF ME.
I WANTED TO FULFILL MY DUTIES WITH HONOR.
I WANTED TO LIVE BEAUTIFULLY.
BUT ALL OF THAT WAS A LIE...
I'M SO SORRY...
...JUST TO BE WITH YOU.

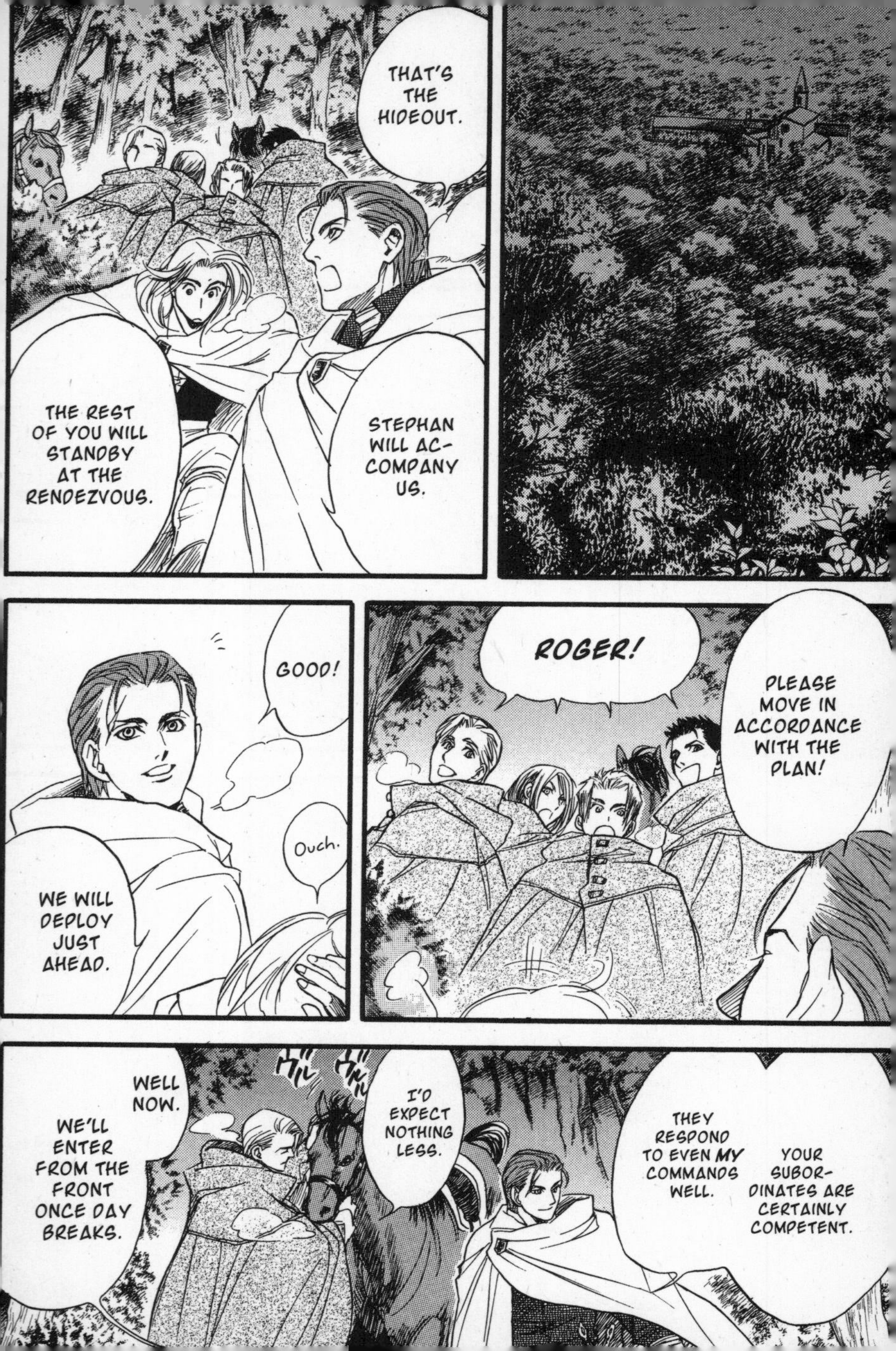
THAT'S THE HIDEOUT.
STEPHAN WILL AC- COMPANY US.
THE REST OF YOU WILL STANDBY AT THE RENDEZVOUS.
PLEASE MOVE IN ACCORDANCE WITH THE PLAN!
ROGER!
GOOD!
Ouch.
WE WILL DEPLOY JUST AHEAD.
YOUR SUBOR- DINATES ARE CERTAINLY COMPETENT.
THEY RESPOND TO EVEN *MY* COMMANDS WELL.
I'D EXPECT NOTHING LESS.
WELL NOW.
WE'LL ENTER FROM THE FRONT ONCE DAY BREAKS.

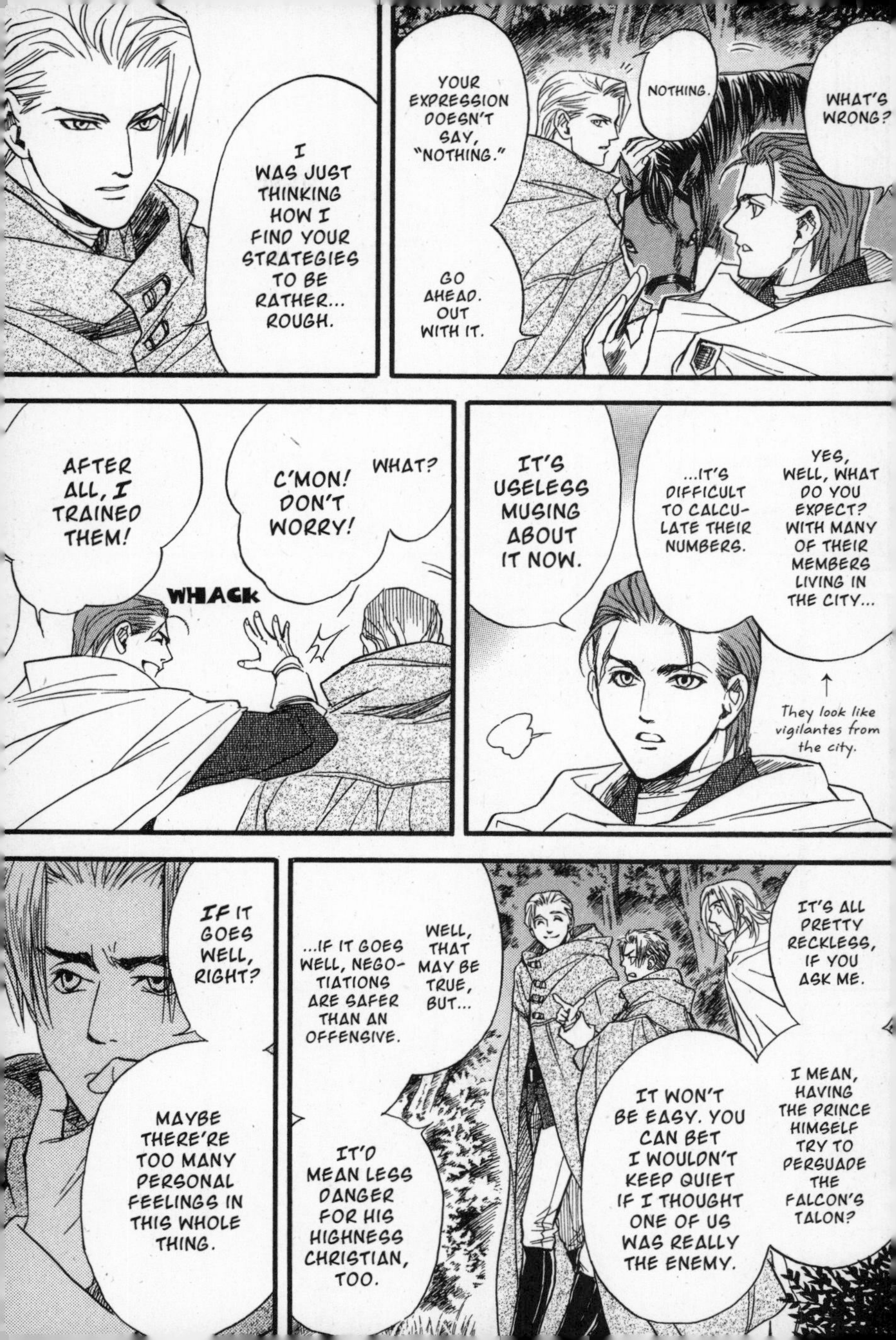
WHAT'S WRONG?
NOTHING.
YOUR EXPRESSION DOESN'T SAY, "NOTHING."
GO AHEAD. OUT WITH IT.
I WAS JUST THINKING HOW I FIND YOUR STRATEGIES TO BE RATHER... ROUGH.
YES, WELL, WHAT DO YOU EXPECT? WITH MANY OF THEIR MEMBERS LIVING IN THE CITY...
...IT'S DIFFICULT TO CALCULATE THEIR NUMBERS.
They look like vigilantes from the city.
IT'S USELESS MUSING ABOUT IT NOW.
WHAT?
C'MON! DON'T WORRY!
AFTER ALL, I TRAINED THEM!
WHACK
IT'S ALL PRETTY RECKLESS, IF YOU ASK ME.
I MEAN, HAVING THE PRINCE HIMSELF TRY TO PERSUADE THE FALCON'S TALON?
IT WON'T BE EASY. YOU CAN BET I WOULDN'T KEEP QUIET IF I THOUGHT ONE OF US WAS REALLY THE ENEMY.
WELL, THAT MAY BE TRUE, BUT...
...IF IT GOES WELL, NEGOTIATIONS ARE SAFER THAN AN OFFENSIVE.
IT'D MEAN LESS DANGER FOR HIS HIGHNESS CHRISTIAN, TOO.
IF IT GOES WELL, RIGHT?
MAYBE THERE'RE TOO MANY PERSONAL FEELINGS IN THIS WHOLE THING.

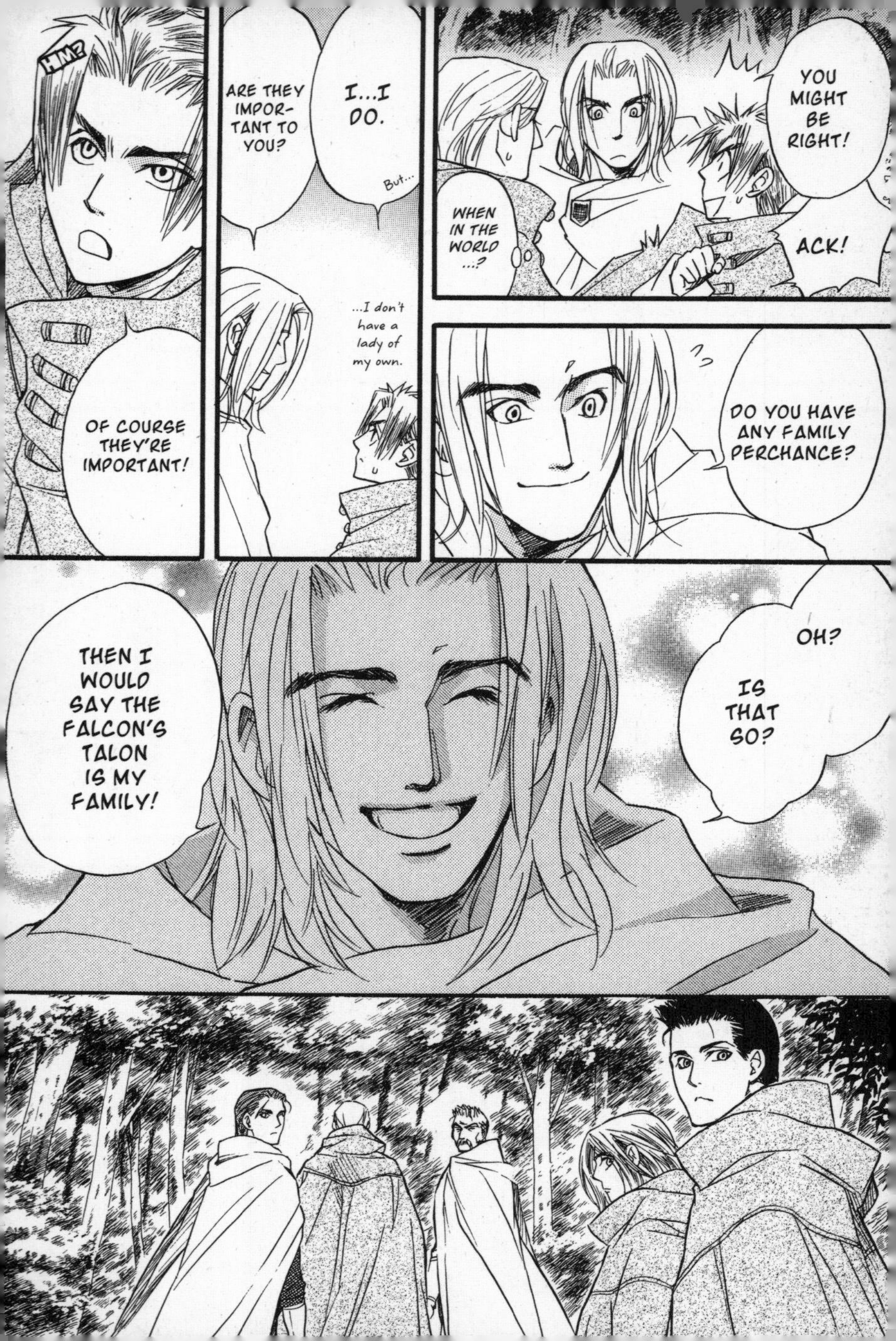
YOU MIGHT BE RIGHT!
ACK!
WHEN IN THE WORLD ...?
DO YOU HAVE ANY FAMILY PERCHANCE?
I...I DO.
ARE THEY IMPOR-TANT TO YOU?
But...
...I don't have a lady of my own.
HM?
OF COURSE THEY'RE IMPORTANT!
OH?
IS THAT SO?
THEN I WOULD SAY THE FALCON'S TALON IS MY FAMILY!

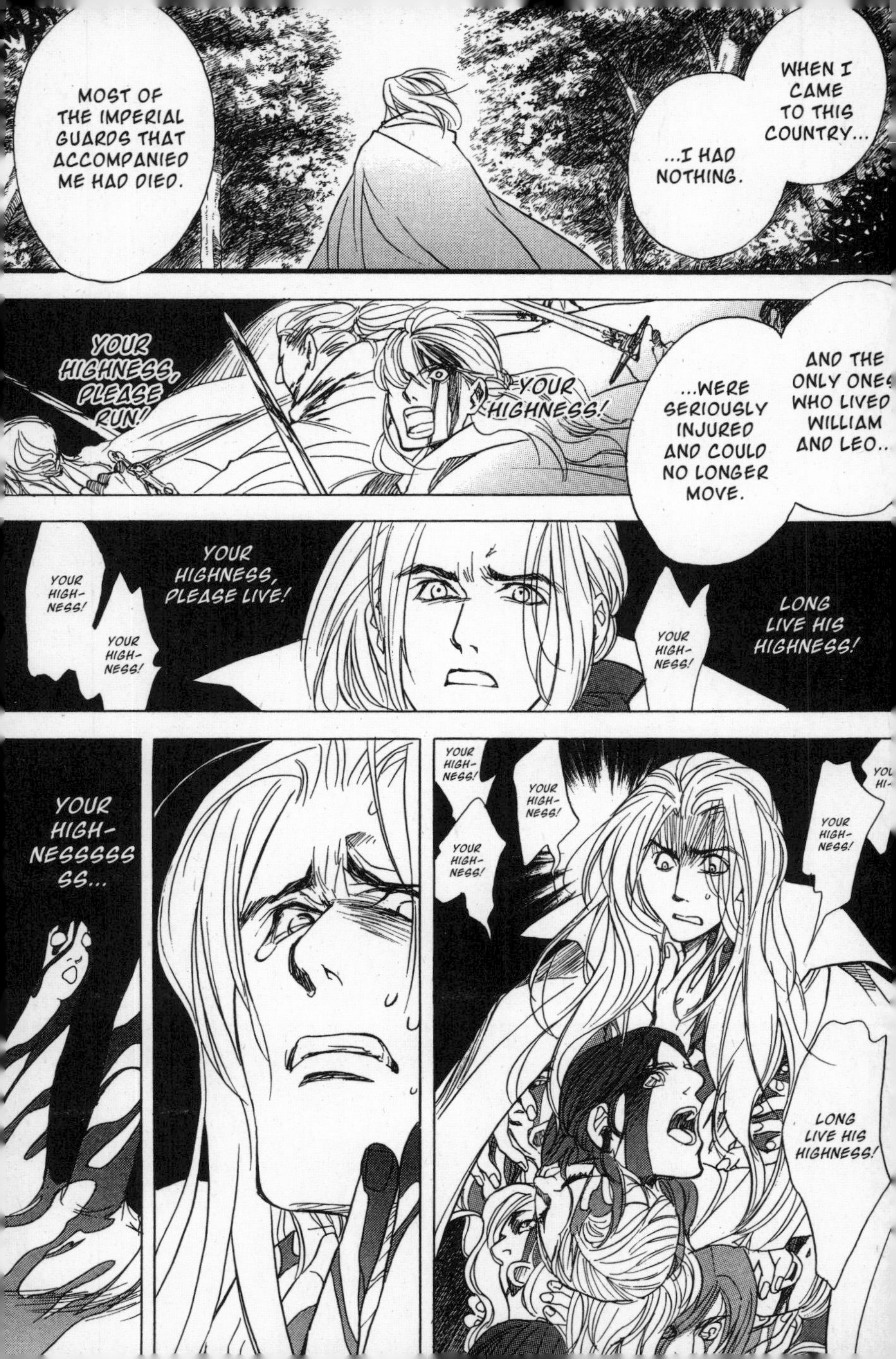
WHEN I CAME TO THIS COUNTRY...
...I HAD NOTHING.
MOST OF THE IMPERIAL GUARDS THAT ACCOMPANIED ME HAD DIED.
AND THE ONLY ONES WHO LIVED WILLIAM AND LEO...
...WERE SERIOUSLY INJURED AND COULD NO LONGER MOVE.
YOUR HIGHNESS!
YOUR HIGHNESS, PLEASE RUN!
LONG LIVE HIS HIGHNESS!
YOUR HIGH-NESS!
YOUR HIGHNESS, PLEASE LIVE!
YOUR HIGH-NESS!
YOUR HIGH-NESS!
YOUR HIGH-NESS!
LONG LIVE HIS HIGHNESS!
YOUR HIGH-NESS!
YOUR HIGH-NESS!
YOUR HIGH-NESS!
YOUR HIGH-NESSSSSSS...

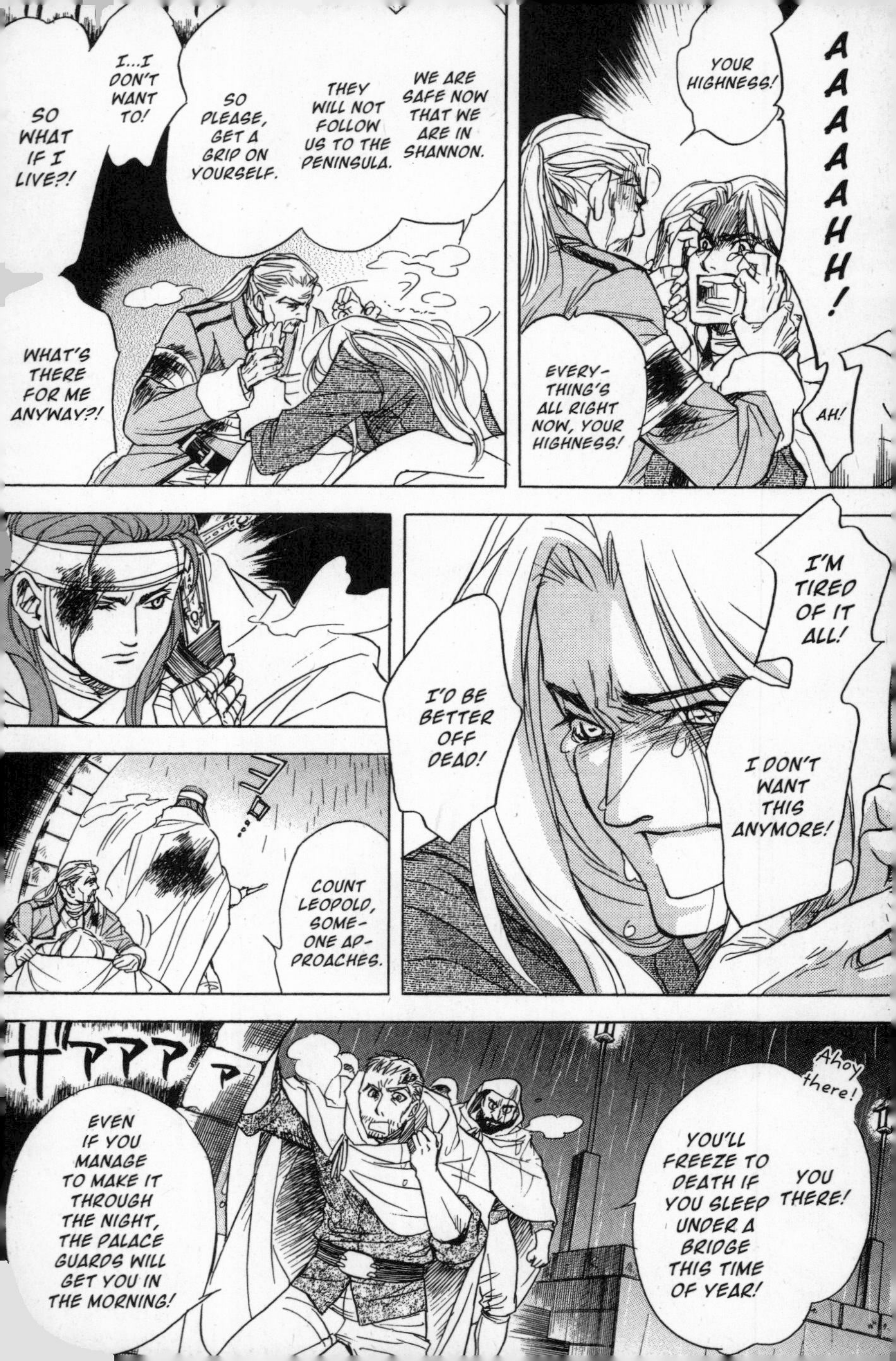
AAAAAAHH!
YOUR HIGHNESS!
AH!
EVERYTHING'S ALL RIGHT NOW, YOUR HIGHNESS!
WE ARE SAFE NOW THAT WE ARE IN SHANNON.
THEY WILL NOT FOLLOW US TO THE PENINSULA.
SO PLEASE, GET A GRIP ON YOURSELF.
I...I DON'T WANT TO!
SO WHAT IF I LIVE?!
WHAT'S THERE FOR ME ANYWAY?!
I'M TIRED OF IT ALL!
I'D BE BETTER OFF DEAD!
I DON'T WANT THIS ANYMORE!
COUNT LEOPOLD, SOME-ONE AP-PROACHES.
Ahoy there!
YOU THERE!
YOU'LL FREEZE TO DEATH IF YOU SLEEP UNDER A BRIDGE THIS TIME OF YEAR!
EVEN IF YOU MANAGE TO MAKE IT THROUGH THE NIGHT, THE PALACE GUARDS WILL GET YOU IN THE MORNING!
ザァァァァ

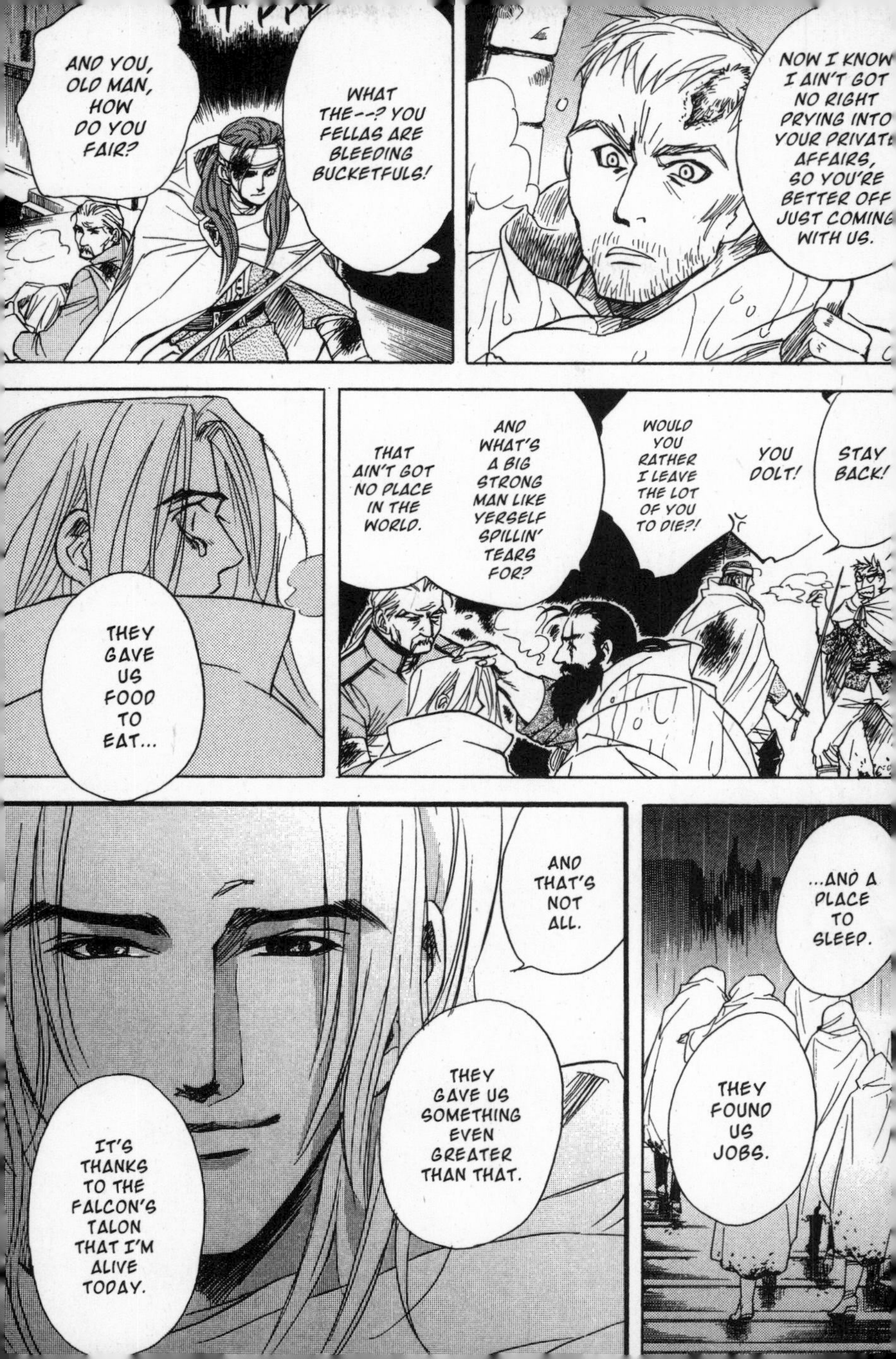
NOW I KNOW I AIN'T GOT NO RIGHT PRYING INTO YOUR PRIVATE AFFAIRS, SO YOU'RE BETTER OFF JUST COMING WITH US.
WHAT THE--? YOU FELLAS ARE BLEEDING BUCKETFULS!
AND YOU, OLD MAN, HOW DO YOU FAIR?
STAY BACK!
YOU DOLT!
WOULD YOU RATHER I LEAVE THE LOT OF YOU TO DIE?!
AND WHAT'S A BIG STRONG MAN LIKE YERSELF SPILLIN' TEARS FOR?
THAT AIN'T GOT NO PLACE IN THE WORLD.
THEY GAVE US FOOD TO EAT...
...AND A PLACE TO SLEEP.
THEY FOUND US JOBS.
AND THAT'S NOT ALL.
THEY GAVE US SOMETHING EVEN GREATER THAN THAT.
IT'S THANKS TO THE FALCON'S TALON THAT I'M ALIVE TODAY.

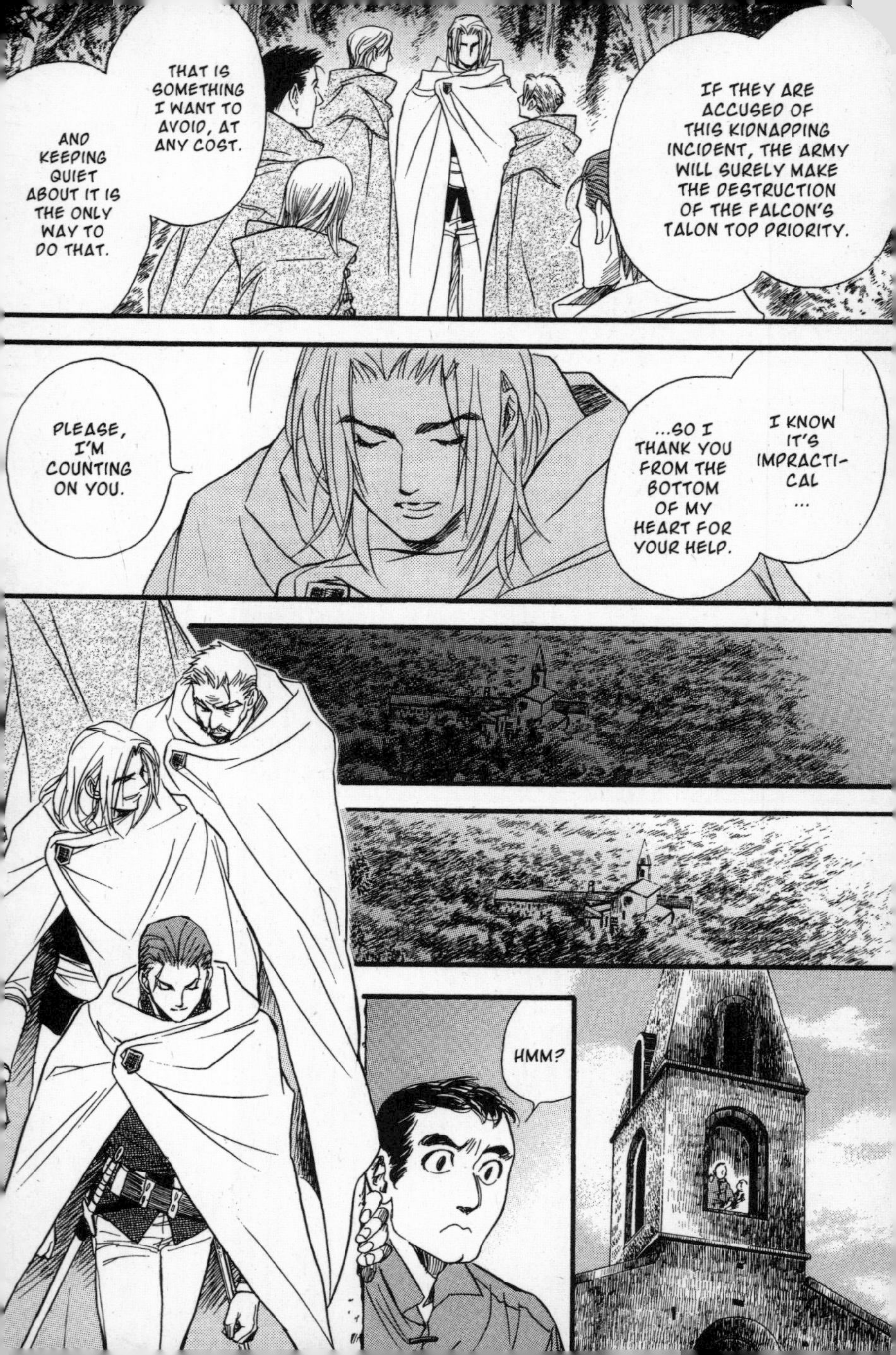
IF THEY ARE ACCUSED OF THIS KIDNAPPING INCIDENT, THE ARMY WILL SURELY MAKE THE DESTRUCTION OF THE FALCON'S TALON TOP PRIORITY.
THAT IS SOMETHING I WANT TO AVOID, AT ANY COST.
AND KEEPING QUIET ABOUT IT IS THE ONLY WAY TO DO THAT.
I KNOW IT'S IMPRACTI-CAL ...
...SO I THANK YOU FROM THE BOTTOM OF MY HEART FOR YOUR HELP.
PLEASE, I'M COUNTING ON YOU.
HMM?

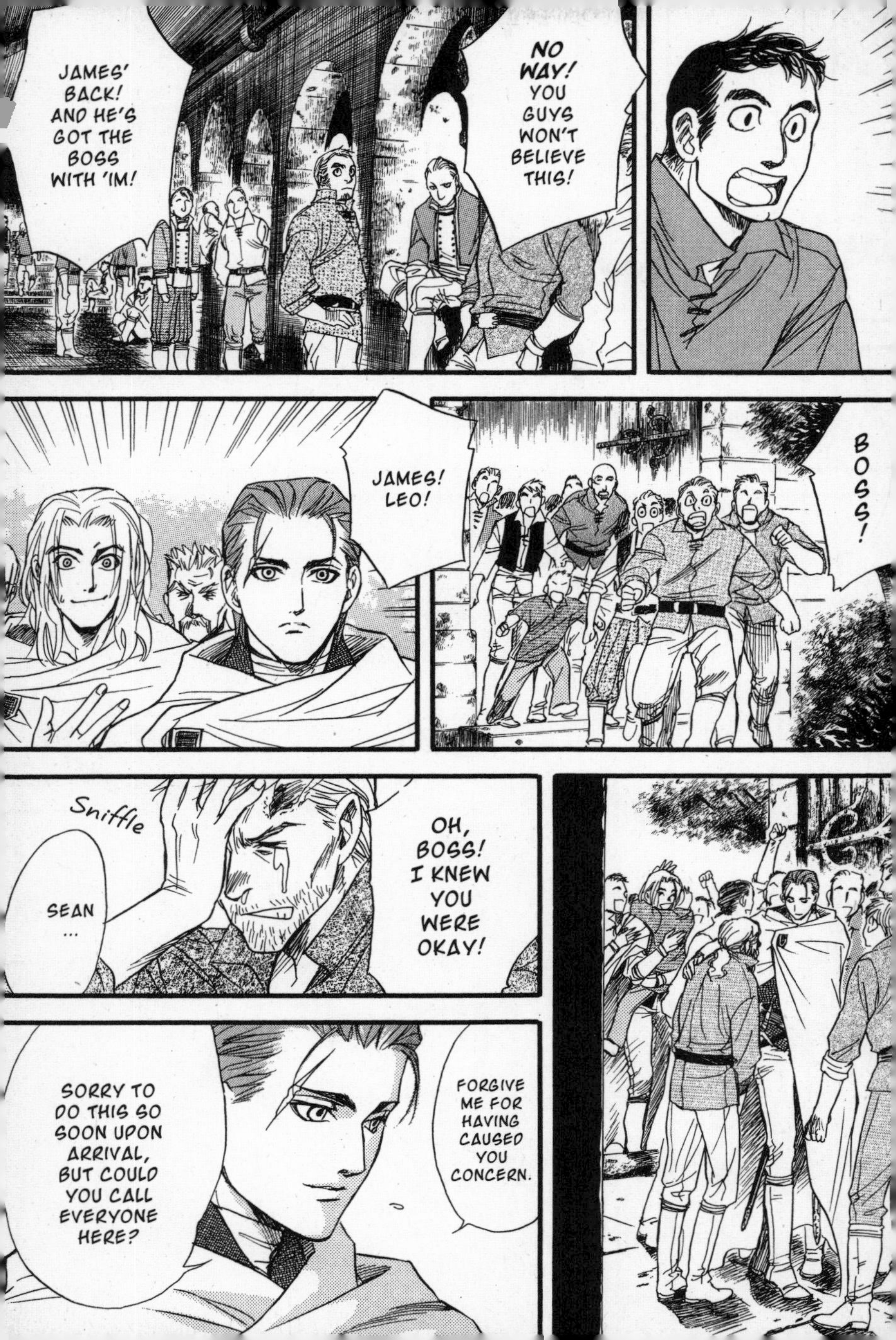
NO WAY! YOU GUYS WON'T BELIEVE THIS!
JAMES' BACK! AND HE'S GOT THE BOSS WITH 'IM!
BOSS! BOSS!
JAMES! LEO!
OH, BOSS! I KNEW YOU WERE OKAY!
Sniffle
SEAN ...
FORGIVE ME FOR HAVING CAUSED YOU CONCERN.
SORRY TO DO THIS SO SOON UPON ARRIVAL, BUT COULD YOU CALL EVERYONE HERE?

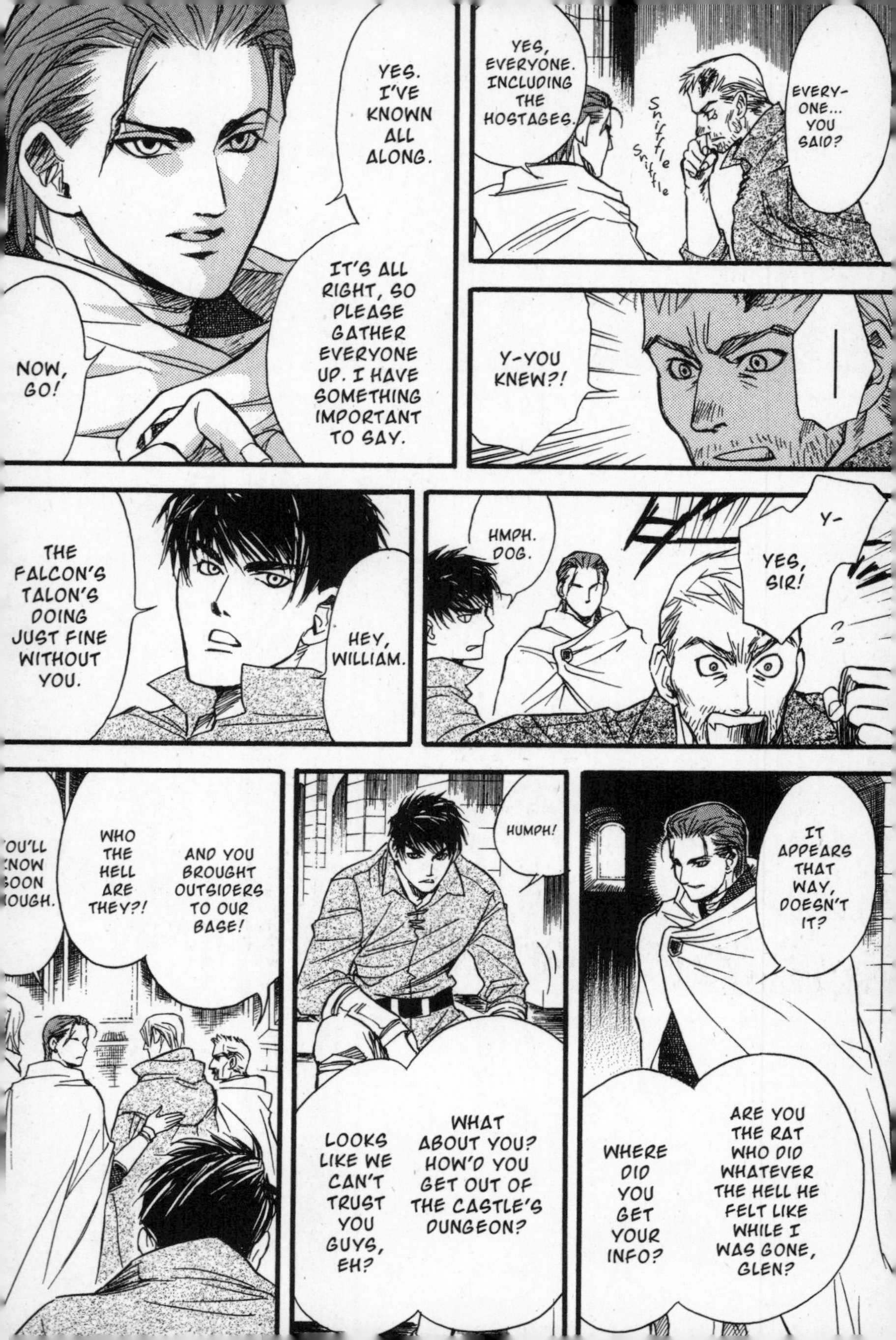
EVERY-ONE... YOU SAID?
YES, EVERYONE. INCLUDING THE HOSTAGES.
Sniffle Sniffle
Y-YOU KNEW?!
YES. I'VE KNOWN ALL ALONG.
IT'S ALL RIGHT, SO PLEASE GATHER EVERYONE UP. I HAVE SOMETHING IMPORTANT TO SAY.
NOW, GO!
Y-
YES, SIR!
HMPH. DOG.
HEY, WILLIAM.
THE FALCON'S TALON'S DOING JUST FINE WITHOUT YOU.
IT APPEARS THAT WAY, DOESN'T IT?
ARE YOU THE RAT WHO DID WHATEVER THE HELL HE FELT LIKE WHILE I WAS GONE, GLEN?
WHERE DID YOU GET YOUR INFO?
HUMPH!
WHAT ABOUT YOU? HOW'D YOU GET OUT OF THE CASTLE'S DUNGEON?
LOOKS LIKE WE CAN'T TRUST YOU GUYS, EH?
AND YOU BROUGHT OUTSIDERS TO OUR BASE!
WHO THE HELL ARE THEY?!

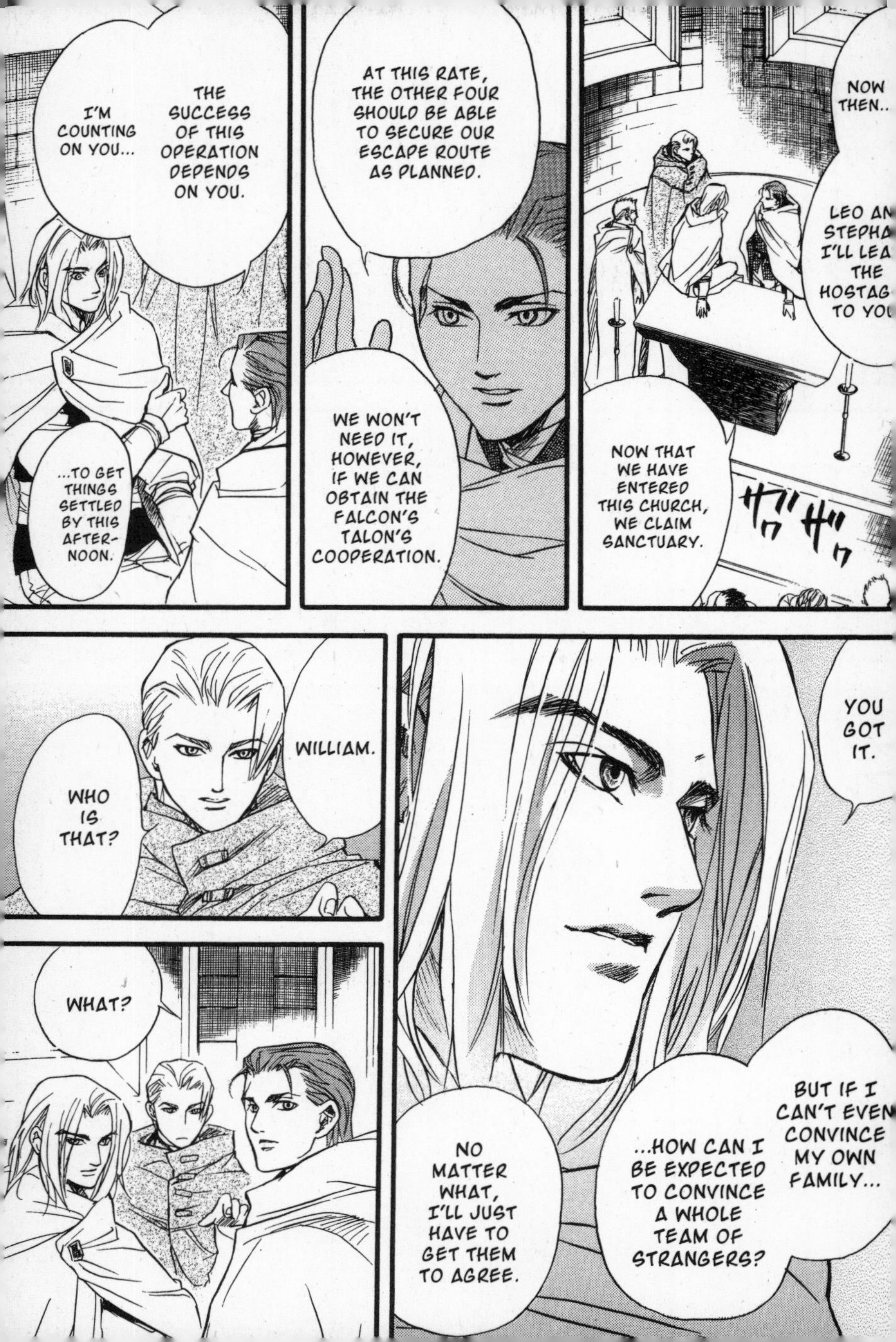
NOW THEN..
LEO AN STEPHA I'LL LEA THE HOSTAG TO YOU
NOW THAT WE HAVE ENTERED THIS CHURCH, WE CLAIM SANCTUARY.
ザワ ザワ
AT THIS RATE, THE OTHER FOUR SHOULD BE ABLE TO SECURE OUR ESCAPE ROUTE AS PLANNED.
WE WON'T NEED IT, HOWEVER, IF WE CAN OBTAIN THE FALCON'S TALON'S COOPERATION.
THE SUCCESS OF THIS OPERATION DEPENDS ON YOU.
I'M COUNTING ON YOU...
...TO GET THINGS SETTLED BY THIS AFTER-NOON.
YOU GOT IT.
BUT IF I CAN'T EVEN CONVINCE MY OWN FAMILY...
...HOW CAN I BE EXPECTED TO CONVINCE A WHOLE TEAM OF STRANGERS?
NO MATTER WHAT, I'LL JUST HAVE TO GET THEM TO AGREE.
WILLIAM.
WHO IS THAT?
WHAT?

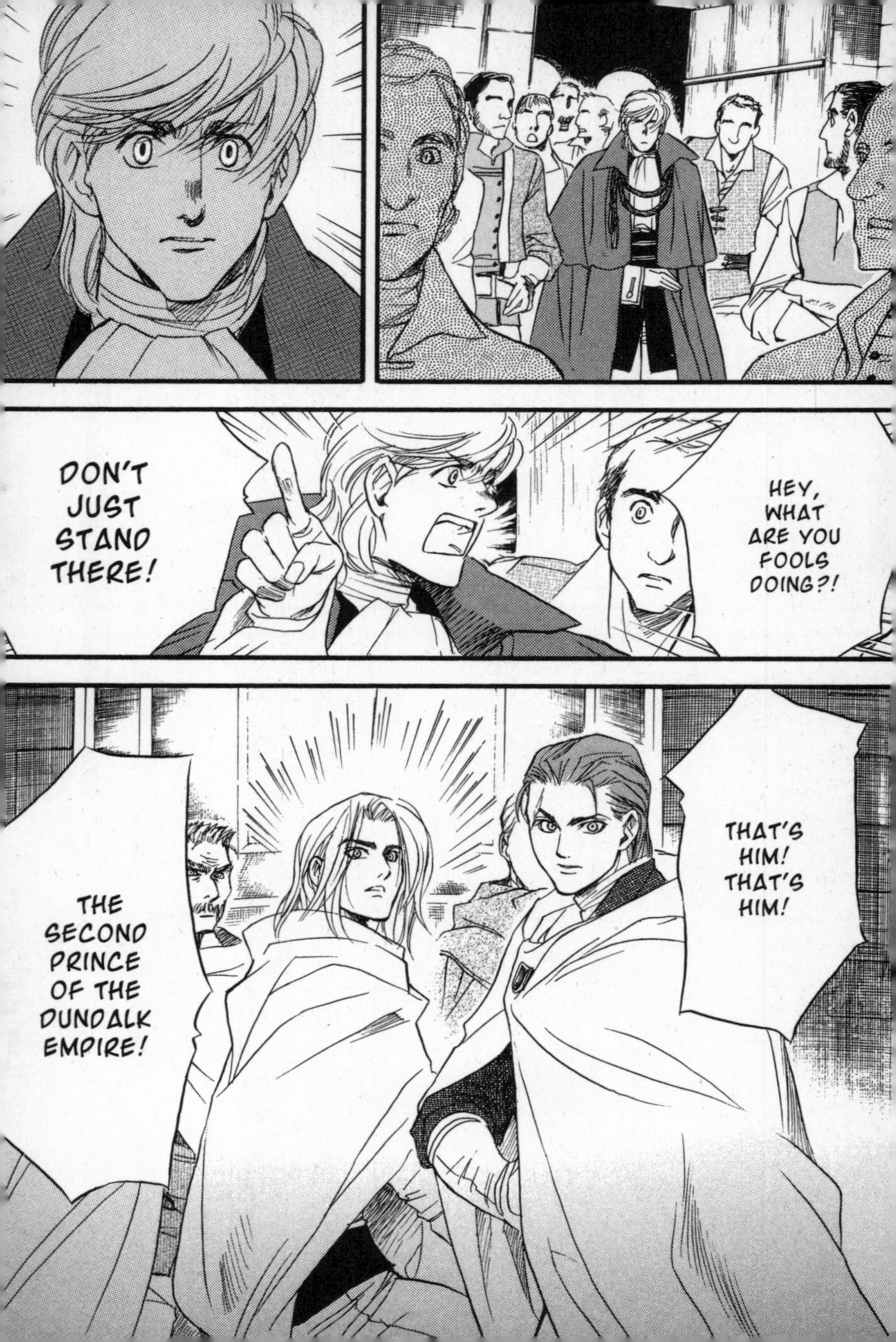
HEY, WHAT ARE YOU FOOLS DOING?!
DON'T JUST STAND THERE!
THAT'S HIM! THAT'S HIM!
THE SECOND PRINCE OF THE DUNDALK EMPIRE!

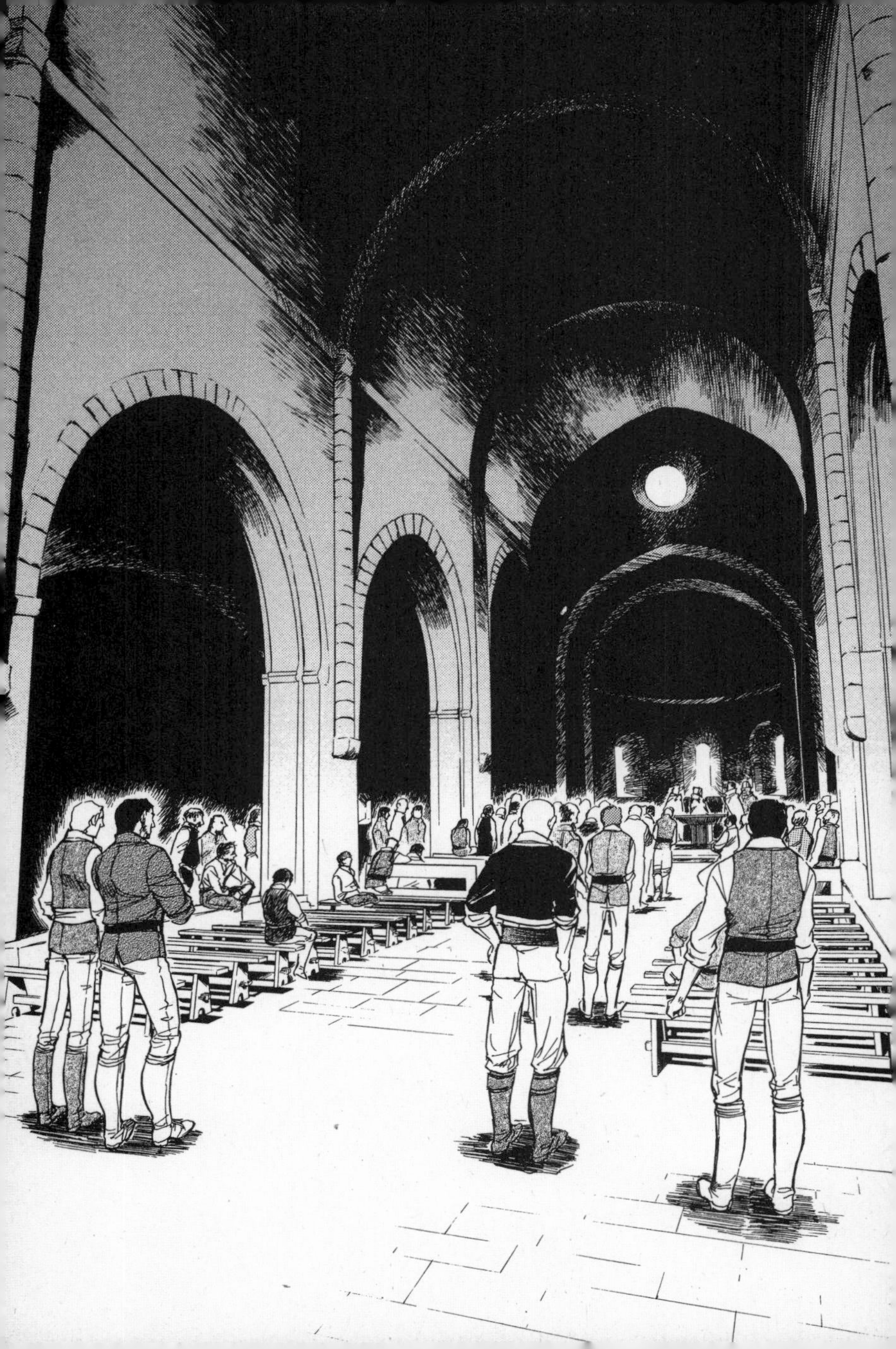

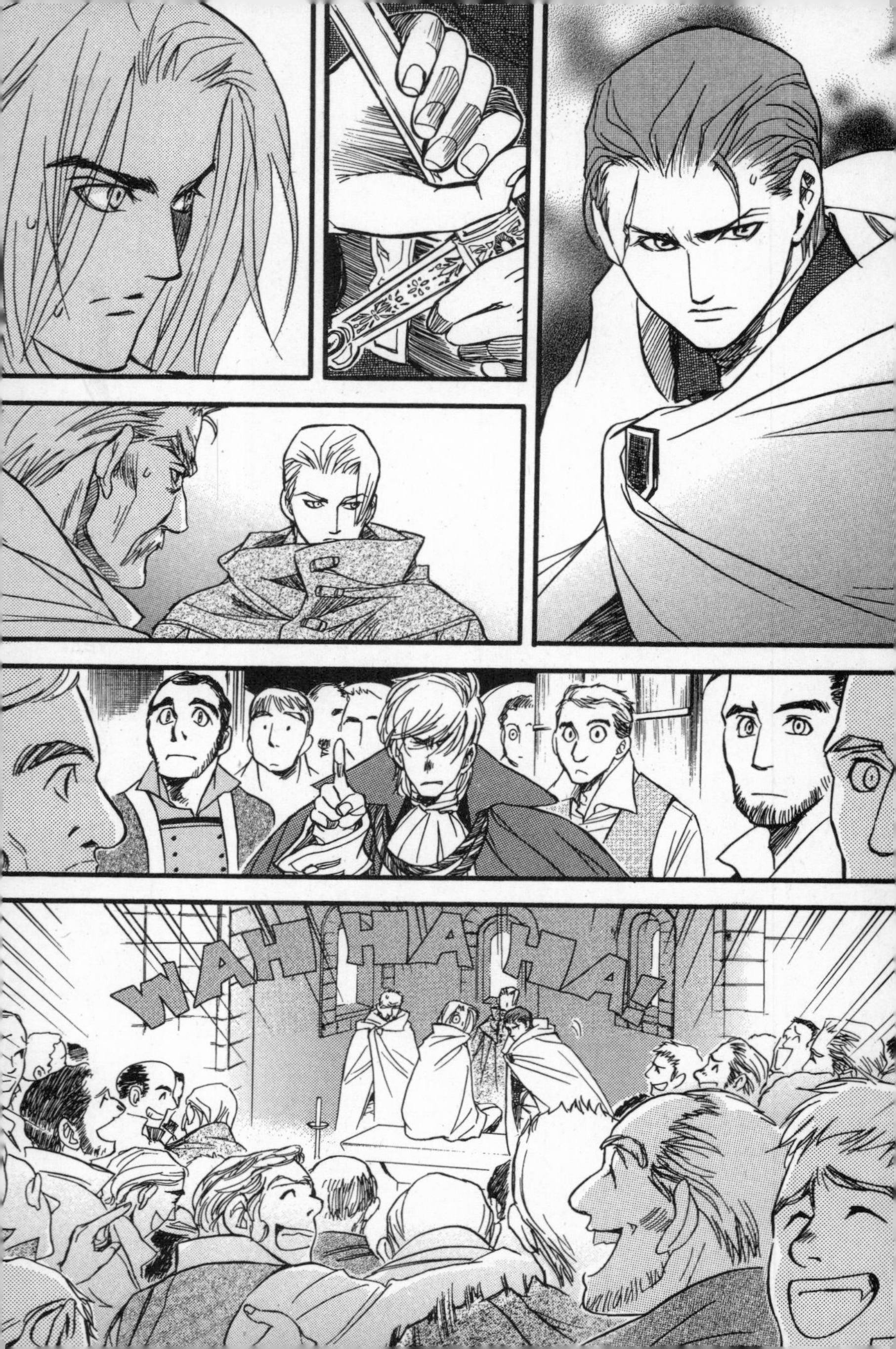
WAH HA HA HA

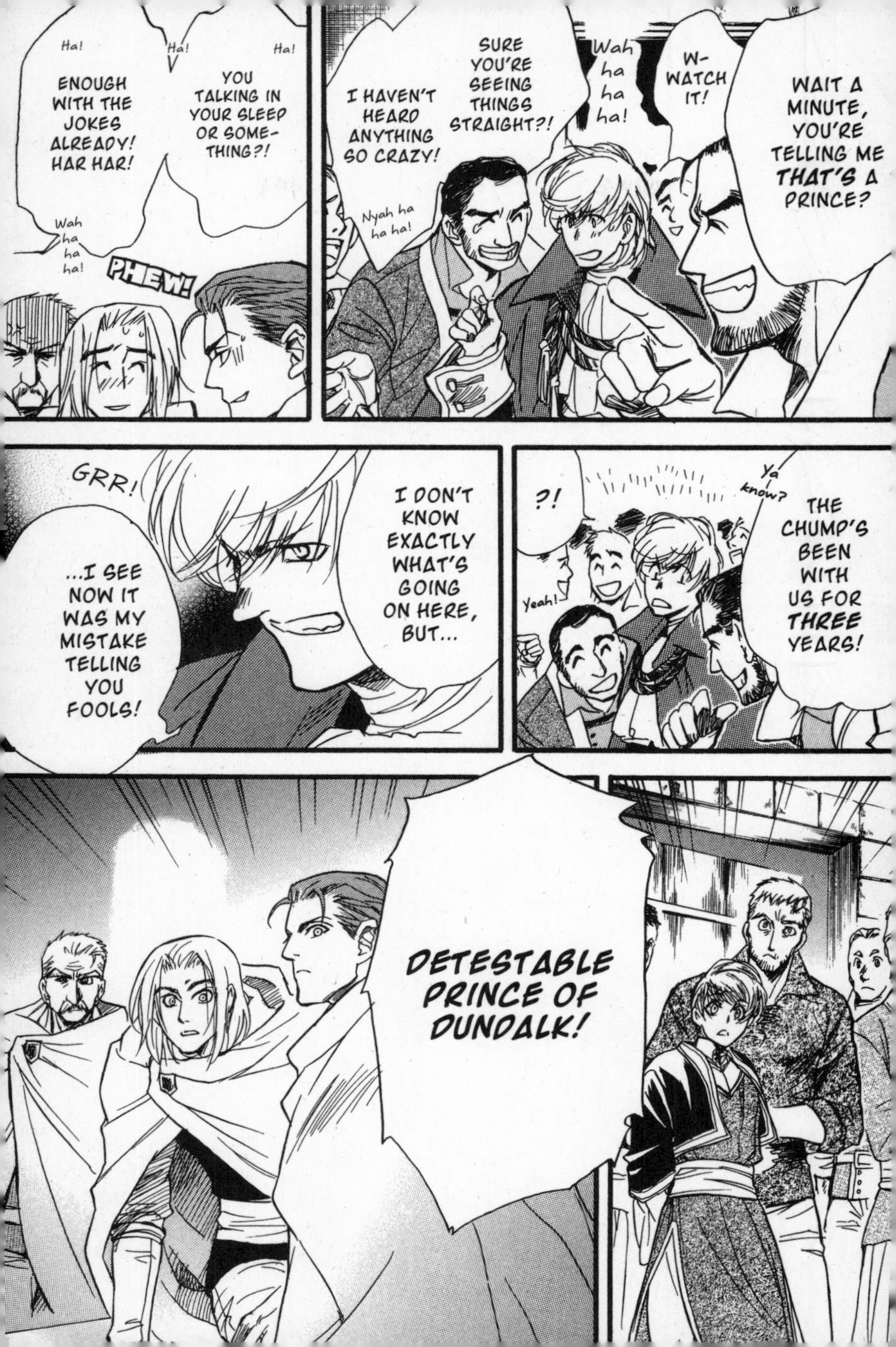
WAIT A MINUTE, YOU'RE TELLING ME THAT'S A PRINCE?
W-WATCH IT!
Wah ha ha ha!
SURE YOU'RE SEEING THINGS STRAIGHT?!
I HAVEN'T HEARD ANYTHING SO CRAZY!
Nyah ha ha ha!
Ha!
Ha!
YOU TALKING IN YOUR SLEEP OR SOMETHING?!
Ha!
ENOUGH WITH THE JOKES ALREADY! HAR HAR!
Wah ha ha ha!
PHEW!
Ya know?
THE CHUMP'S BEEN WITH US FOR THREE YEARS!
?!
Yeah!
I DON'T KNOW EXACTLY WHAT'S GOING ON HERE, BUT...
GRR!
...I SEE NOW IT WAS MY MISTAKE TELLING YOU FOOLS!
DETESTABLE PRINCE OF DUNDALK!

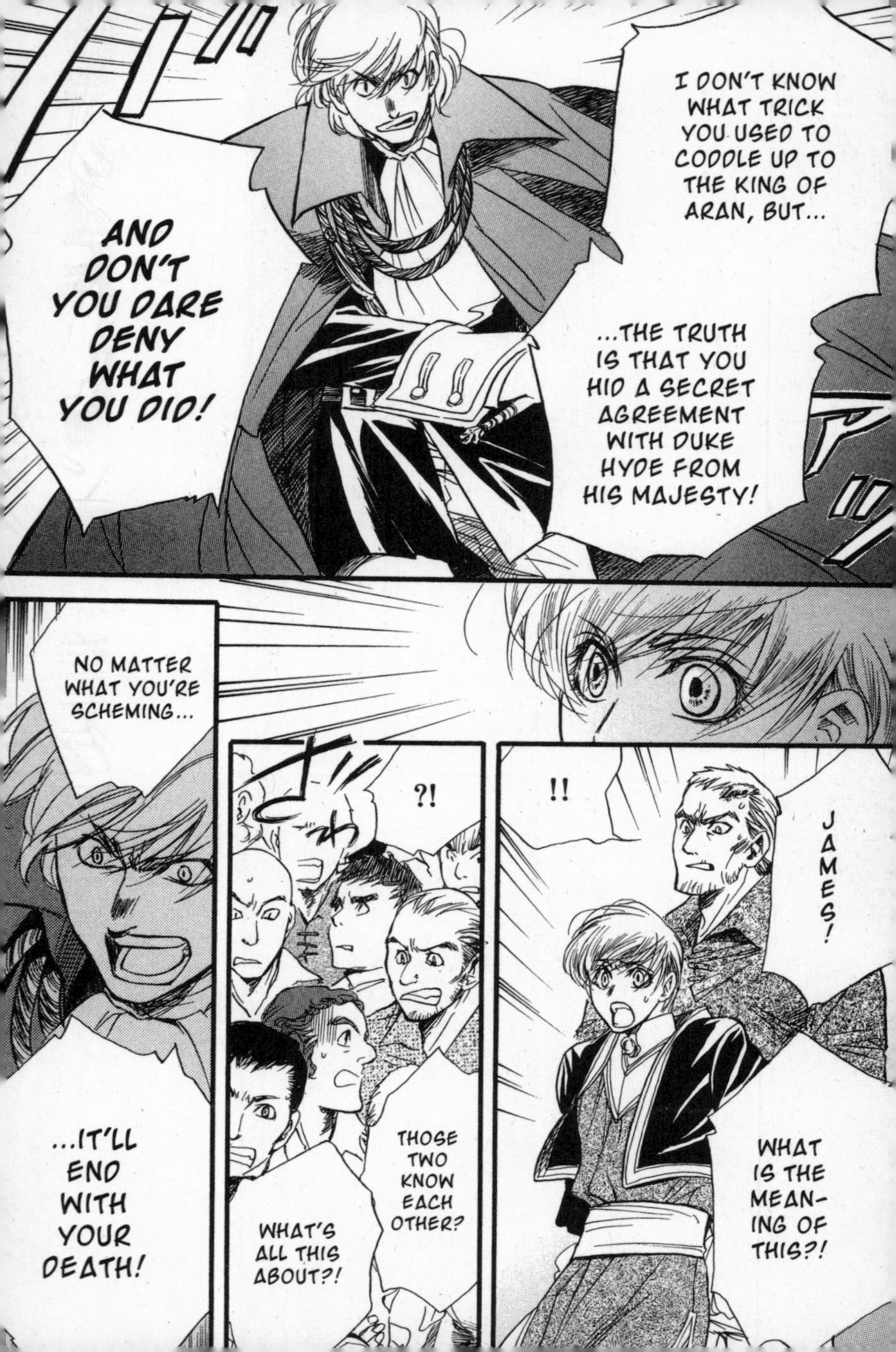
I DON'T KNOW WHAT TRICK YOU USED TO CODDLE UP TO THE KING OF ARAN, BUT...
...THE TRUTH IS THAT YOU HID A SECRET AGREEMENT WITH DUKE HYDE FROM HIS MAJESTY!
AND DON'T YOU DARE DENY WHAT YOU DID!
!!
JAMES!
WHAT IS THE MEANING OF THIS?!
?!
THOSE TWO KNOW EACH OTHER?
WHAT'S ALL THIS ABOUT?!
NO MATTER WHAT YOU'RE SCHEMING...
...IT'LL END WITH YOUR DEATH!

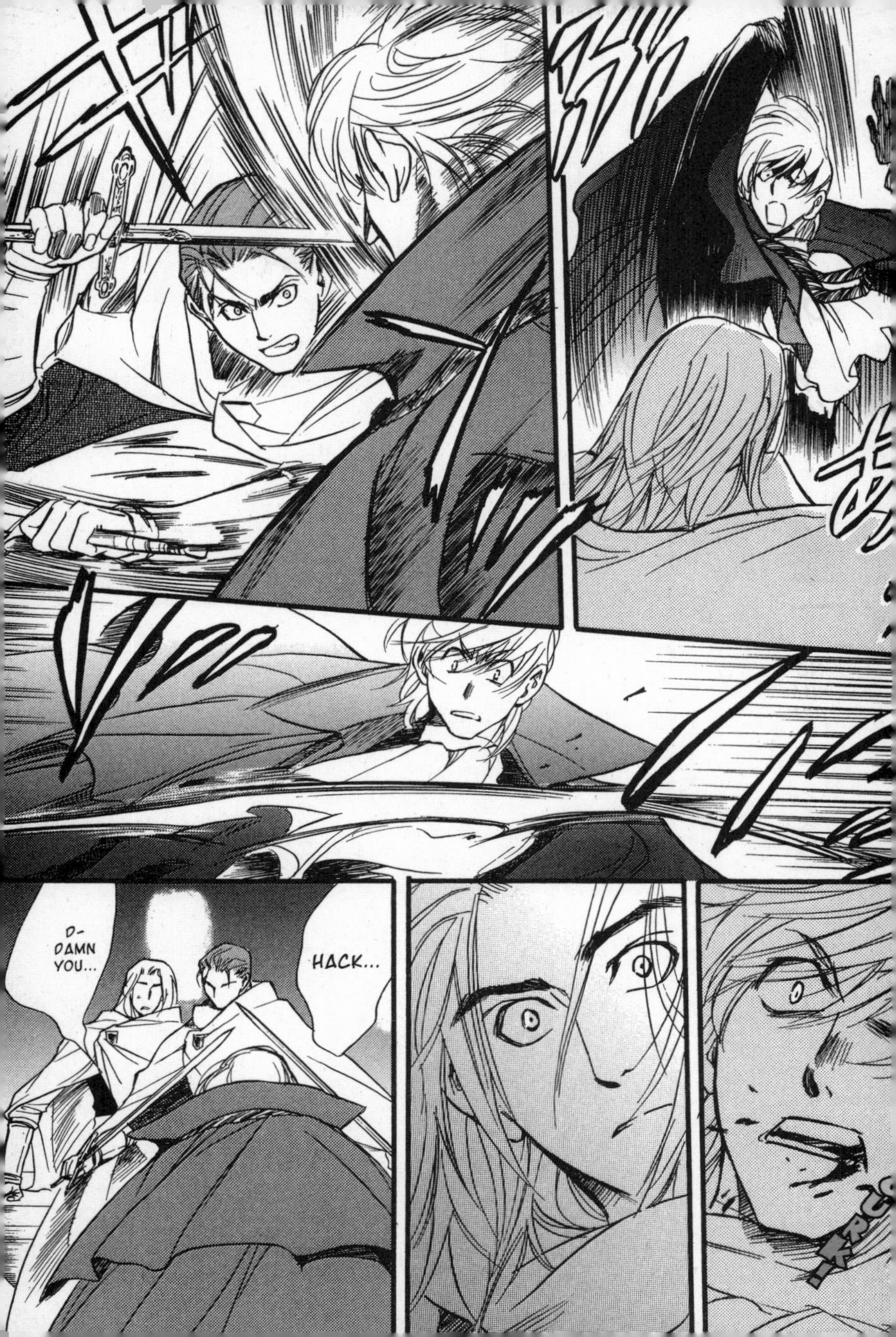
HACK...
D-DAMN YOU...

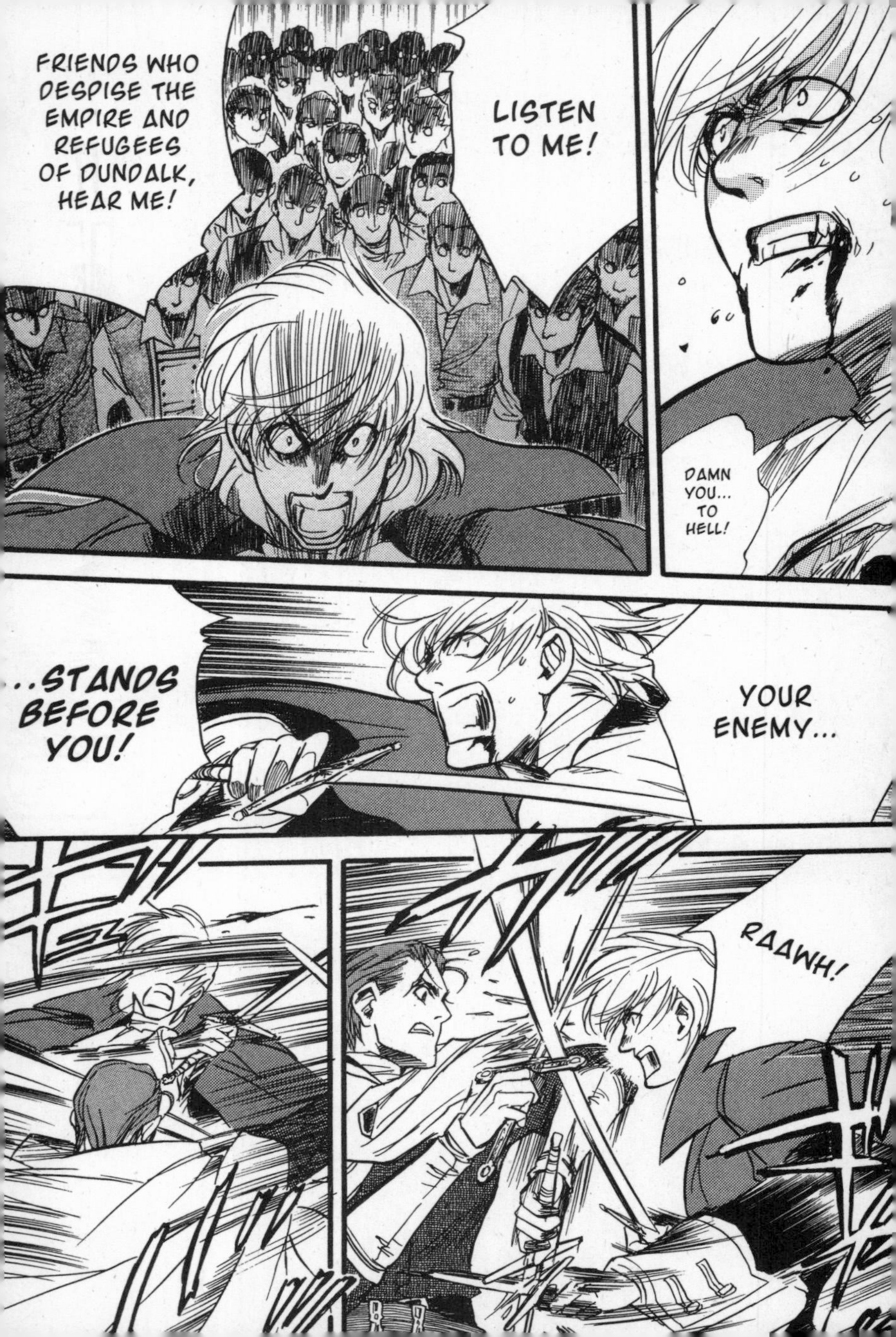
DAMN YOU... TO HELL!
LISTEN TO ME!
FRIENDS WHO DESPISE THE EMPIRE AND REFUGEES OF DUNDALK, HEAR ME!
YOUR ENEMY...
..STANDS BEFORE YOU!
RAAWH!

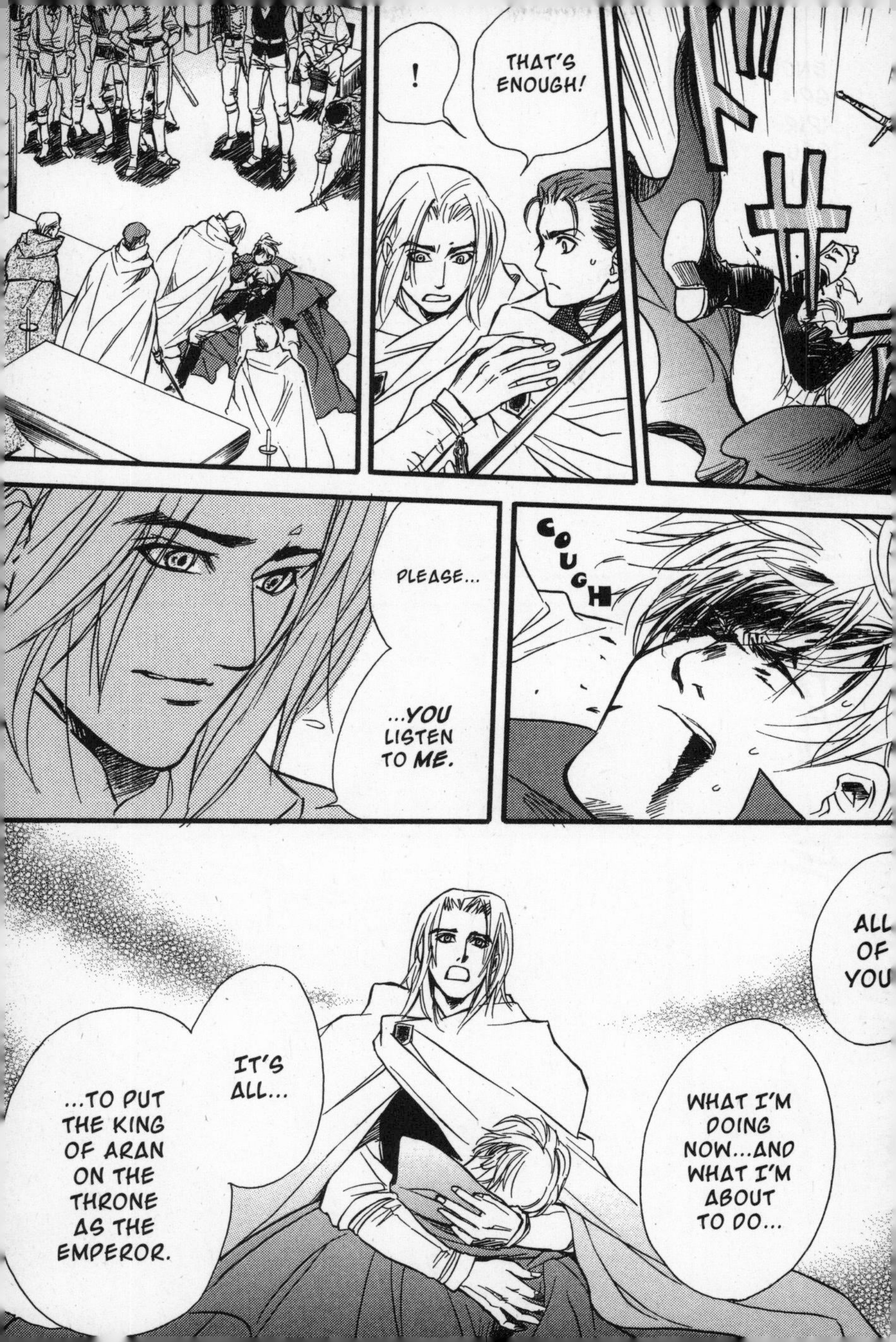
THAT'S ENOUGH!
!
COUGH
PLEASE...
...YOU LISTEN TO ME.
ALL OF YOU
WHAT I'M DOING NOW...AND WHAT I'M ABOUT TO DO...
IT'S ALL...
...TO PUT THE KING OF ARAN ON THE THRONE AS THE EMPEROR.

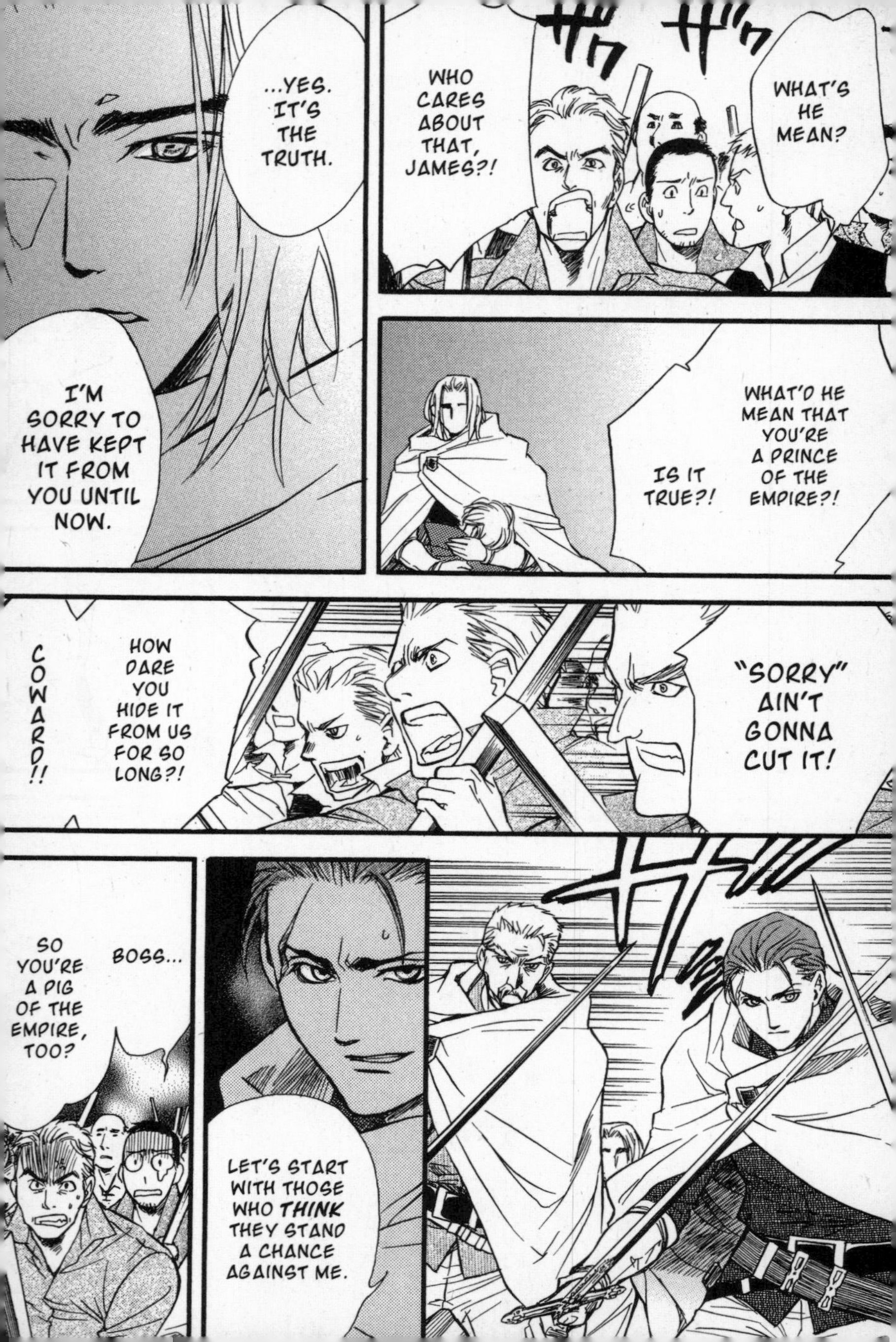
ザワ ザワ
WHAT'S HE MEAN?
WHO CARES ABOUT THAT, JAMES?!
WHAT'D HE MEAN THAT YOU'RE A PRINCE OF THE EMPIRE?!
IS IT TRUE?!
...YES. IT'S THE TRUTH.
I'M SORRY TO HAVE KEPT IT FROM YOU UNTIL NOW.
"SORRY" AIN'T GONNA CUT IT!
HOW DARE YOU HIDE IT FROM US FOR SO LONG?!
COWARD!!
LET'S START WITH THOSE WHO *THINK* THEY STAND A CHANCE AGAINST ME.
BOSS...
SO YOU'RE A PIG OF THE EMPIRE, TOO?

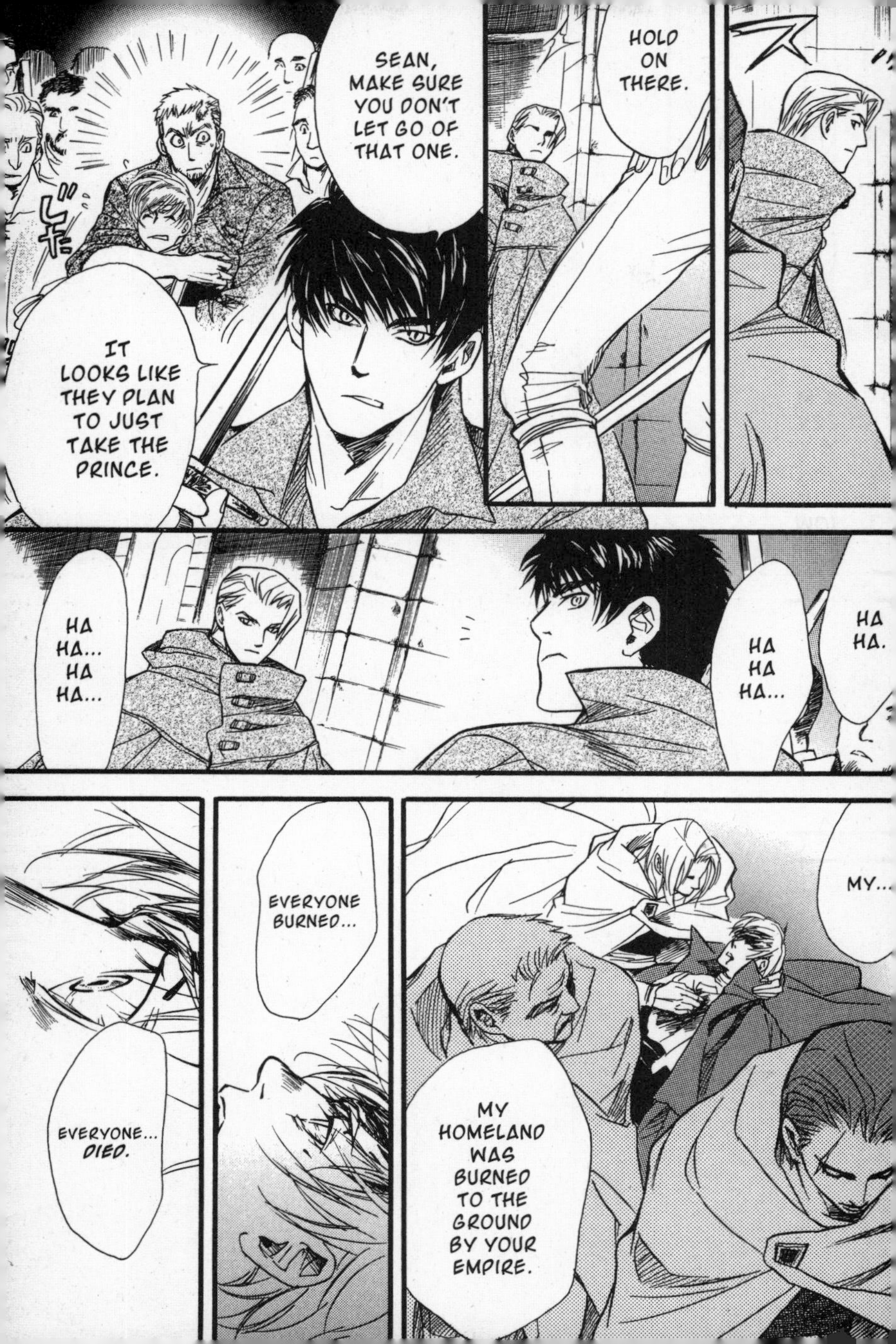
HOLD ON THERE.
SEAN, MAKE SURE YOU DON'T LET GO OF THAT ONE.
IT LOOKS LIKE THEY PLAN TO JUST TAKE THE PRINCE.
HA HA.
HA HA HA...
HA HA... HA HA...
MY...
MY HOMELAND WAS BURNED TO THE GROUND BY YOUR EMPIRE.
EVERYONE BURNED...
EVERYONE... DIED.

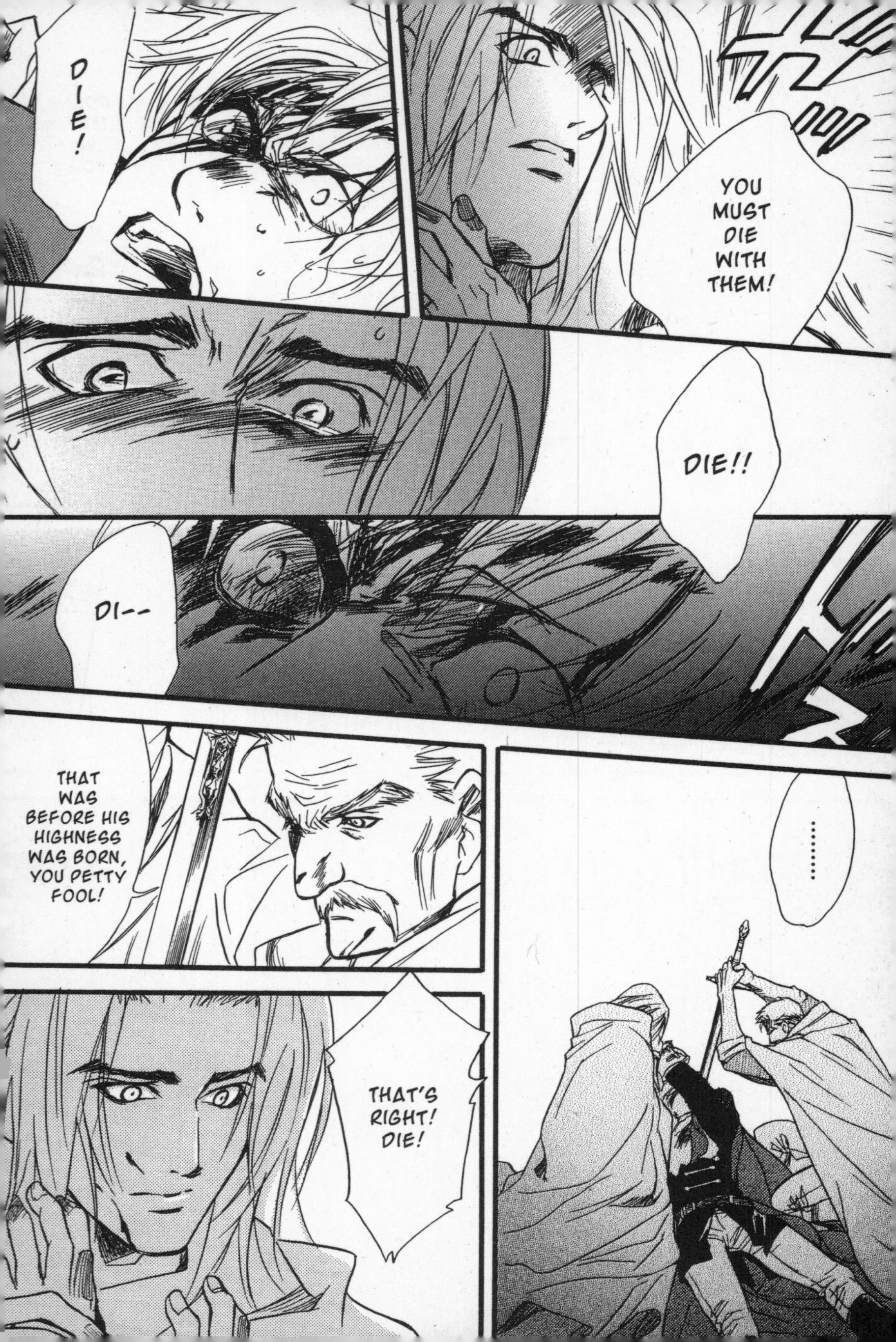
YOU MUST DIE WITH THEM!
DIE!
DIE!!
DI--
......
THAT WAS BEFORE HIS HIGHNESS WAS BORN, YOU PETTY FOOL!
THAT'S RIGHT! DIE!

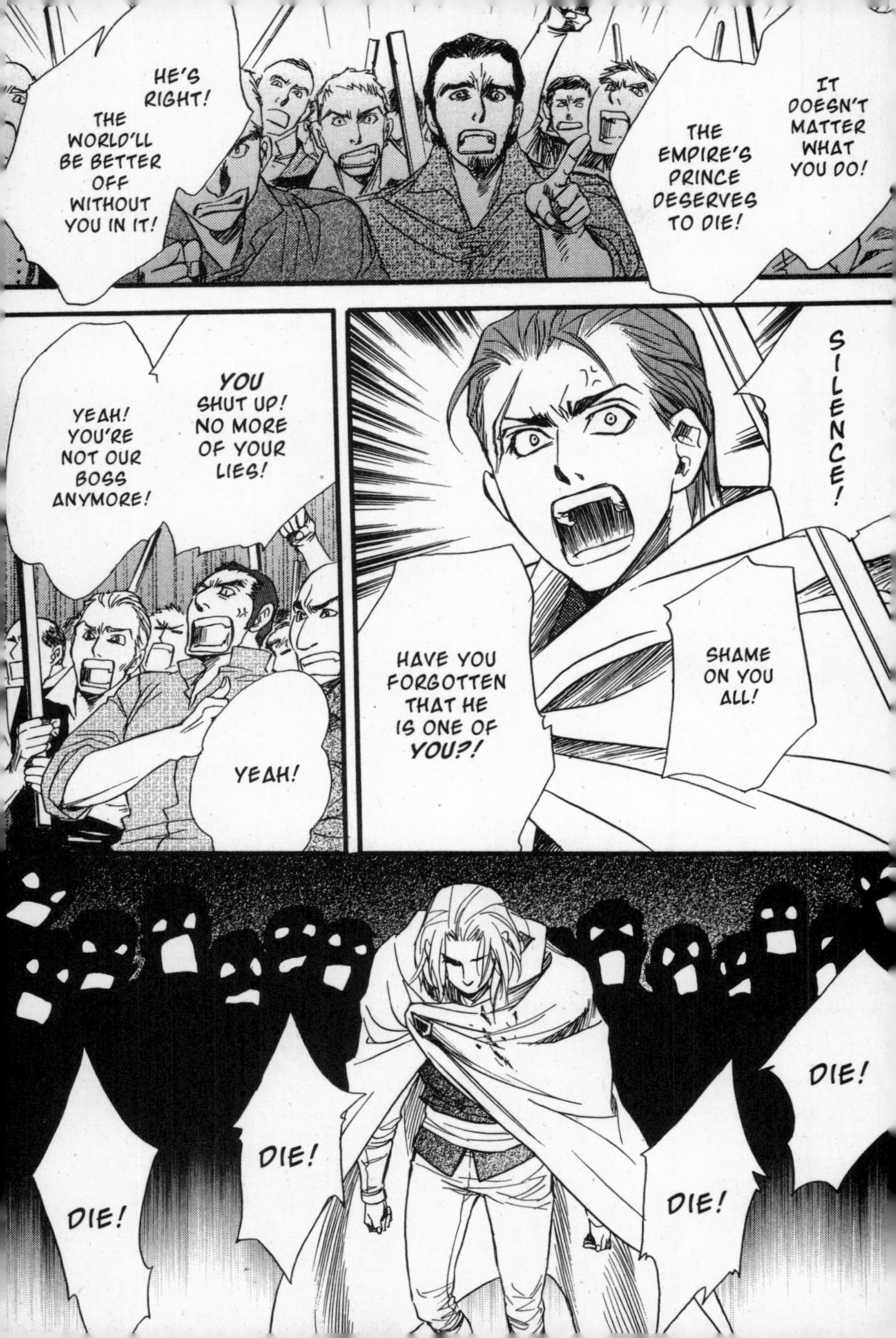
IT DOESN'T MATTER WHAT YOU DO!
THE EMPIRE'S PRINCE DESERVES TO DIE!
HE'S RIGHT!
THE WORLD'LL BE BETTER OFF WITHOUT YOU IN IT!
SILENCE!
SHAME ON YOU ALL!
HAVE YOU FORGOTTEN THAT HE IS ONE OF YOU?!
YOU SHUT UP! NO MORE OF YOUR LIES!
YEAH! YOU'RE NOT OUR BOSS ANYMORE!
YEAH!
DIE!
DIE!
DIE!
DIE!

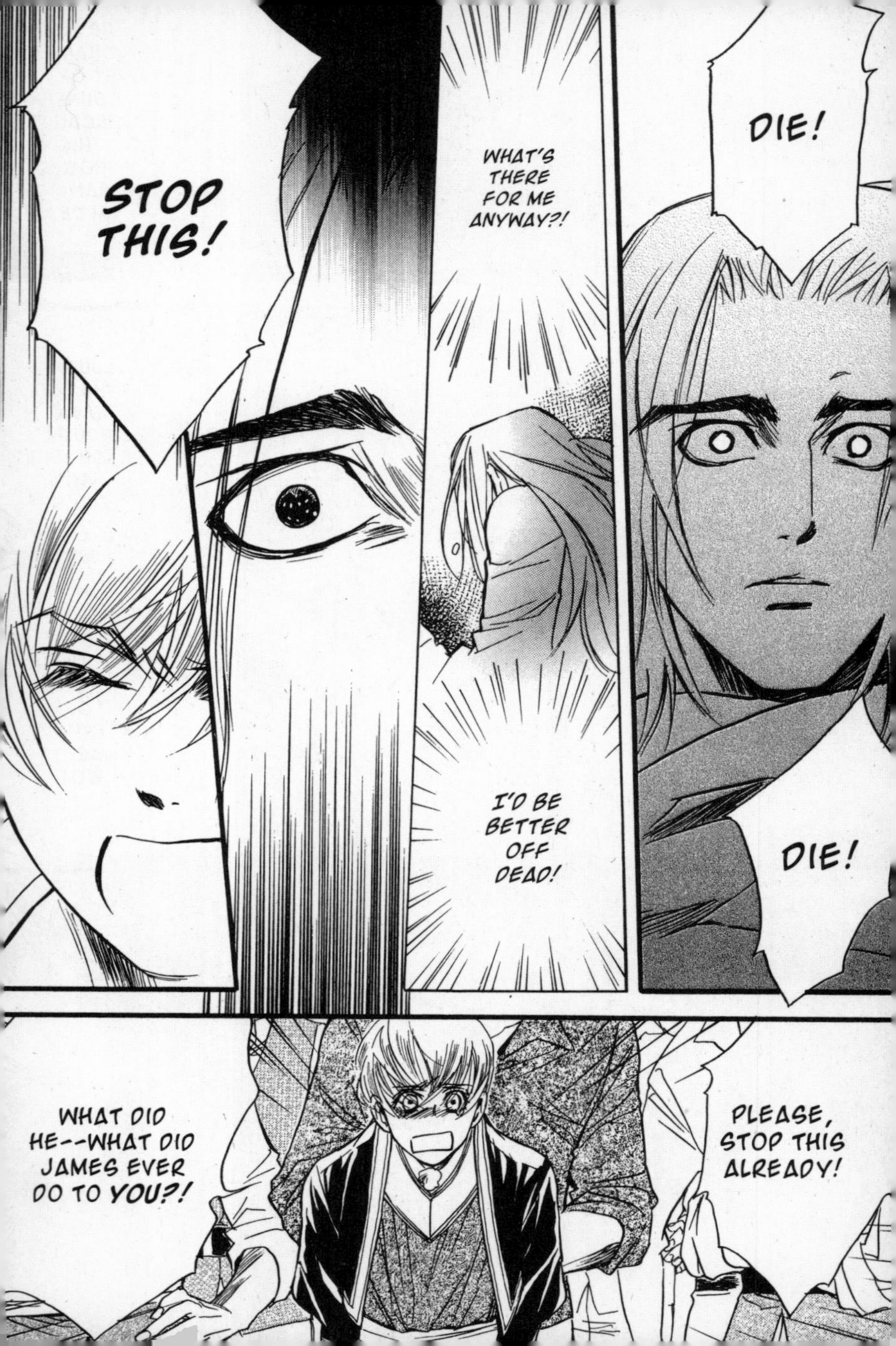
DIE!
DIE!
WHAT'S THERE FOR ME ANYWAY?!
I'D BE BETTER OFF DEAD!
STOP THIS!
PLEASE, STOP THIS ALREADY!
WHAT DID HE--WHAT DID JAMES EVER DO TO YOU?!

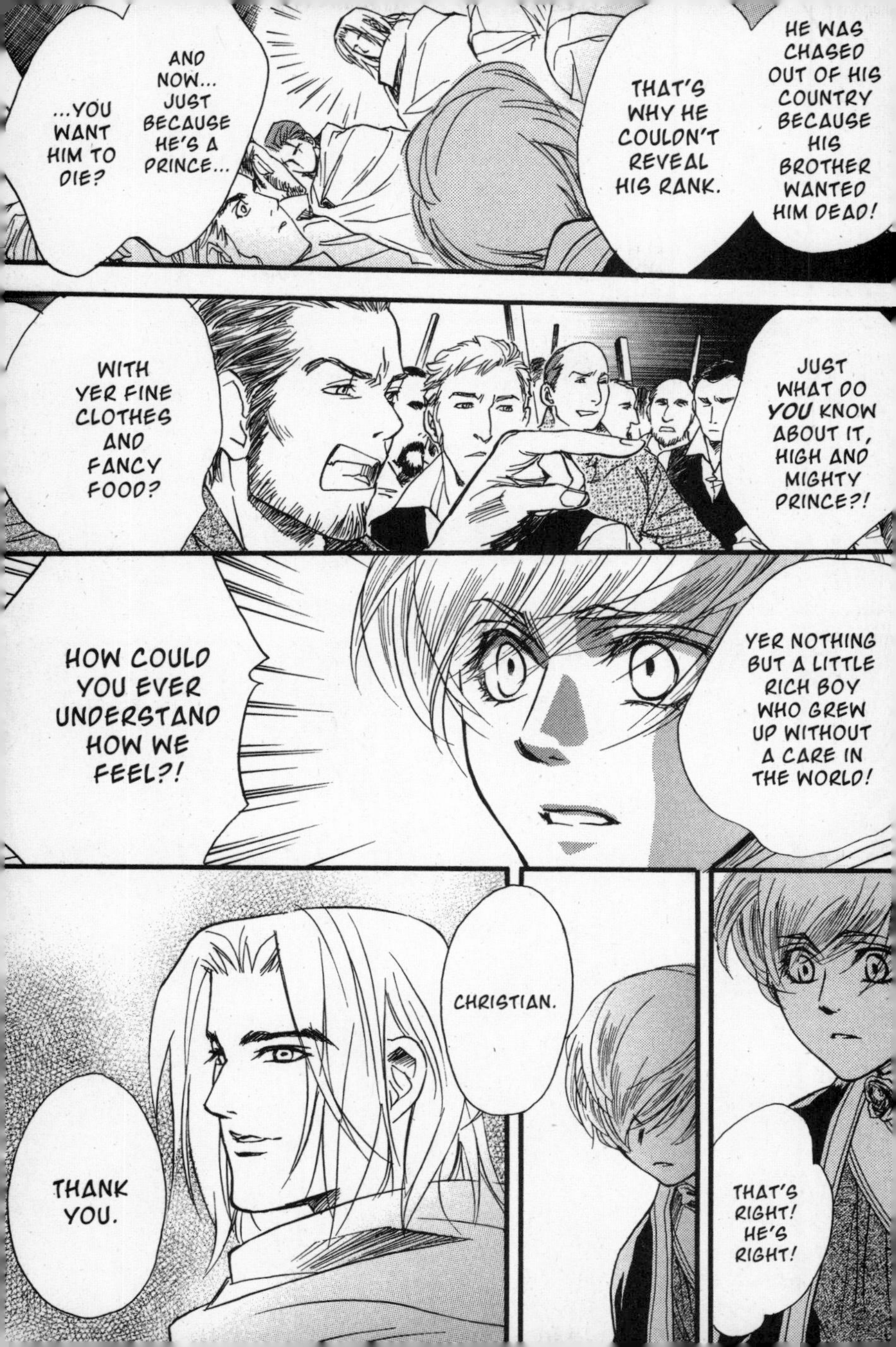
HE WAS CHASED OUT OF HIS COUNTRY BECAUSE HIS BROTHER WANTED HIM DEAD!
THAT'S WHY HE COULDN'T REVEAL HIS RANK.
AND NOW... JUST BECAUSE HE'S A PRINCE...
...YOU WANT HIM TO DIE?
JUST WHAT DO *YOU* KNOW ABOUT IT, HIGH AND MIGHTY PRINCE?!
WITH YER FINE CLOTHES AND FANCY FOOD?
YER NOTHING BUT A LITTLE RICH BOY WHO GREW UP WITHOUT A CARE IN THE WORLD!
HOW COULD YOU EVER UNDERSTAND HOW WE FEEL?!
THAT'S RIGHT! HE'S RIGHT!
CHRISTIAN.
THANK YOU.

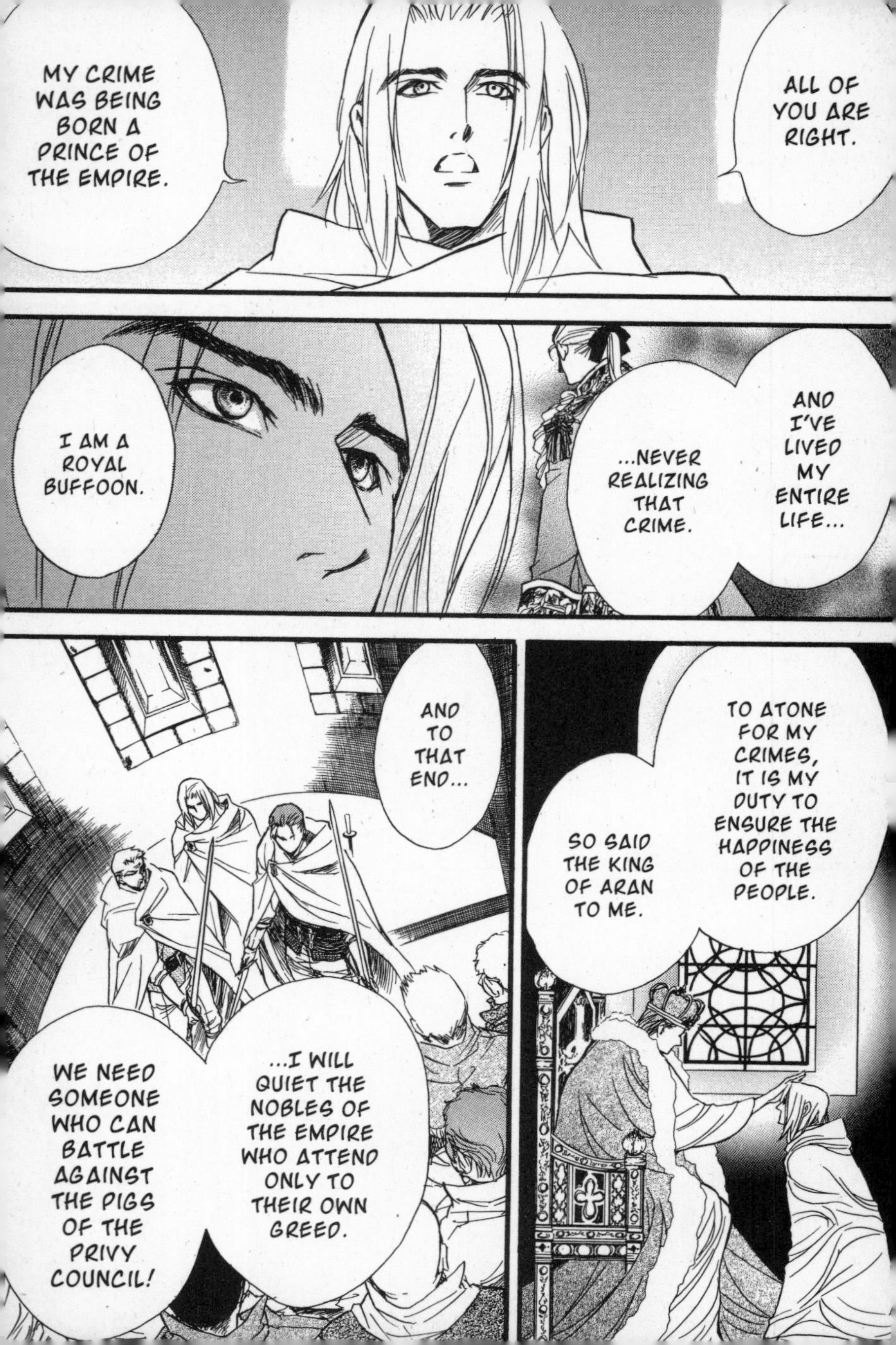
ALL OF YOU ARE RIGHT.
MY CRIME WAS BEING BORN A PRINCE OF THE EMPIRE.
AND I'VE LIVED MY ENTIRE LIFE...
...NEVER REALIZING THAT CRIME.
I AM A ROYAL BUFFOON.
TO ATONE FOR MY CRIMES, IT IS MY DUTY TO ENSURE THE HAPPINESS OF THE PEOPLE.
SO SAID THE KING OF ARAN TO ME.
AND TO THAT END...
...I WILL QUIET THE NOBLES OF THE EMPIRE WHO ATTEND ONLY TO THEIR OWN GREED.
WE NEED SOMEONE WHO CAN BATTLE AGAINST THE PIGS OF THE PRIVY COUNCIL!

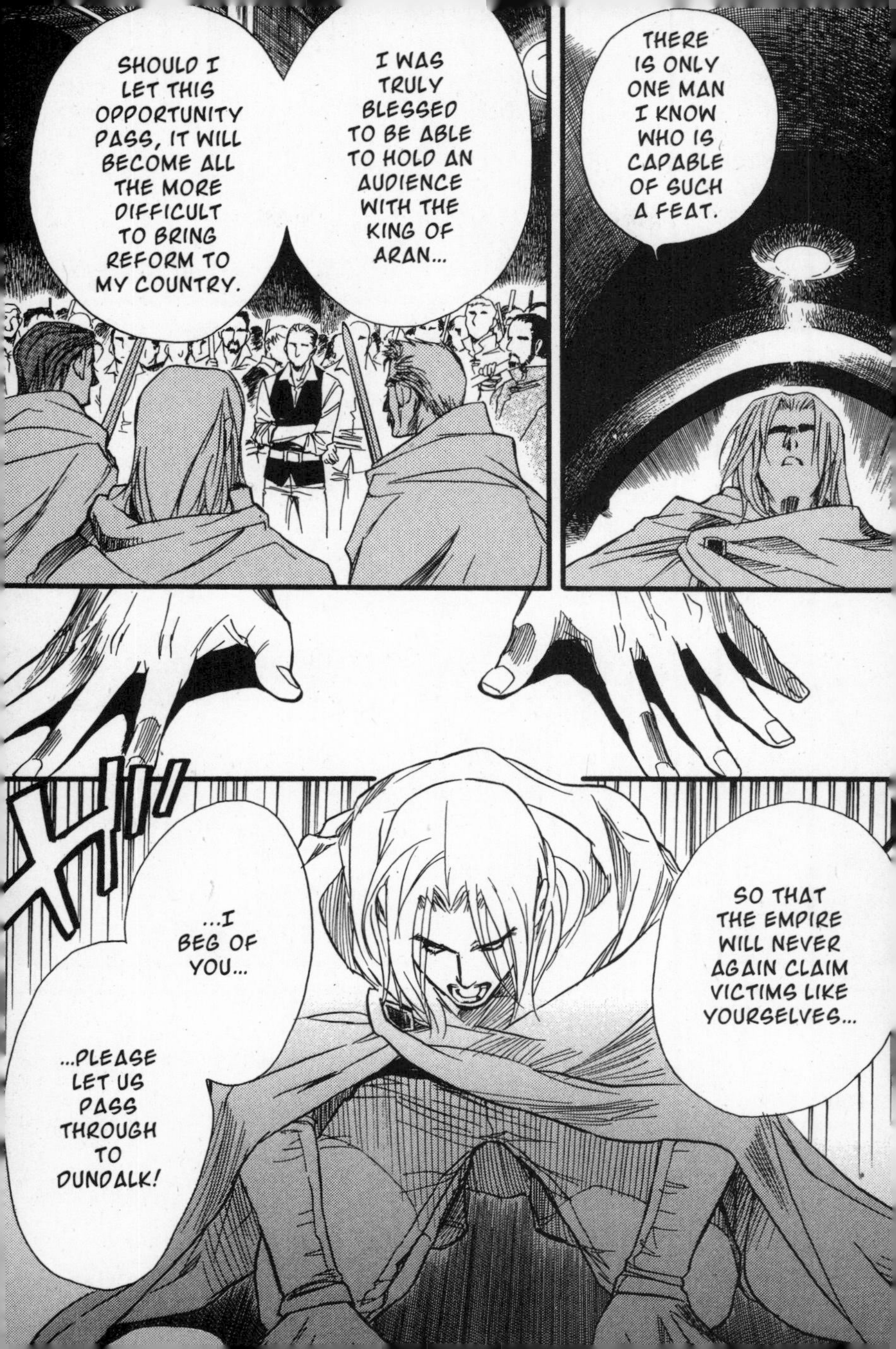
THERE IS ONLY ONE MAN I KNOW WHO IS CAPABLE OF SUCH A FEAT.
I WAS TRULY BLESSED TO BE ABLE TO HOLD AN AUDIENCE WITH THE KING OF ARAN...
SHOULD I LET THIS OPPORTUNITY PASS, IT WILL BECOME ALL THE MORE DIFFICULT TO BRING REFORM TO MY COUNTRY.
SO THAT THE EMPIRE WILL NEVER AGAIN CLAIM VICTIMS LIKE YOURSELVES...
...I BEG OF YOU...
...PLEASE LET US PASS THROUGH TO DUNDALK!

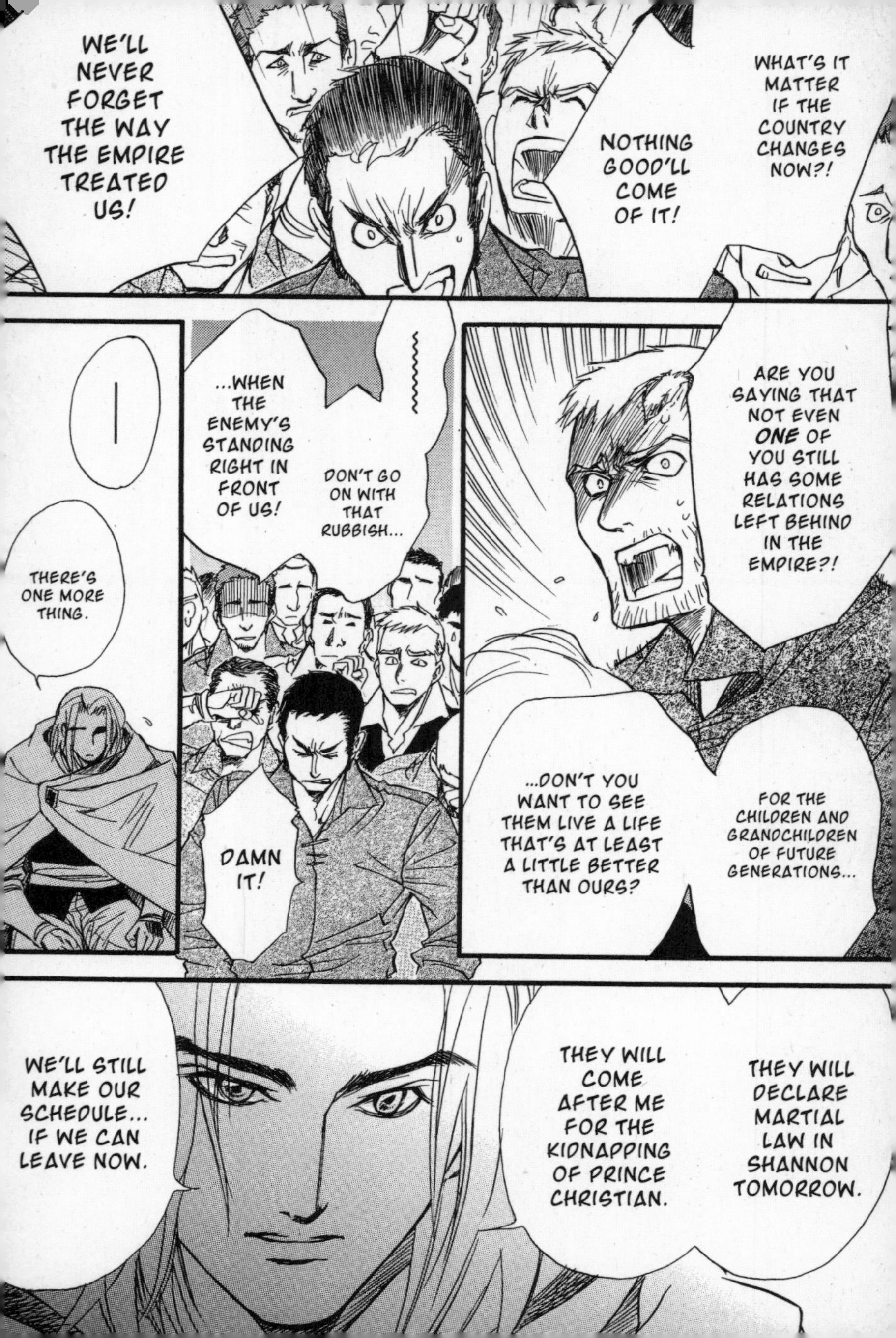
WHAT'S IT MATTER IF THE COUNTRY CHANGES NOW?!
NOTHING GOOD'LL COME OF IT!
WE'LL NEVER FORGET THE WAY THE EMPIRE TREATED US!
ARE YOU SAYING THAT NOT EVEN ONE OF YOU STILL HAS SOME RELATIONS LEFT BEHIND IN THE EMPIRE?!
FOR THE CHILDREN AND GRANDCHILDREN OF FUTURE GENERATIONS...
...DON'T YOU WANT TO SEE THEM LIVE A LIFE THAT'S AT LEAST A LITTLE BETTER THAN OURS?
DON'T GO ON WITH THAT RUBBISH...
...WHEN THE ENEMY'S STANDING RIGHT IN FRONT OF US!
DAMN IT!
THERE'S ONE MORE THING.
THEY WILL DECLARE MARTIAL LAW IN SHANNON TOMORROW.
THEY WILL COME AFTER ME FOR THE KIDNAPPING OF PRINCE CHRISTIAN.
WE'LL STILL MAKE OUR SCHEDULE... IF WE CAN LEAVE NOW.

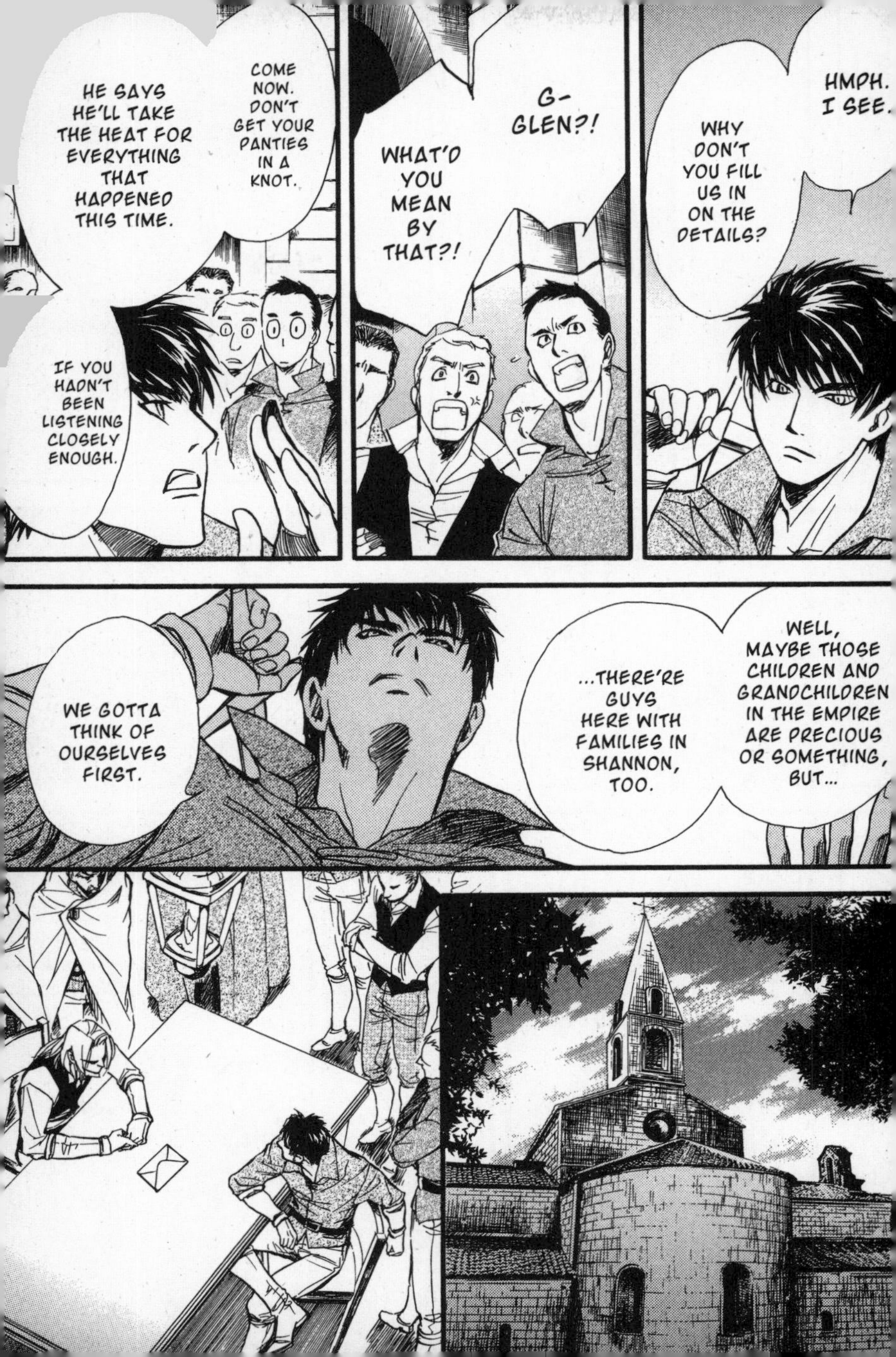
HMPH. I SEE.
WHY DON'T YOU FILL US IN ON THE DETAILS?
G-GLEN?!
WHAT'D YOU MEAN BY THAT?!
COME NOW. DON'T GET YOUR PANTIES IN A KNOT.
HE SAYS HE'LL TAKE THE HEAT FOR EVERYTHING THAT HAPPENED THIS TIME.
IF YOU HADN'T BEEN LISTENING CLOSELY ENOUGH.
WELL, MAYBE THOSE CHILDREN AND GRANDCHILDREN IN THE EMPIRE ARE PRECIOUS OR SOMETHING, BUT...
...THERE'RE GUYS HERE WITH FAMILIES IN SHANNON, TOO.
WE GOTTA THINK OF OURSELVES FIRST.

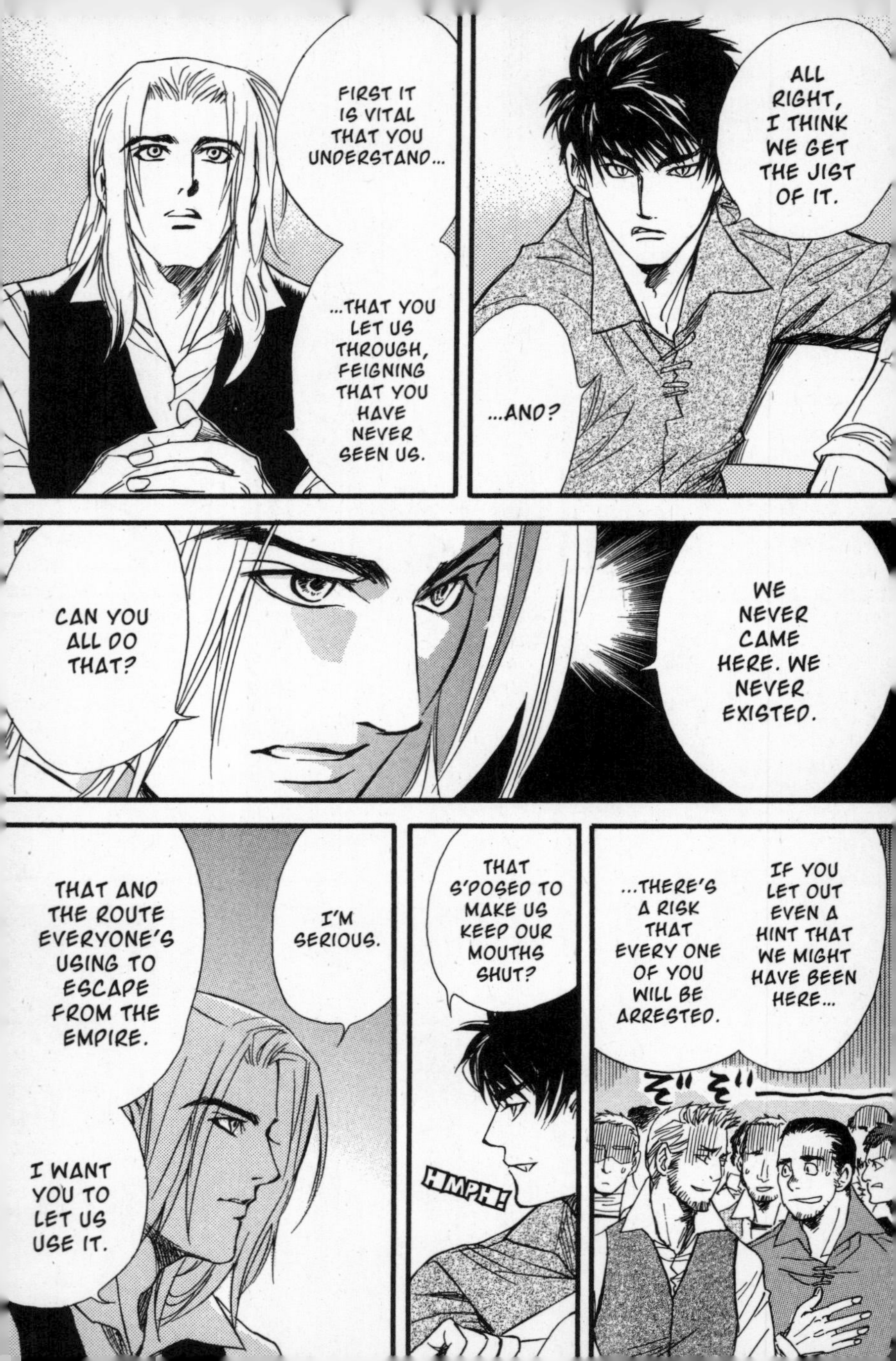
ALL RIGHT, I THINK WE GET THE JIST OF IT.
...AND?
FIRST IT IS VITAL THAT YOU UNDERSTAND...
...THAT YOU LET US THROUGH, FEIGNING THAT YOU HAVE NEVER SEEN US.
WE NEVER CAME HERE. WE NEVER EXISTED.
CAN YOU ALL DO THAT?
IF YOU LET OUT EVEN A HINT THAT WE MIGHT HAVE BEEN HERE...
...THERE'S A RISK THAT EVERY ONE OF YOU WILL BE ARRESTED.
THAT S'POSED TO MAKE US KEEP OUR MOUTHS SHUT?
HMPH!
I'M SERIOUS.
THAT AND THE ROUTE EVERYONE'S USING TO ESCAPE FROM THE EMPIRE.
I WANT YOU TO LET US USE IT.

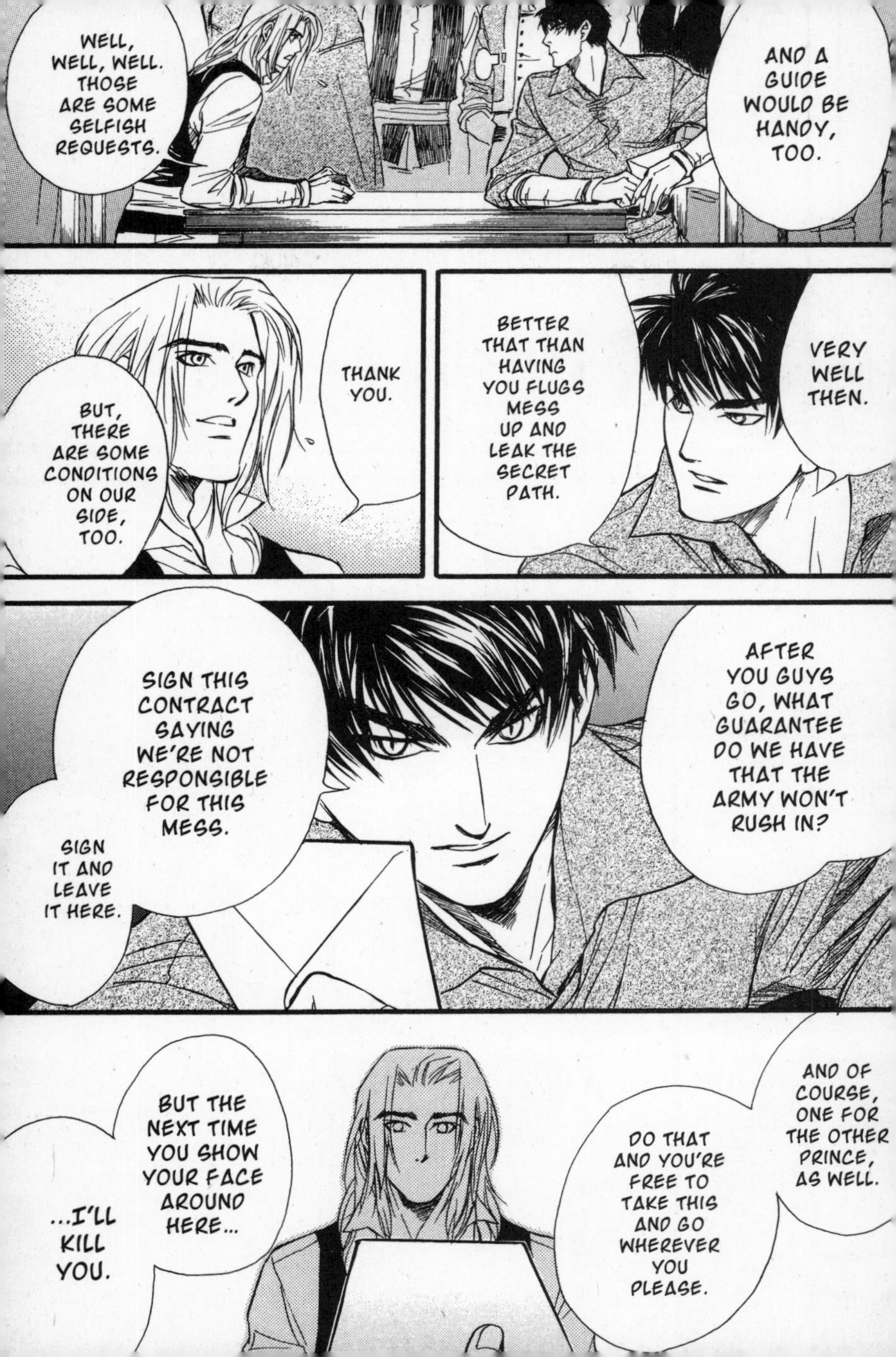
AND A GUIDE WOULD BE HANDY, TOO.
WELL, WELL, WELL. THOSE ARE SOME SELFISH REQUESTS.
VERY WELL THEN.
BETTER THAT THAN HAVING YOU FLUGS MESS UP AND LEAK THE SECRET PATH.
THANK YOU.
BUT, THERE ARE SOME CONDITIONS ON OUR SIDE, TOO.
AFTER YOU GUYS GO, WHAT GUARANTEE DO WE HAVE THAT THE ARMY WON'T RUSH IN?
SIGN THIS CONTRACT SAYING WE'RE NOT RESPONSIBLE FOR THIS MESS.
SIGN IT AND LEAVE IT HERE.
AND OF COURSE, ONE FOR THE OTHER PRINCE, AS WELL.
DO THAT AND YOU'RE FREE TO TAKE THIS AND GO WHEREVER YOU PLEASE.
BUT THE NEXT TIME YOU SHOW YOUR FACE AROUND HERE...
...I'LL KILL YOU.

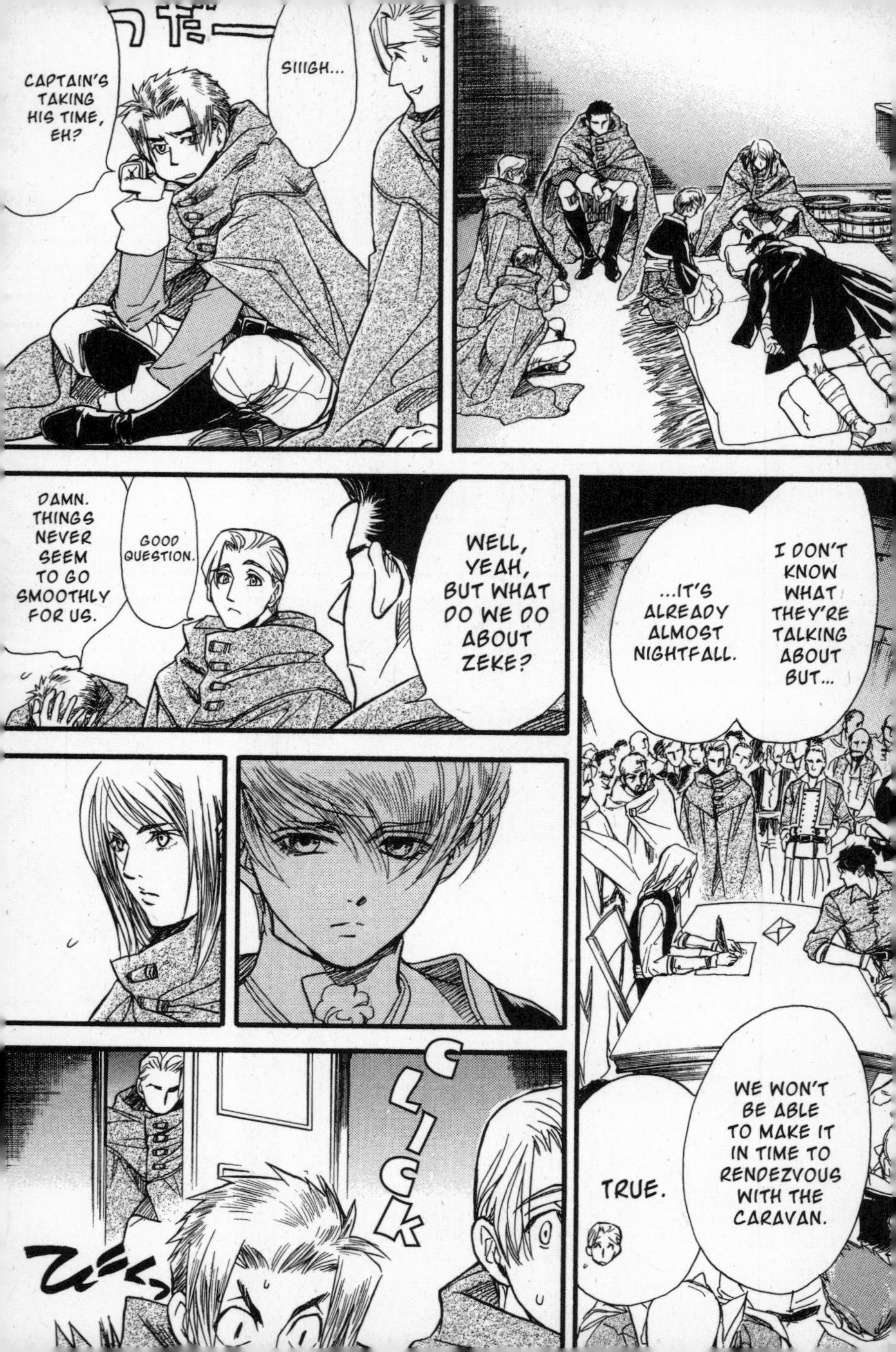
SIIIGH...
CAPTAIN'S TAKING HIS TIME, EH?
I DON'T KNOW WHAT THEY'RE TALKING ABOUT BUT...
...IT'S ALREADY ALMOST NIGHTFALL.
WE WON'T BE ABLE TO MAKE IT IN TIME TO RENDEZVOUS WITH THE CARAVAN.
TRUE.
WELL, YEAH, BUT WHAT DO WE DO ABOUT ZEKE?
GOOD QUESTION.
DAMN. THINGS NEVER SEEM TO GO SMOOTHLY FOR US.
CLICK

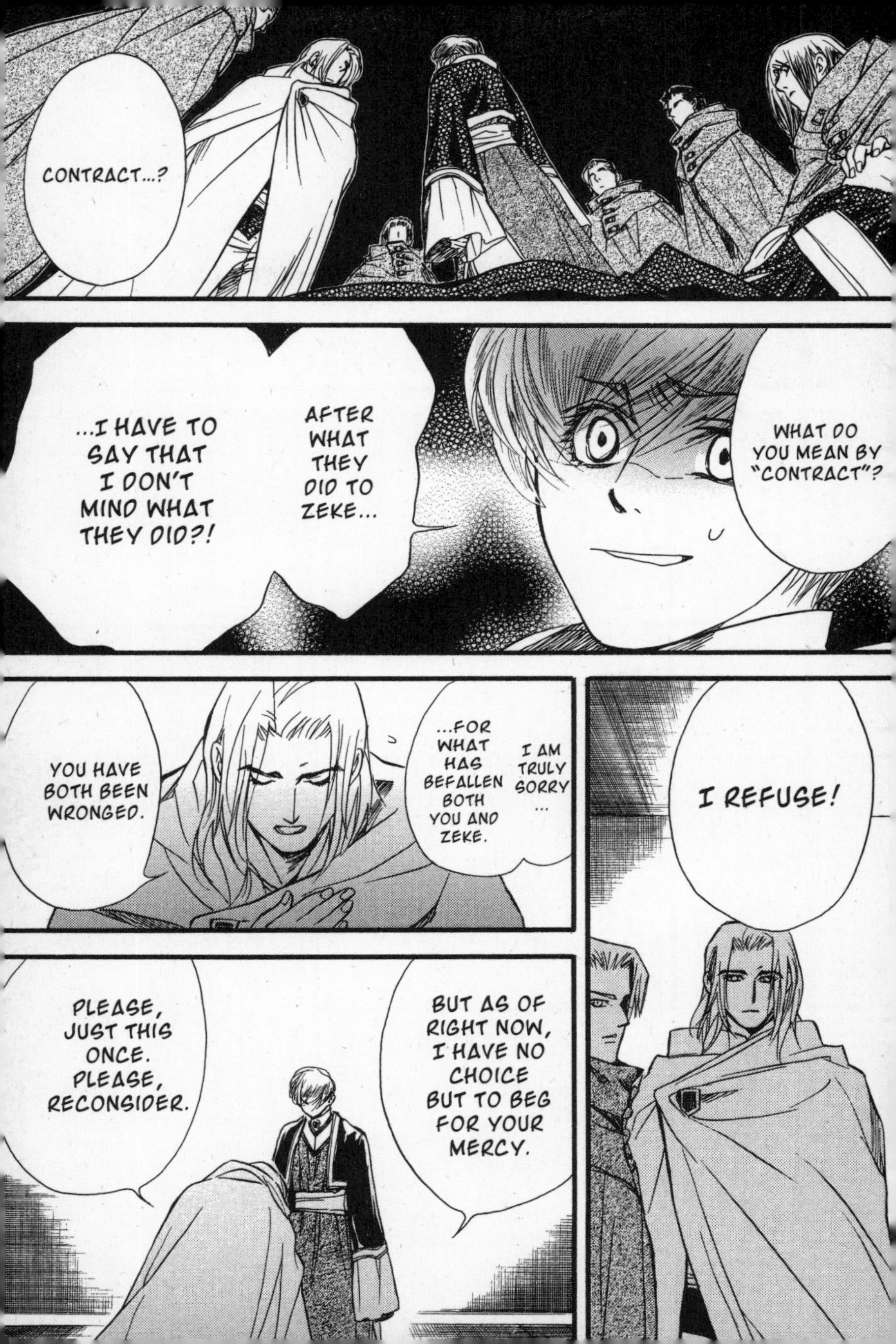

CONTRACT...?
WHAT DO YOU MEAN BY "CONTRACT"?
AFTER WHAT THEY DID TO ZEKE...
...I HAVE TO SAY THAT I DON'T MIND WHAT THEY DID?!
I REFUSE!
I AM TRULY SORRY...
...FOR WHAT HAS BEFALLEN BOTH YOU AND ZEKE.
YOU HAVE BOTH BEEN WRONGED.
BUT AS OF RIGHT NOW, I HAVE NO CHOICE BUT TO BEG FOR YOUR MERCY.
PLEASE, JUST THIS ONCE. PLEASE, RECONSIDER.

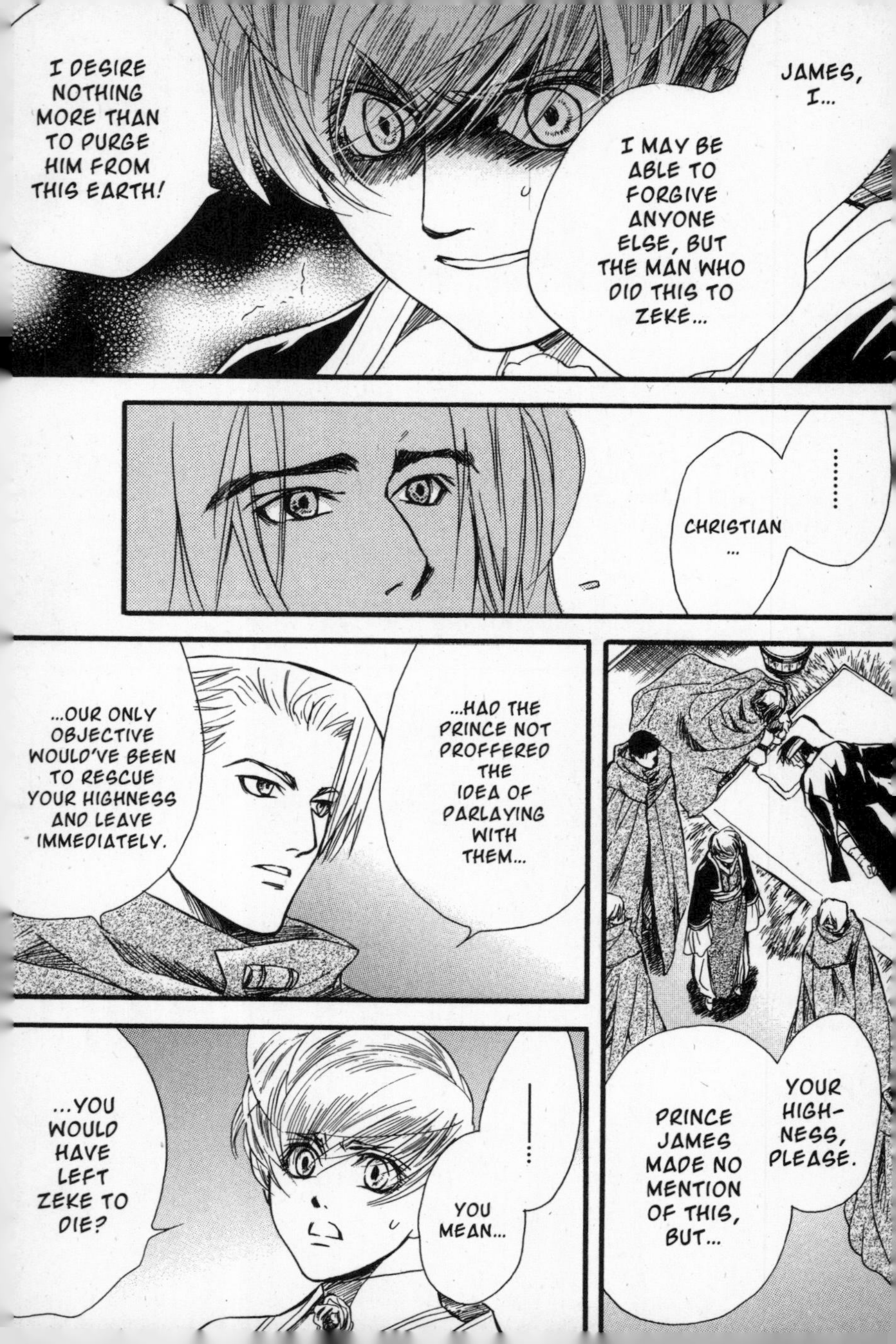
JAMES, I...
I MAY BE ABLE TO FORGIVE ANYONE ELSE, BUT THE MAN WHO DID THIS TO ZEKE...
I DESIRE NOTHING MORE THAN TO PURGE HIM FROM THIS EARTH!
......
CHRISTIAN ...
YOUR HIGH-NESS, PLEASE.
PRINCE JAMES MADE NO MENTION OF THIS, BUT...
...HAD THE PRINCE NOT PROFFERED THE IDEA OF PARLAYING WITH THEM...
...OUR ONLY OBJECTIVE WOULD'VE BEEN TO RESCUE YOUR HIGHNESS AND LEAVE IMMEDIATELY.
—......
YOU MEAN...
...YOU WOULD HAVE LEFT ZEKE TO DIE?

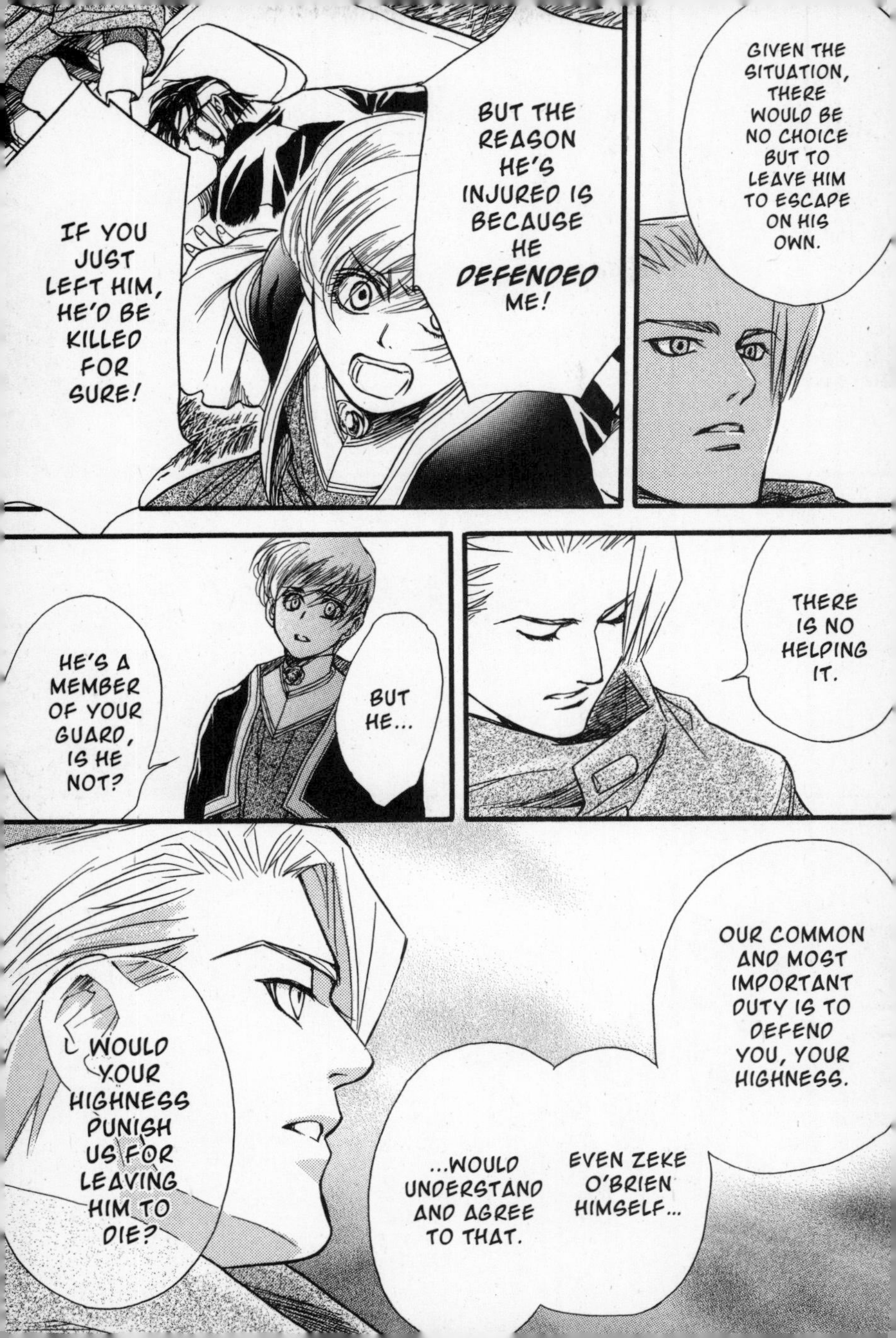
GIVEN THE SITUATION, THERE WOULD BE NO CHOICE BUT TO LEAVE HIM TO ESCAPE ON HIS OWN.
BUT THE REASON HE'S INJURED IS BECAUSE HE *DEFENDED* ME!
IF YOU JUST LEFT HIM, HE'D BE KILLED FOR SURE!
THERE IS NO HELPING IT.
BUT HE...
HE'S A MEMBER OF YOUR GUARD, IS HE NOT?
OUR COMMON AND MOST IMPORTANT DUTY IS TO DEFEND YOU, YOUR HIGHNESS.
EVEN ZEKE O'BRIEN HIMSELF...
...WOULD UNDERSTAND AND AGREE TO THAT.
WOULD YOUR HIGHNESS PUNISH US FOR LEAVING HIM TO DIE?

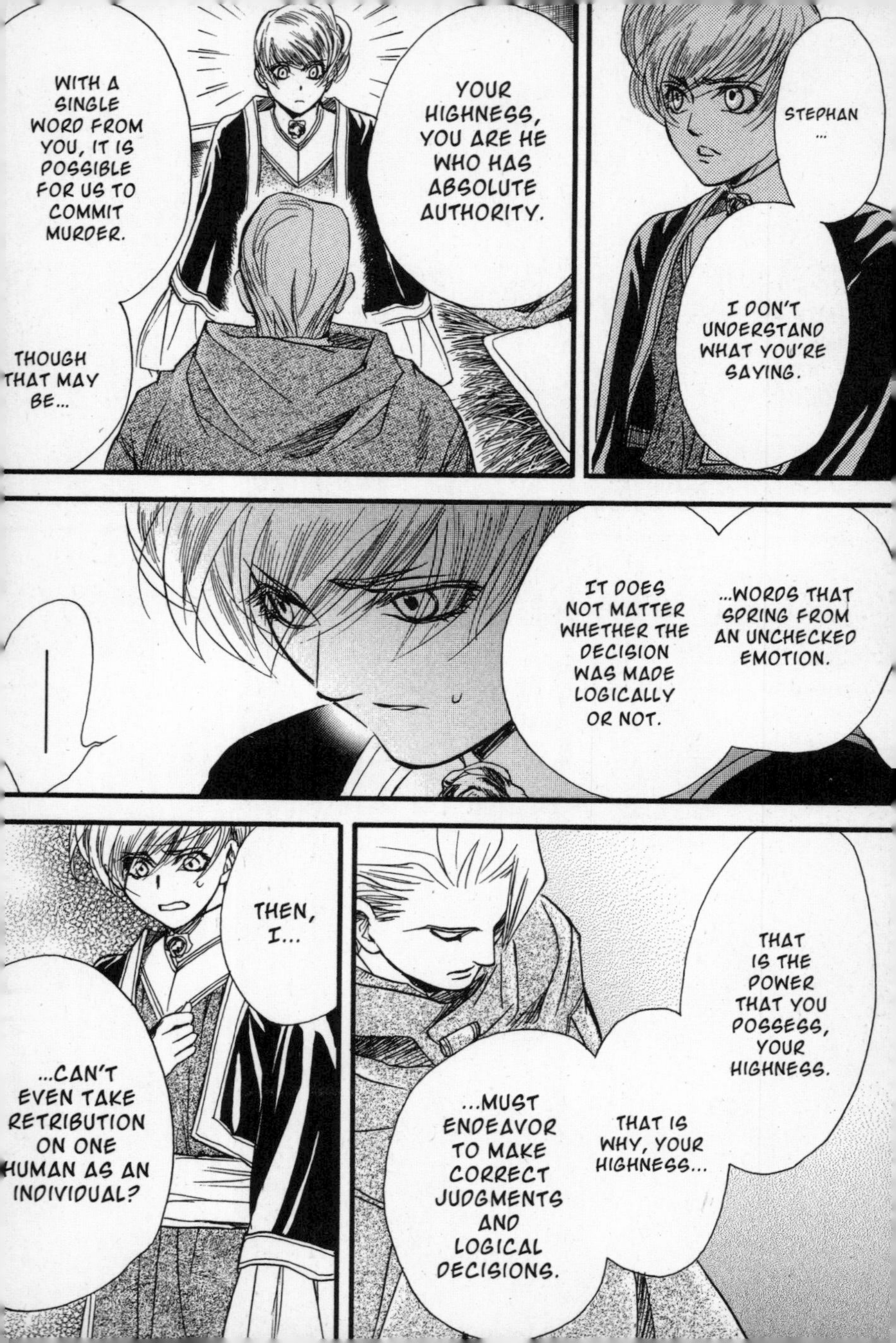
STEPHAN ...
I DON'T UNDERSTAND WHAT YOU'RE SAYING.
YOUR HIGHNESS, YOU ARE HE WHO HAS ABSOLUTE AUTHORITY.
WITH A SINGLE WORD FROM YOU, IT IS POSSIBLE FOR US TO COMMIT MURDER.
THOUGH THAT MAY BE...
...WORDS THAT SPRING FROM AN UNCHECKED EMOTION.
IT DOES NOT MATTER WHETHER THE DECISION WAS MADE LOGICALLY OR NOT.
THAT IS THE POWER THAT YOU POSSESS, YOUR HIGHNESS.
THAT IS WHY, YOUR HIGHNESS...
...MUST ENDEAVOR TO MAKE CORRECT JUDGMENTS AND LOGICAL DECISIONS.
THEN, I...
...CAN'T EVEN TAKE RETRIBUTION ON ONE HUMAN AS AN INDIVIDUAL?

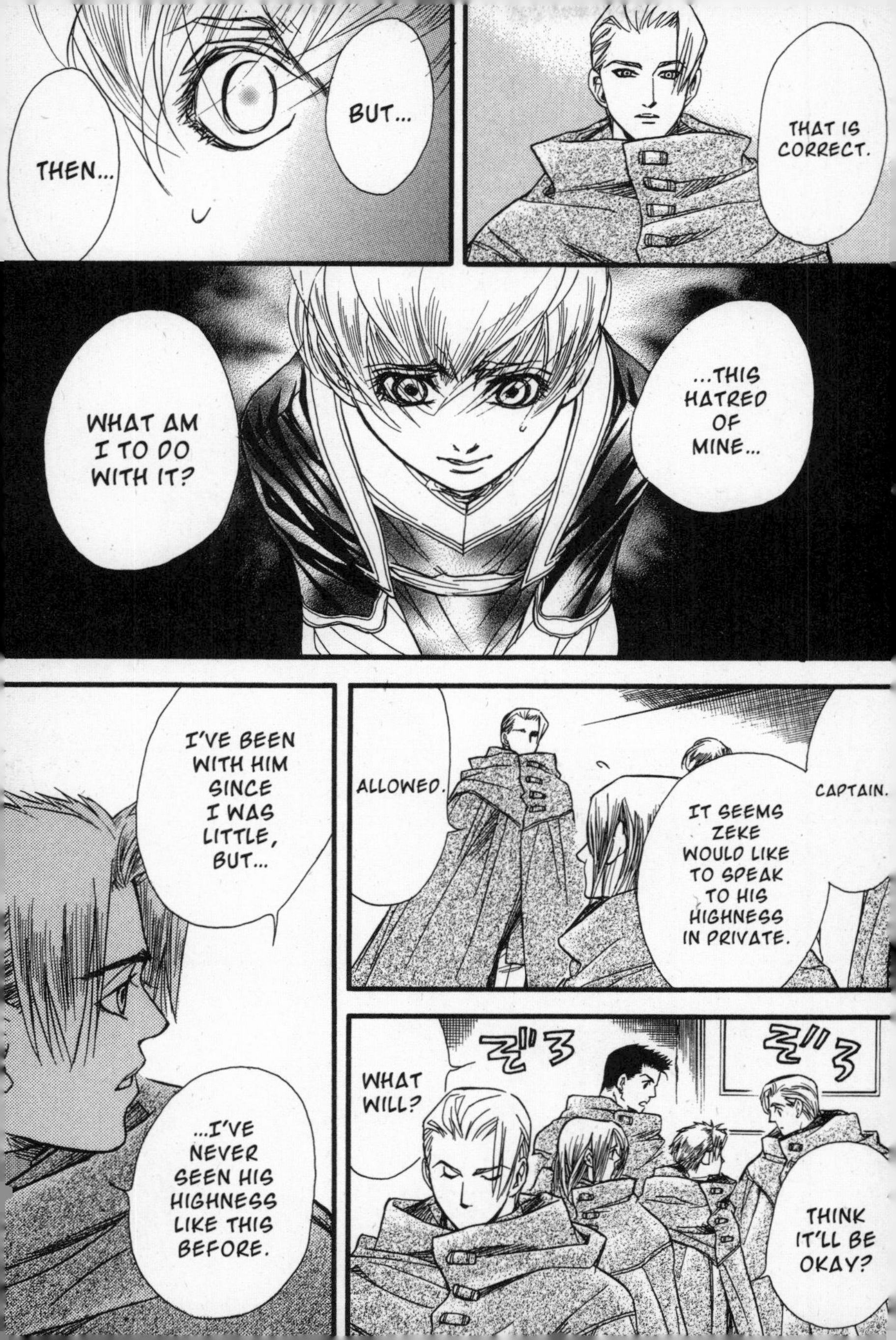
THAT IS CORRECT.
BUT...
THEN...
...THIS HATRED OF MINE...
WHAT AM I TO DO WITH IT?
CAPTAIN.
IT SEEMS ZEKE WOULD LIKE TO SPEAK TO HIS HIGHNESS IN PRIVATE.
ALLOWED.
THINK IT'LL BE OKAY?
WHAT WILL?
I'VE BEEN WITH HIM SINCE I WAS LITTLE, BUT...
...I'VE NEVER SEEN HIS HIGHNESS LIKE THIS BEFORE.

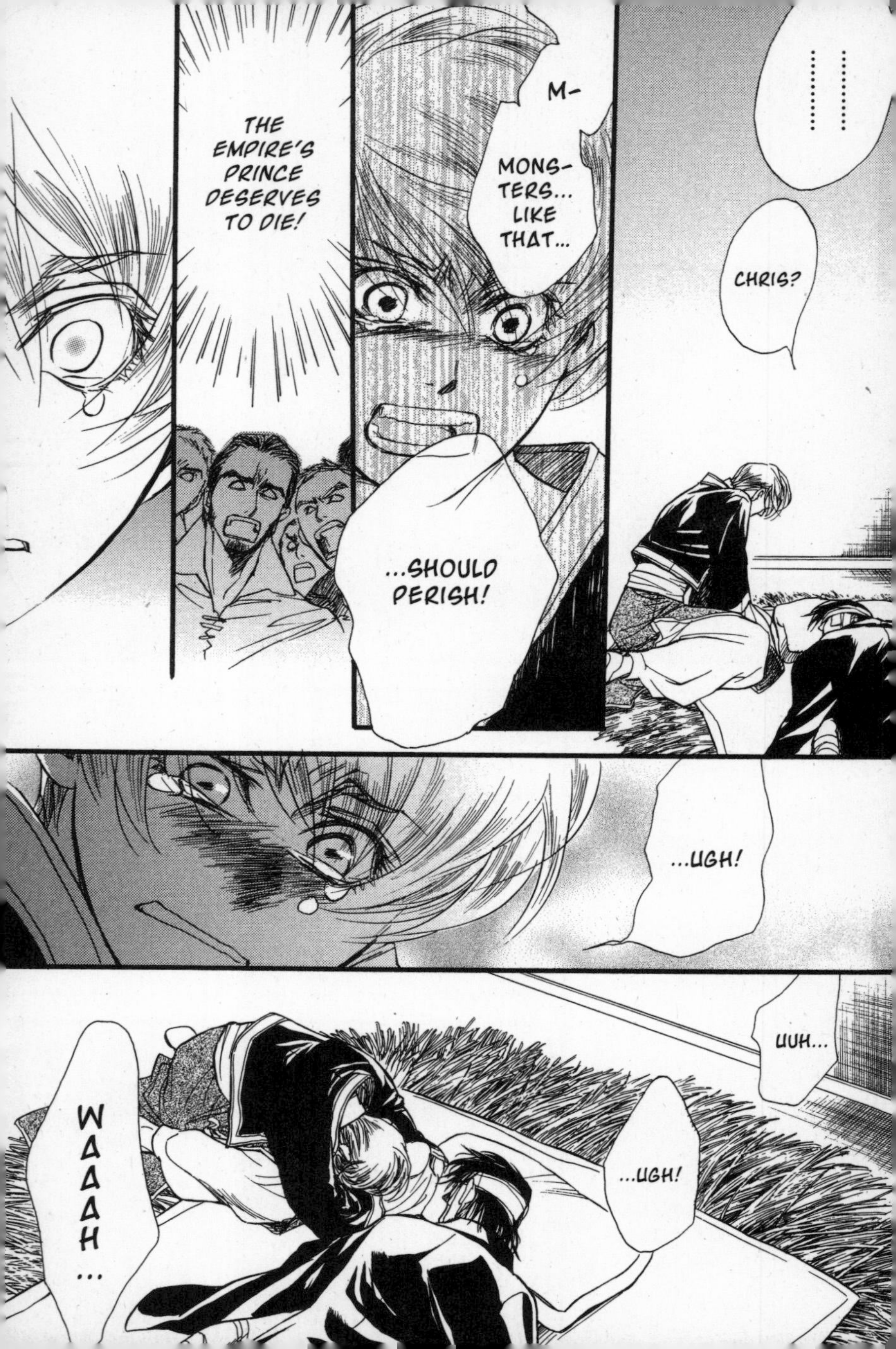
……
CHRIS?
M-
MONSTERS... LIKE THAT...
...SHOULD PERISH!
THE EMPIRE'S PRINCE DESERVES TO DIE!
...UGH!
UUH...
...UGH!
WAAAAH...

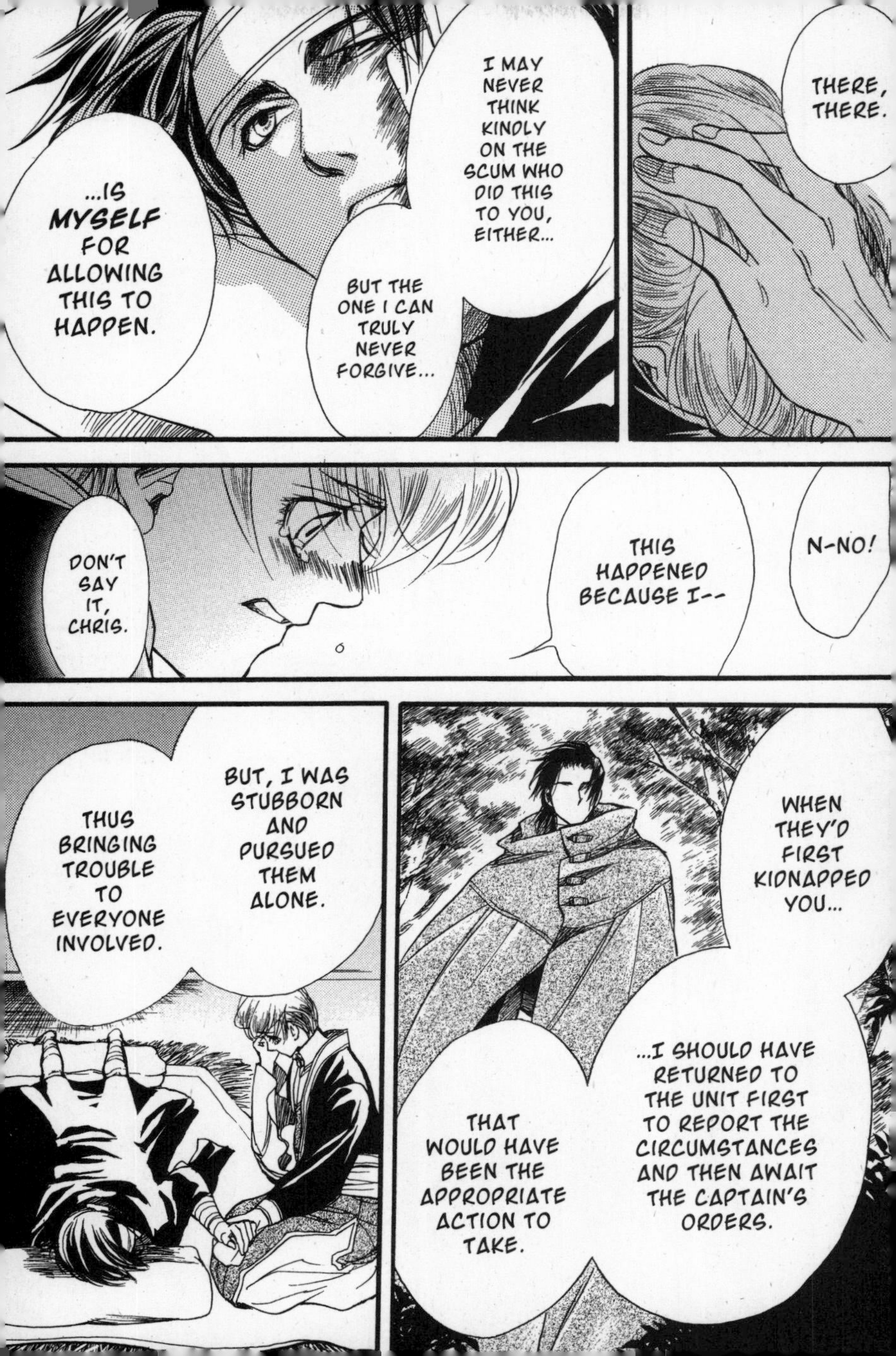
THERE, THERE.
I MAY NEVER THINK KINDLY ON THE SCUM WHO DID THIS TO YOU, EITHER...
BUT THE ONE I CAN TRULY NEVER FORGIVE...
...IS **MYSELF** FOR ALLOWING THIS TO HAPPEN.
N-NO!
THIS HAPPENED BECAUSE I--
DON'T SAY IT, CHRIS.
WHEN THEY'D FIRST KIDNAPPED YOU...
...I SHOULD HAVE RETURNED TO THE UNIT FIRST TO REPORT THE CIRCUMSTANCES AND THEN AWAIT THE CAPTAIN'S ORDERS.
THAT WOULD HAVE BEEN THE APPROPRIATE ACTION TO TAKE.
BUT, I WAS STUBBORN AND PURSUED THEM ALONE.
THUS BRINGING TROUBLE TO EVERYONE INVOLVED.

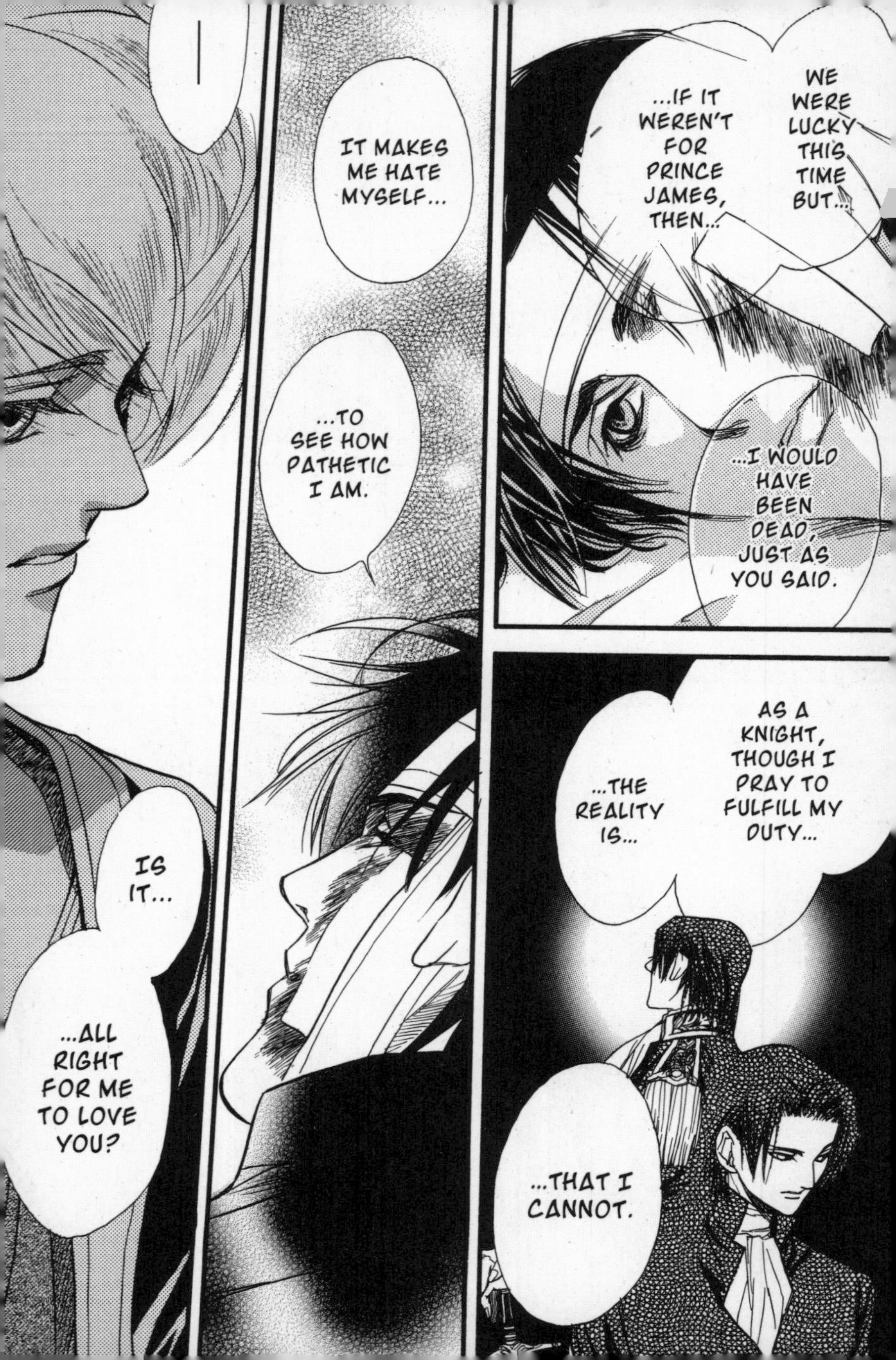
WE WERE LUCKY THIS TIME BUT...
...IF IT WEREN'T FOR PRINCE JAMES, THEN...
...I WOULD HAVE BEEN DEAD, JUST AS YOU SAID.
AS A KNIGHT, THOUGH I PRAY TO FULFILL MY DUTY...
...THE REALITY IS...
...THAT I CANNOT.
IT MAKES ME HATE MYSELF...
...TO SEE HOW PATHETIC I AM.
IS IT...
...ALL RIGHT FOR ME TO LOVE YOU?

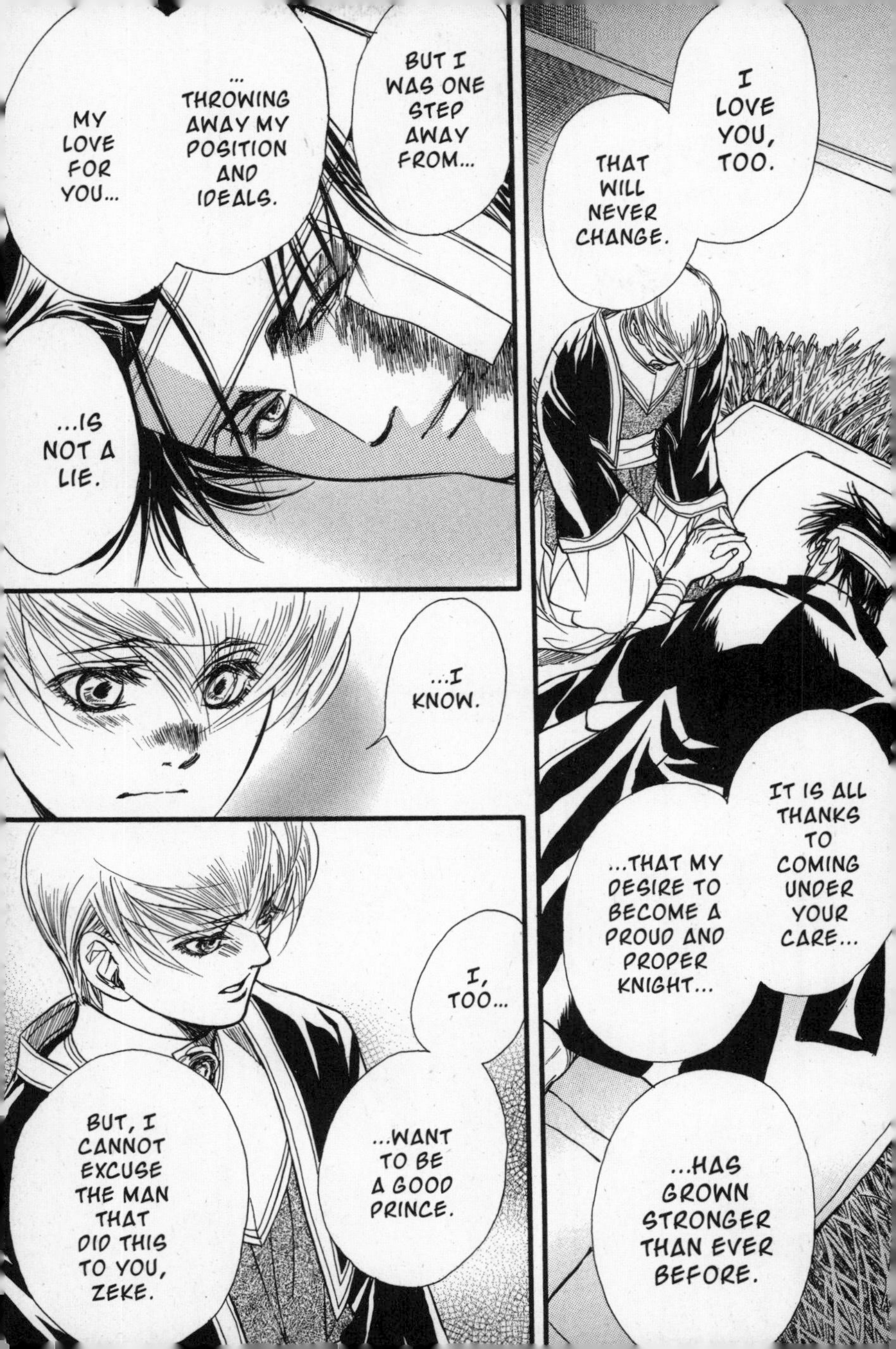
I LOVE YOU, TOO.
THAT WILL NEVER CHANGE.
IT IS ALL THANKS TO COMING UNDER YOUR CARE...
...THAT MY DESIRE TO BECOME A PROUD AND PROPER KNIGHT...
...HAS GROWN STRONGER THAN EVER BEFORE.
BUT I WAS ONE STEP AWAY FROM...
...THROWING AWAY MY POSITION AND IDEALS.
MY LOVE FOR YOU...
...IS NOT A LIE.
...I KNOW.
I, TOO...
...WANT TO BE A GOOD PRINCE.
BUT, I CANNOT EXCUSE THE MAN THAT DID THIS TO YOU, ZEKE.

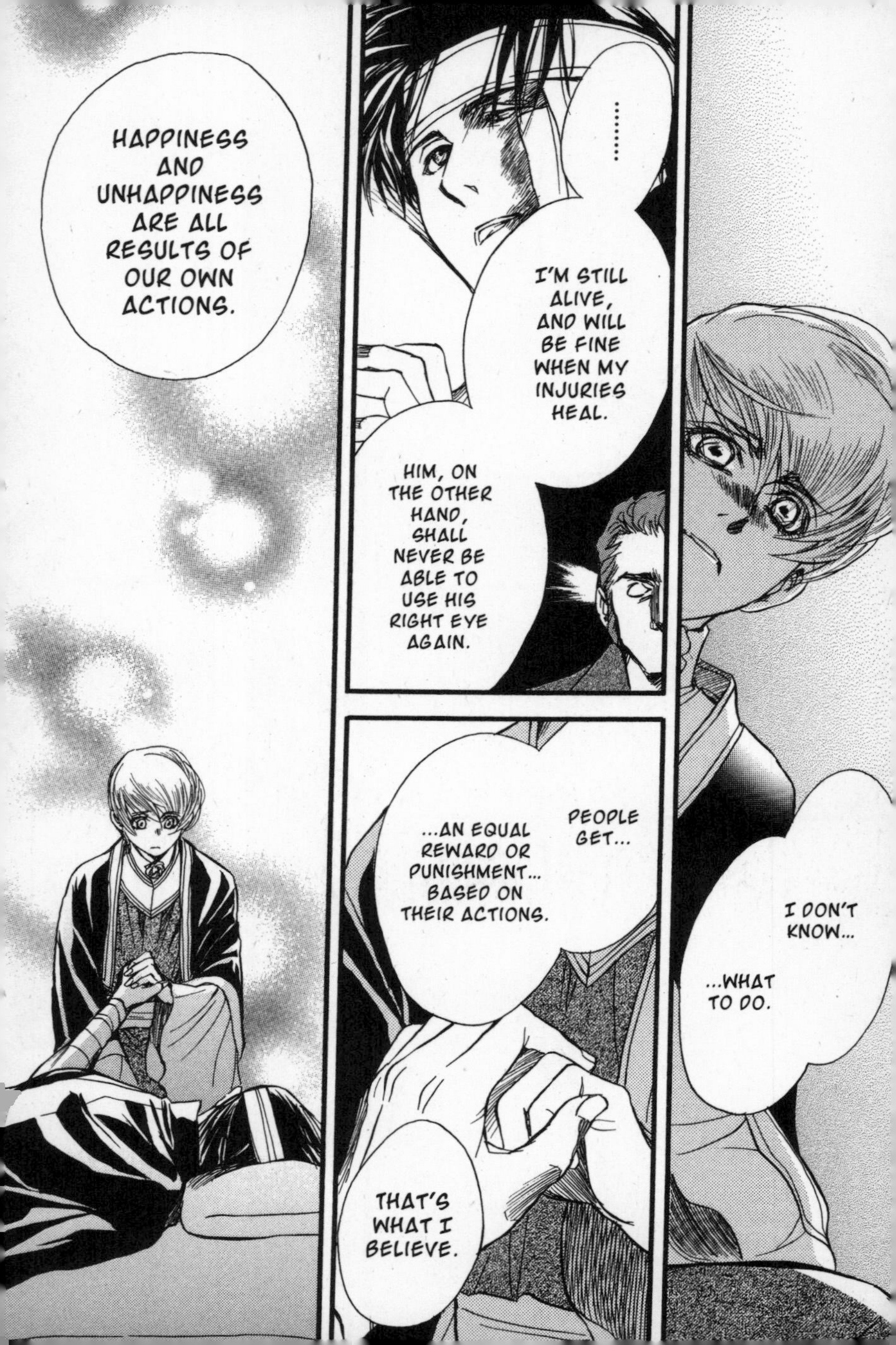
……
I'M STILL ALIVE, AND WILL BE FINE WHEN MY INJURIES HEAL.
HIM, ON THE OTHER HAND, SHALL NEVER BE ABLE TO USE HIS RIGHT EYE AGAIN.
I DON'T KNOW...
...WHAT TO DO.
PEOPLE GET...
...AN EQUAL REWARD OR PUNISHMENT... BASED ON THEIR ACTIONS.
THAT'S WHAT I BELIEVE.
HAPPINESS AND UNHAPPINESS ARE ALL RESULTS OF OUR OWN ACTIONS.

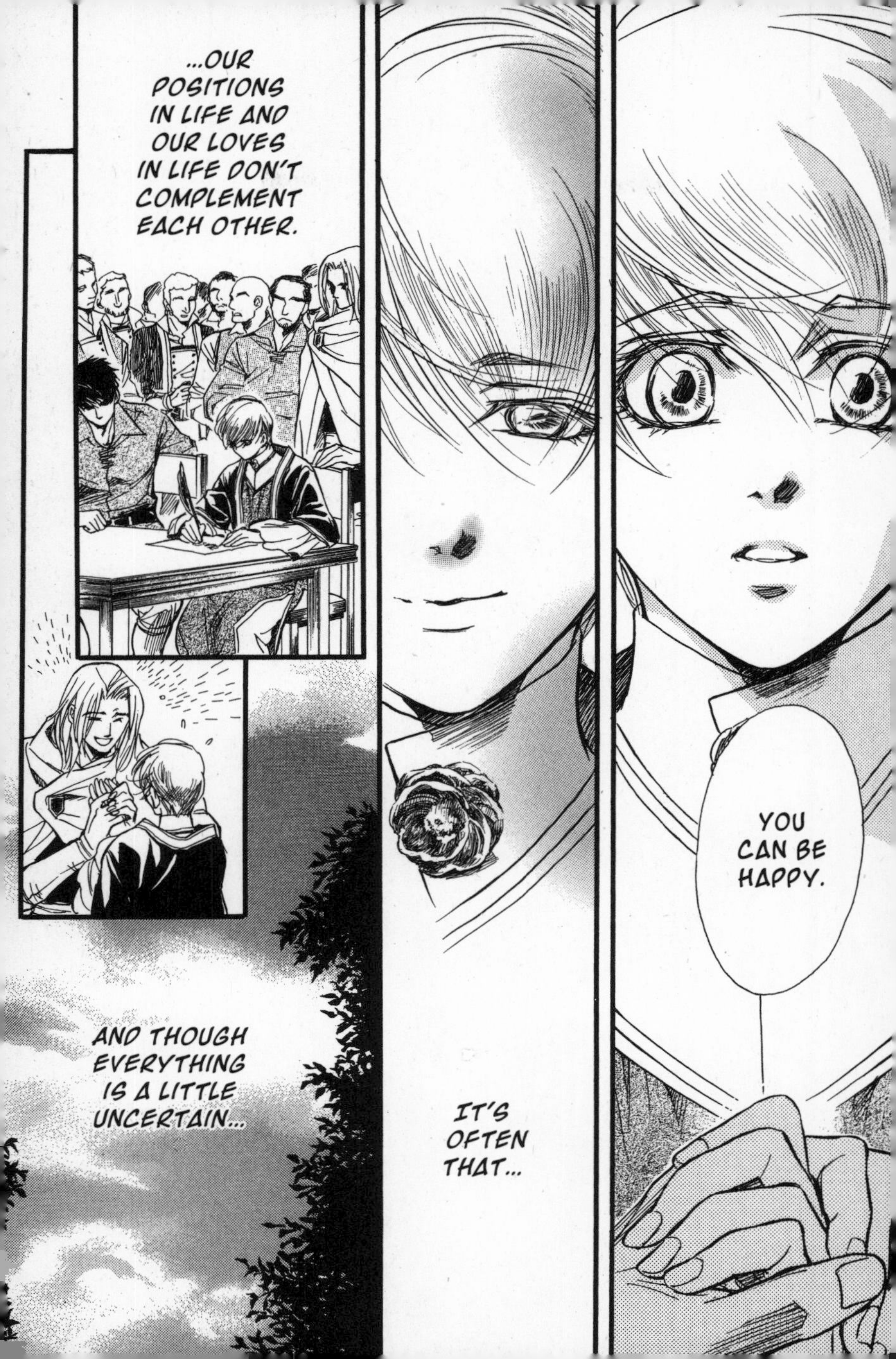
YOU CAN BE HAPPY.
IT'S OFTEN THAT...
...OUR POSITIONS IN LIFE AND OUR LOVES IN LIFE DON'T COMPLEMENT EACH OTHER.
AND THOUGH EVERYTHING IS A LITTLE UNCERTAIN...

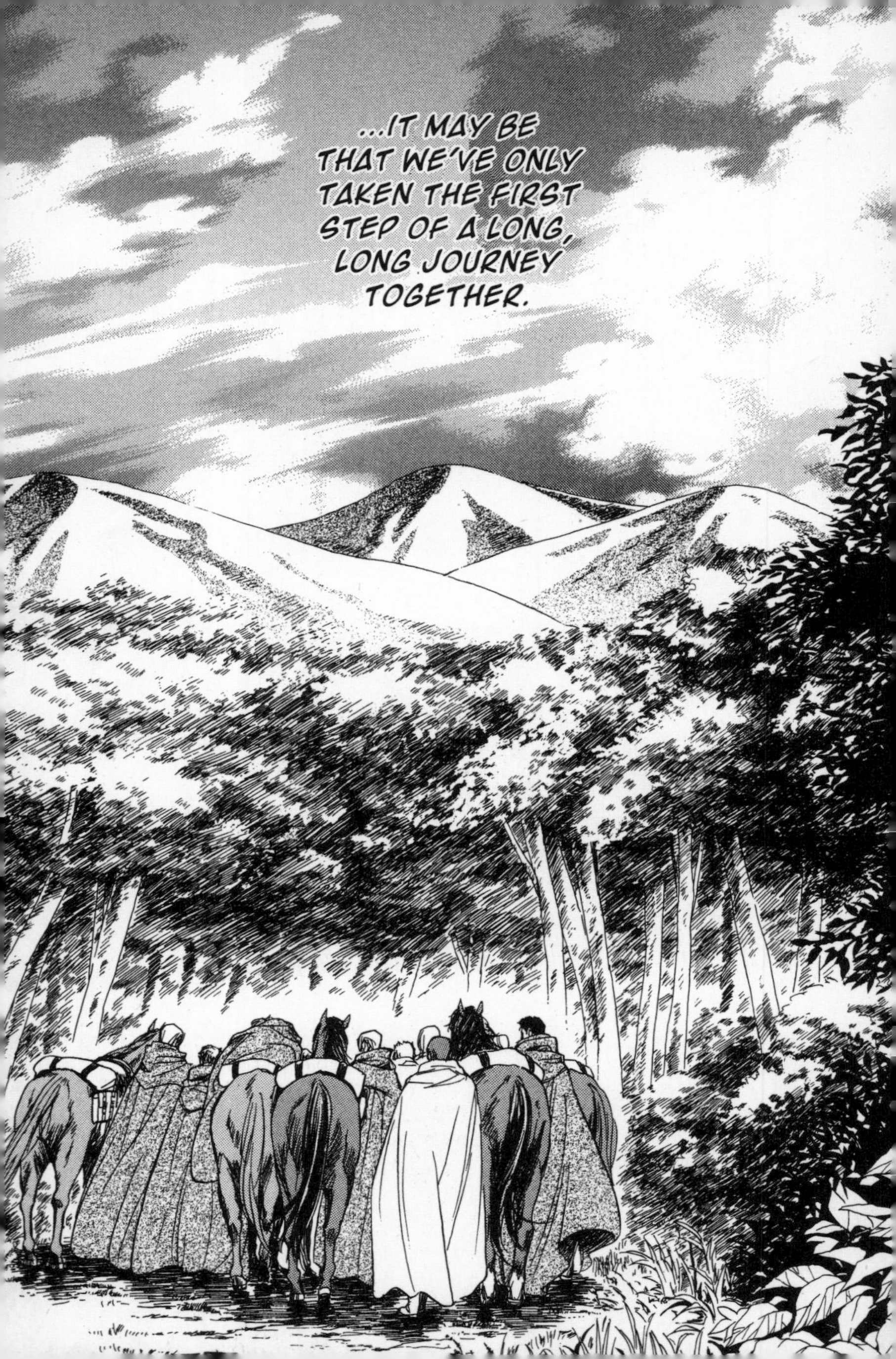
...IT MAY BE THAT WE'VE ONLY TAKEN THE FIRST STEP OF A LONG, LONG JOURNEY TOGETHER.

THE JOURNEY BEGINS / END

THE
BLACK
KNIGHT

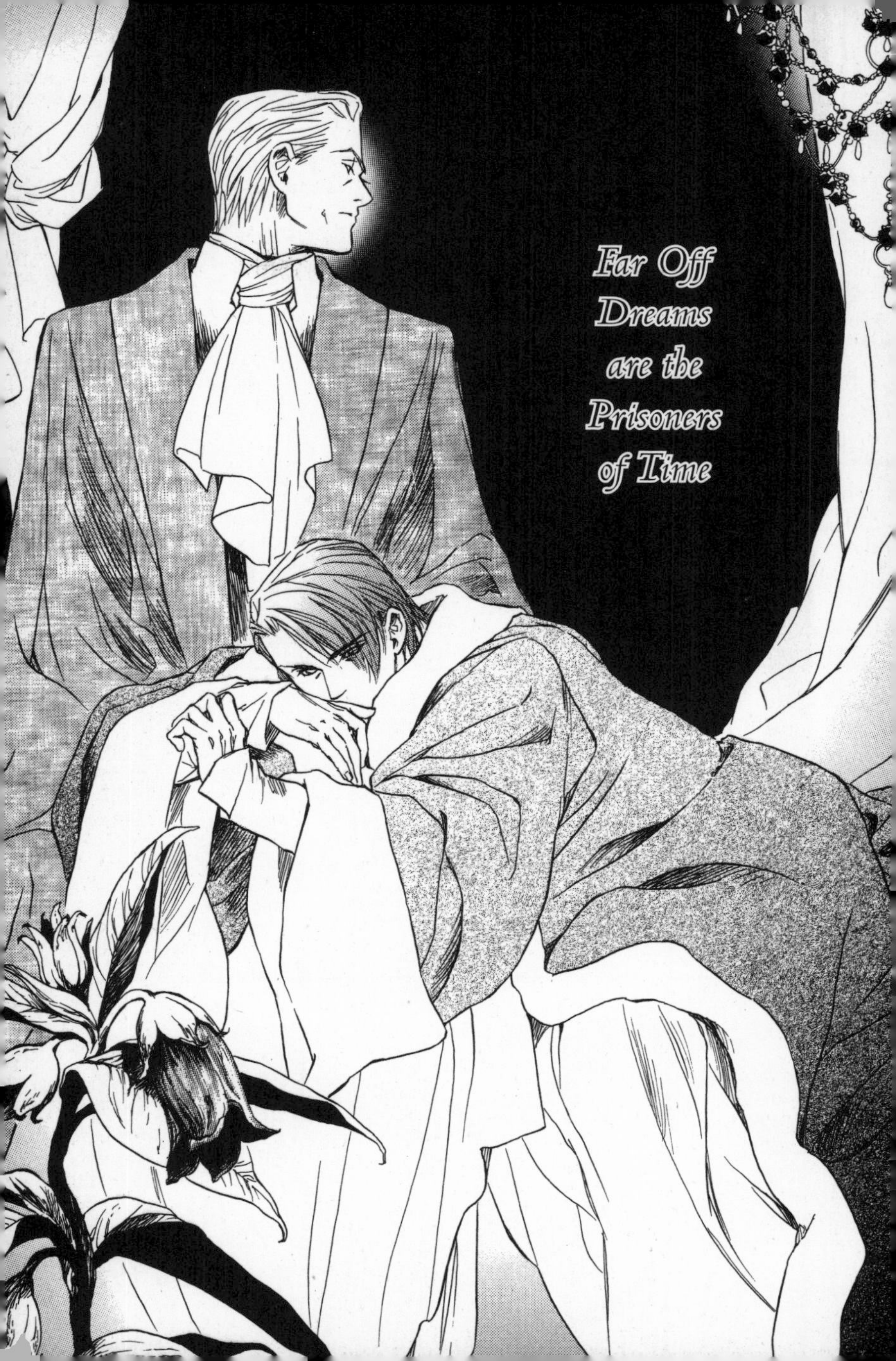
Far Off Dreams are the Prisoners of Time

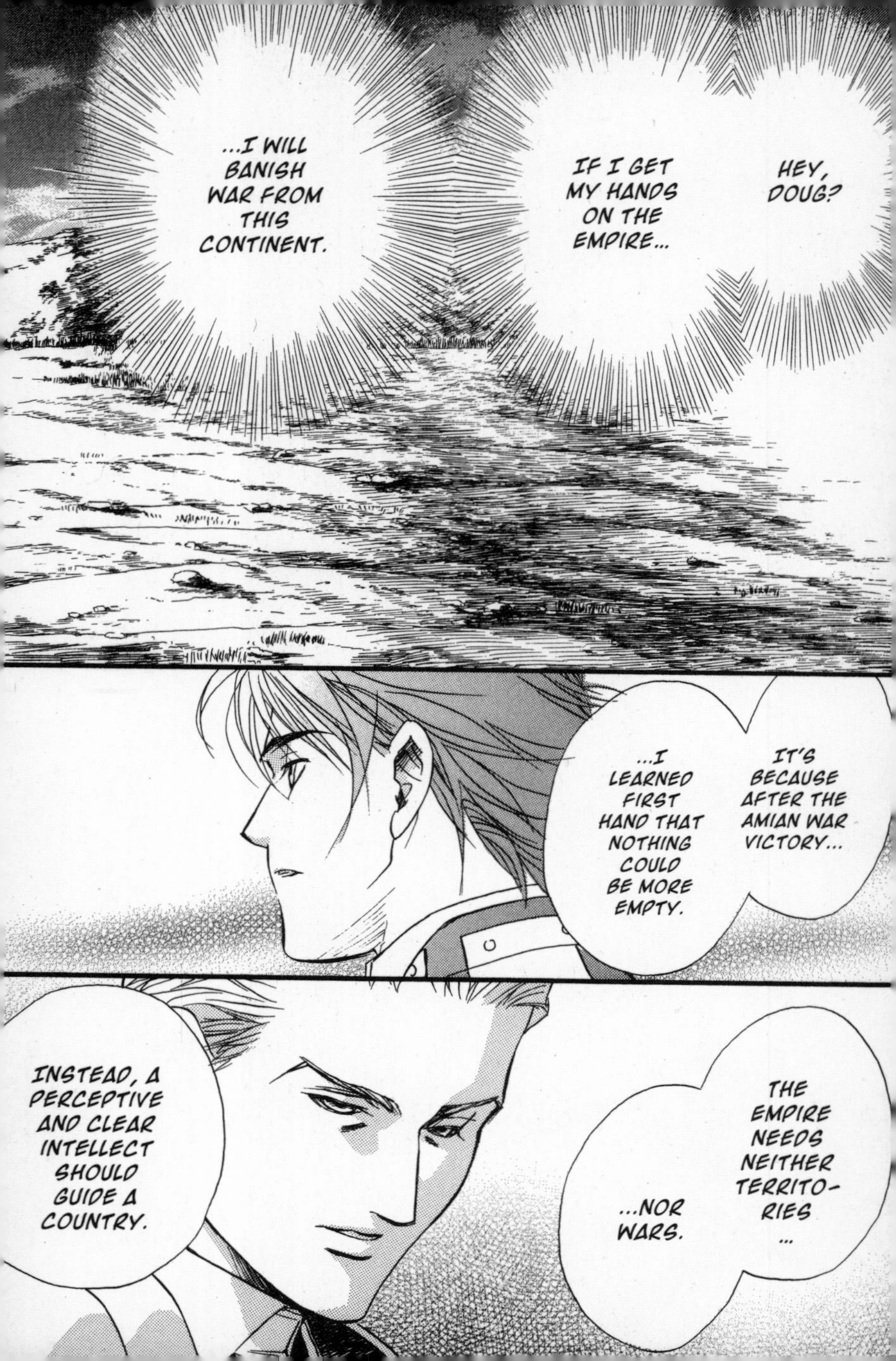
HEY, DOUG?
IF I GET MY HANDS ON THE EMPIRE...
...I WILL BANISH WAR FROM THIS CONTINENT.
IT'S BECAUSE AFTER THE AMIAN WAR VICTORY...
...I LEARNED FIRST HAND THAT NOTHING COULD BE MORE EMPTY.
THE EMPIRE NEEDS NEITHER TERRITO-RIES ...
...NOR WARS.
INSTEAD, A PERCEPTIVE AND CLEAR INTELLECT SHOULD GUIDE A COUNTRY.

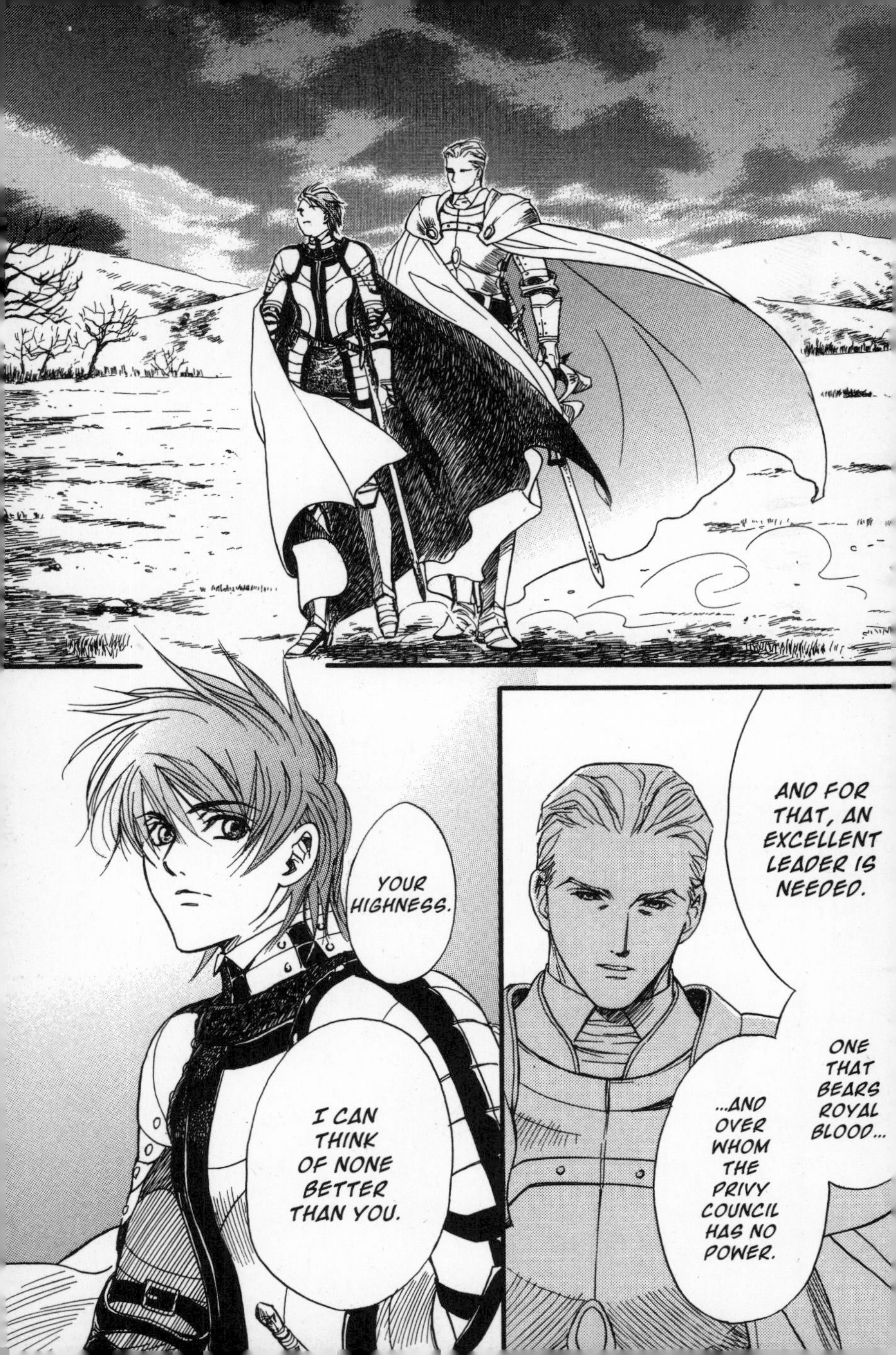
AND FOR THAT, AN EXCELLENT LEADER IS NEEDED.
ONE THAT BEARS ROYAL BLOOD...
...AND OVER WHOM THE PRIVY COUNCIL HAS NO POWER.
YOUR HIGHNESS.
I CAN THINK OF NONE BETTER THAN YOU.

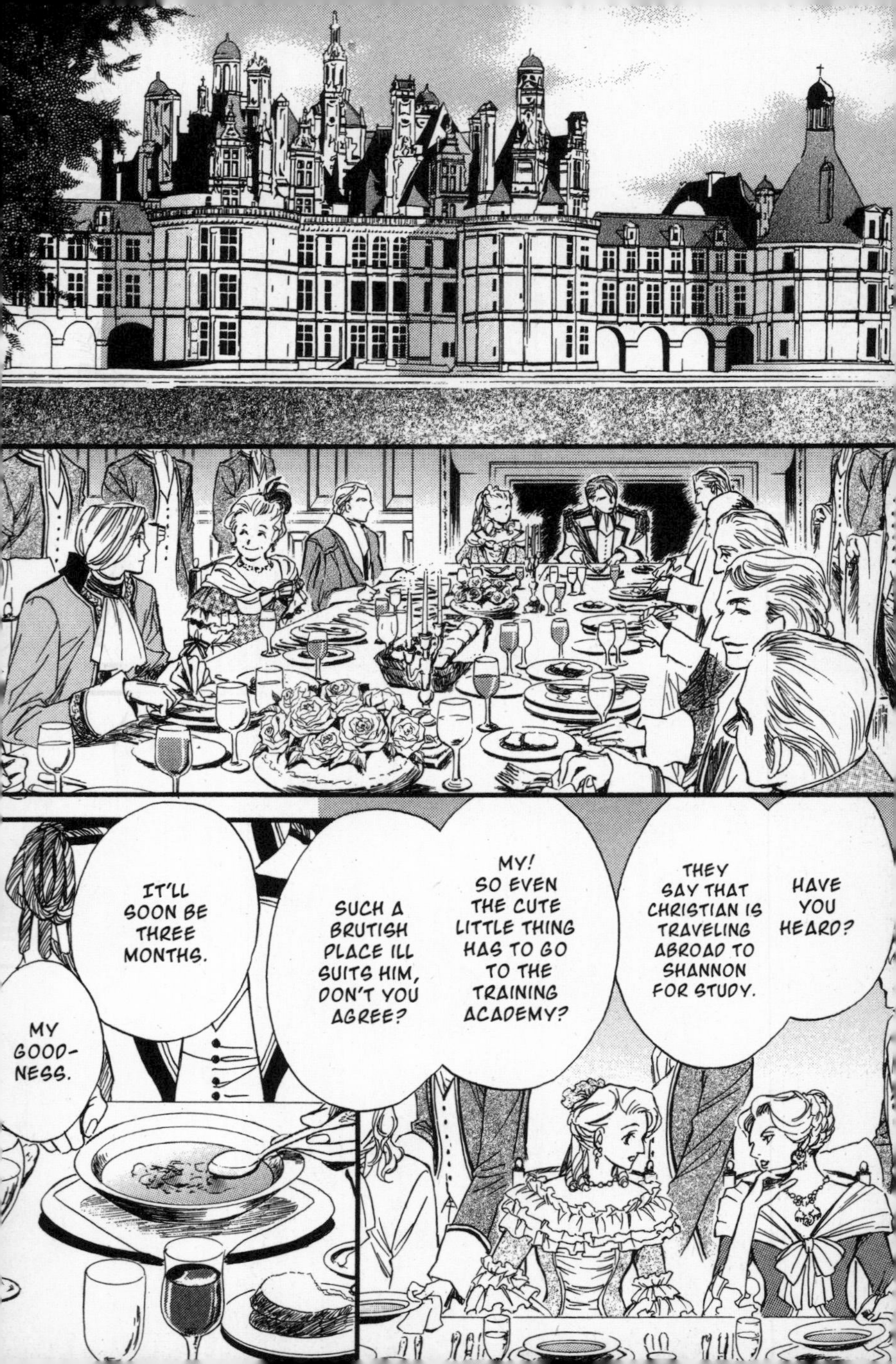
HAVE YOU HEARD?
THEY SAY THAT CHRISTIAN IS TRAVELING ABROAD TO SHANNON FOR STUDY.
MY! SO EVEN THE CUTE LITTLE THING HAS TO GO TO THE TRAINING ACADEMY?
SUCH A BRUTISH PLACE ILL SUITS HIM, DON'T YOU AGREE?
IT'LL SOON BE THREE MONTHS.
MY GOODNESS.

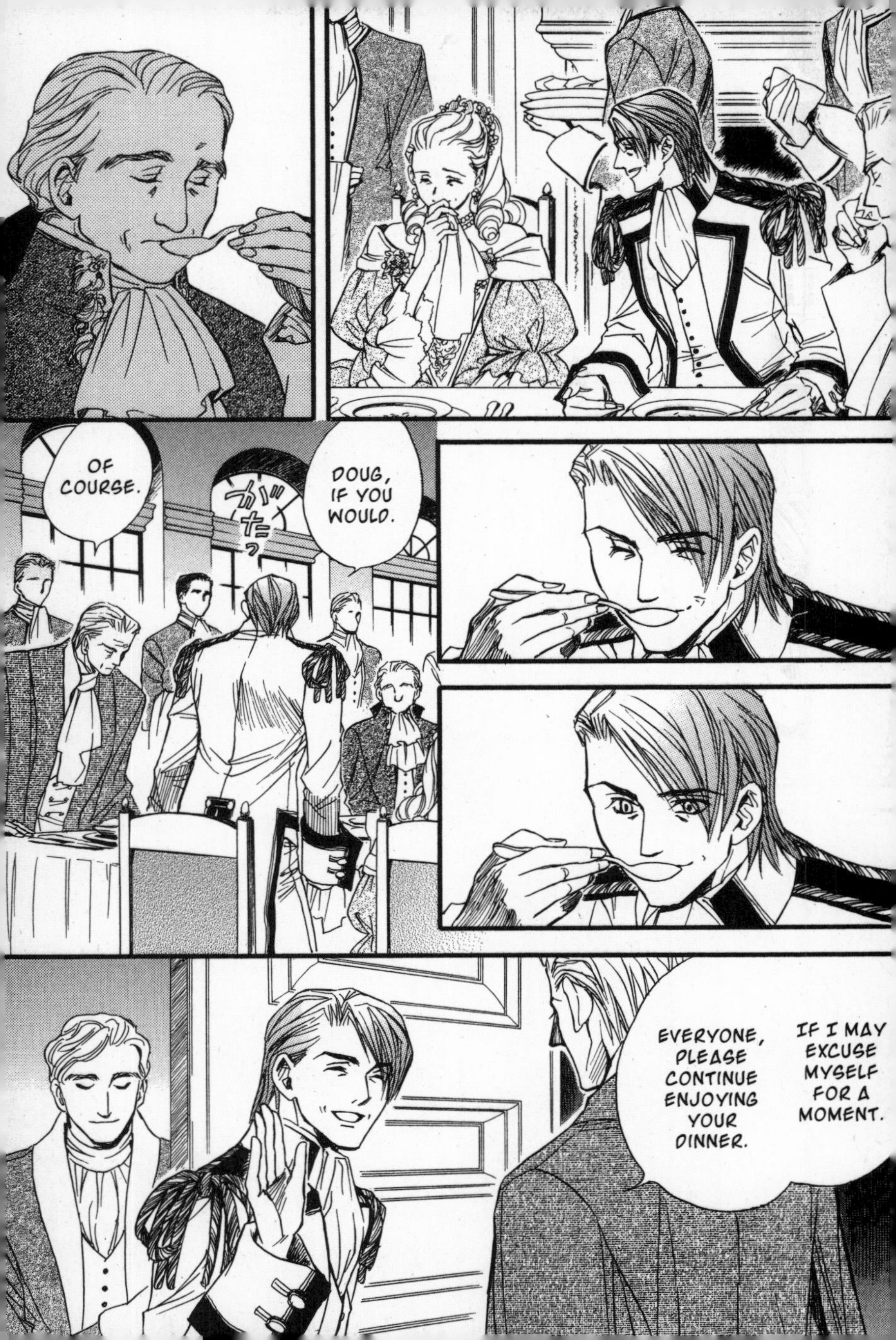
DOUG, IF YOU WOULD.
ガタッ
OF COURSE.
IF I MAY EXCUSE MYSELF FOR A MOMENT.
EVERYONE, PLEASE CONTINUE ENJOYING YOUR DINNER.

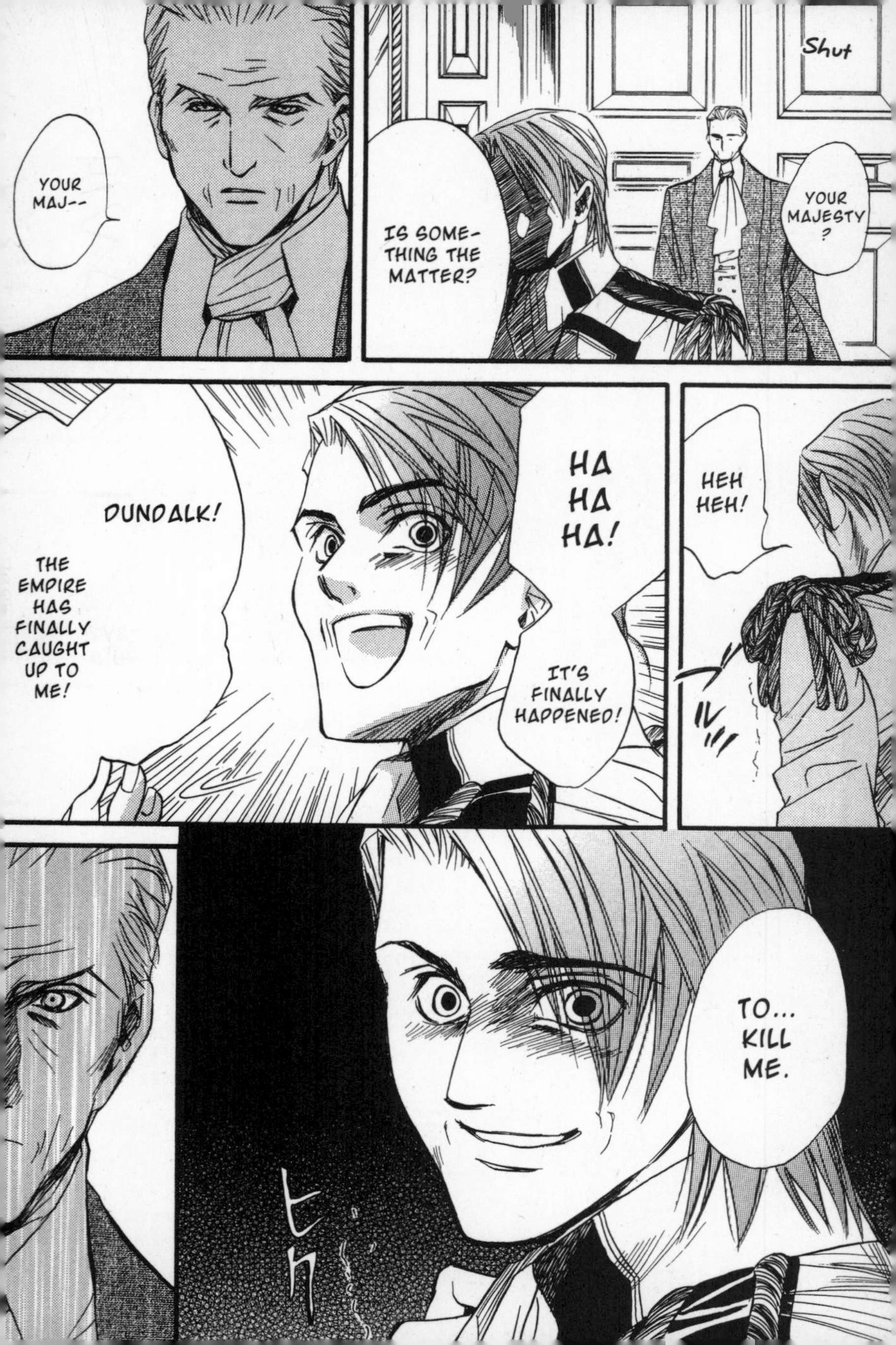
Shut
YOUR MAJESTY ?
IS SOME-THING THE MATTER?
YOUR MAJ--
HEH HEH!
HA HA HA!
IT'S FINALLY HAPPENED!
DUNDALK!
THE EMPIRE HAS FINALLY CAUGHT UP TO ME!
TO... KILL ME.
ヒク

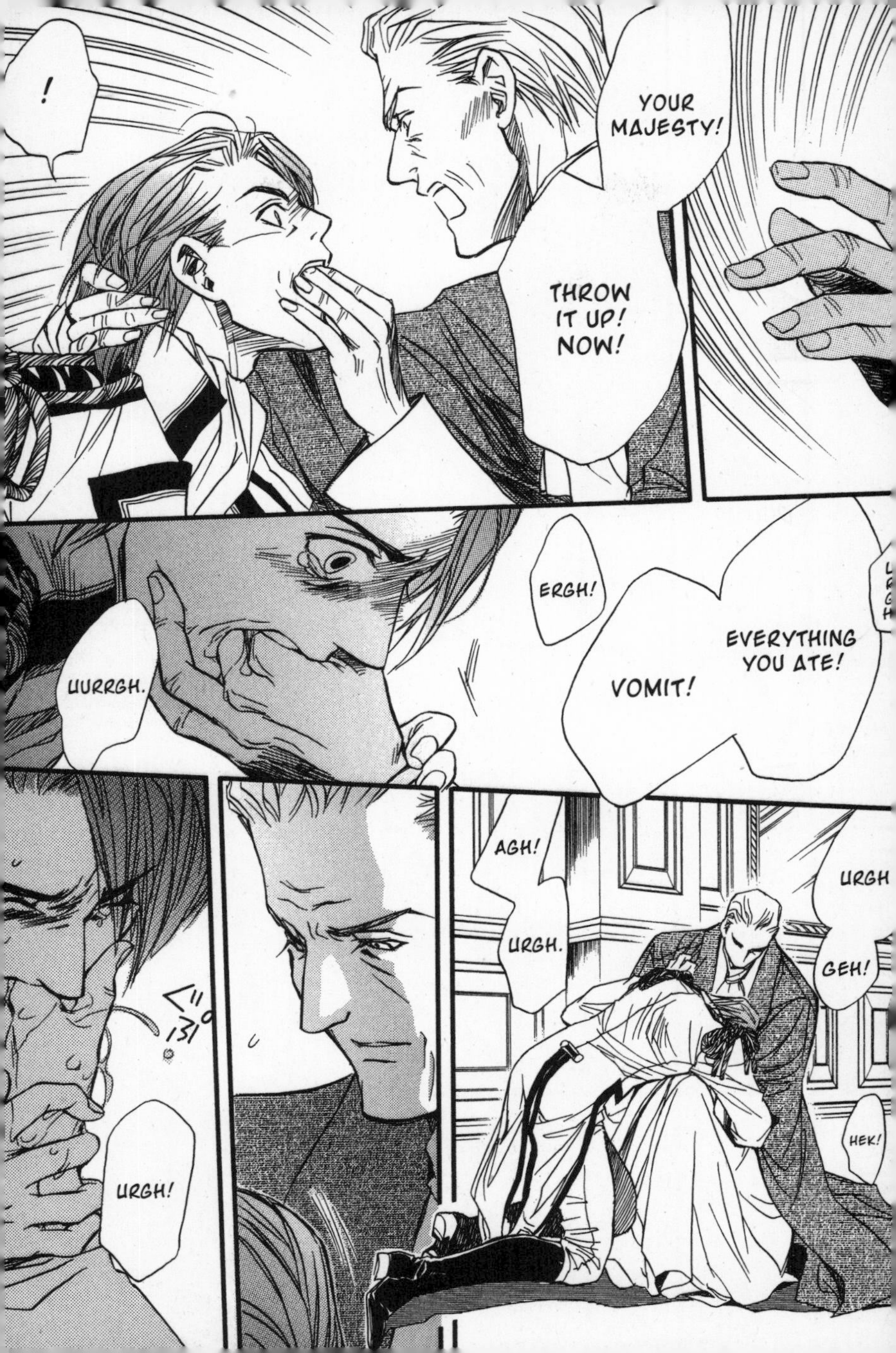
YOUR MAJESTY!
THROW IT UP! NOW!
!
VOMIT!
EVERYTHING YOU ATE!
ERGH!
UURRGH.
URGH
GEH!
HEK!
AGH!
URGH.
URGH!

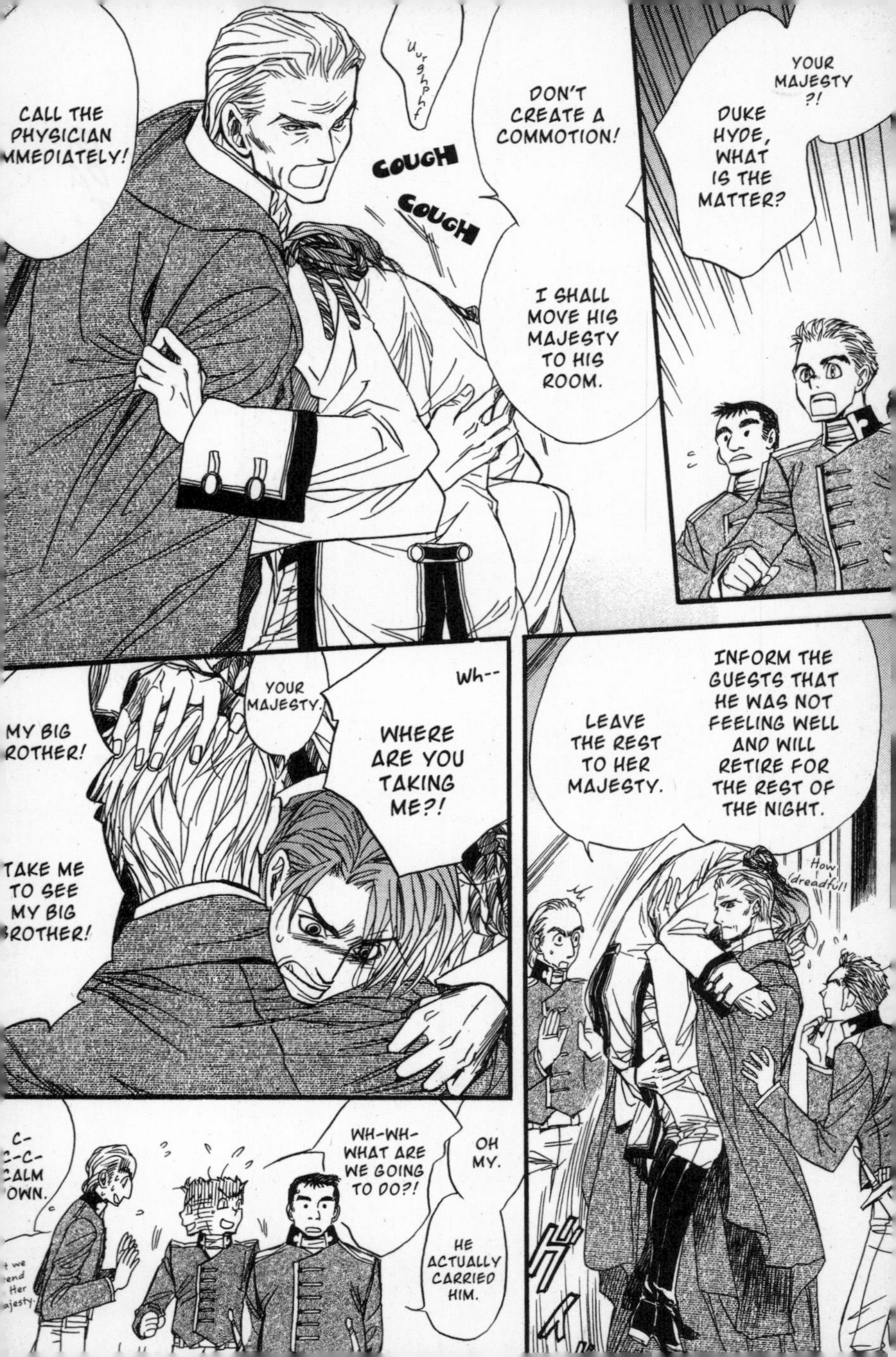
YOUR MAJESTY ?!
DUKE HYDE, WHAT IS THE MATTER?
DON'T CREATE A COMMOTION!
I SHALL MOVE HIS MAJESTY TO HIS ROOM.
Uurghphf
COUGH
COUGH
CALL THE PHYSICIAN MMEDIATELY!
INFORM THE GUESTS THAT HE WAS NOT FEELING WELL AND WILL RETIRE FOR THE REST OF THE NIGHT.
LEAVE THE REST TO HER MAJESTY.
How dreadful!
Wh--
WHERE ARE YOU TAKING ME?!
YOUR MAJESTY.
MY BIG ROTHER!
TAKE ME TO SEE MY BIG ROTHER!
OH MY.
HE ACTUALLY CARRIED HIM.
WH-WH-WHAT ARE WE GOING TO DO?!
C- C-C- ALM OWN.
t we tend Her ajesty.

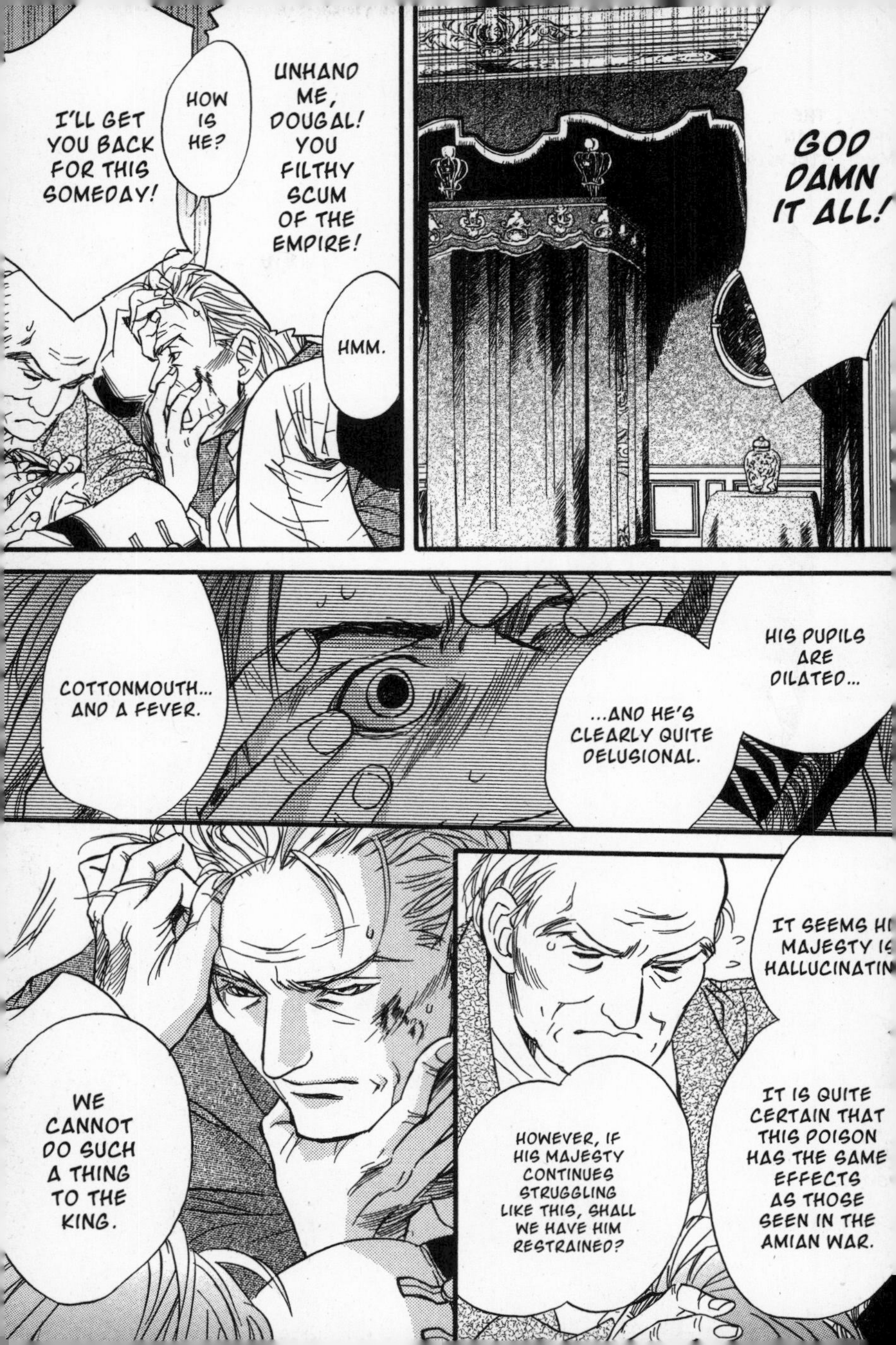
GOD DAMN IT ALL!
UNHAND ME, DOUGAL! YOU FILTHY SCUM OF THE EMPIRE!
HOW IS HE?
I'LL GET YOU BACK FOR THIS SOMEDAY!
HMM.
HIS PUPILS ARE DILATED...
...AND HE'S CLEARLY QUITE DELUSIONAL.
COTTONMOUTH... AND A FEVER.
IT SEEMS HI MAJESTY IS HALLUCINATIN
IT IS QUITE CERTAIN THAT THIS POISON HAS THE SAME EFFECTS AS THOSE SEEN IN THE AMIAN WAR.
HOWEVER, IF HIS MAJESTY CONTINUES STRUGGLING LIKE THIS, SHALL WE HAVE HIM RESTRAINED?
WE CANNOT DO SUCH A THING TO THE KING.

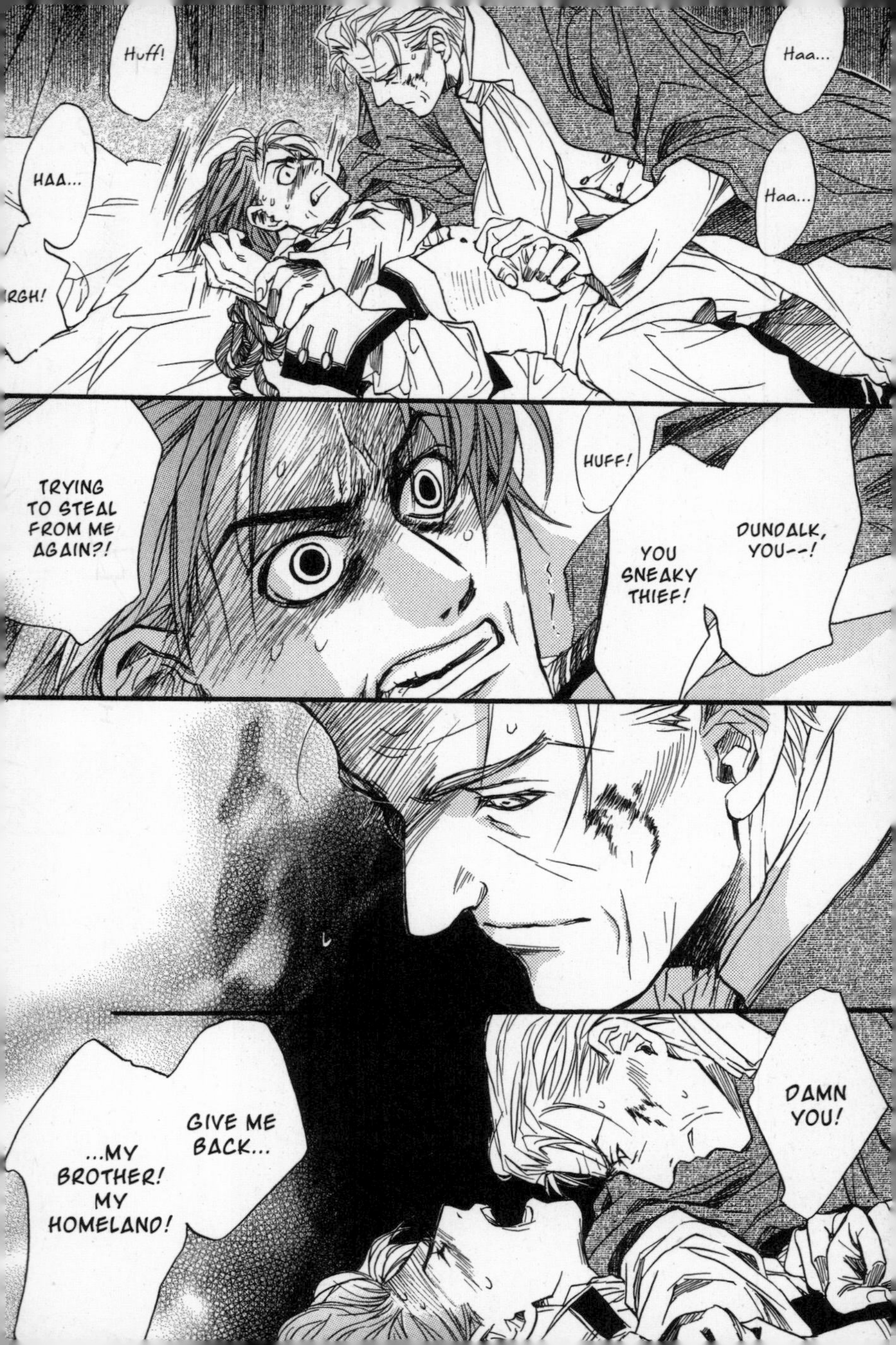
Haa...
Haa...
Huff!
HAA...
RGH!
HUFF!
DUNDALK, YOU--!
YOU SNEAKY THIEF!
TRYING TO STEAL FROM ME AGAIN?!
DAMN YOU!
GIVE ME BACK...
...MY BROTHER! MY HOMELAND!

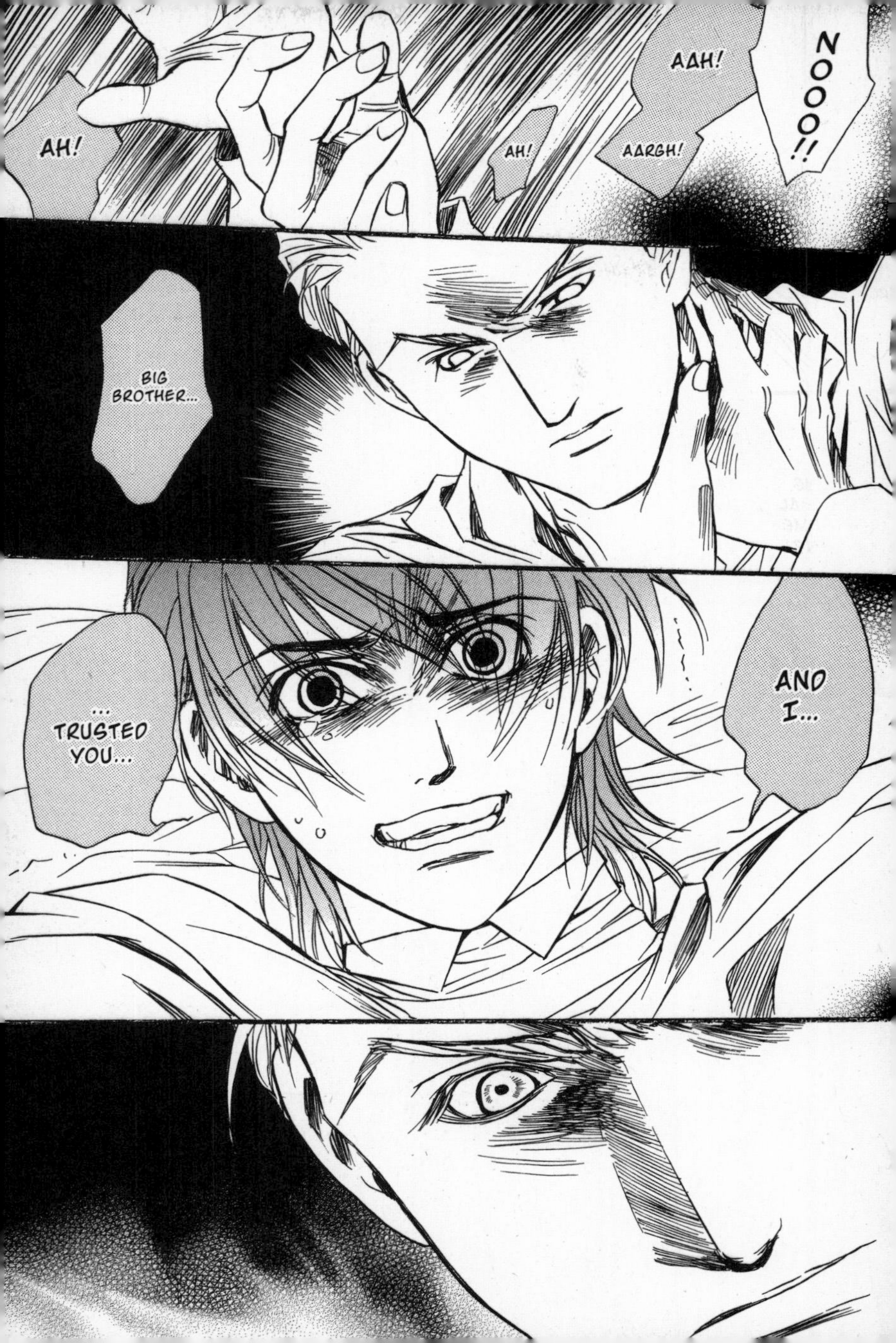
NOOOO!!
AAH!
AARGH!
AH!
AH!
BIG BROTHER...
AND I...
... TRUSTED YOU...

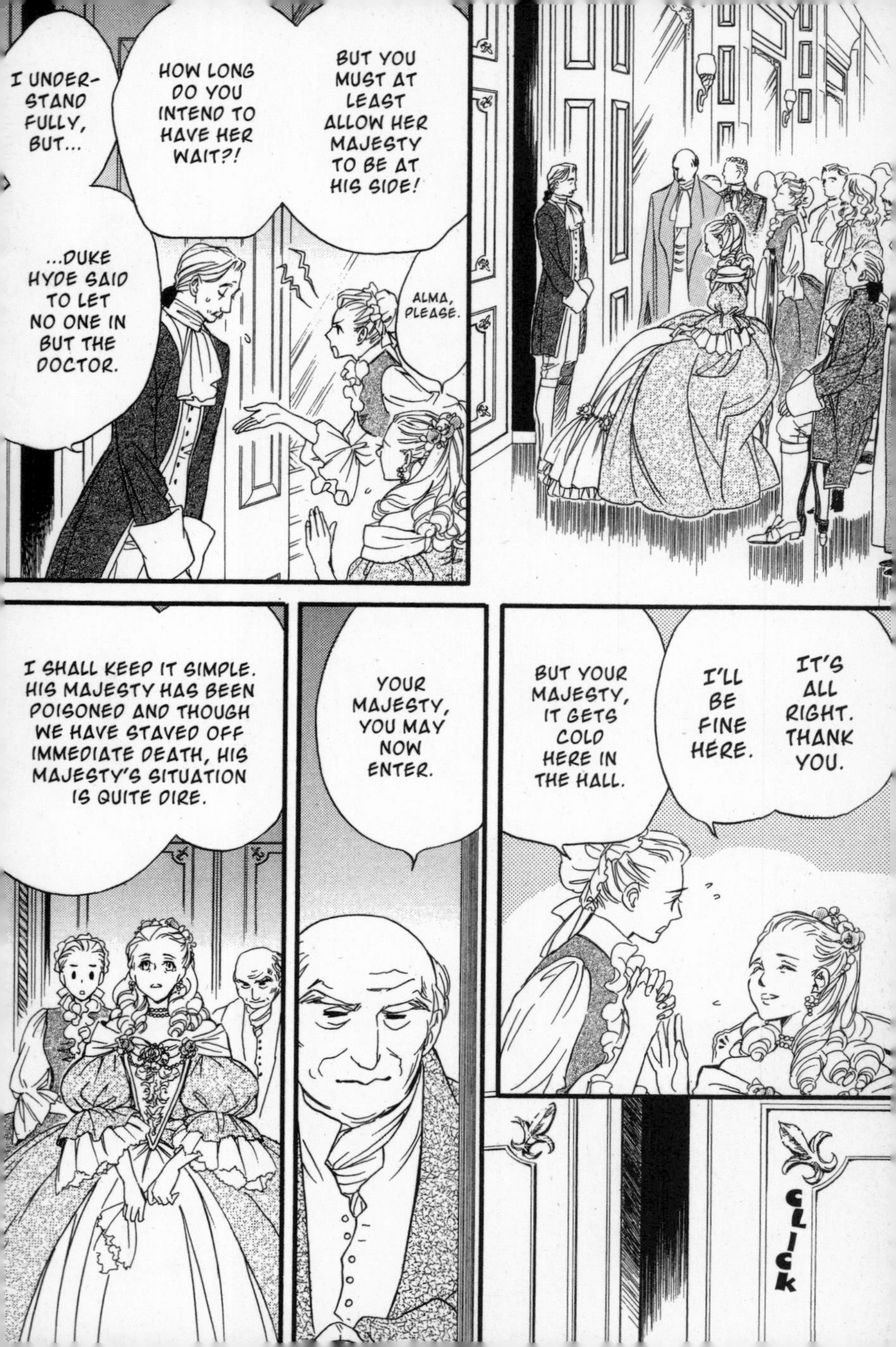
BUT YOU MUST AT LEAST ALLOW HER MAJESTY TO BE AT HIS SIDE!
HOW LONG DO YOU INTEND TO HAVE HER WAIT?!
I UNDER-STAND FULLY, BUT...
...DUKE HYDE SAID TO LET NO ONE IN BUT THE DOCTOR.
ALMA, PLEASE.
IT'S ALL RIGHT. THANK YOU.
I'LL BE FINE HERE.
BUT YOUR MAJESTY, IT GETS COLD HERE IN THE HALL.
CLICK
YOUR MAJESTY, YOU MAY NOW ENTER.
I SHALL KEEP IT SIMPLE. HIS MAJESTY HAS BEEN POISONED AND THOUGH WE HAVE STAVED OFF IMMEDIATE DEATH, HIS MAJESTY'S SITUATION IS QUITE DIRE.

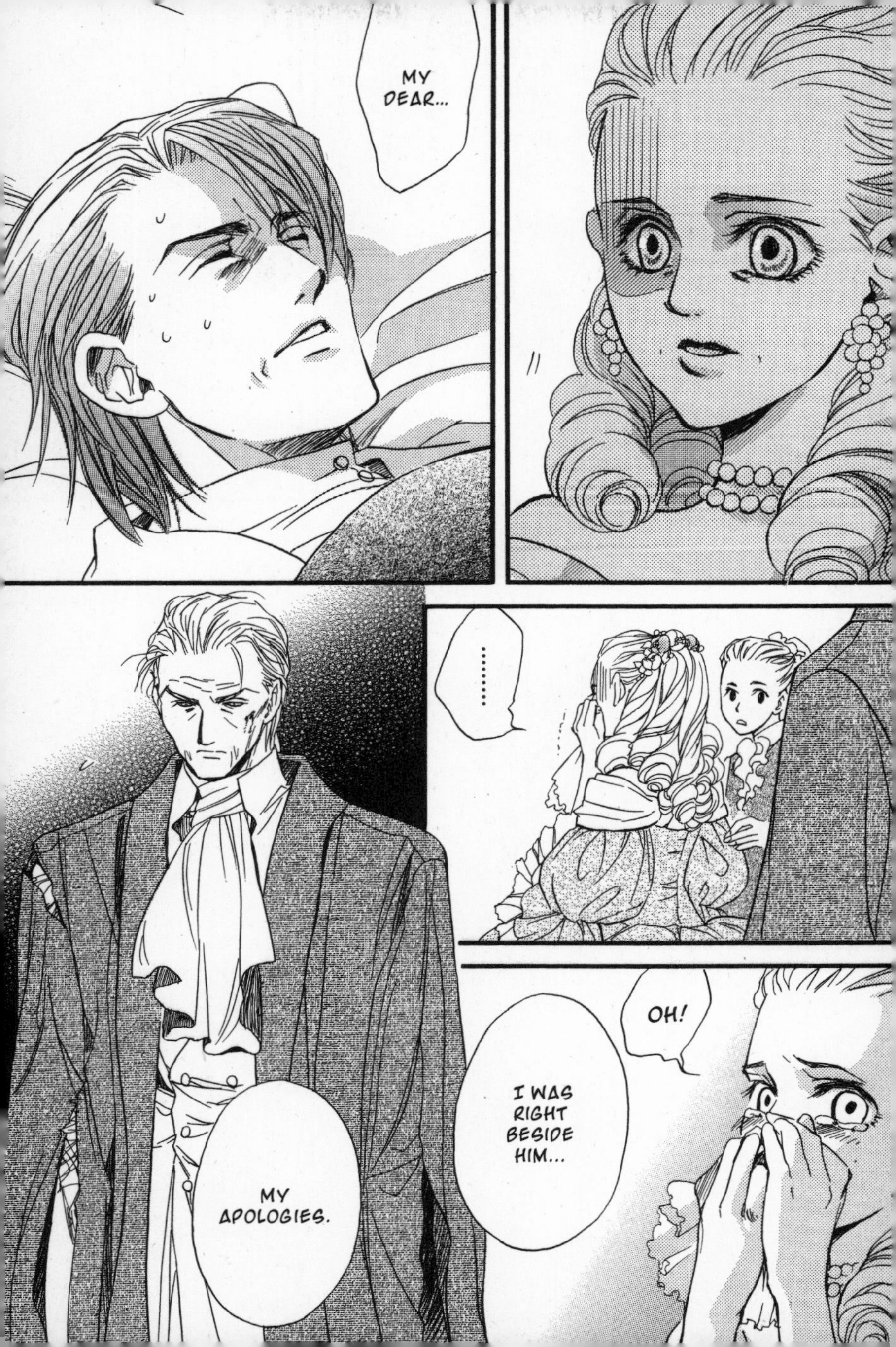
MY DEAR...
......
OH!
I WAS RIGHT BESIDE HIM...
MY APOLOGIES.

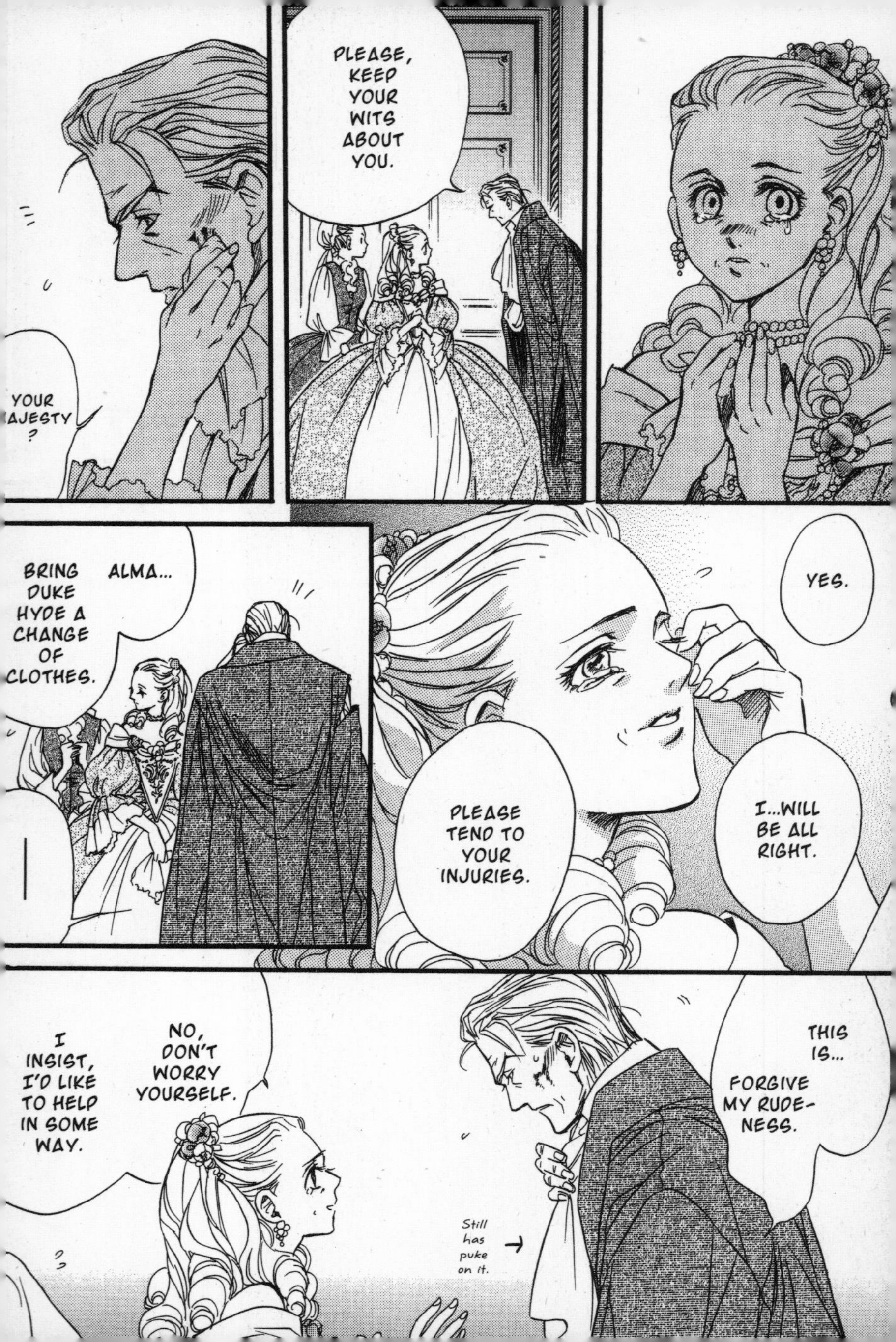
PLEASE, KEEP YOUR WITS ABOUT YOU.
YOUR AJESTY?
YES.
I...WILL BE ALL RIGHT.
PLEASE TEND TO YOUR INJURIES.
ALMA...
BRING DUKE HYDE A CHANGE OF CLOTHES.
THIS IS...
FORGIVE MY RUDE-NESS.
Still has puke on it.
NO, DON'T WORRY YOURSELF.
I INSIST, I'D LIKE TO HELP IN SOME WAY.

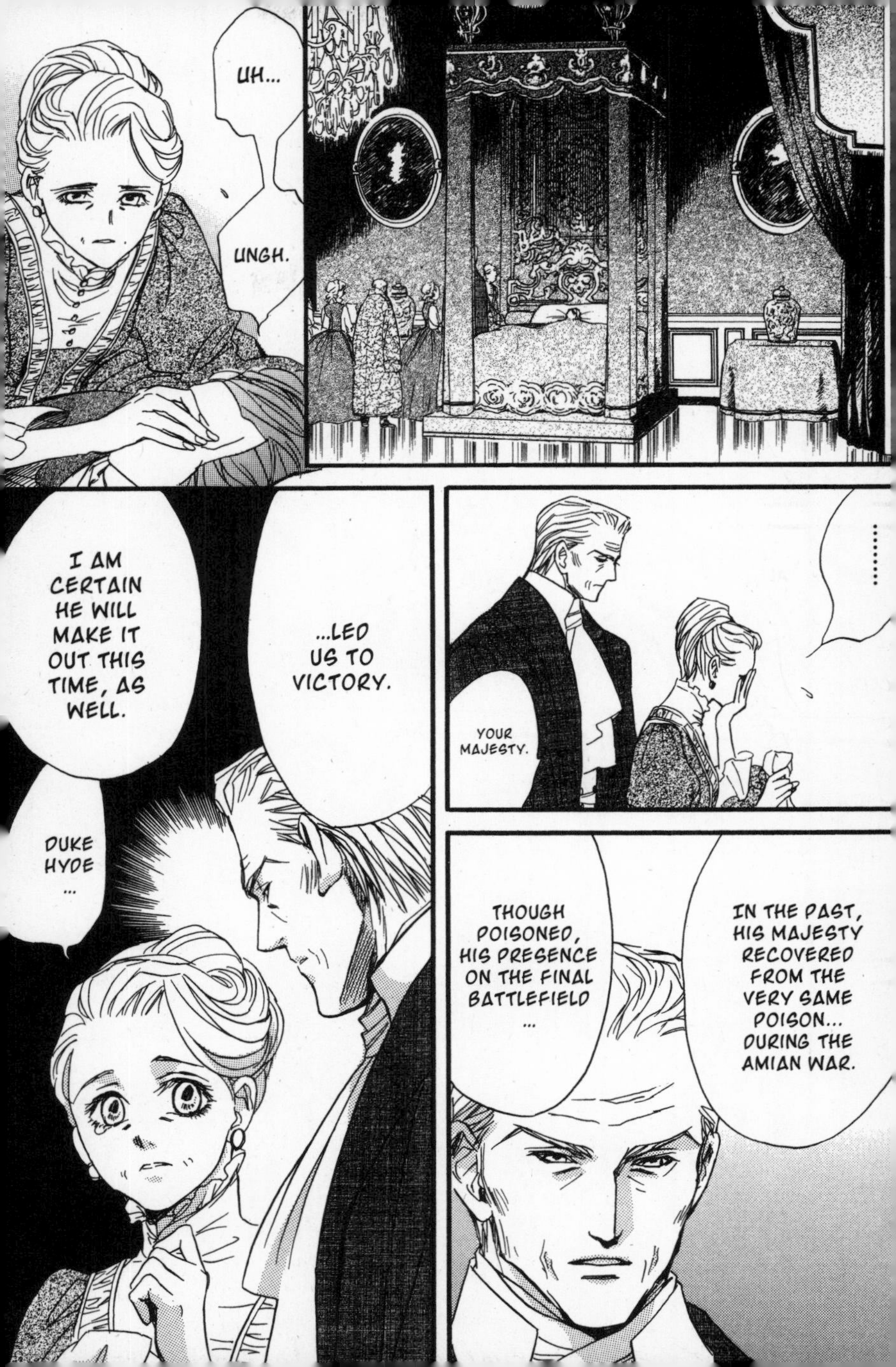

UH...
UNGH.
......
YOUR MAJESTY.
IN THE PAST, HIS MAJESTY RECOVERED FROM THE VERY SAME POISON... DURING THE AMIAN WAR.
THOUGH POISONED, HIS PRESENCE ON THE FINAL BATTLEFIELD ...
...LED US TO VICTORY.
I AM CERTAIN HE WILL MAKE IT OUT THIS TIME, AS WELL.
DUKE HYDE ...

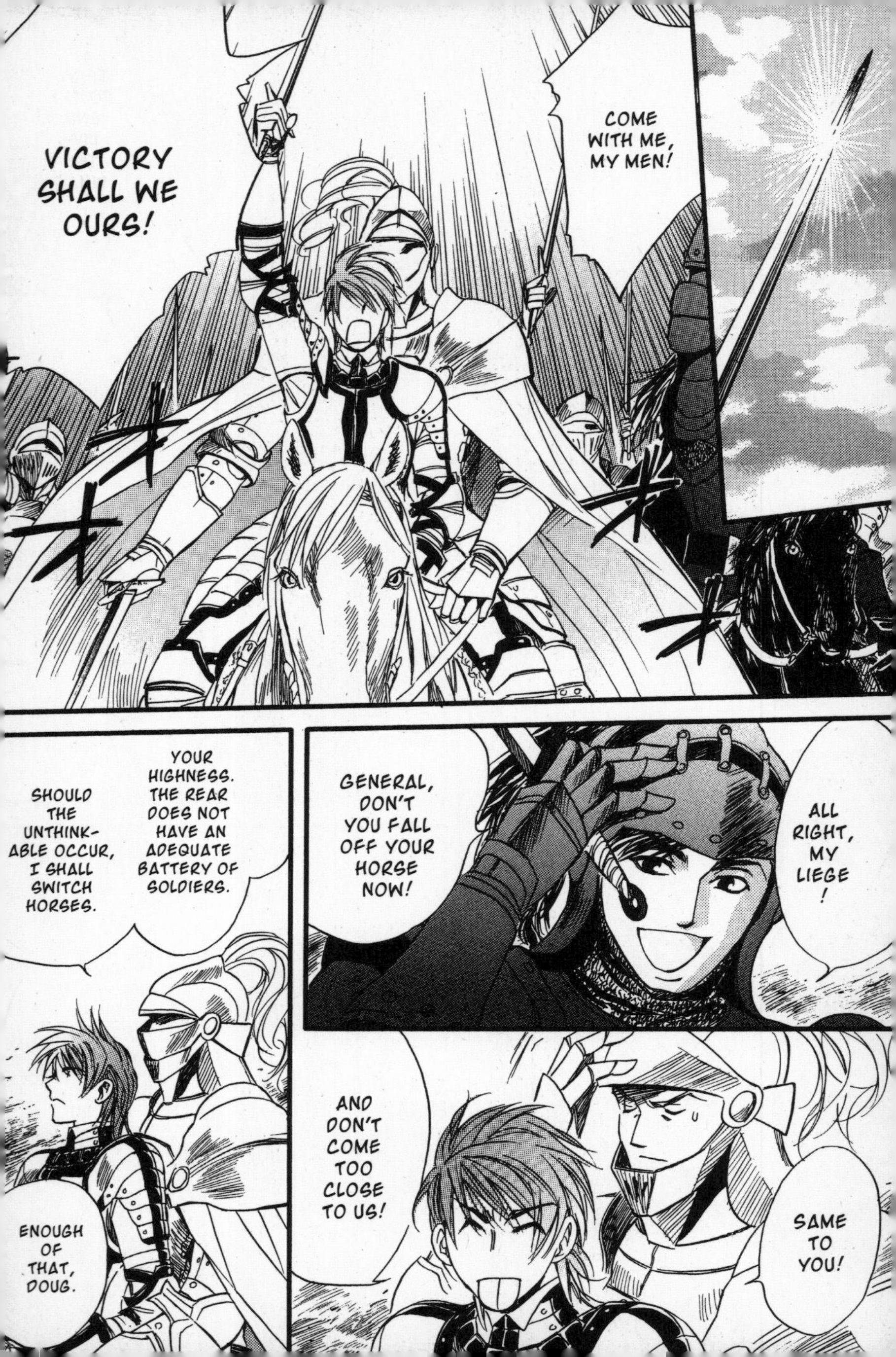
COME WITH ME, MY MEN!
VICTORY SHALL WE OURS!
ALL RIGHT, MY LIEGE!
GENERAL, DON'T YOU FALL OFF YOUR HORSE NOW!
SAME TO YOU!
AND DON'T COME TOO CLOSE TO US!
YOUR HIGHNESS. THE REAR DOES NOT HAVE AN ADEQUATE BATTERY OF SOLDIERS.
SHOULD THE UNTHINKABLE OCCUR, I SHALL SWITCH HORSES.
ENOUGH OF THAT, DOUG.

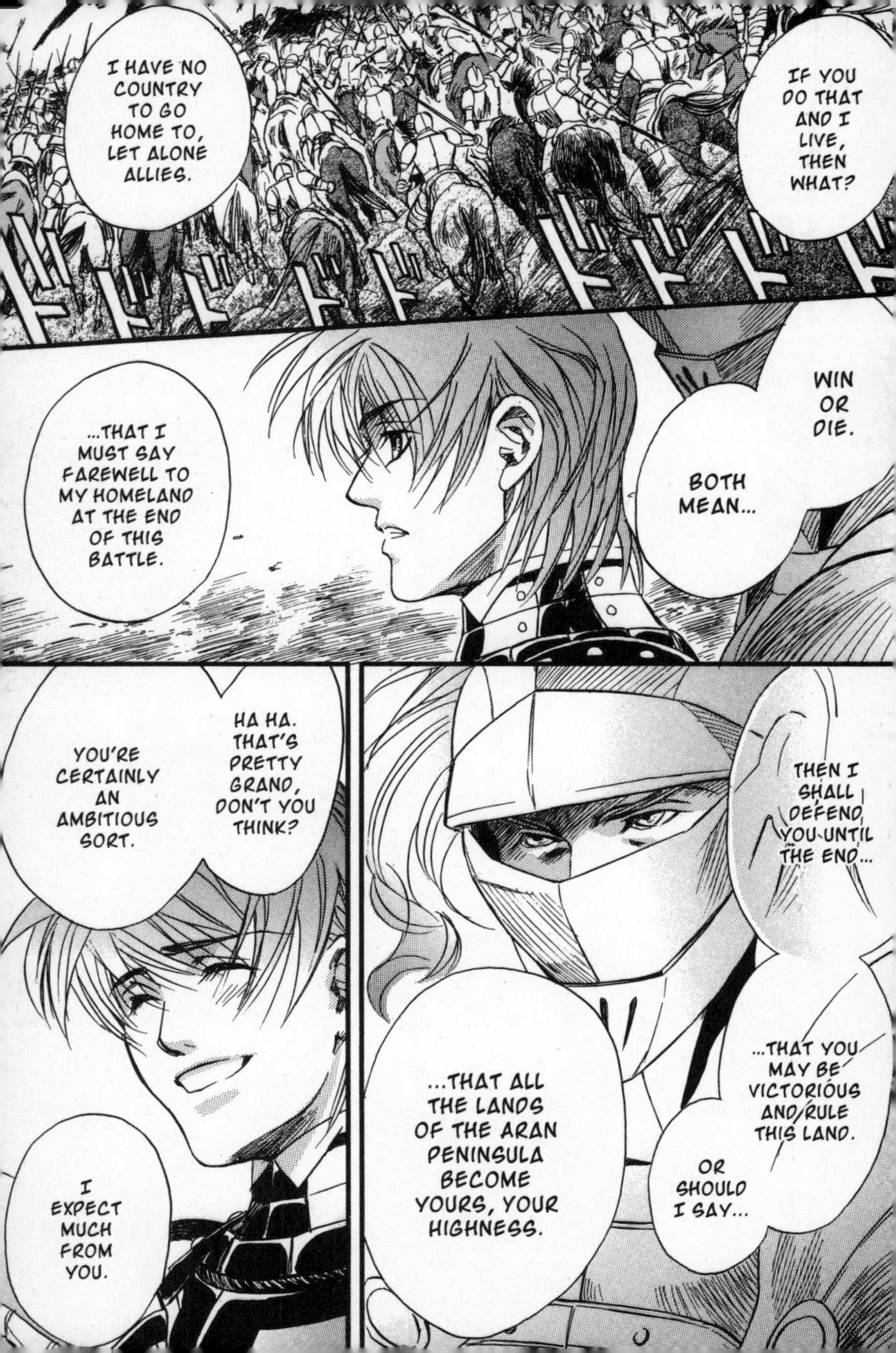
IF YOU DO THAT AND I LIVE, THEN WHAT?
I HAVE NO COUNTRY TO GO HOME TO, LET ALONE ALLIES.
WIN OR DIE.
BOTH MEAN...
...THAT I MUST SAY FAREWELL TO MY HOMELAND AT THE END OF THIS BATTLE.
THEN I SHALL DEFEND YOU UNTIL THE END...
...THAT YOU MAY BE VICTORIOUS AND RULE THIS LAND.
OR SHOULD I SAY...
...THAT ALL THE LANDS OF THE ARAN PENINSULA BECOME YOURS, YOUR HIGHNESS.
HA HA. THAT'S PRETTY GRAND, DON'T YOU THINK?
YOU'RE CERTAINLY AN AMBITIOUS SORT.
I EXPECT MUCH FROM YOU.

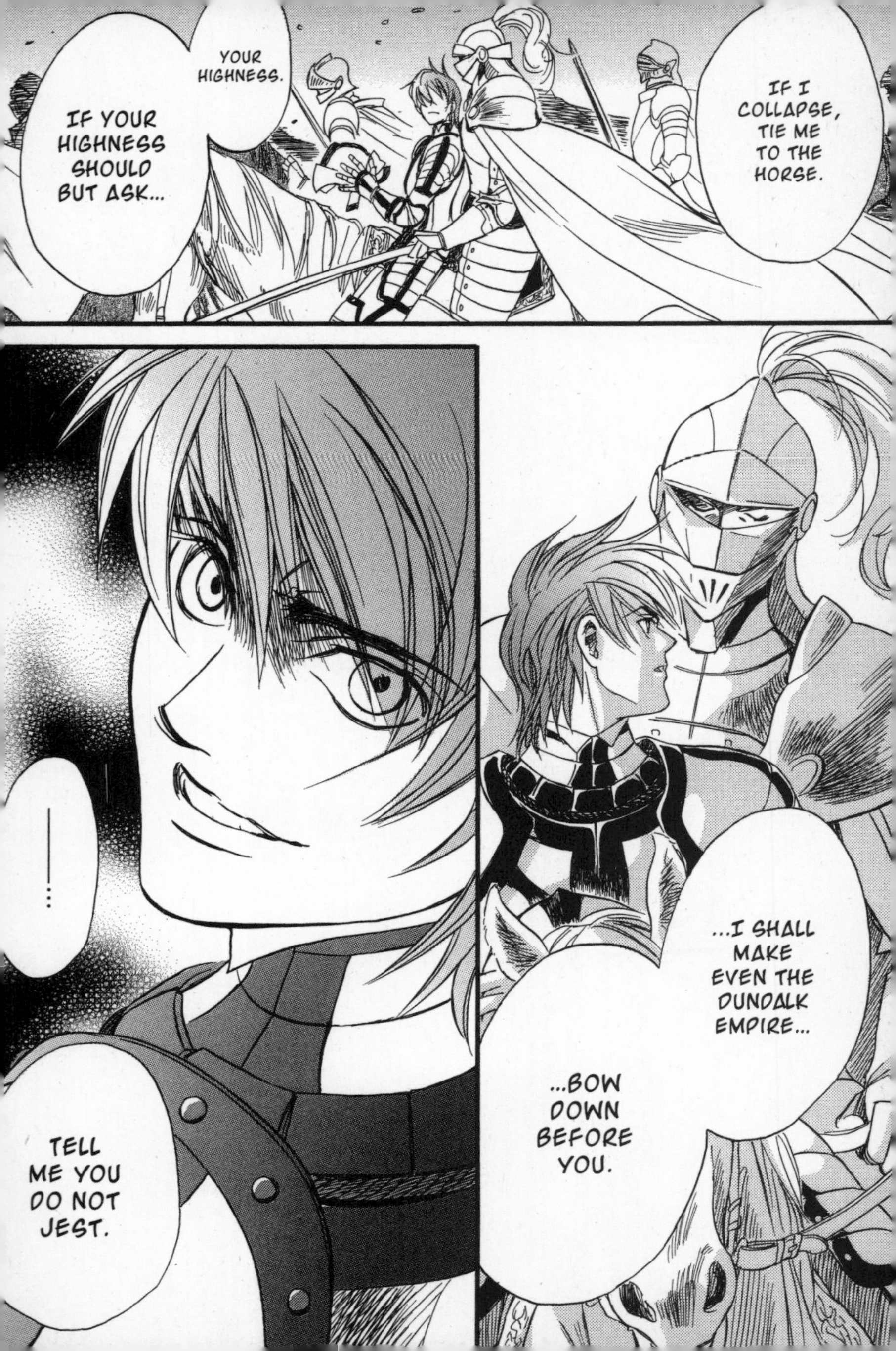
IF I COLLAPSE, TIE ME TO THE HORSE.
YOUR HIGHNESS.
IF YOUR HIGHNESS SHOULD BUT ASK...
...I SHALL MAKE EVEN THE DUNDALK EMPIRE...
...BOW DOWN BEFORE YOU.
—...
TELL ME YOU DO NOT JEST.

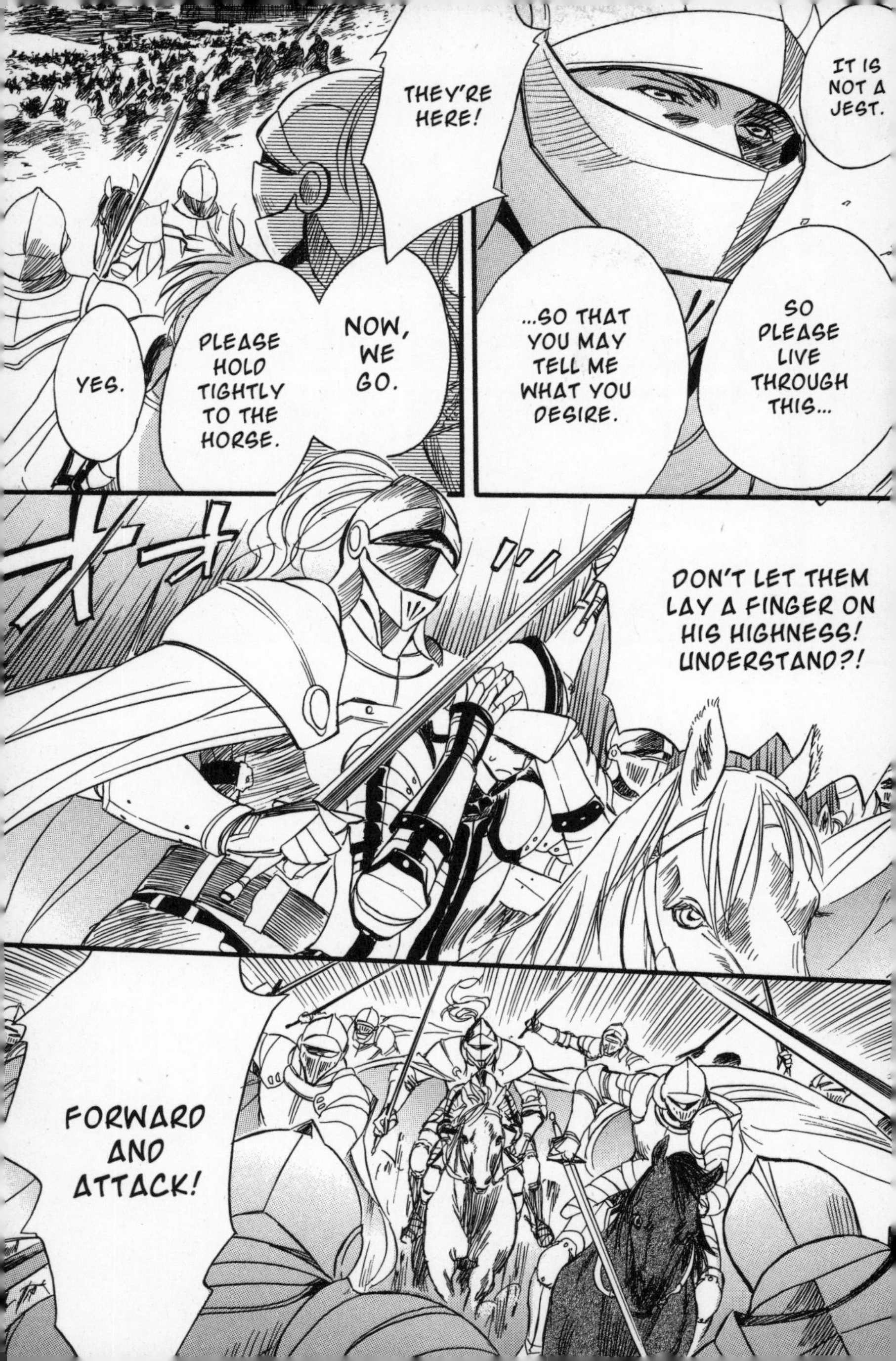
IT IS NOT A JEST.
SO PLEASE LIVE THROUGH THIS...
...SO THAT YOU MAY TELL ME WHAT YOU DESIRE.
THEY'RE HERE!
NOW, WE GO.
PLEASE HOLD TIGHTLY TO THE HORSE.
YES.
DON'T LET THEM LAY A FINGER ON HIS HIGHNESS! UNDERSTAND?!
FORWARD AND ATTACK!

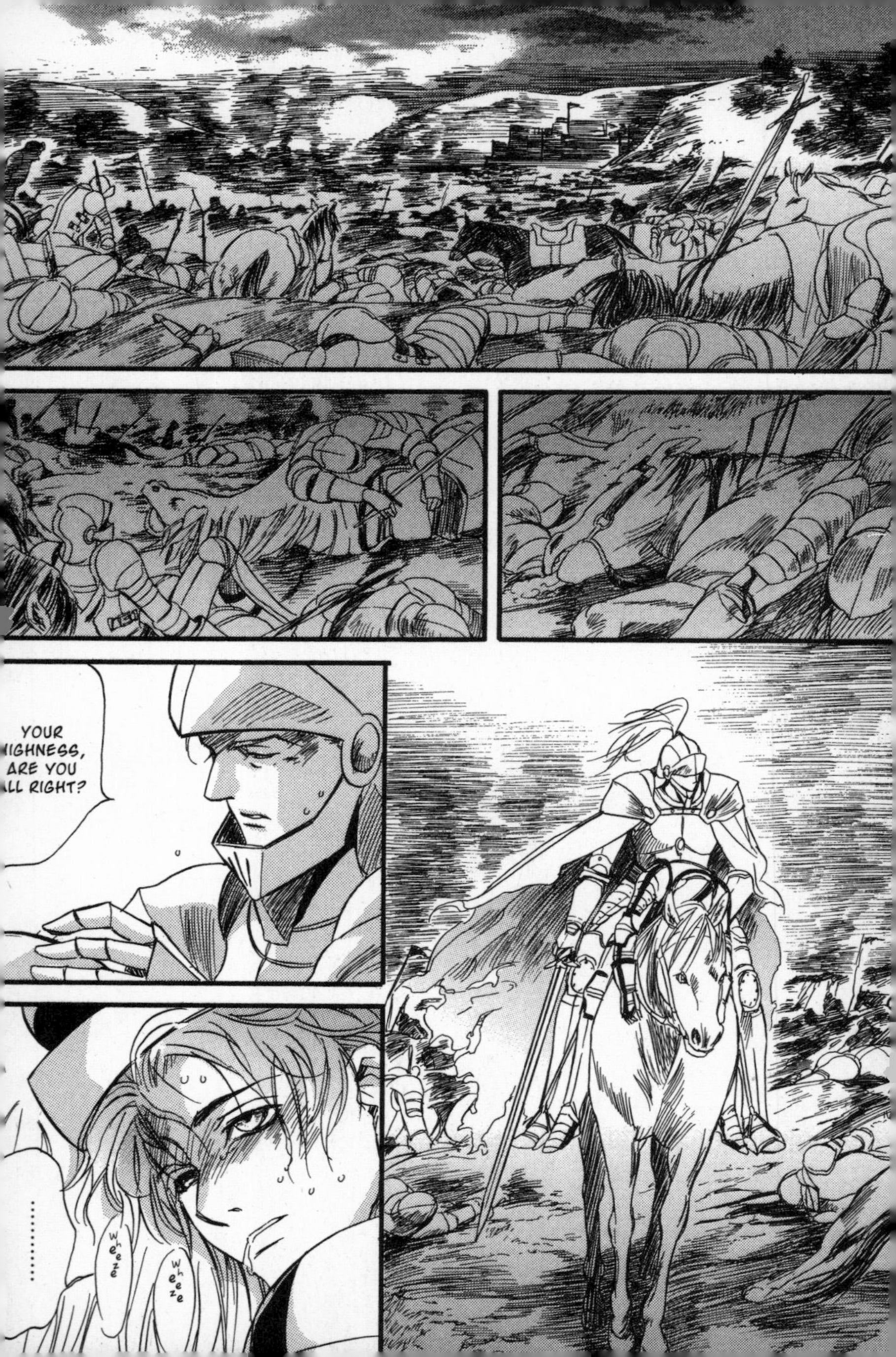
YOUR
IGHNESS,
ARE YOU
LL RIGHT?
wheeze
wheeze
....

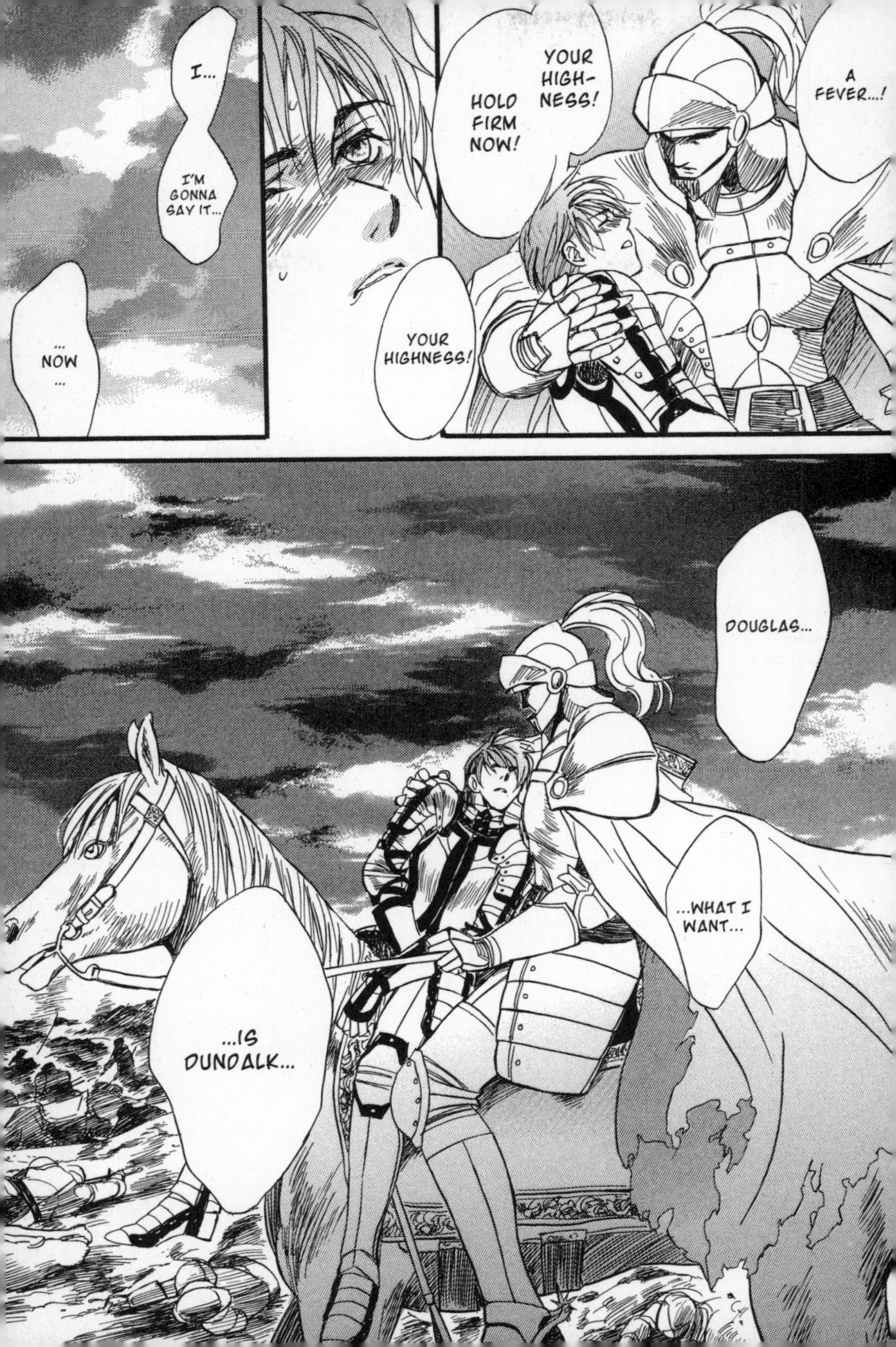
A FEVER...!
YOUR HIGH-NESS!
HOLD FIRM NOW!
YOUR HIGHNESS!
I...
I'M GONNA SAY IT...
...NOW...
DOUGLAS...
...WHAT I WANT...
...IS DUNDALK...

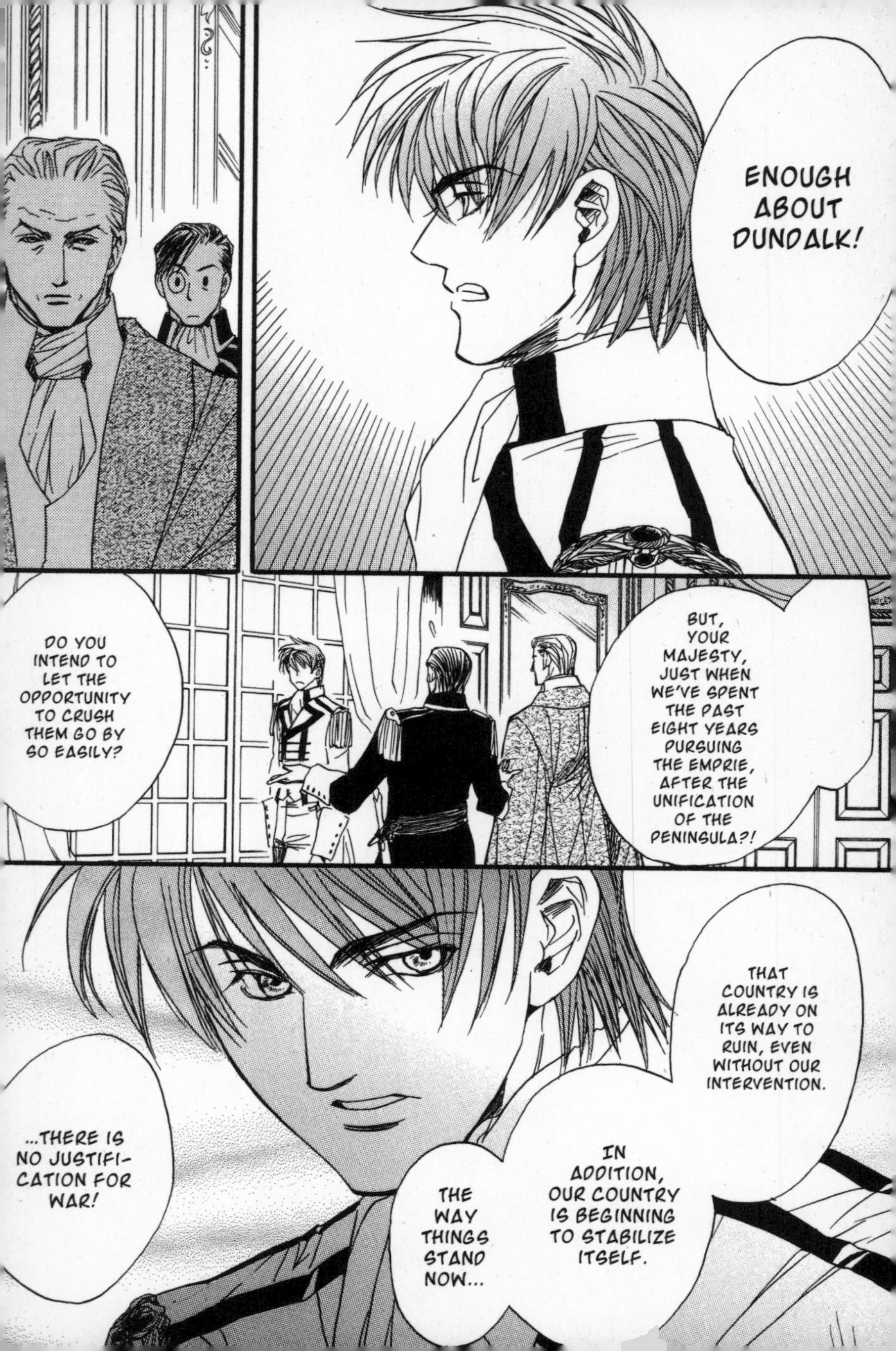
ENOUGH ABOUT DUNDALK!
BUT, YOUR MAJESTY, JUST WHEN WE'VE SPENT THE PAST EIGHT YEARS PURSUING THE EMPRIE, AFTER THE UNIFICATION OF THE PENINSULA?!
DO YOU INTEND TO LET THE OPPORTUNITY TO CRUSH THEM GO BY SO EASILY?
THAT COUNTRY IS ALREADY ON ITS WAY TO RUIN, EVEN WITHOUT OUR INTERVENTION.
IN ADDITION, OUR COUNTRY IS BEGINNING TO STABILIZE ITSELF.
THE WAY THINGS STAND NOW...
...THERE IS NO JUSTIFI-CATION FOR WAR!

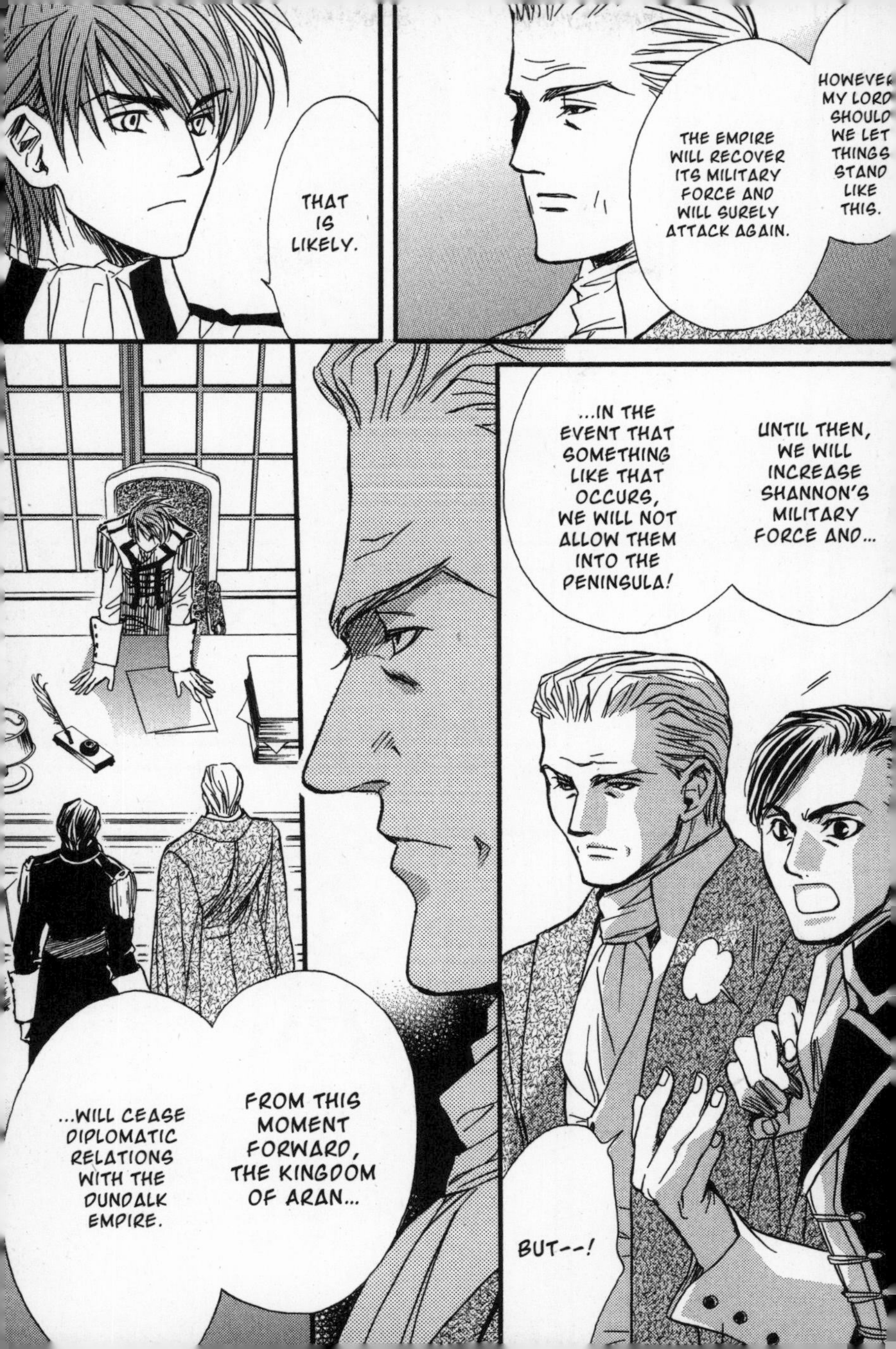
HOWEVER MY LORD SHOULD WE LET THINGS STAND LIKE THIS.
THE EMPIRE WILL RECOVER ITS MILITARY FORCE AND WILL SURELY ATTACK AGAIN.
THAT IS LIKELY.
UNTIL THEN, WE WILL INCREASE SHANNON'S MILITARY FORCE AND...
...IN THE EVENT THAT SOMETHING LIKE THAT OCCURS, WE WILL NOT ALLOW THEM INTO THE PENINSULA!
BUT--!
FROM THIS MOMENT FORWARD, THE KINGDOM OF ARAN...
...WILL CEASE DIPLOMATIC RELATIONS WITH THE DUNDALK EMPIRE.

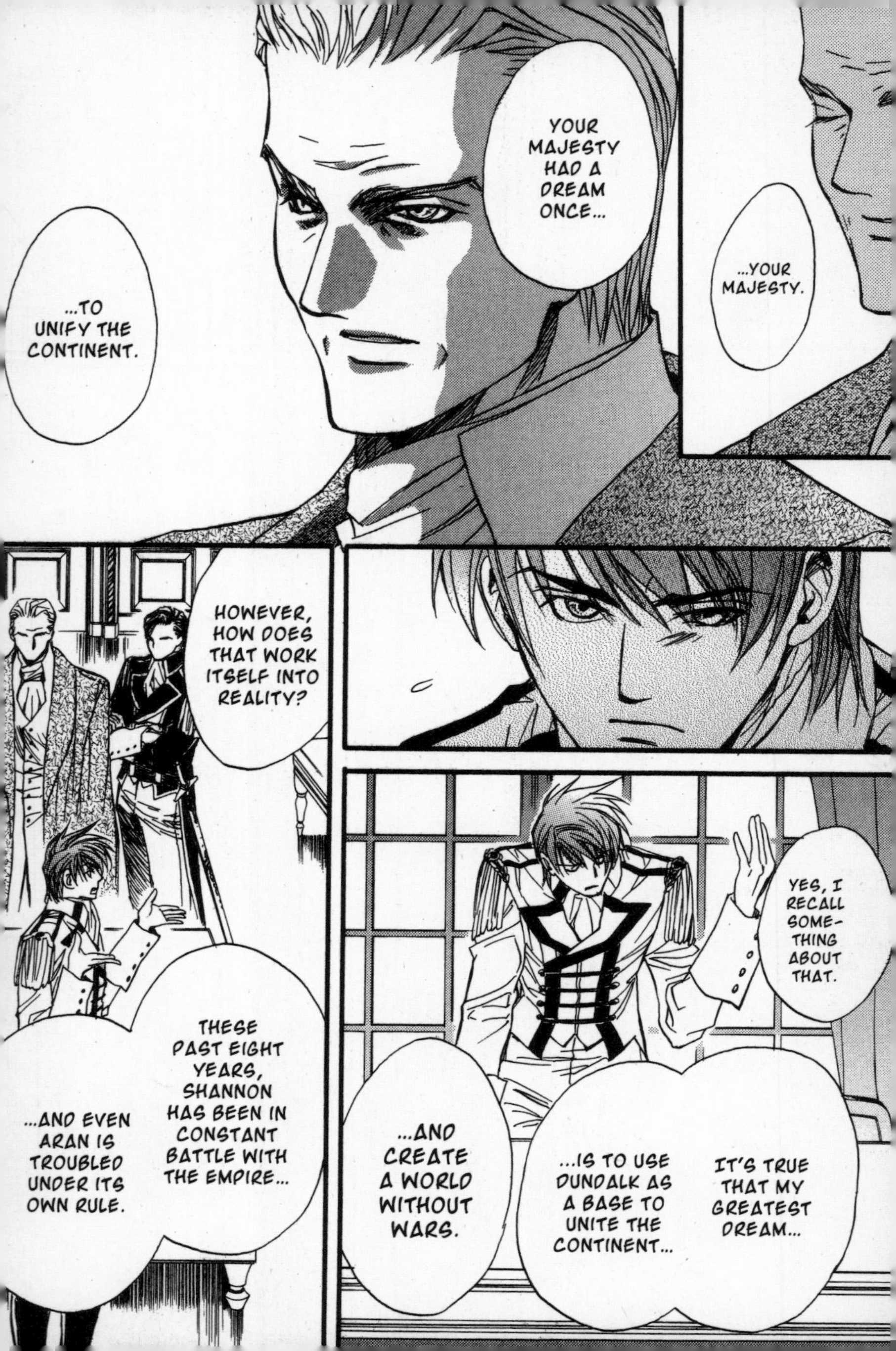
...YOUR MAJESTY.
YOUR MAJESTY HAD A DREAM ONCE...
...TO UNIFY THE CONTINENT.
YES, I RECALL SOME-THING ABOUT THAT.
IT'S TRUE THAT MY GREATEST DREAM...
...IS TO USE DUNDALK AS A BASE TO UNITE THE CONTINENT...
...AND CREATE A WORLD WITHOUT WARS.
HOWEVER, HOW DOES THAT WORK ITSELF INTO REALITY?
THESE PAST EIGHT YEARS, SHANNON HAS BEEN IN CONSTANT BATTLE WITH THE EMPIRE...
...AND EVEN ARAN IS TROUBLED UNDER ITS OWN RULE.

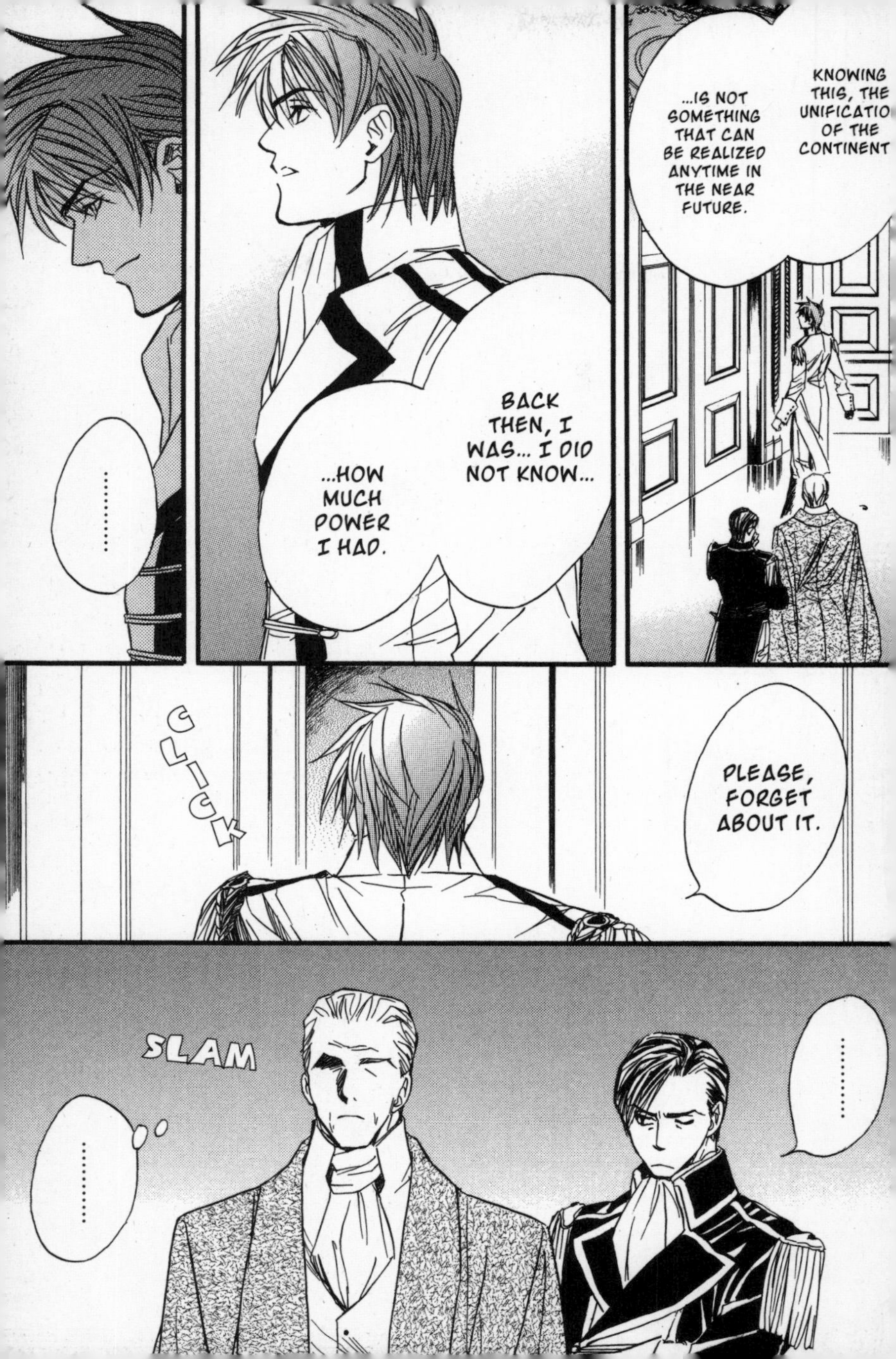
KNOWING THIS, THE UNIFICATIO OF THE CONTINENT
...IS NOT SOMETHING THAT CAN BE REALIZED ANYTIME IN THE NEAR FUTURE.
BACK THEN, I WAS... I DID NOT KNOW...
...HOW MUCH POWER I HAD.
......
PLEASE, FORGET ABOUT IT.
CLICK
......
SLAM
......

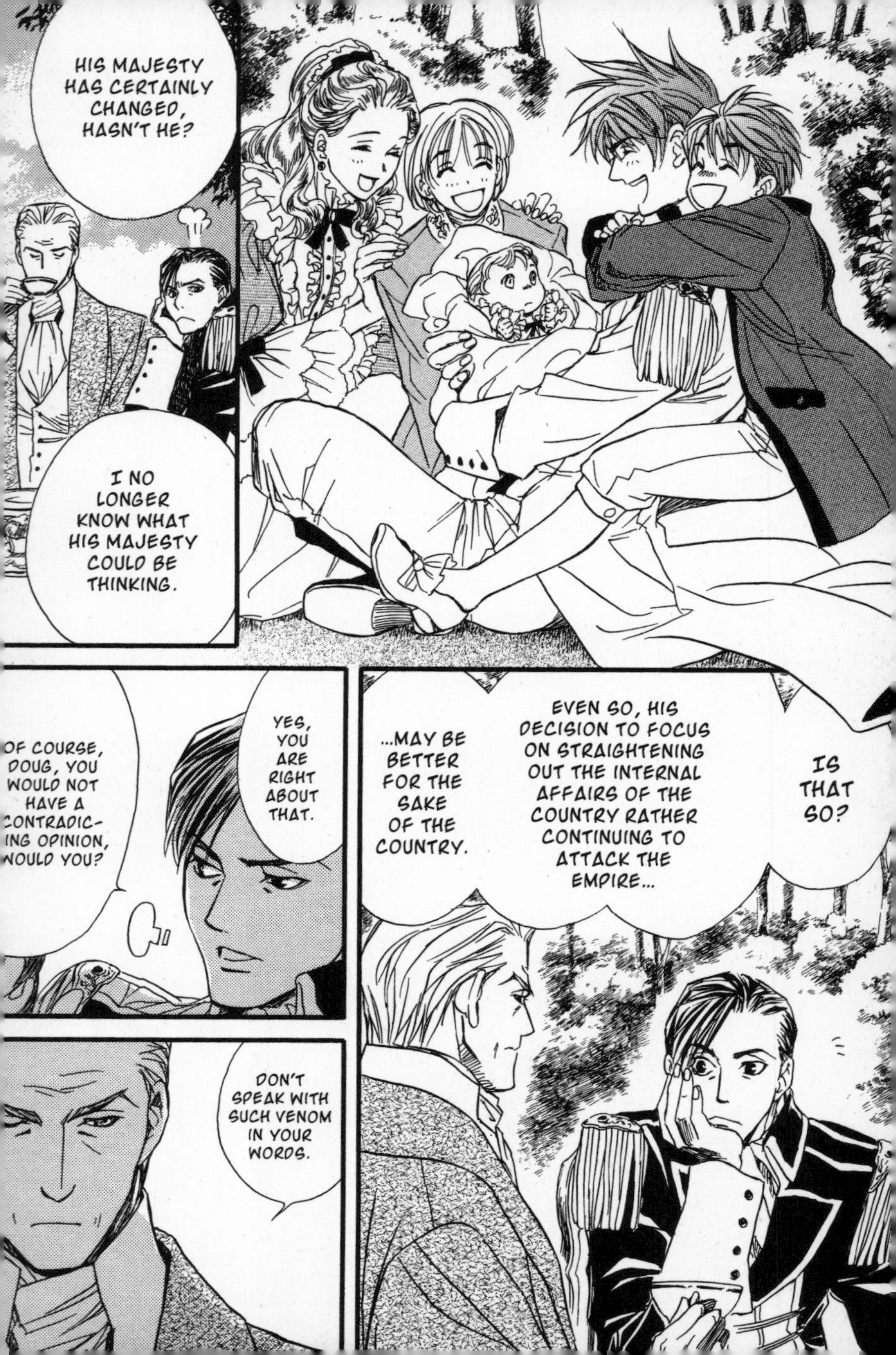
HIS MAJESTY HAS CERTAINLY CHANGED, HASN'T HE?
I NO LONGER KNOW WHAT HIS MAJESTY COULD BE THINKING.
IS THAT SO?
EVEN SO, HIS DECISION TO FOCUS ON STRAIGHTENING OUT THE INTERNAL AFFAIRS OF THE COUNTRY RATHER CONTINUING TO ATTACK THE EMPIRE...
...MAY BE BETTER FOR THE SAKE OF THE COUNTRY.
YES, YOU ARE RIGHT ABOUT THAT.
OF COURSE, DOUG, YOU WOULD NOT HAVE A CONTRADIC-ING OPINION, WOULD YOU?
DON'T SPEAK WITH SUCH VENOM IN YOUR WORDS.

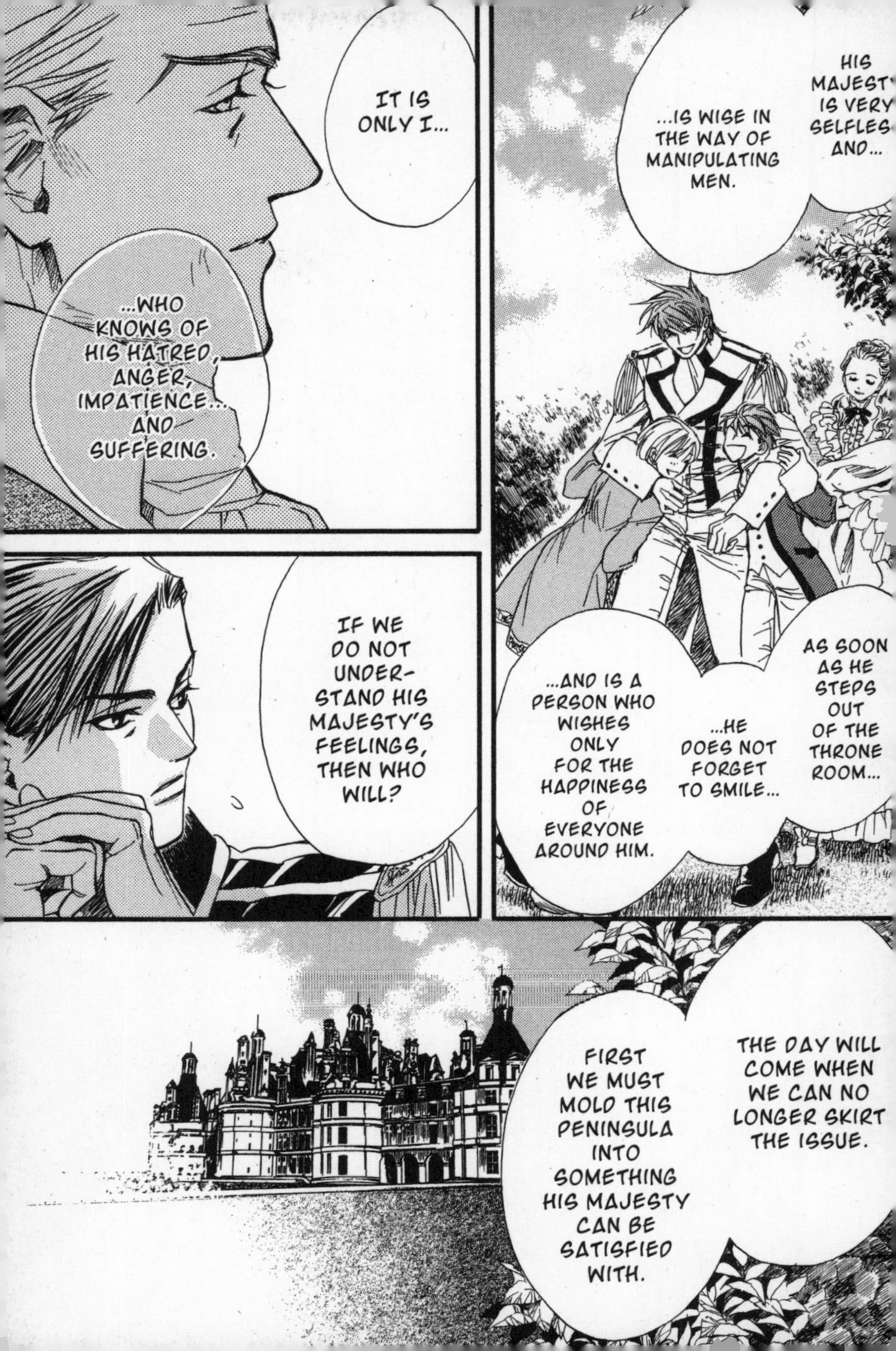
HIS MAJEST IS VERY SELFLES AND...
...IS WISE IN THE WAY OF MANIPULATING MEN.
AS SOON AS HE STEPS OUT OF THE THRONE ROOM...
...HE DOES NOT FORGET TO SMILE...
...AND IS A PERSON WHO WISHES ONLY FOR THE HAPPINESS OF EVERYONE AROUND HIM.
IT IS ONLY I...
...WHO KNOWS OF HIS HATRED, ANGER, IMPATIENCE... AND SUFFERING.
IF WE DO NOT UNDER-STAND HIS MAJESTY'S FEELINGS, THEN WHO WILL?
THE DAY WILL COME WHEN WE CAN NO LONGER SKIRT THE ISSUE.
FIRST WE MUST MOLD THIS PENINSULA INTO SOMETHING HIS MAJESTY CAN BE SATISFIED WITH.

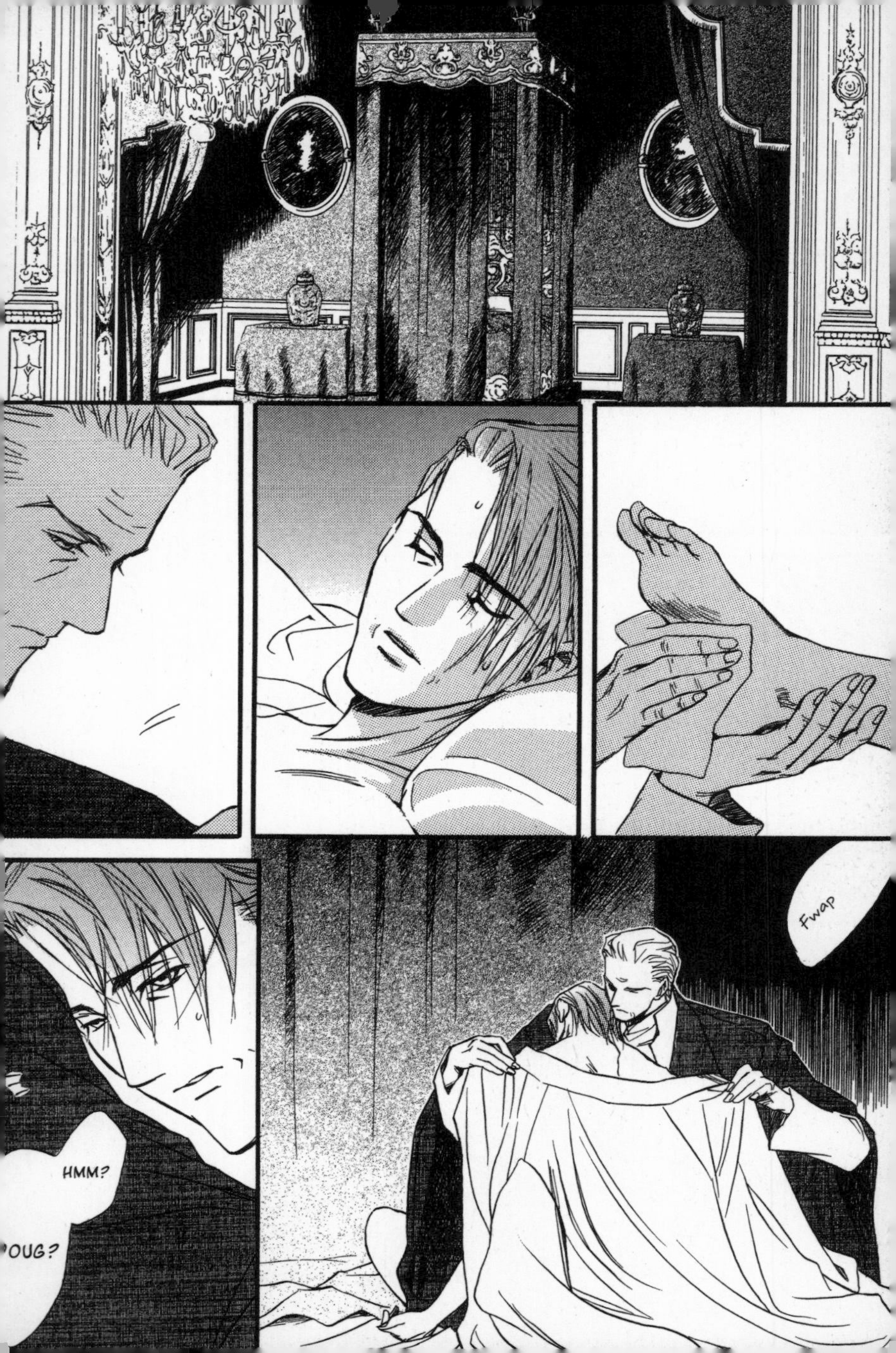
Fwap
HMM?
OUG?

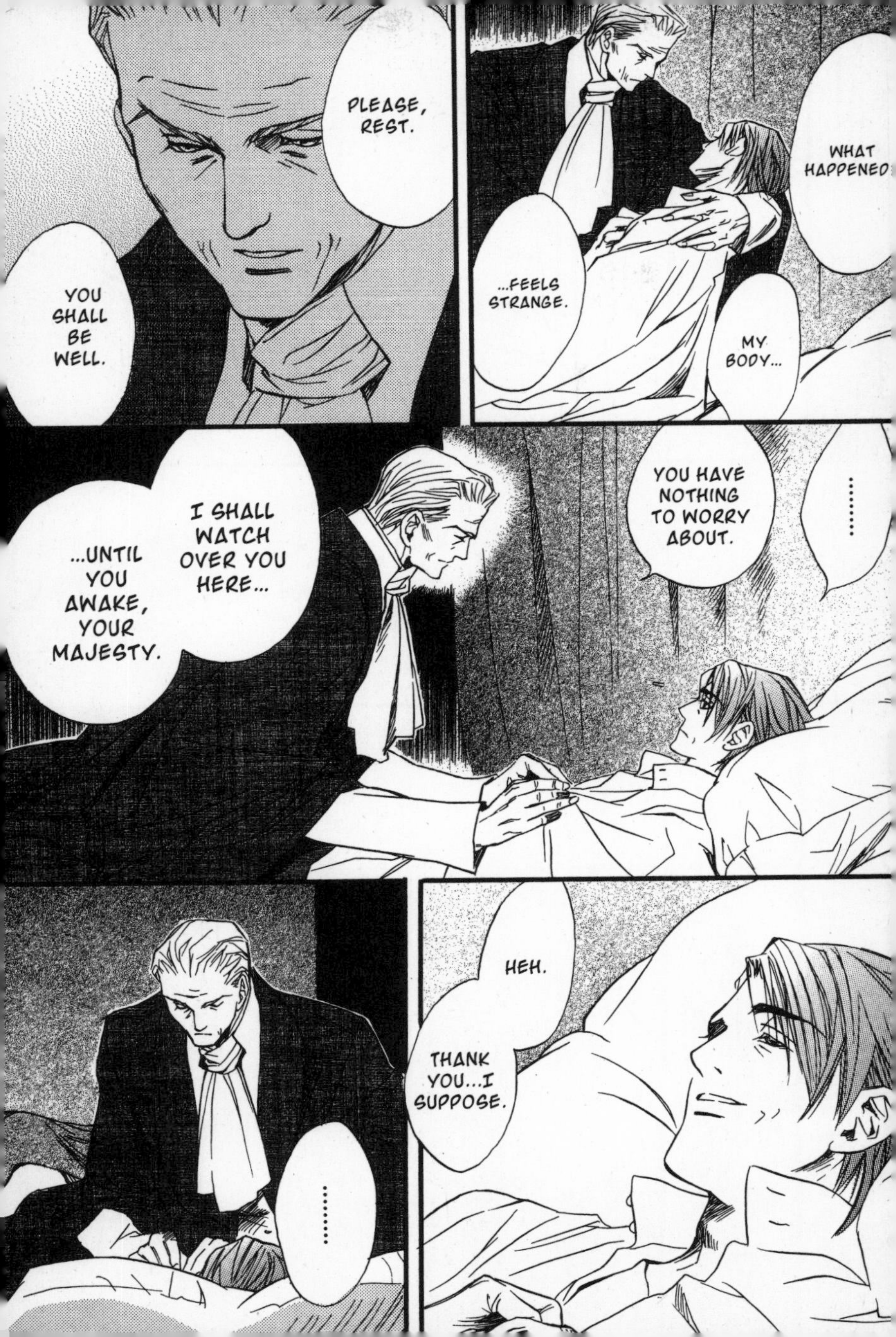
WHAT HAPPENED
MY BODY...
...FEELS STRANGE.
PLEASE, REST.
YOU SHALL BE WELL.
......
YOU HAVE NOTHING TO WORRY ABOUT.
I SHALL WATCH OVER YOU HERE...
...UNTIL YOU AWAKE, YOUR MAJESTY.
HEH.
THANK YOU...I SUPPOSE.
......

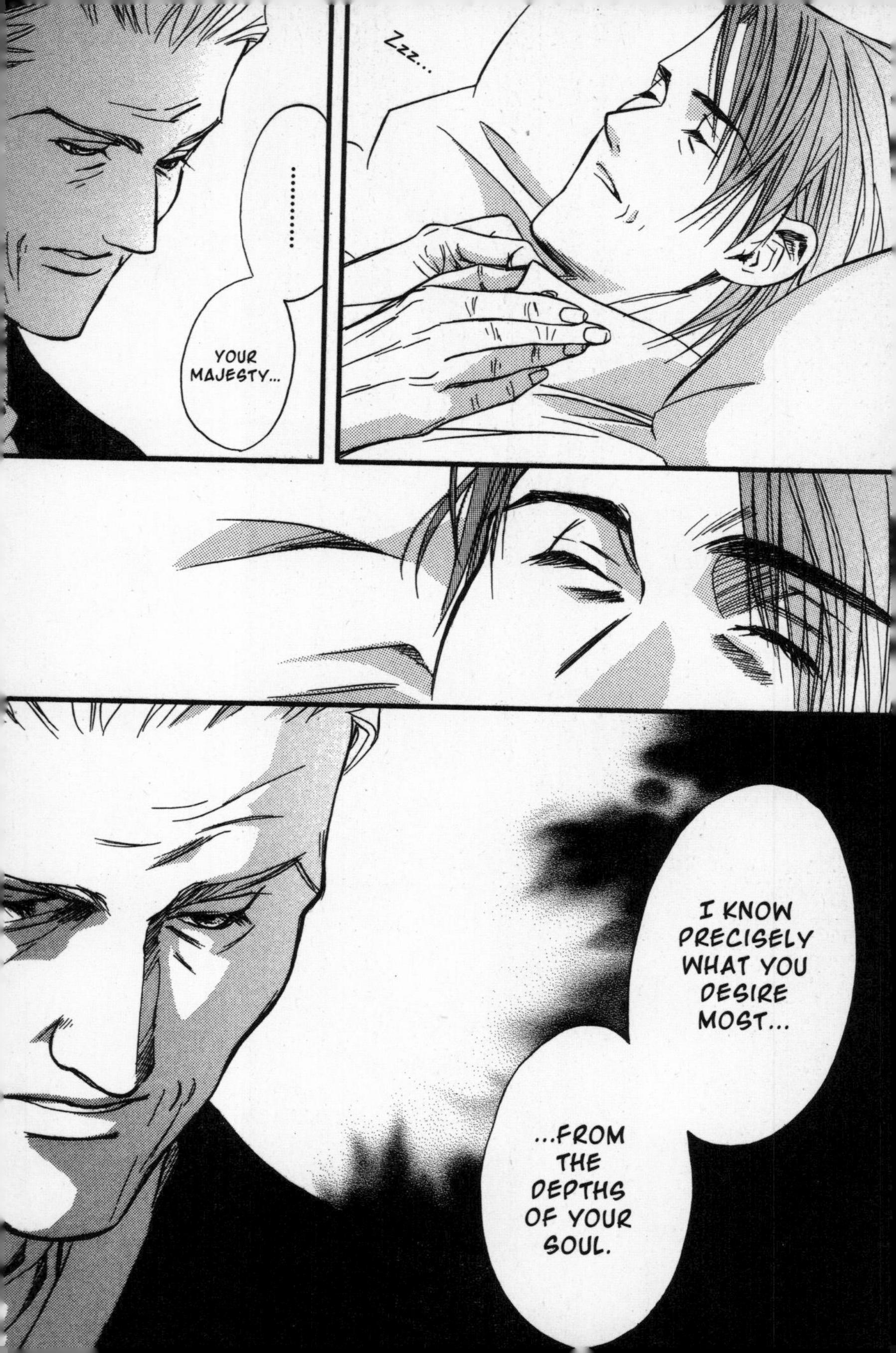
Zzz...
......
YOUR MAJESTY...
I KNOW PRECISELY WHAT YOU DESIRE MOST...
...FROM THE DEPTHS OF YOUR SOUL.

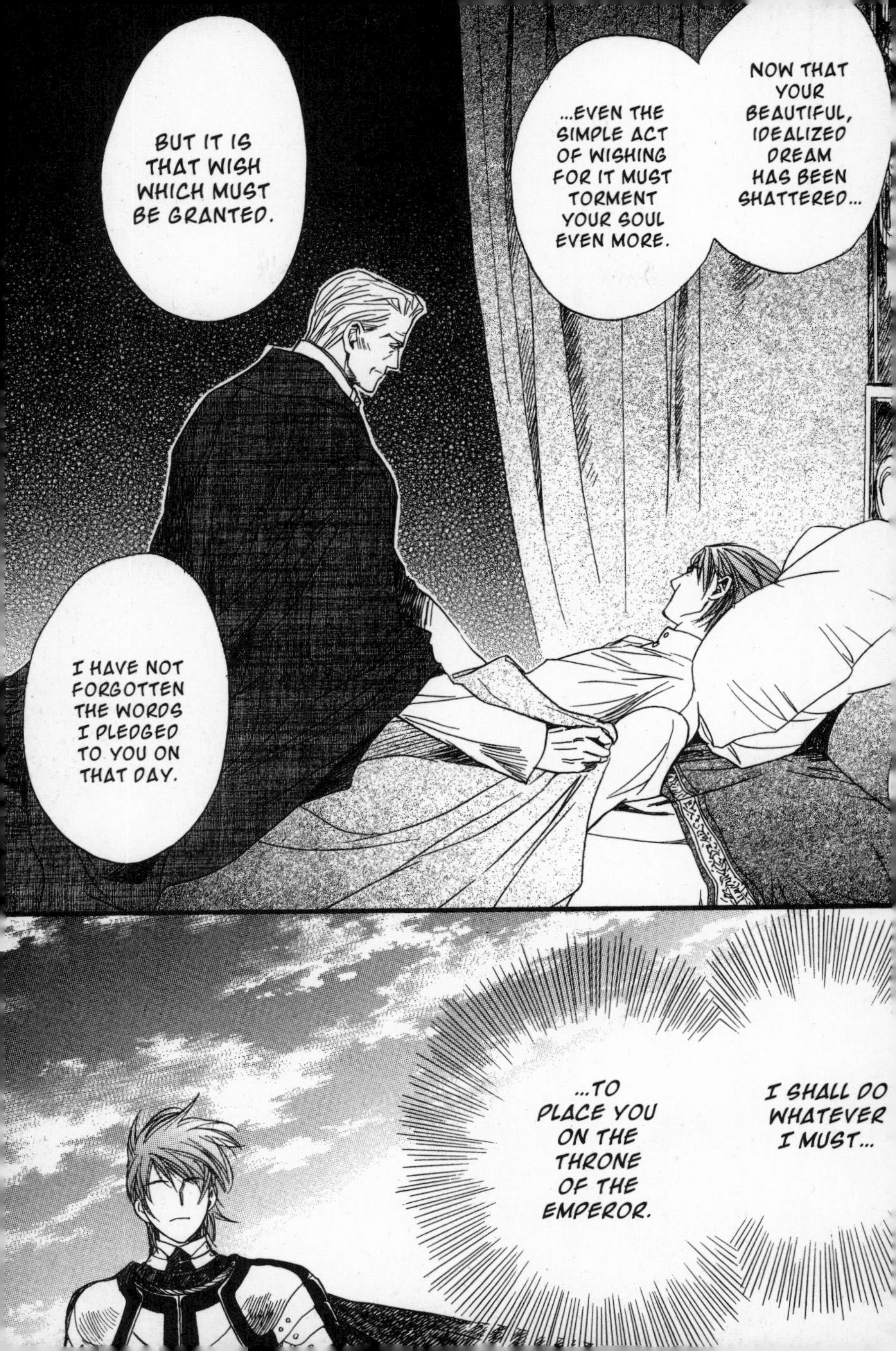
NOW THAT YOUR BEAUTIFUL, IDEALIZED DREAM HAS BEEN SHATTERED...
...EVEN THE SIMPLE ACT OF WISHING FOR IT MUST TORMENT YOUR SOUL EVEN MORE.
BUT IT IS THAT WISH WHICH MUST BE GRANTED.
I HAVE NOT FORGOTTEN THE WORDS I PLEDGED TO YOU ON THAT DAY.
I SHALL DO WHATEVER I MUST...
...TO PLACE YOU ON THE THRONE OF THE EMPEROR.

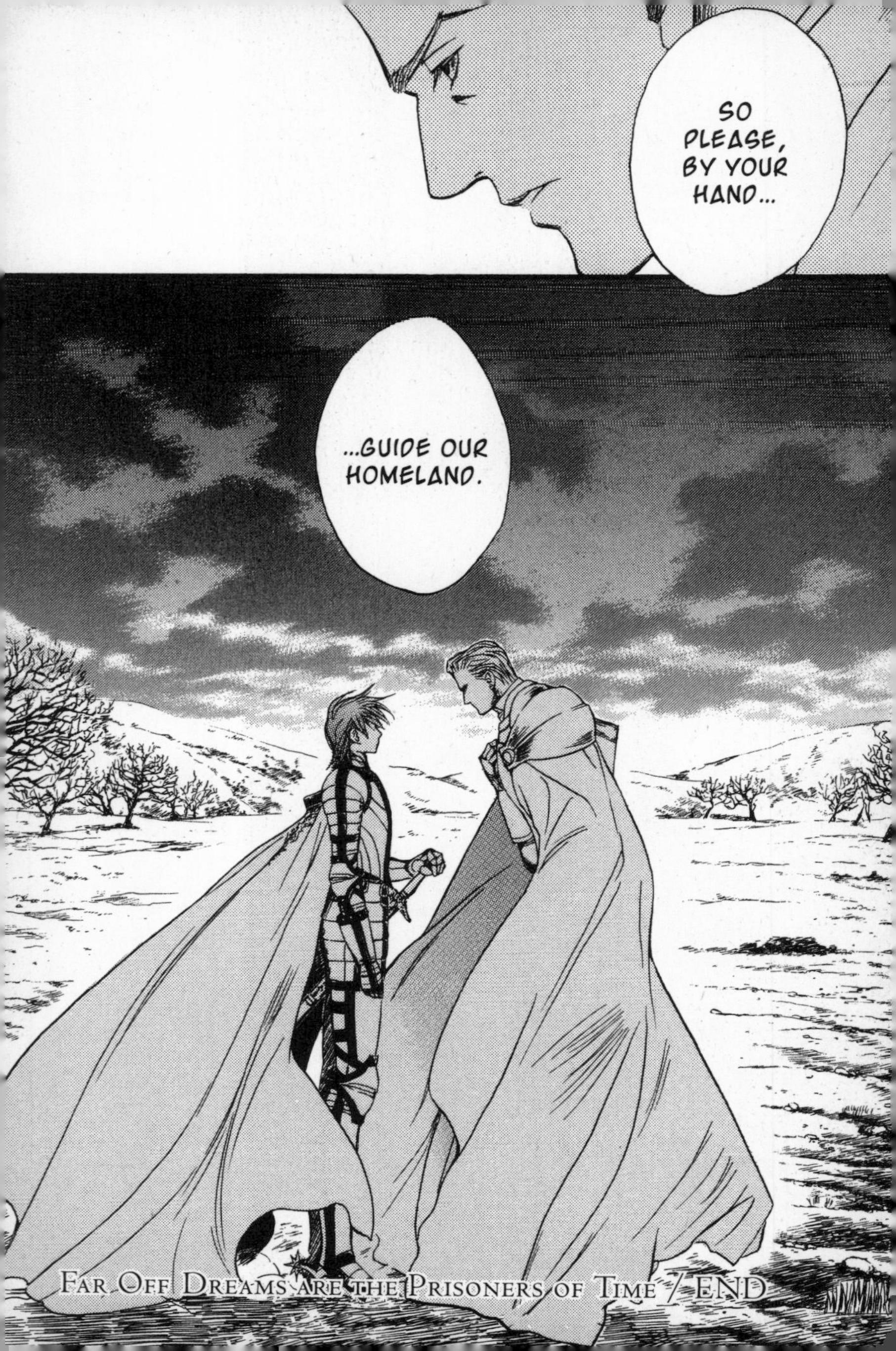
SO PLEASE, BY YOUR HAND...
...GUIDE OUR HOMELAND.
FAR OFF DREAMS ARE THE PRISONERS OF TIME / END

THE
BLACK
KNIGHT

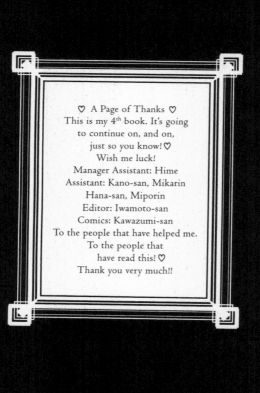

♡ A Page of Thanks ♡
This is my 4th book. It's going
to continue on, and on,
just so you know! ♡
Wish me luck!
Manager Assistant: Hime
Assistant: Kano-san, Mikarin
Hana-san, Miporin
Editor: Iwamoto-san
Comics: Kawazumi-san
To the people that have helped me.
To the people that
have read this! ♡
Thank you very much!!

THE
BLACK
KNIGHT

The Black Knight

BLACK KNIGHT VOL. 3
Created by Kai Tsurugi

ISBN: 978-1-59816-524-1

First Printing: March 2007
10 9 8 7 6 5 4 3 2 1
Printed in the USA

igh school is difficult enough, especially when you live in the shadow of your stunningly attractive older brother...

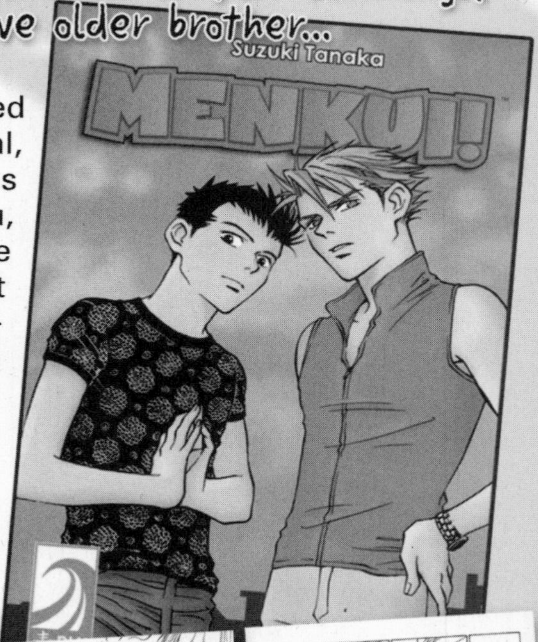
Suzuki Tanaka
MENKUI!

Kotori is often teased for being superficial, and with a gorgeous brother like Kujaku, you can't really blame him for thinking that looks are everything. However, once Akaiwa steps into the picture, Kotori's life is heading for a lesson in deep trust, self-confidence, and abiding love.

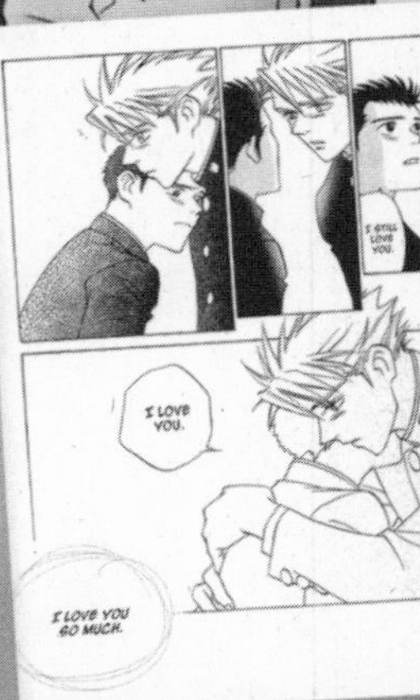
I STILL LOVE YOU.
I LOVE YOU.
I LOVE YOU SO MUCH.

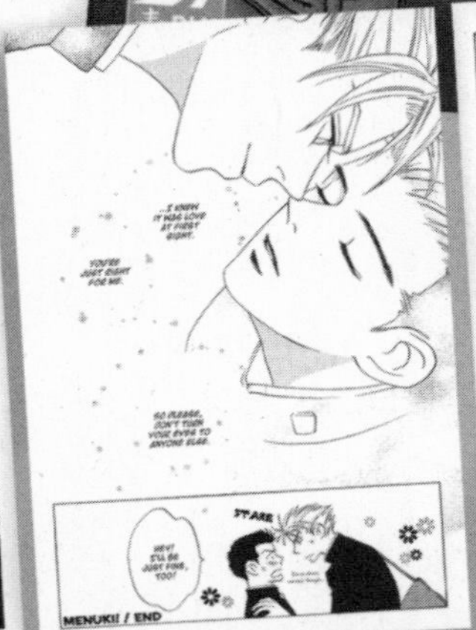
YOU'RE JUST RIGHT FOR ME.
SO PLEASE, DON'T TURN YOUR EYES TO ANYONE ELSE.
STARE
HEY! I'LL BE JUST FINE, TOO!
MENUKI! / END

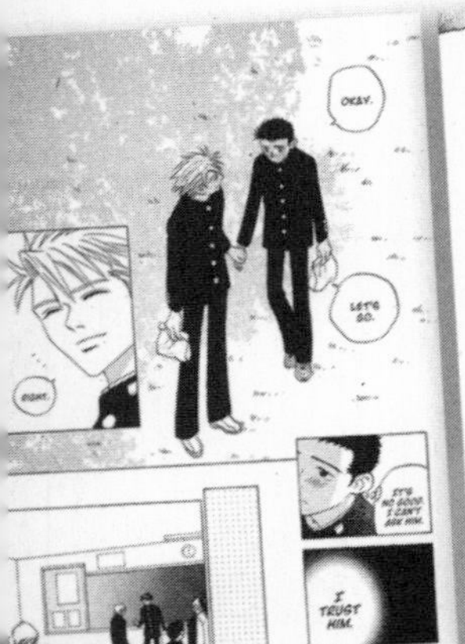
OKAY.
LET'S GO.
I TRUST HIM.

'rice: $9.99
ıvailable Now!

r information about where to buy BLU MANGA titles, visit www.BLUMANGA.com

OT
OLDER TEEN

青 BLU

Here's a dog that will make you beg

When Ukyo rescues a stray dog and names it Kuro, he soon learns that he may have found a rare breed—his new dog can talk and magically transform into a hunky human! With his dog now taking the form of a hot man and licking him in various places, what is Ukyo to do?!

From the creator of BLU's *Wild Rock*.

This "Pure Romance" is anything but...

Passing his college entrance exams isn't the only thing Misaki has to worry about! Being romanced by a suave and older tutor is the concern, especially when the tutor in question is his brother's best friend and a famous porn novelist! Suddenly Misaki's "normal" life transforms into an educational journey filled with unfamiliar feelings and nonstop insanity.

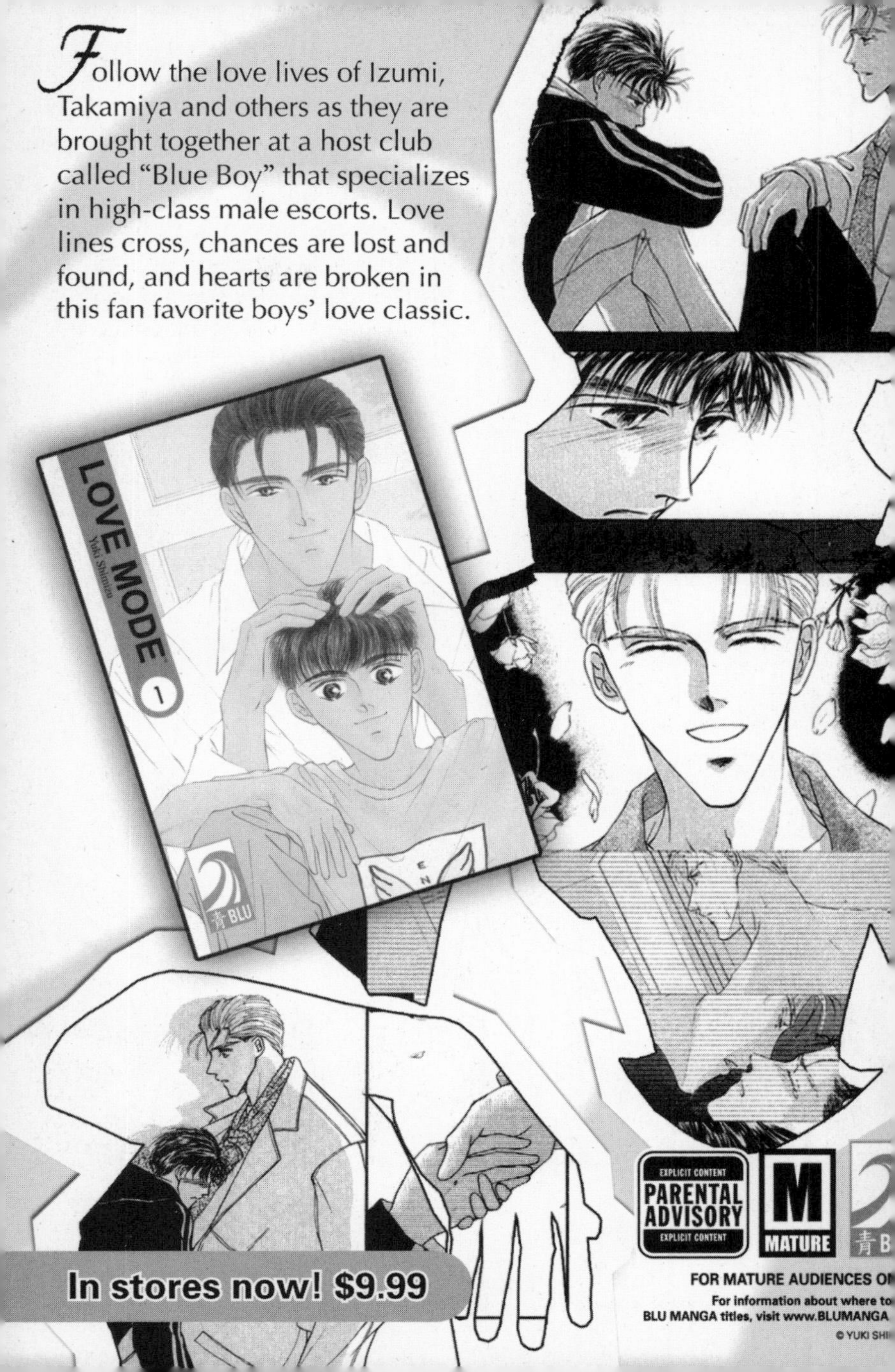
Follow the love lives of Izumi, Takamiya and others as they are brought together at a host club called "Blue Boy" that specializes in high-class male escorts. Love lines cross, chances are lost and found, and hearts are broken in this fan favorite boys' love classic.
LOVE MODE
Yuki Shimizu
1
BLU
In stores now! $9.99
EXPLICIT CONTENT
PARENTAL ADVISORY
EXPLICIT CONTENT
M
MATURE
FOR MATURE AUDIENCES O
For information about where to
BLU MANGA titles, visit www.BLUMANGA
© YUKI SHI

stop

blu manga are published in the original japanese format

go to the other side and begin reading